I0831860

JOURNAL OF EMILY SHORE

Victorian Literature and Culture Series

Karen Chase, Jerome J. McGann, *and* Herbert Tucker, *General Editors*

DANIEL ALBRIGHT
Tennyson: *The Muses' Tug-of-War*

DAVID G. RIEDE
Matthew Arnold and the Betrayal of Language

ANTHONY WINNER
Culture and Irony: *Studies in Joseph Conrad's Major Novels*

JAMES RICHARDSON
Vanishing Lives: *Style and Self in Tennyson, D. G. Rossetti, Swinburne, and Yeats*

JEROME J. McGANN, Editor
Victorian Connections

ANTONY HARRISON
Victorian Poets and Romantic Poems: *Intertextuality and Ideology*

E. WARWICK SLINN
The Discourse of Self in Victorian Poetry

LINDA K. HUGHES and MICHAEL LUND
The Victorian Serial

ANNA LEONOWENS
The Romance of the Harem
Edited and with an Introduction by Susan Morgan

ALAN FISCHLER
"Modified Rapture": *Comedy in W. S. Gilbert's Savoy Operas*

BARBARA TIMM GATES, Editor
Journal of Emily Shore,
with a new Introduction by the Editor

JOURNAL OF EMILY SHORE

Edited and with an Introduction by

Barbara Timm Gates

UNIVERSITY PRESS OF VIRGINIA

Charlottesville and London

THE UNIVERSITY PRESS OF VIRGINIA

First published 1991

Library of Congress Cataloging-in-Publication Data

Shore, Emily, 1819–1839.
Journal of Emily Shore / edited and with an introduction by Barbara Timm Gates.
p. cm. — (Victorian literature and culture series)
Reprint. Originally published: London : K. Paul, Trench, Trübner, 1891.
Includes bibliographical references and index.
ISBN: 978-0-8139-1355-1
1. Shore, Emily, 1819–1839—Diaries. 2. England—Social life and customs—19th century. 3. Authors, English—19th century—Diaries. 4. Young women—Great Britain—Diaries. 5. Children—Great Britain—Diaries. I. Gates, Barbara T., 1936–
II. Title. III. Series.
PR5450.S5Z468 1991
828'.803—dc20 91-12009
[B] CIP

Contents

Introductory

Sept. 20, 1989—Hunting through a stack of Victorian nature journals, I pick up a fragile blue-green covered volume entitled the *Journal of Emily Shore*. What immediately strikes me are the white spaces of the title page. None of the standard puffing of Victorian journals here. Nothing to indicate whether Emily Shore represents a real woman or a pseudonym. No mention of any editor. Even more intriguing is the date. The journal is published in 1891, yet I see that Emily Shore died in 1839, at the age of nineteen. What, I wonder, is the reason for a time lag of over fifty years between the writing and the publishing? And who saw to the publishing of this journal? And why in the 1890s? I feel intrusive as I enter the book's covers and discover not just the nature diary I had expected but the intense and wide-ranging world of an extraordinary young woman who seems to have lived life fiercely, knowing it would be brief. Unable to put down this record of her life, I acknowledge the shrewdness of the Emily Shore who at age fourteen can tell her unknown reader: "If we are going to read a book, how much impression the name of the author makes on us! And yet it ought to make no difference" (132). How well this applies to her own surprising work.

Sept. 21—Shore's identity is established. *The Dictionary of National Biography* lists Margaret Emily Shore (1819–39) as the deceased elder sister of Louisa Shore (1824–95), a "poetess and miscellaneous writer," and notes that a selection from Margaret Emily's "Journal" was "published by her sisters in 1891" (151). A third sister, Arabella, a poet, critic, and translator, seems often to have been Louisa's coauthor and to have survived both Louisa and Emily. She must then have been sole editor of the second edition of

Shore's journal, which was printed in 1898. So here is a mystery lost and a whole family of literary ladies found—with the two survivors "early and enthusiastic advocates of the cause of women," according to the *DNB*.

Sept. 25—Putting aside preconceptions, I decide to meet Emily Shore on her own terms. Shore's *Journal* unfolds as the record of a remarkable young life—a book of days about study and books, natural history and family, politics and world events, a girl's coming of age and a young woman's struggle against death. Yet what is here is only a fraction of what was written. The introduction says there were once twelve octavo volumes of about 160 pages each; that makes 1,920 pages, and we have just over 350. Where, I wonder, are the rest? I begin to feel that this unique *Journal* should be reissued, probably reedited, for the centenary of its first publication. There were also Shore drawings "even more precocious than her writings" (xii). How instructive it would be to find the entire cache of Shore papers, with Emily Shore's histories of the Jews and Greeks and Romans, and her epics, three novels and three books of poems, to say nothing of the "Brief Diaries" that ran concurrently with the journal but reflect a more private world. If the Shore sisters took care to preserve the journal for over half a century, they must surely have willed their papers to some relative or repository.

Oct. 31, Halloween—A university press would like to reprint Shore's *Journal,* possibly including previously unpublished sections, but the original remains elusive. Here then is a new mystery: where can I find that original? My check of the publishers' records of Kegan Paul, Trench Trübner & Co. shows only ledgers of sales and payments to Arabella Shore. The Bedfordshire Record Office, listed in John Batts's *British Manuscript Diaries of the Nineteenth Century* as holding the twelve volumes of Shore's diary, actually holds no more than a typed extract from the journal I have already seen—or so they assure me over the long-distance telephone.

Dec. 22—More discouraging news about Shore's manuscripts. A correspondent for the Royal Commission on Historical Manuscripts' National Register of Archives writes that the register "includes no reference to Miss Shore's journal other than that in Batts's *British Diaries*." I S.O.S. a friend in London for help, and she promises to "trot down" to Somerset House and check the Shores' wills.

Jan. 11, 1990—My jubilant friend writes, "Arabella Shore died 9 Jan. 1901 and left a will dated 5 Aug. 1899 with a codicil including these welcome words, 'I bequeath the manuscripts and drawings of my sisters Emily and Louisa Shore to the Trustees of the British Museum to be preserved in the department of manuscripts.' " In six or seven months I will be in London to actually touch and see those manuscripts and drawings for myself. I sit down and write a letter of relief and hearty thanks.

June 26—Newly in London at long last, I collect a waiting letter from David Sutton of the Location Register of English Literary Manuscripts and Letters. Responding—long since—to a December letter of mine, he too has been stumped by the lack of records of Shore's manuscript material. But now, kindled to an excited anticipation in the new light of the will, I am off to the British Library, hoping to inspect that very manuscript material.

July 14—The British Library thinks I have made some mistake. They simply have no reference to Shore manuscripts. After two weeks of daily visits, trying the nerves of three separate librarians, I am inclined to agree: there is indeed a mistake—somewhere.

July 15—A legal friend sends me to Somerset House to find out whether the will was probated and who was the lawyer. Crossing a line of people waiting for entry into the new Courtauld Gallery, I enter the Dickensian setting of the hall of death records. Clerks bustle about, an old man with tears in his eyes checks a list two columns long against several large books, and other people sit at small tables poring over wills mounted and preserved in even larger books that nearly fill the tables. I am told to look up my Shore in the 1901 record book of wills and to request seeing the will. Half an hour later I hear what sounds like the word "Shaw" called out several times. I wake up to the realization that my American ear has misheard "Shore," claim my will, and soon see that on "the 22nd day of March 1901" both Arabella Shore's will and its two codicils were probated and granted to "Charles Russell Shore the sole Executor." Later in the day I find that W. Whitfield of Surrey Street, Strand, the legal firm listed, is long dissolved. Desperate, I search through the London phone book, which yields no Shores with the name Charles or Russell or any of the other Shore names I have come to know. In a last-ditch effort to find my manuscript, I will write all of the Shores in the London phone book for help.

July 25—The British Library finally agrees to check all bequests and correspondence from 1900 to 1910 to find a possible Shore bequest. It will be another three-week delay. Meanwhile, they remind me, I can search the records of the Natural History branch.

Aug. 3—On this hot, hot, near 100 degree day, my search for the Shore manuscripts dead-ends, along with most of the rest of busy life in London. Overheated animals in the London Zoo get hosed down, and the curator of manuscripts at the British Library writes that "departmental records for the period 1901–1913 contain no trace of a Shore bequest." The letter goes on "many bequests and donations were declined with thanks in this period, but these refusals were documented. It is possible that Arabella Shore's executors did not discharge their obligations." If true, how thoughtless of them.

Aug. 25—Back in the United States, letters from the Shores in London have accumulated in my absence. I am told by one kind and obliging Shore of his family business history—the cotton trade; I find that there are Shores from as far afield as Canada, Israel, Russia, and Poland; and I have even been asked as a return favor to keep an eye out for a man from Milwaukee who subsequently emigrated to South Africa. But there is no sign of Arabella Shore's relatives. I shall have to press on without them or the manuscripts and introduce a printed text.

Sept. 7—Brainstorming about introducing the *Journal of Emily Shore* raises questions upon questions. To begin with, the editing. Since there is no finding the manuscripts, I must work with the 1890s editions of an 1830s journal. Who, then, is the author of these 351-page condensations? Arabella Shore, whose name is on the publisher's records? Or both she and Louisa Shore, who died in 1895 and so may have had a hand in the 1891 editing? As they unfold, the original introductions alternate between "I" and "we." Whichever sister was editor, she certainly parleys with the journal, sometimes intrusively within the text. This editorial voice cannot be ignored.

Sept. 8—Another problem: the Shores are like the Brontës—writing sisters with a family history that is haunted by consumption and early death. It might be satisfying to let their journal reappear without featuring their story and its parallels, and an exceptional work might then quietly drift into the literary canon on its own merits. But do Victorian women still need to enter the literary canon by first being canonized as saints, like Charlotte Brontë in Elizabeth Gaskell's *Life of Charlotte Brontë?* Or as subtle, lonely outwitters of the patriarchy, like Barrett Browning, or Christina Rossetti, who enter through stories of stifling lives overcome or endured? One could easily depict young Emily Shore as a shorter-lived contemporary of Emily Brontë, with parallel commitments to nature and imagination, or as a forerunner of the scholarly prodigy Elizabeth Barrett. Would readers then lose the Shore text in the shadow of the life? Judging from the past, it is clear that canonized personae have clouded the word in women's texts. Uncanonized, perhaps this young woman could help shift literary history.

Sept. 10—I also wonder whether Emily Shore, self-conscious and self-aware, lived the life she wrote. Does a journal like hers represent a life or does it construct one? Leaving questions of canonization aside, I am not certain whether one can or should try to escape the obvious pitfalls of biographical criticism. Readers, even contemporary readers, do like life stories—true or false ones—and do like to believe they are true.

They also like to think that an individual's life—especially in its mundane aspects—represents those of its time and its gender. The Shores' composite book is a representation of one woman's days, yet the voices here are full of authority about far more than the day-to-day. The Shores are telling the story of a special woman; their selectivity shows this. How then do these voices join with those of other Victorian women? Can I go on to generalize from the Shores? My historical sense thinks not.

Sept. 20—Some of the references in Shore's journal are obscure. But if I annotate this text, my annotations will then place emphasis on Emily Shore's world rather than on her represented self. This troubles me because I would like her or the dialogue with her 1890s editor(s) to have center stage. One thing I will not do is to override or extend the Shore sisters' bottom-of-the-page annotations.

Oct. 31—For over a month I have been immersed in Arabella and Louisa Shores' essays and introductions and Emily Shore's journal. From what they tell us about themselves and each other, the Shores emerge as a remarkable family. The mother, Margaret, was a nature lover and walker; the father, Thomas, an author and teacher who declined preferment in the church because his unorthodox views on religion would not permit him to subscribe to the Thirty-nine Articles, doctrinal statements of the Church of England. Instead, he took in pupils to support his family of five children. Thomas also taught his eldest, Margaret Emily, and she in turn taught her younger siblings—how and what she tells us in her journal. From the pages of that journal Thomas emerges as a gentle and principled man, a view seconded by Arabella Shore in her memoir of Louisa, where their father is described as a person "of high cultivation and singular moral worth; the subordination of private interests to considerations of conscience was the habit of his life" (4). All three Shore sisters got guidance from this father, whom Emily represents as encouraging her interests in everything from silk to the cruelty of fox hunting to devotional literature; and all three emerged from his tuition as authors and as questioners of authority. Arabella, next in age to Emily, wrote a *Dante for Beginners* (Chapman and Hall, 1886) and worked with Louisa on at least four volumes of poems in addition to editing Louisa's *Poems* in 1896, after Louisa's death, and the *Journal of Emily Shore* in 1891 and 1898. And as early as 1874, Louisa wrote an influential essay on the emancipation of women for the *Westminster Review*. According to Arabella, this piece was later reprinted as a pamphlet, *The Citizenship of Women Socially Considered*.

Nov. 5—I decide that the "citizenship" of women seems not to have been a problem for the young Shore sisters. From the very beginning of her journal, Emily Shore assumes a tone of authority usually associated with the male voice. If, as Julia Kristeva says, the woman writing her life must raise self to "the stature of her father" (28), Shore does this with relative ease. The always helpful, liberal father—himself something of an outsider—appears to have encouraged an intellectual rigor in his willing eldest daughter, a rigor that can be misread by the uninitiated reader of the *Journal*.

I look for critical readings of Shore but find only a tiny handful and note that, to a man, Shore's male critics have been troubled by Shore's authoritative, learned persona. In his 1927 collection *More English Diaries*, Arthur Ponsonby describes Shore's as the "diary of an infant prodigy whose extraordinary capacity for absorbing knowledge charged her with an abnormal amount of erudition" (204). Abnormal for whom? Not for Shore, but for some nonexistent, generic, young nineteenth-century woman, I suspect. The hyperbolic Ponsonby goes on to decide that Shore's work "presents an almost ludicrous contrast to a social diary kept by young ladies of her age" (204). A social diary was obviously what Ponsonby had expected to find between the blue-green covers. Some twenty years later, and in contrast to Ponsonby, James Aitken introduced a selection from the *Journal* by simply denying the intellectual Shore voice. To his mind, the journal "is the record of a unique girl, simple, unaffected, affectionate, marvellously gifted, lovable" (139). The trouble is, many of Aitken's selections belie his judgments—from Shore's mention of her cutting anti–Reform Bill verses quoted at the beginning of his text, to her tongue-in-cheek observations at being seen as one of a "glorious phalanx of ladies" at its end.

Far from being simple and unaffected, Shore speaks with one or another kind of appropriate authority throughout her journal. I try to define Shore's voices of authority for myself. Emily Shore is a tough critic of the arts and politics, a keen and experienced observer of nature, and a young woman who knows what she is about as she creates her own personae. She fittingly holds authority over the ins, outs, ups, and downs of a young girl's life. She does inscribe the woman's days as a projective male reader might expect her to, but she does much more as well, particularly in the earlier sections of the text. What this all comes down to is that Shore speaks in several authoritative tongues. She critiques the intellectual world in tones that may seem manly for her time and place, but she also speaks with a woman's voice and, most importantly, with an artist's. By relying on sexual stereotypes, Ponsonby and Aitken miss Shore's polyphony.

Nov. 8—I am beginning to see that Shore's critiques of the artist's world are her most extensive and have to do with her own learning process. But then so does the entire journal. Had Shore lived, we might have thought of this book as her "Portrait of the Artist as a Young Woman." From the journal's beginning, Shore is weeding out bad art from good. As early as page three, she faults Sir Thomas Thornhill's paintings for St. Paul's dome as "very ill done" (3). Shore herself drew from a very young age; her sisters' introduction says she did a drawing of the armory at Warwick Castle "*from memory, five weeks after seeing it, at six years and a half old!*" (xii). I am coming to believe that all of her short life, Shore looked—and did nearly everything else—primarily in order to learn. In 1834 she saw some pencil drawings, done in very few strokes, that would revolutionize her own artwork. On December 10 of that year, she decided "it is this style of drawing at which I aim, and I shall neglect shading almost entirely, for I see that in clever hands it is quite unnecessary in producing effect. I cannot bear what the *Quarterly Journal of Education* calls the neat sampler-like style, practised by so many ladies" (87). Here, then, is Shore's voice of authority over her own destiny. She does not wish to deny being a lady or to deny the style practiced by other ladies. She simply wants to aim at something else, and aim she does.

With even more evident intensity than she views drawing, Shore reads and criticizes literature. She likes Sir Walter Scott, but not his essays on the Ten Commandments nor the last part of *Ivanhoe*. Her own closure would have been different; "the book should have finished when Rebecca leaves the room" (172), she tells us. And Shakespeare's Henry VIII, Katherine, and Wolsey are, she feels, "not half so vigorously drawn as I had expected, or as I could, methinks, have done myself" (173). I warm to Shore's archaic "methinks," a word that lends enough humor to her criticism to keep it from pomposity. Here she reads as the apprentice writer she certainly was.

Thinking about Shore's apprenticeships and her range of authoritative personae, I realize that her conscious use of reading to inform her own writing extended to her work in natural history. In 1835 she copied into her journal six months of brief notes observing the onset of spring, "in imitation of [notes] in the *Penny Magazine*" (106–7). Three years later, she published her bird observations in that magazine. In this case, her *Journal* provides both a record of her apprenticeship and an instance of the apprentice at work. Shore validates her scientific self by showing its evolution. So this journal is a writer's life in process; Shore's words construct a self as it constructs itself.

Nov. 13—I wonder about the other Margaret Shore, Margaret Emily's mother. Shore's love of natural history possibly got its impetus from this other nature lover. I think too of Annis Pratt's concept of a "green world"—the margin to one side of civilization where women's imprisoned energies can be released, the innocent place of preenclosure where the preadolescent girl can possess "*herself*" (17). Shore certainly lived in and wrote about a green world, but her sisters' introduction claims that in the world of "Nature," Emily Shore was "her own sole teacher" (vi). Here again Shore seems self-authorized, if validated by homelife at Woodbury. The journal itself does not show Margaret imprinting Emily with a love of nature. Emily's dropping of her mother's name, Margaret, for the title of her journal (if she in fact did title it) suggests a desire for independence from the maternal. And even if her mother did teach her, Shore prefers to image herself as the teacher of her young brother Mackworth, whose boyish delight in snakes and owls thrills his oldest sister. Like Wordsworth's younger sister Dorothy, Shore's brother Mackworth mirrors Emily Shore's developing self. It looks as though the Shore sisters were right, and Shore, again like Wordsworth, "let Nature be her teacher." The *Journal* would lead me to think so: "I believe," says Shore the naturalist, "that if I were chained for life to Woodbury, and never allowed to ramble from it more than three or four miles . . . I should for ever be discovering something new" (92). Woodbury, not the home but the place, was her own "green world," a place she observed with scientific scrutiny, noting that "in the study of natural history it is particularly important not to come too hastily to conclusions, but to study facts from observation frequently and most carefully before any inference is drawn from them" (119). She goes on to say that even though she carefully follows her own advice, "still it is provoking to find myself often making blunders from want of observing with sufficient carefulness at first" (119). Greenness for Shore was not a retreat into romance, or even romanticism, but another area for concentrated learning—a place to watch mason-wasp behavior for two hours straight and to record that behavior every few minutes in what suggests a verbal, slow-motion videotape of the animal (111). Emily Shore was without doubt at work to claim the authority of the painstaking observer.

Nov. 17—When I turn from Shore's quest for learning and the authority of her voice to the art of the journal according to Emily

Shore, learning becomes central yet again. On April 30, 1836, Shore ended the fifth volume of her journal with a vow to continue journal writing for the rest of her life. Her reason: "the use of the pen is amongst the most valuable means of improving the mind" (138). Ever the learner, Shore was already expert in structuring a journal, and this April 30 entry shows one of Shore's deftest devices for noting time. Shore picked key dates—the end of a journal volume; her birthday on December 25; "one year ago"; "three years ago"—to give structure to her written life. In that authored life, I find the birthday heroine is one of the most interesting characters and the one who most noticeably alters from entry to entry. In 1832 the narrating Shore shows the narrated Shore as the excited recipient of Babbage's *Economy of Manufactures* and marks the day simply by saying, "This is my birthday. I am thirteen years old" (28). By her sixteenth birthday, her entry becomes an occasion to look back, check her vivid memory of her fifth and eleventh birthdays, muse about the swiftness of passing time, and reconfirm how busily employed Emily Shore has always been. To mark age seventeen, the entry alters to a meditation on her onetime happiness and current illness and an announcement of self-hatred over her slow spiritual development. This is followed at eighteen by a short notation only to confirm the closeness of death and the brevity of life. Shore's final birthday entry, in Madeira, turns away from self after a quick look at the unlikeliness of another birthday, and shifts to a description of the fruit market in Funchal. Is the outer world brought in here to block out inner pain?

From the birthday entries, I would like to generalize about Shore's life and counter Robert Fothergill, who claims we cannot really find development in diaries because they are concerned with particulars—but the sisters Shore raise their arms and put a stop to me. Emily Shore's final entry has been edited—pierced with four tiny dots . . . stop signs between the self and the fruit market in Funchal! I look back to see that others of the birthdays have been deleted altogether. Brought up short, I remember again that this is a doubly edited text—first chosen and arranged by Emily Shore, recollecting her days, and then by her sisters, reviewing and controlling those days. The sisters were orchestrating a memoir; Emily was unfolding a life. Even the plots could differ. Certainly Arabella and Louisa Shore ultimately control time in this journal. I remember now that on the fourth page they inserted a passage "to remind us that it is but a child who writes." They could make their big sister Emily as old or as young as they liked. Selectivity was always their option.

Nov. 18—Sidetracked now by the sisters' editing, I return to that vexed issue that troubled me in September: Who is author of this book? Now I reassure myself that it is not a sidetrack. In a sense, this is a book by three sisters, consisting of Shore's representation of her life and Arabella and Louisa Shores' presentation of that text. Different temperaments, more than fifty intervening years of differing acculturation—these things really matter. At the beginning of chapter ten—and the chaptering, too, must be the surviving Shores' work, since Emily marked off her larger divisions by volume—the editors pause, like novelists, to summarize. They tell us that from around age seventeen the text cannot give us the whole picture. Emily became sadder and wiser as she grew from the student and observer to the young woman. Both piety and "passionate friendships" (177), they declare, altered her. It sounds as though she developed a crush; but Arabella and Louisa resort to hinting here and reveal that only their mother knew something of its nature. They cover themselves by saying that in any case Emily's parents were her first and real loves. I am sure that this is where their need to control the text shows the most. They turn the plot from its concentration on learning to the young girl's adolescent interests—the more conventional social diary that Ponsonby was looking for in Shore's narrative. Toward the beginning of Emily's own first entry in chapter ten, their control is still very evident. Here the capitalized "Ed." feels obliged to reinforce Emily Shore's taste by agreeing with her literary assessments (179). They are given a stamp of approval. Is this the patronizing result that can follow the piety-and-passion character summary that readers have just been offered? I begin to find the younger sisters Shore too invasive.

Looking at the remainder of the text, I notice how strongly this vein continues. The progress of Shore's illness, so well documented in the text, is supplemented with a countertext determining exactly when Shore caught the cold that led to her death (196). The mysteries of Shore's adolescent love are again alluded to in an aside (206–7), along with a "passionate love for Mary W." and further innuendoes about the return of an unnamed friend are inserted to compensate for six months of the journal that are deleted. The omission, we are told, was made because the descriptions of the reunion were "so mixed up with morbid depression from the poor journalist's own sinking health" (266). Dear editorial ladies, you go too far. Are you bowdlerizing or just playing coy? I think maybe you are helping create what Sidonie Smith calls the "good woman fiction" of women's autobiography, suppressing "female eroticism, though not, of course self-effacing love and devotion" (55).

In the end, the sister editors parley with the text. As Shore grows weaker and has doubts about her own good nature when she returns home after a ten-month absence, her sisters become the final authorities on the matter. In a footnote they say that if Emily had morally deteriorated, "No one else discovered it" (337). Did they know her better than she knew herself? Near the end, on the last page of the journal, they take the liberty of glossing and encroaching on Shore's assessment of her own death portrait. And at the very end they will have the last word, appropriating and omitting Emily Shore's own closure, "written in a tremulous, yet quite legible hand, on June 24th, a fortnight before her release" (351). I now fear these editors may have tailored for their protagonist a life nearly as fictional as Gaskell's life of Brontë.

Nov. 19—An unexpurgated Shore will never come my way, but I have made what small peace I can with the other sisters Shore and can turn back to Emily Shore's own art of journal writing. Granting the overall shape of her book may be her sisters', Shore's own narrative art shines through. To begin with, Emily Shore is indeed polyvoiced; she creates a Bakhtinian *heteroglossia.* Entries come in the form of questions, questions and answers, dialogues, and retellings. There are observations by Shore and by others, and short narratives or tales within the context of entries. I follow the antics and life span of a pet lark from day to day in the summer of 1833. This ministory is shaped to intrigue, with ups and downs, denouements and closure.

Sometimes Shore's entries are staccato and matter of fact, sometimes metaphoric and poetic. A traveler's voice comes in to talk about the sights of London or of Exeter, or a sea voyage to Madeira, or Madeira's people and landscape. It has a different kind of authority mixed with modesty. Always, though, I sense a characteristic Emily Shore authenticity. When, for example, Shore takes over a story secondhand and reinflects a man's voice, as she does so often, she gives us her sense of the man first, then what seems his, not her, story. So we hear Charles Shore on Sweden (13) and Shore's father on fox hunting (24–25) and later, when Shore is older, a Mr. W. on the supernatural (201–2)—and for a moment we enter their lives too.

These twice-told tales and other representations of an outer world are counterpointed by Shore's more inward musings about the art and nature of journals. There is no doubt in my mind that Shore's journal offers an excellent example of a diarist reflecting on the implications of journal writing. I recall that the only two experts on diaries who have discussed Shore in any detail have also thought this. Ponsonby wrote that "no diarist, not even Amiel himself, can have examined more profoundly the whole psychology of diary writing and faced the problems of the honesty of introspection and the questions of motive in writing and the eventual fate of a diary with greater perspicacity than this girl writing at the age of eighteen after keeping a journal for seven years" (205). More recently, Harriet Blodgett has remarked that Shore confronted the "problem that self-consciousness poses for the diarist" (60) as well as anyone has ever done. Both Ponsonby and Blodgett cite my favorite, clear-sighted entry by Shore (July 6, 1838) to prove their points:

> *I am sure it [her journal] is a memoir of my character, and the changes and progress of my mind—its views, tastes, and feelings.*

> *But I am conscious that, at the same time, it is far, far from being as complete as with this end it ought to be. . . . it has become to me a valuable index of my mind, and has been the record of faults and follies which have made my cheek burn on the re-perusal. I have poured out my feelings into these later pages; I have written them on the impulse of the moment, as well as from the coolness of calm deliberation. I have written much that I would show only to a very few, and much that I would on no account submit to any human eye. Still, even now, I cannot entirely divest myself of an uncomfortable notion that the whole may some future day, when I am in my grave, be read by some individual, and this notion has, even without my being often aware of it, cramped me, I am sure. I have by no means confessed myself in my journal; I have not opened my whole heart; I do not write my feelings and thoughts for the inspection of another—Heaven forbid!—but I imagine the vague fear I have above mentioned has grown into a sort of unconscious habit, instinctively limiting the extent of my confidence in ink and paper, so that the* secret chamber of the heart . . . *does not find in my pen a key to unlock it. (261–62)*

Shore goes on to say that this journal will be open to her current family and, poignantly, some day to her children, but from July 3 on, she will keep a second journal into which she can pour "*all* the secret feelings of my heart" (263).

I now begin to think that Emily Shore, the apprentice author and writer of published essays on birds, had it in mind to publish the nonsecret journal that we now know only through her sisters. She handled it like a professional, even providing the volumes with indexes. And her other entries on her writer's art show a self-conscious candor and a thoughtfulness about craft. On April 24, 1837, Shore reflects that "I am always apt to see things in richer colours at first sight, and then, writing about them while my fancy is yet heated, I unintentionally exaggerate" (195). She is also acutely aware of the inadequacy of even the most exaggerated language to catch a summer's day (194). And she knows too that with writing come not just sequence and succession but selectivity and choice of tone. These she also ponders in 1837, wondering whether or not to ridicule an evening party. "I think not," she decides, "though such subjects would give variety to my journal" (233). By 1837, after a half-dozen years of daily writing, Shore was enough at ease with her form to talk to her journal about itself.

Nov. 21—This year and more of journal keeping about Shore's work leads me to see the seductions of the form. Linearity is not essential, doubling back makes sense, and one can move from the outer world to any degree of interiority with some ease. Shore, I think, liked all of this, especially that move from outer to inner. The journal consistently shows her reactions to family, friends, the natural world, and the world of books and presents her personal history in intersection with the history of her time—the Reform Bill of 1832, the New Poor Law of 1834, the newly opened London Zoo. But as it evolves, the journal most of all reveals Shore's representations of alternative Shore protagonists within the text. In writing about self, Shore constructs many alternate selves. The long passage I quoted from July of 1838 as much as tells us so. Emily Shore had written a "memoir of my character, and the changes and progress of my mind" (261), but in the course of the writing, her journal altered from one about a mind as an intellect and entity to one about a mind on a spiritual voyage. As I review it yet again, I discover that Shore's journal encodes the progress of at least three prominent selves: the student self, the girl–young woman self, and the dying self, struggling to accept its own termination. These selves both crisscross each other and, at times, coalesce.

Nov. 22—I have spent the morning scanning the text to ferret out the evolution of the student self. She is omnipresent, but less prominent as the dying self takes over. I note that this student is as self-conscious in her methodology, and as self-critical, as is the journal keeper. On February 10, 1835, she determines to study botany differently, for, she tells the journal, "I have hitherto been a very superficial botanist, attending to little besides the classification, and not studying the habits, properties, and uses of plants, as I do the habits of birds" (89). Student Shore, it seems, has a different plan of attack for her various studies. Herodotus she plunders for stories to feed her own intended dramas and narrative poems (125); the weather she measures with barometer and thermometer three times a day, at 8:30 A.M., 1:00 P.M., and 8:00 P.M. (151); the architectural plans she draws she afterwards writes "minute descriptions of . . . , with the measurements, furniture, uses, etc., of all the apartments" (136); chronology she memorizes in slots of time represented on charts—by November of 1837 she has learned 365 separate dates with the intention of adding to that number continually (224); and history she learns by reading different books on the same historical period (224). When her tastes change, she analyzes why. Fiction has less appeal by 1837, but that must be an acceptable change of taste because it gives her "a greater enjoyment of soberer and more useful reading" (184).

As the journal progresses, the voracity and intensity of Shore's study decrease. Shore matures but simultaneously faces death and is forced to treat her education differently. By the beginning of 1838 she lightens up her tone—"I have crammed a good deal of fresh information into my pate to-day" (237)—and begins thinking about self-cultivation not in and of itself but as it is useful to others. It is part of her new piety. Nevertheless, as an honest young woman, she also mourns the loss of strength for her rambles and observations of nature and her studies. In her last half year she admits how much happier she was as a child, fully engaged in those pursuits. Most poignant of all is the day she sorts out her manuscripts in Madeira, two months before her death, and smiles at her own eclecticism:

> *I was highly amused at the curious mixture of every kind of subject which I found in these confused heaps of manuscripts. Fragments of unfinished poems, Latin exercises, and rough reports of conversations, scribbled over one sheet; sketches of epics, translations from Greek plays, notes of sermons, and algebraical calculations, mixed together on a second; on another, grammatical rules for an imaginary language, references to a plan for an*

> *invented palace, sums in arithmetic, scenes of unfinished dramas, and lists of* dramatis personae *are scribbled and scrawled all over with heads and figures of men and horses, likenesses of unconscious sitters, and outlines of trees and flowers. So miscellaneous have been my studies and amusements. (340–41)*

Miscellaneous indeed! In reviewing Shore's studies, I notice that the sisters do not quite approve of their rigor. At thirteen Shore sketched out her daily regimen of study: from being up before seven thirty memorizing Greek and Latin, through to reading Fuseli's lectures to her mother, to lessons with papa, to more Greek and Latin. In their note, the editors want to make sure that we realize that this severe timetable was voluntary and often interrupted by nature rambles (31). We are not, they remind us, to blame the other Shores for imposing such rigor on young Emily; it may have been what killer her.

In about 1836, Shore's narrative of learning begins to give way to representations of her young-woman self, and it is possible that adolescent insecurity may account for the refocusing of the journal that both Shore and her sisters gloss. Protagonist Shore is more self-consciously and traditionally feminine in the later volumes of the journal. To begin with, her new amusements are more socially and humanly directed. She visits and walks out with friends, and she consents to net a purse for a young male friend. Out for the evening to a concert, she reflects on and resists the stereotyping of the "bright eyes and sweet smiles" of the ladies (213). It is in these same last years that Shore begins to look at Mackworth as her child self, passionately pursuing natural history, and to think about the possibility of her own children reading her journal. And she tones down her assertive critical self, passing judgment on Shakespeare's *Timon of Athens* but claiming to be "ill qualified . . . to pass any opinion on the matter" (228). Her room, she finds, suits her—yet it is "grotesque and singular" (218), a space, perhaps to suit the more awkward self she feels she has become. She is indeed "a different creature from what [she] was three years ago" (280), one more vulnerable to the opinion of others (269). This suggests that women autobiographers may interrupt their own male-identified selfhood—in Shore's case her intellectual childhood—when the suppressed story of a part of their femaleness can no longer be kept in check. For awhile, however, Shore, the narrator, keeps the two stories going side by side.

Nov. 29—Rethinking the idea of the two stories I believe now that it was really Shore's representation of her dying self more than her young-woman self that began to silence the energetic voices of her childhood. I ache to see that by her journal's end young Shore is writing a kind of holy dying. Death already begins to stalk its pages before the midpoint of the journal, just after Shore's first visit to a London physician in the summer of 1836 for a consultation about her illness. After this, the mortality rate of a nearby family—who have lost four of their young people—stuns Shore, who devotes her entire entry for August 18 to their quick deaths, possibly by consumption. From this point on death dominates. Shore the narrator seems never to miss discussing any youthful deaths brought to her attention. Nor does she miss recording the illnesses of friends and examining their mental attitudes toward illness, nor empathizing with other consumptives like her relative Winthrop Praed or the other people who are, like her, in warmer Madeira as a last resort. The Shore way of reading changes, too. Not only does the dying Shore read devotional literature, but she rereads works like *Hamlet,* now emphasizing the pain and melancholy of the central hero.

For awhile, Shore's student self heroically struggles with the dying self. The brain gets "muddy and rusty" (165) during long bouts of illness, and Shore the student regrets all of 1836 as a year "wasted, as far as study is concerned" (171). But she fights back, sadly suspecting all along that those who say too much study can cause consumption may be right. She will put herself on a new regimen because she "cannot bear the idea of living, even in sickness, without systematically acquiring knowledge" (221), and she will put off the more difficult subjects until she is "quite restored to health" (221). There is high drama in these inner conflicts and even more in the irony that comes from knowing the sad outcome of Shore's story before she does.

The last chapter of Shore's dying comes in Madeira, where she has been taken for the beneficial climate. Her eye is now trained on death. From aboard ship, she sees another ship in mourning, painted in a special blue stripe. She would like to be intrigued by Madeira, but it is a "beautiful stranger" (319), and she herself is in mourning for the natural world of England. She watches Portuguese funeral processions and visits the English cemetery where she knows she will be laid to rest. Through all this, she sometimes feels she is improving in health; in March she excitedly arranges her books in new shelves. In May, however, she admits that "on the 4th of April I broke a blood-vessel, and am now dying of consumption, in great suffering, and may not live many weeks. God be merciful to me a sinner" (350). Weak as she is, Shore's dying self takes up the pen as long as she can hold it. And I must stop retelling her story.

Dec. 5—I speak to my publisher and decide that our edition will be a centenary reproduction of the first edition, the 1891 journal. I have a last look at its 1898 counterpart, identical in text but revealing the busy hand of Arabella Shore still at work in yet other ways. Three new features were added in 1898: a table of contents with a list of illustrations; a number of Emily Shore's own sketches, alluded to in the Shore sisters' introduction; and an index, which may or may not have been drawn from Emily Shore's original categories in her own volume indexes. The index and three of the pictures can be retained for our edition.* Accustomed now to Arabella Shore's ways, I am not surprised at her choice of pictures. Natural history is not represented, just as the London Zoo was not, and important men, including all the Shore men, dominate the selections, all of which are of people, not places or things.

*The 1898 index and frontispiece portrait and Emily Shore's pencil sketches of her beloved father and brother Mackworth appear on pages 363–70 of this text.

People, especially family and anecdotes about them, seem to have delighted the younger Shore sisters. I recall how, as editor, Arabella or Louisa could not resist refining one of Emily Shore's descriptions of her mother's sisters, the Twopenys, by adding a clever footnote recalling that collectively, on account of their beauty, the six sisters were called the "Splendid Shilling."

With respect to the pictures, I am most intrigued by the ingenious choice of frontispieces for the two editions. In 1891, the frontispiece is the death portrait mentioned on the last page of the text (351)—Emily Shore, facing her viewer head on, with her stuffed birds, the hoopoe and bee eater, on her lap. Weak and dying, Shore herself had heard this was an excellent likeness and cared enough to say so at her journal's close. But in 1898, the frontispiece is by Emily Shore, a self-portrait. It is inscribed "Your *very* affectionate sister, Emily Shore—Monday, 1837" and faces away from the title page. Positioned in this way, Emily Shore's figure seems to be turning its back on her text, inscribing not just the picture but the journal to one of the sisters who in the end determined the shape of that journal for posterity. To me, far preferable is the serene, direct gaze of "Margaret Emily Shore, Aged Nineteen Years" with birds in lap, fronting us as does her name on the journal's title page just opposite.

Mar. 1—The eleventh hour has passed. Two weeks ago, the University Press of Virginia did a quick, thorough copyediting of my typescript and I an equivalently quick return. For all practical purposes, we are in print with our centenary edition of the 1891 text. And now this news from London. Anne Summers, curator of manuscripts at the British Library, has sent on an announcement of an auction at Phillips, Son & Neale, New Bond Street. As I read that two manuscript volumes of the journal have surfaced and will be auctioned on 14 March 1991, at one o'clock, I think about my letters of inquiry to the Shores and wonder what desk or attic has yielded up its treasures. I look carefully to see which volumes are to be sold: volume seven, running from 6 October 1836 to 10 April 1837, describing life at Exeter and including an index, and volume twelve, the death volume. Phillips advises potential buyers that these two appear to be "random survivals"; the whereabouts of the rest of the manuscripts are still unknown.

As I scrutinize the announcement, I am confirmed in my discomfort with the sister editors. From even the short abstracts printed by Phillips, it is apparent that editing did radically change the nature of Emily Shore's journal. What Phillips calls "the final harrowing page of the journal" has, for example, been deleted. Characteristically, the editors ended their text with images of their family, but Emily Shore went on painstakingly to describe her solo battle to accept death and Providence and to detail her declining existence, right down to her daily intake of nourishment—goat's milk and fruits. Editing also altered the focus of a Heaven-earth dichotomy that troubled the nature-loving young woman at the onset of summer's warmth. Much as she might have liked to, Shore refused to cling to her beloved earth. Nevertheless, she tells us, she would have liked more time to come to peace with the idea of Heaven. In the light of these printed fragments from the manuscripts, Shore's death now appears even more heartrending than her sisters allowed. And according to the Phillips announcement, so is the deterioration of her handwriting. The editors conclude her journal by telling us that Shore's last words were written "in a tremulous, yet quite legible hand" (351); the announcement, however, reports a "dramatic deterioration of her once meticulous handwriting [that] gives these last entries a poignancy to rival that of Scott's Antarctic journal."

Like the final volume, the volume of 1837 also seems to have been heavily edited. One of its omitted passages reveals Shore's disdain for the wiles of Victorian courtship ritual. With relief, Emily Shore notes that her own education has been different from those of young women who have been trained by their mothers expressly to be attractive to young gentlemen, as if that were their sole purpose in life. She herself refuses to become plagued with an obsession to marry. Should marriage come, it will come naturally, as do other things in the universe. Here, once more, the sisters Shore appear to have expurgated one of Margaret Emily's self-representations of adolescent sexuality and to have minimized her divergence from Victorian norms. In another passage that never entered the published versions, this earlier volume also directs attention to Shore's ill health, indicating her long-time concern with the discomfort of her consumption and describing a cough that feels nailed onto her lungs. This allusion to a crucifying, Christ-like burden may have seemed a religious impropriety to the editors, who chose to eliminate it from their text. Finally, the Phillips announcement reveals an unpublished conclusion to the 1837 volume. This is another segment on journal-writing and one in which Shore confesses—perhaps to her sisters' dismay—that the journal, not family or friends, is her closest companion. With a fanfare of exclamations, Shore bids a dramatic and loving farewell to her volume—the trusted holder of secrets imparted to no human being, a confidante that anyone might envy, and the vessel for intimate feelings of self and soul.

For readers of this current edition, it now appears that despite her own farewells and mine, there will be more of the indomitable, resilient Emily Shore to anticipate. After 14 March 1991, doors may open for another look at this remarkable young polymath who, after years in obscurity, has resurfaced twice in her centenary year—once in this edition and now once more in these newly available manuscripts. Long may her resurrections continue.

References

Aitken, Robert. *English Diaries of the XIX Century 1800–1850*. New York: Penguin Books, 1944.

Batts, John Stuart. *British Manuscript Diaries of the Nineteenth Century: An Annotated Listing*. Totowa, N.J.: Rowman and Littlefield, 1976.

Blodgett, Harriet. *Centuries of Female Days: Englishwomen's Private Diaries*. New Brunswick, N.J.: Rutgers University Press, 1988.

The Dictionary of National Biography. London: Oxford University Press, 1921.

Fothergill, Robert A. *Private Chronicles: A Study of English Diaries*. London: Oxford University Press, 1974.

Kristeva, Julia. *About Chinese Women*, trans. Anita Barrows. London: Boyars, 1977.

Ponsonby, Arthur. *More English Diaries: Further Reviews of Diaries from the Sixteenth to the Nineteenth Century with an Introduction on Diary Writing*. London: Metheun, 1927.

Pratt, Annis. *Archetypal Patterns in Women's Fiction*. Bloomington: Indiana University Press, 1981.

Shore, Arabella. *Dante for Beginners*. London: Chapman and Hall, 1886.

———, ed. *Poems by Louisa Shore with a Memoir by her Sister Arabella Shore*. London: John Lane, 1897.

Shore, Louisa. "The Emancipation of Women." *Westminster Review* 45 n.s. (1874): 137–74.

Shore, Margaret Emily. *Journal of Emily Shore*. London: Kegan Paul, Trench Trübner & Co., 1891 and 1898.

Smith, Sidonie. *A Poetics of Women's Autobiography: Marginality and the Fictions of Self-Representation*. Bloomington: Indiana University Press, 1987.

The original copy of the 1891 edition of the *Journal of Emily Shore* was provided through the courtesy of Musselman Library, Gettysburg College, Gettysburg, Pennsylvania.

MARGARET EMILY SHORE

AGED NINETEEN YEARS

JOURNAL

OF

EMILY SHORE

"Thy leaf has perished in the green,
And, while we breathe beneath the sun,
The world that credits what is done
Is cold to all that might have been."

"So be it; *there* no shade can last
In that deep dawn behind the tomb,
But clear from marge to marge shall bloom
The eternal landscape of the past."

LONDON
KEGAN PAUL, TRENCH, TRÜBNER & CO., LTD.
1891

INTRODUCTION.

A LIFE whose light was blown out half a century ago, and whose whole span did not complete twenty years; a girl's life, which budded, blossomed, and faded in the close shade of a quiet English country-home ;—here, it may be said, are scarcely materials of interest for the present generation. Nevertheless, it has been decided to present to the readers of our day a picture of that life as it is given in the journal of Margaret Emily Shore, kept regularly for eight years of her teens, and ending only with her death. This self-revelation, it is thought, will serve better than any formal biography to preserve a memory, not only cherished by surviving love, but deemed worthy of perpetuation by others who have known her only through these pages. I venture to quote the judgment pronounced by one of these, a highly qualified friendly critic, as the justification—or, shall I say, the defence ?—of this publication. "She," whose portraiture is here found, "will obtain favour with those finer spirits who love what is delicate-textured, exquisite, and unique in human shape, as cognoscenti love a fine bronze, whereof the mould, after serving but once, has been destroyed. She belongs to the order of beings of whom Nature makes no replica."

And it may be suggested that the half-century which has elapsed since this record was closed, adds something, not only to the impression of definiteness and uniqueness left by its truthful disclosures, but to its general present value. A voice speaking to us in such distinct and living tones across so wide a gulf is a witness in some degree of that change in feeling and point of view which on a large scale makes up the history of thought.

In one not unimportant particular it affords some matter for comparison with the present day, some possible bearing on certain educational problems which we are now busy in trying to solve. Emily Shore, I need not say, went to no High School, no College, no Lectures, passed no Examination, and competed with no rivals; her teaching was that of Nature and of Love. Her education had two characteristics: it allowed her own individuality, with all its tastes and tendencies, freely to expand; and it was an education of pure and good home influences. Her sole instructors were her parents, especially her father; but much, very much, was done by herself. She made her whole existence a happy schoolroom. Besides the father's lessons so eagerly assimilated and followed out, she had two worlds in which she was her own sole teacher—the world of Nature and the world of Imagination.

Her passion for Natural History will appear in the earlier journals; it was, indeed, in a great degree to her wanderings at dawn of day in the dewy woods, and her late watchings at open windows with a telescope, collecting plants and studying the habits of birds and insects, that she owed the attack of lung-disease which terminated so fatally and so soon. Her almost equal love of Poetry and of historical knowledge gathers strength through all the later pages. In drawing she had no instructor but her mother; but the taste came spontaneously, and was as marked as that for any of the serious studies we have mentioned. From six years old she was accustomed to use her pencil, copying every object she saw. We may add here that she was born in 1819, on Christmas Day, at Bury St. Edmund's, Suffolk, spent all her life at home, and, dying of consumption in Madeira, on July 7, 1839, about nightfall, aged nineteen years, six months, and fourteen days, was laid to rest under the cypresses and orange-trees of the Strangers' Burial-ground in the town of Funchal.

Nothing more need be prefixed to the tale told by herself than that her father, to whom she owed so much, and whom she loved so deeply, was the Rev. Thomas Shore, M.A., of Wadham College, Oxford, who for the first twenty years of his married life maintained his family by private tuition, taking into his house and preparing for college five or six young men, many of whom were of a high social position, and became known in the political world. Some attained to distinction, and of all of them it may safely be said that they carried away a high esteem and regard for him. During the first half of this life he had occasional duty, and often assisted gratuitously in performing the church services. But he declined preferment when offered to him, because doubts which arose in his mind during the constant study of theology made subscription to the Thirty-nine Articles impossible to him; and he continued to support his family by teaching, till age and infirmities compelled him to seek retirement and repose. What he was in domestic life, the pages of his daughter's journal will in a great measure unfold.

JOURNAL.

The journal is in twelve octavo volumes, beginning July 5, 1831, when the writer wanted five months of her twelfth birthday, and ending June 24, 1839, a fortnight before her death. The number of pages in each volume is on an average a hundred and sixty. It is all through written in a printing hand, varying but little from first to last. As the facsimile of a page is given, I need only say that all the twelve volumes are executed in precisely the same style, and with the same care and completeness; and that the whole was written *impromptu*, without a rough draft, in the midst of as busy a life as ever young creature led!

The selection of extracts from these journals has been a task of much difficulty. In the whole long work of nearly two thousand pages, there is scarcely a passage which, at least to partial eyes, did not seem to possess some charm, some interest of its own. But as a limit was absolutely necessary, it was resolved to be guided by the object of exhibiting individual character as much as possible, without violation of what, even at this distance of time, are felt to be the sacred privacies of the soul, or intrusion on other personalities. A great deal of what is interesting and characteristic, especially of the almost daily notices of her studies and observations on natural history, had to be omitted. But nothing which has been suppressed would tend to give a different idea of her character from what the published extracts convey.

Several passages, too, have been retained as marking the difference, outside and inside, in the aspect of great towns and the life of the country, the intellectual movements and material progress of the England of fifty years ago and the England of to-day.

We subjoin a list of some of her principal compositions, in prose and verse, from the age of eight to that at which she died—nineteen and a half.

1. A little book, with a paper cover, on which is printed in capitals, "Natural History, by Emily Shore, being an Account of Reptiles, Birds, and Quadrupeds, Potton, Biggleswade, Brook House, 1828, June 15th. Price 1 shilling." Inside are sixteen pages of writing in pencil, in a clear but very childish hand, and very few misspellings. The contents are evidently the result of her own observation or oral teaching, for the language is simplicity itself, and the facts

such as she could not get from books. Here is an account of the green fly :—

"Towards the end of spring, in the month of May, the rose and currant trees are greatly infested by an insect called the green fly. These insects are little more than a quarter of a quarter of an inch in length. They have six legs, each about the length of their bodies. These legs are thinner than a hair. They have three tails, each of which are black." A footnote adds: "The tails of these insects are very curious. One tail, which is green all over, sticks out horizontally behind; the two others, which are black, stick out higher up, and rather perpendicularly." "They have two feelers placed on the top of their heads. Their legs have one joint. Here is a drawing of this little insect." (A rude but very correct sketch follows.) "The colour of the insect is green; the body is covered with stripes. Limewater is a good thing to take away these insects. If made too strong it will make the leaves of the tree white. In the currant trees it swells the leaves and lays its eggs in them. They spoil the roses very much. In the older insects the joints of the legs and the bases of the feelers are black; but the little ones are green all over. These troublesome insects also frequent the honeysuckles in very great numbers. In the currant trees they make purple swellings, and there they live."

2. A translation of seven chapters of the first book of Xenophon's "Anabasis," very literally and faithfully done, and, as usual, very skilfully printed—date 1838.

3. A History of the Jews, begun before she was eleven years old, and finished on completing her twelfth year. It is in a hand as clear and regular as type, with an Introduction and Index, a beautiful map, and twelve illustrations, composed out of her own head, and two of them coloured. These two are "Dagon falling before the Ark," and "David taking away Saul's Cruse and Spear." The first shows

the pillared temple of Ashdod, the richly carved copper and smoking tripod, the shattered idol, the rich-robed priest entering, men following with gestures of horror; the second, a scene of yellow moonlight, the bare waste tufted with grass and broken by palm-trees, the tent in which Saul lies sleeping, with shield, spear, and cruse beside him, a man holding open the tent folds, and David cautiously approaching.

4. A History of Greece, finished August 9, 1833, abridged
1 from Frederick Malkin's. As she says in the Preface, "It is true that we may in some instances be accused of plagiarism, where we have nearly copied word for word the corresponding passage in Malkin; but children are to be our critics" (the condescending author was thirteen years and seven months old), "and if the language is plain and intelligible, no matter the source whence it came."

The book ends with a poem, from which I shall quote only one stanza—

> "And still her radiant isles, on every side,
> Spotted the azure main like fallen stars;
> A thousand gems risen from the waters wide,
> A thousand halcyons calming ocean's roars."

5. A History of Rome, in the same style, still more beautifully turned out.

6. A number of books, containing Imaginary Histories of England from 1840 to 2354, a "Collection of Celebrated Parliamentary Speeches" (fictitious), and a "Life of the Right Honourable Charles George Howard" (equally so).

7. An account of an imaginary country in the heart of Australia; nearly twelve chapters are given to the geography, natural history, manners and customs, religion, science, literature, language, with the alphabet and grammar, and finally the "political history." In this work, the most remarkable features are the mechanical execution and the

pretty and spirited illustrations, bits of landscape, imaginary squirrels, birds, flowers (coloured), with "three-celled capsule"; "shepherds, wild sheep, and a hut thatched with large leaves;" figures of men, women, and children; soldiers armed for battle, with weapons very ingeniously constructed; musical instruments, coinage, and canoes. (Fourteen years old.)

8. An unfinished Conversation between herself and the Shade of Herodotus, in which she supposes herself to inform him of all the changes that have taken place in the world since his time. (Fifteen and a half years old.)

9. Fragments of two epics, "Witikind the Saxon," of which one book was completed in such style that centuries hence it would be looked on as a matchless specimen of the manuscript of our age; and "Cosmurania." (About fifteen years old.)

10. Three novels, completed, of the romantic order, of course conventional in handling and formal in language, yet made her own by vividness of conception and vigour of execution—"The Emigrants' Tale," written in 1835; and "Devereux," in two volumes, which sprang out of the first, the history of a precocious boy, who escapes from his home, turns pirate, and redeems a career of crime by one act of splendid and pathetic self-sacrifice (1836 and 1837). She had neither read nor heard of Trelawney's "Adventures of a Younger Son" when she wrote it. Both these works show book-knowledge of other countries, an eye for localities, and skill in describing nature. The printed manuscript of "Devereux" is, perhaps, the most beautifully executed of all her works; it is, in fact, perfect.

11. Three small square books of Poems, written between the ages of ten and nineteen, collected, bound, titled, and prefaced by herself in 1838, the contents being either copied literally from, or remaining in, the original text, thus showing the changes in her printing hand in the course of nine

years, as well as the growth of intelligence, but all equally regular and exact in execution.

A few extracts will be given from each volume. The third, left off not long before her death, contains but few pieces, which, written, as they are, from the very heart, and ringing with melancholy passion, have a far deeper interest than the former ones. But whether they indicate a future and finished poet, whose verses might not be left to die, readers must decide for themselves.

11. Three volumes, "Brief Diaries," begun April 1, 1835, and ended April 3, 1839, containing merely the common facts of daily family life. It was carried on simultaneously with the fuller journals, and with the same neatness and completeness, even to her latest day of living life, the day before that incident—the bursting of a blood-vessel—which sealed her doom.

I must make some mention of her drawings, which were even more precocious than her writings. As a specimen, there is a drawing of the armoury of Warwic Castle, as she spells it, in childish hand, with the weapons faithfully portrayed, *done from memory, five weeks after seeing it, at six years and a half old!* From that age she was always using her pencil, copying every object she saw—her nursery and its furniture, the family group, the farmyard, the hay-cart, cows milked and pigs fed, a hunt with horses and dogs, the watchman and his lantern, a man falling from his horse, a wild-beast show with lion and tiger; all was noticed, carried away, and reproduced with a quaint and vivid exactitude. Her sketches were like little dramas, full of human action; where she had not seen she invented, or took hints from the books she had read. Thus we have "Martyrs," "A Man hanging from a Gallows," "A Prisoner in Chains," "Persian Robbers." At about twelve years old she took to drawing likenesses, though seldom, if ever, requiring her subjects to sit to her; she sat in a corner, when the room was full of company, and sketched them in characteristic attitudes. Forbidden to take the portraits of strange visitors, lest the act should be discovered, but unable to resist the temptation, on one particular occasion she sketched the face (that of a sporting parson), as Hogarth did once, on her thumb-nail. She found subjects amongst her father's pupils, as well as amongst household dependents, and, from the nobleman to the laundress, their likenesses remain to this day as caught by her faithful but not very flattering pencil. To this branch of art succeeded one inspired by her passion for Natural History, that of flower-painting. She conceived the idea of representing in a kind of natural garland or bower the wild flowers proper to every month of the year, with the chief songster of that month placed within it. Sketching then became a passion; a year in Devonshire filled her sketch-book with landscapes, mixed with figures of all that hit her fancy; she sketched even from coach-windows (for railways were then unknown), and beautiful little bits of church architecture filled the corners of her pages. She also drew plans and copied machines with great accuracy.

JOURNAL OF EMILY SHORE.

CHAPTER I.

[At from eleven and a half to twelve years old.]

From July 5 *to Dec.* 30, 1831.—*Brook House, Broadstairs, Ramsgate, Brook House, Woodbury.*

Our family consists of papa, mamma, and five children. Papa is curate, during part of the year, for Mr. Cust, Rector of Cockayne Hatley, a little village two miles and a half from us. We live at Potton, a little market town on the confines of Bedfordshire and Cambridgeshire. Papa takes pupils; his greatest number is six.

Potton is four miles from the post town of Biggleswade, on the north road. The nearest adjoining villages to Potton are Hatley Cockayne, or Cockayne Hatley, two miles and a half distant; Wrestlingworth, about the same distance; Gamlingay, about three miles; Everton, two miles and a half; Sutton, scarcely one mile, and much the prettiest of them all; and Sandy, four miles.

The nearest gentlemen's places are those of Mr. Pym, whose place is called "The Hassels," near Sandy; Mr. Astell's, at Everton; and Captain Foley, at the little hamlet of Tetworth, in the parish of Everton; also Woodbury, in the parish of Gamlingay, an estate of Mr. Wilkinson's. There is, or rather was, that of Sutton, a manor of Sir John Burgoyne's; but he does not inhabit it himself, and in the time of the last tenant, Mr. Russell, the house was burnt down by accident. The estate is now going to ruin apparently. The park is a very pretty one, with some fine old oaks. It is on the Biggleswade road, which is decidedly the prettiest about Potton.

The principal persons in Potton, besides papa and Mr. Whittingham, the vicar, are Mr. Keal and Mr. Moor, surgeons; Mr. Youd, a wool merchant; and Mr. Smith, a rich farmer.

Potton contains no less than thirteen public-houses, besides beer-shops. There is a market every Saturday, a statute and horse fair once a year, and occasionally a show of wild beasts.

The church is ordinary in appearance, but contains some architectural curiosities. Potton is famous for fires; about forty years ago it was almost entirely burnt down, and four cottages were destroyed by fire last year. It contains about fifteen hundred inhabitants.

Our house in Potton is called Brook House. It stands just without the town, in front of a little brook or ditch.

In the spring of 1831 we were all five of us taken ill at once with a most dreadful fever, and were all very dangerously ill. When we were all recovered in some degree, so as to be able to walk, and were nearly as strong as in health, papa and mamma determined to take us to Broadstairs, to spend the summer holidays by the seaside.

July 5.—We took the coach to London, and filled it inside and out, with ourselves and three servants. The road to London is in some parts very pretty. At about one o'clock we entered London, and put up at the Spread Eagle, Gracechurch Street.

We first went to see the new London Bridge. This bridge is very beautiful, but not yet completed; it is of

white stone, and consists of very wide semi-circular arches, thrown across the Thames just above the old bridge, which is a heavy, ugly fabric. We were likewise much pleased with the Thames itself, which is filled with vessels of all
kinds. The Monument is very near; it looks immensely 2
tall, but we did not ascend it. I have read of a man getting over the rails at the top, and throwing himself over; he was dashed to pieces. I believe he was insane. I do not much like the urn at the top of the Monument; it is very ugly. We next went to see St. Paul's Cathedral, which I admire extremely. The exterior is too immense for me to see correctly enough to describe, but when we entered it, it was most beautiful. The pavement is black and white marble, as well as the whole interior. I have, however much I admire the building, two objections to our adopting the Grecian architecture (or rather the Roman). One is that there is nothing like an arch in pure Grecian; the other is that there ought not to be more than one story of columns, which does not look at all well. The Dome is immense. Papa took Richard and me up to the Whispering Gallery, which extends round it, and looks down into the church. Everybody in the church looked like dolls or monkeys from it, it was so high up.
The Dome is covered with paintings by Sir James Thornhill, 3
representing the life of St. Paul; they are very ill done. On leaving the Whispering Gallery, we went some hundred steps higher to a large stone gallery extending all round the outside of the Dome. From thence we had a view of a great part of London, and the tops of the highest churches appeared a vast distance beneath us. We went no higher than this, but descended after we had walked round it. I had not much time to examine the monuments; there were some by Flaxman, and others by Banks and Bacon. I also remember two representing Admiral Nelson and Lord Cornwallis.

After seeing St. Paul's we went to the little church of St. Stephen's, Walbrook, which is admired all over Europe. It is completely enclosed by buildings, and actually an odious little cobbler's stall is built up against the steeple! There is nothing remarkable outside, but the interior, though small, is very elegant, and beautifully proportioned. The carving on the dome and on the capitals of the pillars is rich. What I believe Richard admired the most of all was a picture, as large as life, representing the stoning of St. Stephen, painted by West, whom Richard adores, but whom I do not love much; and the picture in question does not increase my admiration of him, for the design is cold and tame, the drawing lifeless and without spirit, and the colouring sufficiently bad.

July 6.—The country about Margate, Broadstairs, and Ramsgate is odious. The soil is chalky, scarce a tree is to be seen, and a hill would be a wonder. The cliffs of chalk have not a broken edge anywhere, and are perfectly the same for miles, extending all along the coast like white walls, as papa says; and, indeed, the similitude is very apt. The journey was very hot, dusty, and fatiguing. We did not see the sea all the way till we came to Broadstairs, and then indeed it broke most beautifully on our sight, of the brightest blue, and perfectly calm. What struck me very much was the way in which it seemed to rise so very high, and extending before us to such an immense distance. The white sails of vessels at a distance look also very beautiful.

Broadstairs is a small town. Mamma describes it by saying that "it has not enough company to make it lively, but it has too much to make it retired."

[To remind us that it is but a child who writes we insert the following:—]

After arriving we had a run on the sands; then we took our tea, arranged the house, and soon after went to bed.

The first thing Mackworth did on his arrival was to get Edward, the footman, to go over the town with him and buy a little wooden ship, worth sixpence, or properly nothing at all. Papa told him that whereas he had spent sixpence on this good-for-nothing ship, Edward would have made him a much better one for nothing (for be it known that Edward is very clever in such little works of ingenuity). It may be worth while to relate the end of this memorable vessel. In a few days it was stripped of all its rigging, and was then used to throw into the sea and take out again. On returning from Broadstairs it still existed, and was tied by a string to the boat which conveyed us to the packet, following the said boat stern foremost. Lastly, having safely gone through the dangers of the voyage, it was lost in the inn when it came to London.*

July 7.—None of us have ever seen the sea before, and therefore I at least was much delighted with it. It is a great pleasure to me to sit on the sands and watch the boats coming out of the harbour, or entering it, especially if the sea be rougher than usual. I think it is also extremely amusing to watch a wave rolling on, gradually increasing in bulk, and at last breaking into foam. The surf of a large wave often runs a great way up the sands, and wets those who are not on their guard. I was once taken by surprise, and found myself suddenly up to the instep in sea-water. A great deal of seaweed is to be found here. One sort is of a shining red brown, or a little like damson colour; it is shaped like a long strap of leather; the consistence of it is also leathery. Another grows like a plant on rocks; its peculiarity is that the leaves are covered with a singular kind of ball inflated with air, which when broken, snaps with a loud hollow noise. Another

* The beginning of this journal, though written at the date given, was copied out, down to the end of August, some months afterwards, and the passage above, as well as the explanatory opening, added.—ED.

sort has similar excrescences, but which are oval and juicy, and of a jelly-like substance. A third sort is of nothing but a multitude of long, fine red hairs, unbranched, and growing from the same root all together. An extremely beautiful species looks like a collection of very small pink ribbons; this, if I remember right, is a little branched. Some of the hair-like kinds are branched, and there are some which are composed of jointed tubes.

July 8.—I think there are a good many flowers about Broadstairs, which is particularly interesting to me, as I am very fond of botany. Though I have looked in vain for samphire and eryngo, which grow near the sea, yet the wild mignonette, which I never saw before, is plentiful on the rocks, as well as another flower, called the little Bermedick. It is a papilionaceous flower, of a yellow colour, and unbranched; the flowers grow in a large woolly tuft on the top of the stalk. The yellow toad's-flax also is to be found, and I once saw, on the rock, a splendid scabious, of a rich crimson-purple colour, which is often seen in gardens, and has a strong sweet scent. Lastly, a sort of red valerian, a very pretty flower, grows on the cliffs.

July 12.—Ramsgate is a large and rather handsome town, with a noble harbour and a great deal of shipping. The harbour is formed by three magnificent stone piers, the finest in the kingdom. The inner harbour is only formed for the reception of boats and small brigs; it is entered by an iron bridge in the cross pier, which lifts up.

July 19.—The star-fish is also very common. This singular zoophyte is in the shape of a star; it is of a pink or purple colour, and each spike is covered with thousands of minute points, by means of which the creature moves.

Aug. 8.—In the evening we all had a nice row on the sea. We saw in the water some crab-nets, which are made of nets stretched over sticks, so as to form a place big enough for a large crab. The entrance is so contrived that it cannot get out again. These traps are fastened at certain distances on a long line, which floats in the water. We saw several crabs already caught in some of these nets. The tide rose particularly high to-day.

Aug. 11.—Near Calais papa and mamma observed a remarkable phenomenon. A large space of ground, at some distance from the sea (as much as two miles, indeed), is entirely composed of a bed of round pebbles, whose depth is said to be interminable. It is not that the ground is stony, but there is nothing to be seen except these pebbles. Query,—Is it possible that the sea has in ancient times retired and left these stones behind it?

Aug. 31.—In the morning mamma took Arabella and me to Burgess' Library to see the printing, which interested us extremely. The types are small, wedge-shaped pieces of metal, at the end of which is a letter in relief; they are of a great many different sizes. On tables are raised things resembling very large desks, all covered with little wooden compartments in which the different letters are kept; they are not arranged alphabetically, but according as they are most wanted. The man who lays the types stands before this table, and takes out one after another all the letters he wants. He fixes each, as he takes it up, in something called a composing-stick, which he holds in his left hand, and which is made of brass and wood; it resembles a little case or box, without a top, and with only three sides. When the case is filled, the types are laid out correctly on another desk (without compartments), and when the sheet is completed, they are transferred to the press. The press is a small table with an edge round the top of it, and with brass lines to separate the pages or columns. A frame is fastened to it on hinges; this frame is as big as the table and has a cloth back; it is made to contain the paper. The little table is attached to the machine part of the press.

The types are arranged in order on the table, and the printer goes to another near it, covered with a particular sort of stiff ink. He then takes a roller, composed of glue, isinglass, and some other elastic materials; this he rolls over the ink, and, when it is thoroughly inked, passes it in like manner over the types. The sheet of paper is then fastened into the before-mentioned frame, which is immediately laid down on the type-table, and thus brings down the paper on the inked types. The table is next rolled under the press, which is screwed down on it; it is then rolled back, and the sheet taken out.

Sept. 16.—Gamlingay heath is famous throughout England for the rare flowers to be found there; I wish we lived nearer to it. Amongst the prettiest flowers I have found on it, at least at this time of the year, are the *Euphrasia officinalis*, or eyebright, and the *Polygala vulgaris*, or milkwort. The eyebright is a purplish white, with dark purple streaks and two yellow spots on the lip of the corolla; it is of the class of ringent flowers. The whole plant is small and delicate. The milkwort is also a small slender plant; it grows in little clumps, and does not rise above three or four inches in height; the stalk is purplish red, the leaves small and oval; the blossom varies considerably in colour, being sometimes blue, sometimes pink, and sometimes white. Of these I think I prefer the blue. The *Erica tetralix*, or cross-leaved heath, grows here in great abundance. It is bell-shaped, and of a beautiful pink.

Oct. 21.—In the morning papa took us all to see certain interesting operations in glass, performed by a man who travels about, and who has come to Potton to exhibit for a day or two. He made, in glass, baskets, candlesticks, birds, horses, etc., etc. The way he did them was as follows:—He sat at a table, and before him was a little furnace, which contained a flame of intense heat, though it was only kept up by tallow. He had a great many glass sticks of various sizes and of every colour; when he wished to make anything—a basket, for instance—he took a small one, which he merely used as a prop; he held the end of it * in the flame till the end of it melted into a sort of paste, which could be drawn out into any fineness. It was then drawn round and round the first stick, so as to make the bottom of the basket horizontally on the stick. In this way he made a vast number of things. One was Charles II. in the oak, another the Lord Mayor's coach, George IV. lying in state, etc. Some of these were very handsome and expensive. We bought a few of the minor things; one was a glass pen, and there was also an elegant and beautiful little ship.

Oct. 31.—Another pupil arrived last night—Mr. Charles Howard, the fifth son of the Earl of Carlisle. He is a tall, fine young man, and I like him a good deal from what I have since seen of him. I believe he is clever, and he is certainly very fond of books, especially of poetry. But his ruling passion is a love of politics, even from the time when he was quite a child. He is a great Whig, Foxite, and Reformer, and always reads the debates in Parliament. The newspaper is his inseparable companion wherever he goes and whatever he does, even at meals; indeed, he is so employed with it at breakfast that Mr. Gower (who is his cousin, Lady Carlisle and Lady Granville being sisters) is often obliged to give him a little kick under the table to remind him that he must eat his breakfast.

Nov. 4, *Friday.*—I had forgot to mention in the proper place that after I came home from Ramsgate I made a pasteboard model of the steam-packet in which we went to Broadstairs. It is nearly a yard long; I finished it a few weeks ago. It cost me a good deal of money, for I had to buy pasteboard and coarse paints in powder. I made it very correct, and furnished and painted all the cabins, even

* Here there is an evident clerical error; it should be "he held another in the flame," etc.

to the staircases. I also rigged it and put the rudder and boat to it, with the paddles, seats, railings, and flags.

Nov. 10, *Thursday.*—Some time ago there was an exhibition of paintings and engravings at Potton; many of the latter were very good. Amongst those I remember best was a very pretty engraving of a cottage-girl and her little dog, from a painting by Gainsborough. But those I liked
4 most were some excellent etchings from Morland, and two very beautiful proofs in mezzotint from the same artist; papa was so much pleased with these that he bought them at a low price. Morland particularly excels in figures, especially in children, but most of all in pigs, which animals he was very fond of, and used to make pets of them. The two proofs were "Blind-man's Buff" and "Bird's-nesting." I think the former is my favourite. The children are admirably represented, especially one little girl holding a dog in her arms; the dog is perhaps the best of the two, the expression of his eyes and his whole air are so very natural. Morland rather fails in his trees, and the shading of his barns and sheds is sometimes a large, unmeaningless mass of heavy strokes.

Nov. 11.—For some little time Louisa has complained of pain in her hip when she walks, and to-day mamma consulted Mr. McGrath about her. Mr. McGrath "confessed that all we had for to do" was to put on a blister, which we accordingly applied to her hip, and she was of course obliged to keep in bed. Blisters are made of the Spanish fly, or cantharides, which is a small insect, whose colour is very beautiful—green, gold, and azure. It is a native of the south of Europe. Their smell is like that of mice; they feed on the leaves of shrubs, especially of ash trees. Their eggs are deposited deep in the ground, where also the larvæ are metamorphosed into perfect insects. The odorous particles emitted by the cantharides often occasion sleep to those who sit under trees on which swarms of them are collected. When dried, fifty of them weigh hardly a drachm. They are used as blisters in a powdered state.

Nov. 17.—It is not perhaps generally known that all kinds of plants have their particular moth or butterfly, and that which feeds on one could not feed on another. Moths may be distinguished from butterflies by the shape of their feelers. All which have clavated feelers—that is, feelers that are of an equal thickness throughout, with a large head at the end—and all which have feelers that grow gradually bigger from the root to the extremity, and have a sort of tuft composed of several threads at the terminating point, are butterflies; while those which have feelers in any way different are moths. These latter are more numerous than butterflies are.

Dec. 24, *Saturday.*—I have long been employed in writing a history of the Jews, which, down to the return from the Captivity, is taken from the Bible, but after that 5
is much abridged from Milman's History. I have illustrated it with several drawings; it is of the size of half a sheet of writing-paper doubled once. It has more than two hundred pages, and is in the printing character. Moreover, it has a frontispiece, title-page, vignette, preface, table of contents, and index, to say nothing of an introduction, conclusion, and poem at the end. It is an inch in thickness, and has a cover of fine blue pasteboard, glued on and decorated with several patterns.

CHAPTER II.

[From twelve to thirteen years old.]

From Feb. 16 *to Dec.* 30, 1832.—*Brook House, Woodbury.*

Feb. 16.—Till lately I have never read Spenser, and therefore was not personally acquainted with his beauties. Neither do I mean to say that now I have read his "Faerie Queene;" but, having accidentally met with an extract from his "Hymn of Heavenly Love," a long poem, I went to papa's study and read the whole poem, which is most exquisitely beautiful, and is perhaps equal to anything Milton ever wrote. It is very simple, but highly poetical, and a pious feeling runs throughout. I was so much delighted with it that I read another, his "Hymne of Heavenly Beautie," which in point of poetic excellence perhaps exceeds the other. He has written a great many more long poems, together with sonnets and epitaphs; but I have not read these. Papa's copy of his poems is a very old edition, printed in the time of Queen Elizabeth, to whom it is dedicated. The illuminations are very curious, and the engravings most laughable; the print is small, and the old words make it rather difficult to read.

March 29, *Thursday.*—This evening we had an unexpected visitor in Mr. Charles Shore, the eldest son of Lord
6 Teignmouth. He is a very agreeable man, and has travelled a good deal, especially in many parts of Norway which are not well known. He has also been in Sweden, and has told us a great deal about both these countries. He says

that the scenery is wild and very magnificent, the glaciers are more extensive than even those of Switzerland, and mentioned some which were of vast size. One of these was nearly six thousand feet high; another was fifty-six miles long. This was the glacier of Upsala. The city of Stockholm is built on seven rocky islands in a lake, where it narrows into a river; the islands are connected by bridges not more than a hundred yards distant from each other. The streets have no pavements for foot travellers; it is, therefore, very dangerous to walk in them, for the sledges make no noise in coming, except, indeed, that each horse has a bell fastened to it. Each sledge has two horses, and is followed by another sledge bearing wheels, if they should be wanted. The post is regular, and as well conducted as ours; the royal palace is a vast square building. The manners of the Swedes are admirable, but the general society is very frivolous, and, though there are some people well informed in French and English literature, yet the greater part are devoted to balls, plays, and other idle amusements. Gustavus III. introduced French into his court, and it was his wish to call Stockholm the Paris of the north, but this did not meet the approbation of his subjects, who aim more at resembling the English. The present king is a very affable man, but possesses a good deal of dignity; he enjoys pretty good health. His countenance is very remarkable; his eye is kind, though large, dark, and piercing; his nose is hooked; but the greatest peculiarity of his face is that his mouth and chin recede a good deal. The queen is a very good-natured woman, but is devoted to balls, and commonly dines at nine o'clock, though the Swedes generally dine from one to three o'clock. Many of the *noblesse* are high aristocrats, and there is a strong party of opposition. The government consists of a diet of four chambers—one of nobles, one of peasants, one of the Church, and one of soldiers. Any decree must go through three of these chambers before it can be passed. The regiments are local. They are a sort of militia; each is drawn from a province and remains there. There are guards, cavalry, and artillery; the colonel possesses lands and a farm.

The Norwegians are a fine, dark-haired, handsome race of people; the women, however, are not generally so. The costume of the common people is very different from ours, but varies in the different provinces. Mr. C. Shore talked Latin with the clergy, who did not understand English. He says that the Swedish is an easy language to learn. He, on one occasion, entered the house of a pastor in one of the wildest parts of Norway, and perceived there the portrait of his father, Lord Teignmouth, who was one of the principal promoters of the Bible Society. He immediately made himself known, and was, of course, received with all hospitality.

[Here is a little bit of child's fun.]

April 5, *Thursday.*—We spent the afternoon also in the
summer-house, and were joined by Mr. Howard and Mr.
Gower. Arabella has a book about Africa, which was given
to her on her birthday. So I having told this to Mr. Howard,
he addressed Arabella with, "You know the Juvenile
7 Library, do not you?" "Oh yes, I do, and I have got one
of its books." "I think they are all very nice books, except one, that about Africa." This put Arabella into a direful
rage, but she immediately retaliated by deprecating Reform, and denouncing the newspapers as only vehicles of
deception. Mr. H. instantly fled away from hearing these
offensive sounds, but she pursued him, exclaiming, "No
8 Reform! no Reform! Down with Grey! hang Brougham!"
To complete his anger, I presented him that same evening
with some verses which I had written against Reform, and
which provoked him extremely.

June 15, *Friday.*—All the mob of Potton made a great
9 riot to celebrate the passing of the Reform Bill, and paraded
the town with the most hideous yells, accompanying a

triumphal car in the shape of a waggon completely covered with fresh boughs and bearing flags. They had also with them a band, and three large flags bearing the following inscriptions: "EARL GREY AND HIS COLLEAGUES," "TAVISTOCK AND PAYNE FOR EVER," "EARL GREY AND RELIGIOUS LIBERTY," "W.R. IV. AND REFORM." I do not suppose that any of them understood what they were so noisy about. The procession took place late in the evening; the band entered our garden and played several tunes, while the flags were all the while waving before the windows.

June 18.—I have been much interested in observing the operations of some ants in one of the garden-walks. These little insects have made very extensive buildings in one of the paths, both underground and above. With the earth which comes from their excavations, they build little domes and arches above ground, near the entrance. It is most interesting to watch the ants bringing out huge lumps of earth to make these domes with. I saw a single ant labouring up the steep sides of its hole, which was almost perpendicular, and carrying with it a lump of earth five times as big as itself. For three successive times the ant fell down with its burden as soon as it reached the top, but its perseverance prevailed, and it succeeded. Another ant, having fallen down, obtained the assistance of two others, and the united strength of the three dragged it quite up.

June 21.—I picked up on the grass a palmer-worm, which is a caterpillar, so named because it travels about like a palmer or pilgrim. It has long, thick tufts of black and red hair, and a very minute gold spot to each ring; it crawls very quickly. It seems to eat chiefly the leaves of the dock, the vine, and the lilac.

June 23.—Richard has found in the garden a beautiful caterpillar, which is now before me; it is nearly two inches long, with a number of thin tufts of hair on its body. There is a broad blue stripe on each of its sides, extending from head to tail, and on every other part are alternate and narrow stripes of orange and black, besides a white stripe along the top of the back. The face is grey, and the eyes black; the hairs beneath the body are of an orange colour; it has ten rings on its body, and six legs before, besides eight holders nearer the tail. I have never before seen such a pretty caterpillar; the different colours are arranged so beautifully, and the blue is so exquisitely speckled with black. Round its neck it has a band of a grey colour, with two black spots, and the under part of the body is black and grey. I think it is much prettier than the palmer-worm, and I wish very much to know its name.

July 2, *Monday.*—Richard and I went to sketch St. Leonard's Monastery, an ancient Norman building now falling to ruins, but there still remain some beautiful arches, with very rich mouldings. I took a drawing of it from a very inconvenient place, and did not succeed very well. The boys in the street threw stones at us, and behaved very impudently, which my aunt attributes to Reform! What an idea!

July 3.—Mr. Cayley found the *Nummularia*, or money-wort, which I had long wanted to see. It is very beautiful, of a delicate gold colour; the class is Pentandria, monogynia; the flowers are strung with the leaves along creeping stalks.

The chief flowers I found in my walks to-day were the *Spiræa ulmaria*, or meadow-sweet, a pretty flower with a very strong smell; the *Veronica anagallis*, or water-speedwell, a blue flower; *Galium palustre*, or white water lady's-bed-straw; the *Ligustrum vulgare*, or privet; and the *Lathyrus pratensis*, or everlasting pea. Of these I like best the water bedstraw. It is extremely beautiful; the plant is small and delicate, and is entirely covered with clusters of very minute white flowers. The pea is a pretty yellow flower, and the stalk climbs round other plants.

July 18, *Wednesday.*—This day was colder and more windy; in my walk I found the nest of some insect, I think it is a spider's. It is formed amongst the gorse bushes, and resembles a deep, narrow thimble, formed of a cottony or silk substance, very thick, and impervious to the rain. It is always slanting, I suppose to prevent the rain from pouring in through the entrance, which is at the top; the edges of the entrance spread far and wide all round into a large and flat web, of the same cotton, which suspends the nest safely among the bushes. The cotton is beautifully woven, thick, and not easily torn.

Of all the caterpillars I brought home on Sunday, eight only remain; the rest have crawled away, and have been lost or trodden to death. Poor little creatures! I shall never keep caterpillars alive again. While they were in the full enjoyment of health and liberty, I took them prisoners, confined them in a box, and shut them up in a house, far from their homes; by which means almost all have been destroyed. It makes me quite unhappy to think of it. I shall certainly set them all at liberty to-morrow, and put them on one of the plants to which they belong.

July 19.—The first thing I did this morning on rising was to set my caterpillars at liberty; and I was very glad I had done it. Louisa afterwards found another of them in my room, crawling about; this, too, I placed with its companions when I walked out.

We went to the sand-rock and had a nice game of play; only we dirtied ourselves terribly, at which Henrietta was much displeased. The sand-rock is very pretty on one side of the road, fronting it; it declines on each side into green hills, covered with fern and larches, which reach to the hedge. This rock is much inhabited by sand-martins, and is completely pierced by the holes which contain their nests. The sand-martin is a very pretty bird, about the size of a swallow; the upper part of the body is a soft brown, underneath it is white; the shape is extremely elegant.

July 20, *Friday.*—This evening, as papa and mamma were out in the gig, they saw at the Biggleswade turnpike road a man stretched out dead by the side of the road; but they thought he was asleep. It has since turned out that this is a case of cholera. If this dreadful disease reaches Potton it will, I fear, from the drunkenness that pervades the place (there being no less than thirteen public-houses, besides beershops), prove very fatal.

At tea-time papa told us a story of an adventure which happened to a lady at Bury St. Edmunds. She and her husband were walking in a field, when a bull attacked them furiously, and ran after them. They happened to have a little dog with them, which increased the fury of the animal. By dint of running as hard as possible they reached a stone fence or wall of some height. Her husband had but just time to throw his wife over, when the bull came up, and made so furiously at the wall that they expected every moment he would be over. The gentleman now thought that his only chance of safety was to throw the dog over to the enraged creature. He told his wife to run on (they had another gate to go through); he took the poor little animal in his arms and threw him over the wall. The dog, of course, ran away, the bull after it; it was tossed and gored. The lady never got over the fright; it eventually caused her death.

July 24, *Tuesday.*—The way —— spends her day is as follows: *—First she will be down in a quarter of an hour, but does not make her appearance till the middle of a breakfast made late on her account. She rustles into the room, laughs, and eats her breakfast. After this she

* This lively picture was drawn on purpose to amuse the lady (a very dear friend, and a very charming one) who was the subject of it.—ED.

dawdles a little while, and then sits down to her drawing. She every minute declares her abhorrence of it, and how she cannot go on with it any longer; however, it contrives to exist till luncheon; then she jumps up, calls on every one to praise her decision of character, and runs up to make away with it. Luncheon is ready, she goes into the parlour and makes a dinner, though it is only one o'clock. When she has finished she sits and talks a little while, then starts up and goes to the window to see the weather. Finding that it is just going to rain, she runs out into the garden, dragging all the house after her. A shower drives her in; on returning she finds one of her paints lost, which is no wonder, for the table is covered with her litters. After setting everybody in the room to look for it, it is found on the top of her paint-box. Dinner is announced. She laughs herself into the parlour, and makes a hearty meal. She concludes the day with gossip and screaming to the sound of the harp.

July 31, *Tuesday.*—We went to Cambridge to-day. Papa and mamma took Richard and me with them. We got up very early and took a slight breakfast; then we set off in the gig, with the two ponies, and went through the most hideous country—all chalky, and in some parts the road was wretched. I, however, noticed a great many beautiful flowers in the hedges, many of which I did not know. When we were about a few miles from Cambridge we came to the top of an exceedingly steep hill, with deep places on each side in one part; here we had to get out and walk while the gig went down to the bottom of the hill. From this road was a very extensive and beautiful view before us; but what made me most glad to get out and walk was that I should be able to gather flowers. The chief of these was a very pretty flower, called the *Campanula rapunculus;* it is of a deep purple colour, and not tall from the ground. I took it home and copied it. Cambridge is about twenty miles from Potton. We reached it at eight o'clock, and had breakfast immediately. Our object in coming was to see the chapels and colleges; so, after having gone shopping some time, we went to see them.

Jesus College is my favourite. The college itself is not worthy of attention, but the chapel is exquisite. It is an admirable specimen of Early English architecture, especially the choir, which is decorated with the most beautiful windows, and arches underneath them, each perfect in their kind, with extremely deep mouldings. One particular sort, called the dog's-tooth moulding, peculiar to Early English, is found here. In the choir are two niches of remarkable beauty. The arches run into each other and twine together; they are surrounded by a square moulding of the dog's-tooth sort; in its being square it somewhat resembles the Perpendicular style.

The chapel is in the form of a cross; but the central tower, instead of being open all the way to the top, is unhappily shut out from the spectator by a nasty ceiling of the same height as the rest of the chapel. I say "unhappily," because what is above is perhaps more splendid even than the choir. We ascended by a dark winding staircase, but when we reached the interior of this tower itself it was exquisite! All round the wall (it was square) there were the most beautiful arches, with extraordinarily deep mouldings, and connected with each other; they were nearly all perfect. It is impossible for those who have not seen it to form an adequate idea of them. The capitals are in many places beautifully carved, and every arch has a cinquefoil belonging to it. I am glad to say that the ceiling is to be removed, and these noble arches will be laid open to view.

The hall in Jesus College contains two portraits—Arch-
10 bishop Cranmer, and the celebrated Sterne. Cranmer is a copy painted by Sir Joshua Reynolds.

Aug. 2, *Thursday.*—Papa in his drive to-day found the *Verbascum tetralix*, or mullein, an extremely beautiful plant. The leaves grow at the root; they are large and very woolly, and crumpled all over. The blossoms are flat, of a very delicate yellow colour; the stamens are large, and completely fringed with purple hairs; the flowers grow in a very long spike, in hundreds together, quite closely, so as to form a most beautiful appearance; the stalks are single, and unbranched. This plant is found by roadsides in a sandy soil.

Aug. 5,* *Saturday.*—We found in our walk to-day a large locust, two inches in length, of a light green colour. He had six legs—the two hinder ones were those he leaped with; all the thighs were speckled with minute black spots. The top of his head was of a dark colour, his eyes black, and from above these, out of green roots, sprung two feelers, longer than his whole body, of a clear reddish yellow, speckled with black. On his neck there was something like a saddle; along his back extended a stripe of the colour of a dead leaf. His knees were brown, and his legs, downwards from his knees, full of little thorny points, and his claws very large. Four little jointed things, like very small legs, came from his mouth; the upper part of his body seemed to be composed of seven or eight broad rings, laid over each other like scales; the under part of the body was green, with two milk-white longitudinal stripes. I drew this creature; he constantly moved, but did not attempt to jump. I caught him in my handkerchief, and kept him an hour or two under a finger-glass turned upside down.

Aug. 7.—I again found the nettle-caterpillar. It has several double rings, each composed of very minute golden spots, which, when seen in a certain light, sparkle like silver or drops of dew; the hairs, too, are silvery. These caterpillars are slow in their motions.

* Evidently a mistake for Aug. 4.

Aug. 15, *Wednesday.*—. . . Besides this, we found a great curiosity, which few people have had an opportunity of seeing. It was discovered by mamma. The butcher-bird is in the habit of killing insects and small birds, and sticking them (sometimes alive) upon thorns; now we found a poor humble-bee stuck, living, on a thorn in a hedge, and, as it is impossible this could be by accident (for the thorn came quite through his body), we have every reason to conclude that the butcher-bird put it there.

As we were passing through a meadow, we saw a shepherd stand at a gate which led into a turnip-field; he called to the sheep, and, without the aid of any dog, they all came scampering from every part of the meadow, though it was a large one, till there was not one left. He then bade them pass into the turnip-field; they obeyed, and this the shepherd said they did constantly. It was quite a singular instance of obedience in sheep.

Aug. 22.—. . . The morning was extremely rainy, but after dinner we all took a walk. We saw a poor miserable woman in a tent by the roadside. Her name is Richardson; she has a bad, drunken husband, who has quite starved her; and, now that they cannot pay their rent, they have been turned out of their house. To add to her miseries, she is very ill, having just given birth to a child, and the hard rain has quite poured through the slender covering of the tent. Mamma has been once or twice to see her, and has given her broth, etc.

Aug. 28.—. . . In the evening papa began to read to us Shakespeare's play of *Julius Cæsar*, and finished it to-day. I like it extremely; it is very fine, and the characters remarkably well drawn. Brutus is my favourite; the scene I like best is where he and Cassius quarrel and are reconciled. I am very fond of Portia also, but not Julius Cæsar, nor Mark Anthony.

The day was so fine and hot that I sat out of doors,

and I employed myself in carving a carrot into the shape of a man.

Oct. 14, *Sunday.*—In our walk to-day, after dinner, we picked up a dead Norway rat, quite a young one; we at first thought it was a mouse, till mamma set us right again. It was four inches long, and the tail three inches; the head was very large; it had no neck; the ears were broad and bare. The eyes are large and black; the whiskers numerous; the mouth placed much under the head. The feet are bare and flesh-coloured; the two fore-feet are destitute of a thumb. The rat is brown; the throat and under-part of the body a greyish white; the tail dark and thinly covered with hairs.

Oct. 17, *Wednesday.*—It is surprising how many hornets we have seen in the last day or two; I am sure there is a nest very near. We caught a very large one to-day, and extremely handsome. We tried to put it to death with oil, but it was above an hour before we succeeded, for I was the performer, and did not know how much to apply. When papa, however, came out from dinner, he put a great quantity, so as completely to saturate it, and it soon died. But I shall never forget the agonies it seemed to suffer! It made an awful sound, rolled over and over, went round and round the glass, and sometimes even stood on its head. It was more painful to bear than even my poor caterpillars. We should have set it at liberty but that it was so dangerous a creature that we could not do it safely. I have got it now in my collection.

Nov. 8, *Thursday.*— . . . It was now settled that we are to do what we have long had in contemplation, viz. to remove to Woodbury, a good house near Everton. The reason is that we find Potton agrees very ill with our health, while Woodbury is remarkably healthy, and is situated on the celebrated Gamlingay heath.

Nov. 10, *Saturday.*—Mr. Howard is, indeed, the most

agreeable pupil papa has ever had. He is exceedingly amiable and good-tempered,* and is constantly with us in the drawing-room. Papa is very fond of him; he says that he does not suppose that in any company he would ever be caught assenting to what he did not feel, for he is remarkably open and candid; and mamma once said (which I dare say is very true) that he has a great deal of fine feeling. He is very intelligent, and has a good deal of information; in short, he is a particular favourite with all of us. To conclude, he has a fine and expressive countenance.

Nov. 13, *Tuesday.*—This evening I read Spenser's poem, called "Mother Hubbard's Tale," a very long one. It is evidently a satire on the court and clergy, and a very bitter one too.

[Then follow three pages of extracts from the above-named poem, very accurately done.]

Dec. 14, *Friday.*—There is going on a sale of Mr. Wilkinson's furniture at Woodbury, and papa went to attend at it. When he returned he told us a story of what had happened. He rode on horseback, and on his way heard the fox-hounds for some time; he knew that they were to throw off that day, and hoped he should not get in their way. However, he arrived safe at Woodbury. The auctioneer, Mr. Carington, was at his work, when a cry was heard of, "There they are!" Behold, the whole set of hounds, pursuing the fox, dashed through the garden, over the beds and everything! Papa was, of course, not highly delighted, but every one else was in ecstasies. The ladies jumped up and clapped their hands; Mr. C. blew a horn which he had in his pocket or somewhere, and leaped out of the window into the garden, with all the ragamuffins after him. Papa, finding it in vain to try and stop them, walked out

* It was a peculiarity of the writer, when a child, always to use the word "good-tempered" for "good-natured."

with Mr. Wilkinson to see if he could not hinder them from doing damage. Mr. W. ordered the door of the courtyard to be opened, that the fox might pass through; but, unluckily, there was no one to open it, and he was obliged to turn back, the dogs quite close to him all the way, and even brushing by papa. The animal made the greatest exertions, but could only reach the greenhouse, and there the hounds killed poor foxey; he was quite unhappy, and with his tail between his legs. Just then the hunters came up; they had taken care to dismount, all except two most ungentlemanly fellows, who leaped over the haw-haw, cutting up the turf sadly. The fox was now handed about to be seen, the hounds surrounding the hunters, and great delight was shown by all; but papa pitied the poor creature, and several times expressed his indignation, not against the intrusion into the garden, for that he could have borne with perfect good temper in the pursuit of any rational amusement, but against the general barbarity and cruelty of fox-hunters, whom he detests. He says that he never before saw a fox so closely pursued. Even after the body was taken away, the place smelt quite offensively.

Dec. 19, *Wednesday.*—The going to Woodbury both costs me something and has given me something. In the first place, two of my stuffed birds are thrown away, because they breed the moth (why this was not discovered before I cannot tell), my pasteboard steam-packet is burnt, to my great grief, and my two chalk figures are also destroyed. However, papa and mamma, to console me for the loss of my steam-packet, which cost me thirteen pennies, very kindly indeed gave me sixpence apiece, and papa offered me a shilling for every stuffed bird I should throw away, but I would not for a guinea.

I asked papa about colleges, and papa, perceiving from my question that I understood but little about it, kindly undertook to explain it to me. He first told me what a corporation was, one person (for it may be one, and is then called a sole corporation) or a united body. He gave me an instance: Mr. Whittingham, Vicar of Potton, constitutes one; he possesses certain emoluments and certain endowments, but not as R. W., but as vicar. As for a corporation of several people, it is formed by a charter from the king; all the members act together, have a common seal, and make laws among themselves, provided they are not in contradiction to the laws of the land. If they buy an estate the deeds are signed by any they shall depute, and the common seal is put to it. A college is a sort of corporation. Some colleges have been endowed as much as eight hundred years ago, but whoever endowed them left for their support the revenues of certain estates, which thenceforth belong to the college, and decided the number of people to compose it—perhaps a master, or warden, or whatever he may be called, and eighteen or twenty Fellows, some of whom act as tutors. All these govern amongst themselves, and make laws, with the head or master as supreme, but not despotic. Besides these, a number of young men as students are admitted to receive instruction, but they are quite independent, and have nothing whatever to do with the government of the college.

The university itself is a much more complex affair. As each college is in itself a corporation, governed by its own laws, so all the colleges together form another grand corporation, which makes its own laws, has common revenues, and whose members occasionally meet to deliberate in Cambridge at a Senate, and in Oxford in Convocation.

The university is represented in Parliament, each by two members which are chosen among them, not for one college or another, but for the whole university. When a student has been three years in college, he is examined, and if he is found sufficiently advanced, he has his first degree conferred on him, Bachelor of Arts; but this is not by his own college, but by the whole university. In three years more, commonly without examination, he is made Master of Arts; and on becoming B.A. he may be elected Fellow, and join in the government of the college. On marrying, though he still retains his degree, and may vote for the member to represent the university, he loses all influence in the government, as is the case with papa.

The university is governed by a nominal chancellor, but all acting power is in the vice-chancellor, who resides always at the place. The chancellor is commonly a nobleman. The Chancellor of Oxford University is now Lord 11
Grenville; that of Cambridge, the Duke of Gloucester. He is a very silly man. Papa told us that one day, as he was riding out, he complained that the flies would get into his mouth, and he could not keep them out. The servant answered, "Perhaps your Royal Highness had better shut your mouth," for he was in the habit of riding with the mouth wide open. Another time he bid his servant fetch his handkerchief from his room, but hesitated, and said, "I am pretty sure I locked the door, but I cannot remember whether I left the key on the inside." These anecdotes made us laugh heartily.

Dec. 23, *Sunday.*—The little girl whom I teach has been here every day for the last week, and came this evening for the last time, as I am going to-morrow, and she is too young to go as far as Woodbury. . . . Perhaps, however, as summer comes on and she is a little older, she may now and then walk over to Woodbury, for it is a pity that, when she seems to be getting on, I should give her up altogether. In the mean time, I have some thoughts of having a few little girls from Everton, if mamma and papa approve of it, which I believe they do.

Every evening of Sunday, after tea, mamma hears us say a hymn of Watts', which we have previously learnt, each saying one verse. After this we say some parts of the

Catechism, mamma commenting as we go on in the simplest manner. I believe none of us are taught anything which is not thoroughly explained, and I am afraid this is too unusual. There is another very common practice, not followed with us, that of sending children very early to church. I think that before the age of eight they can rarely understand the Liturgy, yet they seem to be supposed to comprehend it even at three or four. If children are taught hymns and prayers before they can perceive anything of their meaning it is likely to produce a superstitious idea that they are to derive good from what they say, and will thereby please God, as the Roman Catholics do with their Latin prayers. But this is not my own idea;
12 I learnt it from Whately, and must not pass it off as original.

Dec. 24, *Monday.*—This was the day we moved to our new house; there was the most indescribable bustle and confusion. Everything went, except a table and a few chairs in the drawing-room, that we might have our dinner. I was even obliged to part with my beloved desk, and had then nothing left to do except now and then to play at cup and ball.

Dec. 25, *Tuesday.*—This is my birthday. I am thirteen years old. When I came down into the library as soon as I was dressed, papa and mamma gave me a birthday
13 present, a beautiful and most interesting book, Babbage's "Economy of Manufactures," which I have long wished for. It is a new edition, with corrections and improvements.

Dec. 27, *Thursday.*—To-day's newspaper announces that Antwerp has capitulated to the French, who are besieging it in behalf of the Belgians, and to whom they are to give it up. The commander of the fortress was General Chasse. The account of the elections was very entertaining; I read it as usual to the children. It always happens that the Reform candidates are cheered and applauded, while the Tories are hissed and assailed with groans. The Tories have been behaving most shamefully, bribing and threatening the electors to the utmost degree; but they are generally unsuccessful.

Dec. 28, *Friday.*—After breakfast, when we were all sitting together in the library, the conversation turned on the late capitulation of the citadel of Antwerp. Papa made some promiscuous remarks on the war, of which I will put down what I remember. "The free navigation of the Scheldt has always been a great object with the other powers, the Dutch have as strenuously opposed it; but it is a free gift of Nature, and ought to belong equally to all the countries through which it runs. . . . The King of Holland is a thorough money-making merchant. He himself trades; he monopolizes at the expense of his subjects."

Dec. 30, *Sunday.*—Papa said also that during the war, when the farmers were rich and flourishing, and were amassing thousands upon thousands, they showed the most brutal indifference to the poor who were perishing around them; but that now their turn came, they were getting poorer and poorer, their rents were not paid, and they were eaten up with the poor rates.

CHAPTER III.

From Jan. 1, 1833, *to May*, 1833.—*Woodbury, Casterton.*

[Written at thirteen years old, and giving the beginning of her life in the new and beautiful home to which her parents removed the preceding Christmas, and where they lived five years.]

*Jan.**—We took a walk with mamma across the cow-pasture, the first of the three fields leading to Everton. It is a very pretty little field, hilly, and partly covered with broom. It slopes down towards Foxhill Wood, the wood at the bottom of our garden. Here we saw a very handsome young bull. He seemed very quiet and innocent, and not disposed to hurt any one; but bulls are never to be trusted.

Jan. 12.—We had a long game of play in the garden. The flower garden, which is very large, is divided from the kitchen garden by a noble laurel hedge. Under this hedge runs a path, and there is another path between it and the kitchen garden, which is surrounded by a brick wall. The second path runs all round the kitchen garden, and is entered in two different places by openings in the laurel hedge, which runs round two sides of it. The laurel hedge is double, and the two rows meet together above, so we found that the interior made a very noble palace. This suggested the idea of playing at kings and queens. We began by making Louisa queen, and Arabella and I were

* Date of day uncertain.

her guards; but Richard and Mackworth were very rebellious. At length we all got tired of her, deposed her, and made Mackworth king. We chose him because, being the youngest, he would probably not control us much; and, in fact, I did get all the acting power myself, being made his principal guard. After dinner we continued the play for some time longer.

Jan. 15.—At dinner Mackworth, having forgotten on one occasion to say "Thank you," put papa in mind of the following story:—A gentleman was driving in his gig to a town in Devonshire; on the way he overtook a little boy, with whom he had some chat, and he ended by inviting the boy to get up into the gig. The lad accepted the offer, and on coming to the town jumped down and ran away. The gentleman called out, "Well, but don't you say 'Thank you'?" But he got only the gruff reply, "It was you axed me, not I axed you." From this we began to talk of dialects and provincialisms. Mrs. Keal remarked that the Pottoners made great use of the odd word "mort"—"there has been a mort of sickness," "a mort of fine weather;" and she told a little anecdote she had from a gentleman, who, going out one morning before breakfast, met a working man, and asked him how he employed his time. The man said, "Why, I gets up early in the morning, and the first thing I does I has no breakfast."

Jan. 21.*—Our daily employments vary but little. As for myself, I rise as soon as I can wake, which is usually as late as half-past seven, and employ myself in doing my Greek and Latin, and learning whatever I have to get by heart. After breakfast I feed the birds with bread-crumbs, and from about that time till twelve o'clock I am usually

* This reads like a severe programme, but it must be remembered that most of her lessons were voluntary, and a great delight to her; also that the time-table was, as we have seen, freely varied in favour of rambles after flowers, and other open-air investigations.—Ed.

employed in teaching the children, and in some of my own lessons. At twelve we go out till dinner; after dinner I amuse myself for half an hour; then I read to mamma, and do my needlework; then we go out again for about an hour and a half; then I and Richard finish our Greek or Latin for papa, and I read Fuseli's Lectures to mamma. This employs me till tea, after which I and R. do our lesson with papa, and then we amuse ourselves till bedtime. This is generally the way in which I, at least, spend my time; of course the coming of visitors sometimes makes a little difference.

Jan. 25.—At tea, papa and mamma always sit at the fire by themselves, and we listen to their conversation; this evening it was peculiarly interesting. Papa began by condemning the idea that the Duke of Wellington's military prowess ought to exempt him from dislike on account of his political opinions or anything else. He instanced Mr. T. Quintin, who would call it quite a shame that, after all he had done for England, he should be so unpopular; but if a man who had been eminent in science, and had made useful discoveries, should fall under general odium for his after conduct or opinions, he would (think) nothing of abusing him. And yet this man would be much more deserving of public esteem, for he would really have been a benefactor to his country; he would not have been employed in cutting throats, in war and massacre, in which men nevertheless glory, instead of considering the business of a soldier a painful necessity. Soon after, mamma remarking that the Conservatives had still a strong party in England, papa assented, and then said that the late election cost Mr. Stuart, the Tory member, £20,000. This was chiefly spent in indirect bribery, by entertaining people in public-houses, "a beastly way of spending money."

Jan. 28.—Poor mamma has had a night of intense suffering, which kept her entirely awake, and very early this morning, before two o'clock, Mr. Keal was sent for. Her pain was in some degree allayed by laudanum, but was succeeded by great sickness and debility. After breakfast, papa called us together, and spoke to us at some length. He began by mentioning the dreadful pain mamma suffered all night, and then said that, though we had never been told so in such plain terms before, he now deemed it proper to inform us that mamma's life was very uncertain, and would probably not last long. It is hardly necessary to add that papa's words made a deep impression on us, and that he left us in tears. Indeed, I cannot think what we could do without mamma; it seems to be that if she died I should never be happy again. At ten o'clock Mr. Magrath and Mr. MacLear [the doctors] came; and at about twelve I went upstairs to see mamma. She was more free from pain, but extremely weak, and scarcely able even to whisper; she looked very pale and ill. I kissed her and then left the room, and finished hearing the children's lessons, about which I was before employed.

Jan. 29.—Mamma is rather better to-day; I sat with her in the evening, while papa was making his usual weekly examination of the children's progress in Greek, which I teach them.

Jan. 30.—We went out of doors as usual, and walked about the garden, the children listening to a story I told them. This has been my practice ever since I was six or seven years old, and is a great amusement both to them and myself. I think I must by this time have told them many thousands of stories. They are of every kind. At one time I used to relate histories of imaginary kings of England or France; sometimes I tell stories about children, generally of noble birth; sometimes of adventures of people cast on desert islands; sometimes the adventures of some hero who encounters dragons, genii, and all sorts of enchantments; sometimes discoveries of unknown lands; sometimes the adventures of Lilliputians in England; and frequently tales in which birds or quadrupeds are the actors; in short, of every kind which can possibly be devised. I always tell these stories extempore.

Jan. 31.—In the afternoon there was a fall of snow, and we began to speculate what we should do if every flake was a piece of gold money. To be sure, this shower of money would break all the windows, destroy the plants, and patter furiously down the chimneys; but then we should get ten thousand times more money than would be sufficient to pay for the repairing of the damage a hundred times over. We then began to settle what we should do with all this money. We should in the first place purchase the whole estate of Woodbury, and rebuild the house on a magnificent scale. Then we should have a splendid garden, filled with all the choicest flowers in the world. And we would have a noble library, and printing-presses for us children, to print all the productions of our pens. In short, there would be no end to the magnificence of our possessions and mode of living. I should like also to have a tame elephant.

Feb. 9.—We did not go beyond the garden, and as usual I told the children a story; but I shall never thoroughly enjoy going out till there are wild flowers for me to find and botanize.

I continue my usual employments of writing, both prose and poetry. I am chiefly employed about "Witikind the Saxon," an epic poem in several books, of which I have completed three. I am also writing "Don Roderick," a poem something in the manner of Sir Walter Scott's. Of this I have finished three cantos, and begun the fourth. In addition to these, several prose works of various sorts.

Cook is a great coward; she is afraid even of slugs, snails, and mice. She complained to me once that the mice used to run over her bed and pillow at night. "And what do you do to them?" I asked. "Why, I buffet them off as well as I can, miss," she replied. To think of battling with mice!

Feb. 12.—Mr. Maclear* called, and as usual entertained us with a great deal of astronomy. He first inquired whether I had studied a little book on that subject which he had given me, and afterwards told us what he was doing in that way. He said that Jupiter and Venus are both now visible in the west. Jupiter is very magnificent, and Venus (though not to the naked eye) is in the shape of a half moon; but she is difficult to manage with a telescope, on account of the flood of light about her, which makes her outline indistinct. The same thing is rather apt to happen with Jupiter; but not so with Saturn, because of his distance from the sun. I asked him, "How near is Saturn's ring to the body of the planet, in its nearest part?" This I said, conceiving it to be an ellipsis; but Mr. Maclear, perceiving my mistake, set me right, and told me that it was perfectly round, and that it seemed oval, because it was not flat before us, like the moon, but we saw it sideways, as it is represented in prints. This ring, he said, is now disappearing, and will soon become so straight before us that we shall see nothing but two little wings on each side. Saturn is the most extraordinary of all the planets. Mr. Maclear kindly promised to send me a telescope through which I can even see Jupiter's four satellites; this telescope he has had seventeen years.

Feb. 13.—At about eight o'clock we were all sitting quietly in the drawing-room, except papa, mamma lying on the sofa, when a tall muffled figure entered. William, who showed him in, said something which sounded like "Mr. Howard," but I was not certain till he said again, "Mr.

* The well-known eminent man of science, afterwards Sir Thomas Maclear, Astronomer Royal at the Cape. He started in life as a medical practitioner in the little town of Biggleswade, in Bedfordshire. —Ed.

Howard." Then we all shouted out, "Mr. Howard!" full of joy and astonishment, and I was so surprised at his totally unexpected arrival that I trembled all over. Mr. Howard laughed, and then went up into Mr. Taylor's room to make himself tidy. Richard was despatched to tell papa, and we did nothing but talk about him, and say how glad we were that he was come. When he came down he told us that he had been at least a fortnight at the Cambridge University, and had set off in horse and gig at three o'clock, but that near Hatley St. George the horse was knocked up, and would go no further, so that he had walked all the rest of the way to Woodbury. Mamma had soup and mutton-chops warmed up for him, as he had eaten nothing for hours, and must necessarily be very hungry. We could scarcely have a more agreeable visitor, or one whom we should be more glad to see. He looks quite as pleasant and good-tempered as he used to do, and talks quite as agreeably.

Feb. 14.—Mr. Howard set us to run races. I won in two of them, and Richard in another. Papa and mamma had dinner at one o'clock, and we all dined with them in the library—a great treat. Mr. Howard went away at about half-past three, not being allowed to stay two nights from college, but he hopes to come and see us several times in the summer.

Feb. 23.—I tried the telescope—it is the new moon, and at length I succeeded in viewing her. I easily saw the whole globe, and perceived where the dark and light parts joined; the edges were quite rough. This was while mamma and papa were at dinner; when mamma entered the drawing-room, we saluted her with exclamations of joy, telling what we had seen. She then looked herself, and next Mr. Taylor. Afterwards we viewed Jupiter; he was extremely bright, but we could not see his satellites.

Feb. 25.—We came in at a quarter past four; I went

up to put on my frock, when the sky grew suddenly black, as if a thunderstorm was coming on. My room looks to the north; there are several fir-trees near it in the garden, and the dark blue-gray sky seen amongst their branches, and which was of a beautifully clear hue, had a most striking appearance. At length a very heavy shower came on; at the same time the setting sun darted from the west, and a splendid rainbow appeared, making a complete arch from north to south, but most brilliant in the north. Above it was seen a very faint reflection of its beauty, but which soon vanished, though the real one remained some time.

Feb. 26.—As for Jupiter, we must make haste in looking at him, for he is getting near the sun. His belts are visible, and though the trees hide him from the drawing-room, I think we can see him from upstairs. Venus is much higher and nearer the moon. Mars and Saturn are to be seen, one in the south-west, the other in the east. Mr. Maclear gave us a great deal of interesting information, of which I will put down what I remember. Saturn's ring gives him light, though it is opaque; his shadow is often seen upon it. Jupiter, though he is so enormous, turns round on himself in nine hours. His belts are atmospheric vapours; they vary continually, and sometimes spots are seen on them. The Georgium Sidus is at an immense distance from us, and not bigger than one of Jupiter's satellites. The sun is supposed (though it is all surmise) to consist of a luminous substance devoid of heat in itself, but whose rays in entering our hemisphere, being dispersed and broken, produce heat by a chemical process. As for the spots, it is imagined that his light is a vapour round him, and that his dark body appears sometimes through the vapour. The Milky Way is a nebula; if we look through the telescope we shall see that it is composed of myriads of stars clustered together, but which are probably very far apart. There is another very beautiful nebula in the sword of Orion.

14 We received to-day new numbers of the *Penny Magazine*, *Penny Cyclopædia*, *Gallery of Portraits*, *Society Maps*, *History of the Church*, *Commerce*, and *Saturday Magazine*. The *Penny* contains many interesting things. Of the engravings, there is the statue of Niobe and her daughter, the very picture of grief, and in a beautiful attitude; there is a woodcut of Mary Queen of Scots, and another of Lady Jane Grey; a portrait of Galileo, and a representation of Notre Dame at Paris; with a spirited wood engraving of Raphael's painting of the death of Ananias. But, above all, it contained a highly interesting and valuable article on the horrible (for it is no less) effect of tight-lacing and want of exercise. The whole body is diseased, every function depraved by this fatal practice. Boarding-schools are nurseries of illness; few girls come from them in health; and in one in particular, all who had been there two years were more or less crooked.

March 6.—I forgot to mention an odd thing Arabella and I did this morning. A. got out of bed early, and woke me. I felt wonderfully tired and sleepy, but got up not very long after. Just as I had done dressing, I heard it strike four o'clock. I hastened downstairs, and found A. in the dark, so I unfastened the shutters of our sitting-room. The sun, of course, had not risen; the moon was shining beautifully in the north-west, and several stars were visible; a very thick fog hung about the trees. It was not light enough to read or write, and nobody was up besides ourselves, so we sat a whole hour in the cold, talking together. Just as it struck six, Richard came down, and at the same time Frederick got up and struck a light, so that we obtained a candle and went to our employments.

March 8.—Mrs. Keal mentioned a curious fact in natural history; a jack (a fish) had been sent to her, and when it was opened a large rat was found inside him, quite whole and unmasticated, and apparently just swallowed. It is not uncommon, papa said,' to find frogs and small fish withinside the jack, which is very voracious.

March 12.—I worked at my garden, which mamma has lately given me; it consists of two beds, but I shall only plant it with wild flowers. One bed is to contain flowers which like damp; in it I am making a little mound of earth and stones for the beautiful potentilla to climb over. I shall also have the money-wort, the willow-herb, the mouse-eared scorpion-grass, and, if I can get them, the flowering-rush and the water-violet.

March 19.—The paths of our gardens have all been nicely sanded; and in lieu of a mound, which I cannot make nicely, I cut away the earth pretty deeply in one part, so as to leave a space standing in the middle, down which the potentilla may climb. I then went with a spade and wheelbarrow to the bottom of the garden. Here we dug up two or three wild plants, two sorts of ranunculus, hyacinths, and strawberry. We then went into the lower part of the cow-pasture, a damp meadow separated from the garden by a paling and low hedge, over which we easily climbed. From thence I got other plants—some *Geranium Robertianum*, primroses, a cowslip, strawberries, and others which I do not know. All these I put in my garden, with the proper soil in which I found them; when blooming they will look very pretty.

March 20.—To make a little shade, I have dug up a few young trees, and planted them among my flowers, and also stuck two long straight and supple sticks, crossing each other in the shape of half-hoops, at whose feet I planted slips of ivy and wild honeysuckle, which I got from Whitewood, to climb up them. The soil I chiefly use is a light kind of black earth, formed from rotten leaves, and very loose.

March 23.—The sunset was most glorious this evening. The sky and clouds were deeply tinged with purple, yellow, and crimson; the sun himself was like a complete ball of fire, with a clear and distinct outline.

March 26.—In order to provide for such plants in my garden as want water, I have ordered a small tub, or more properly a pail without handles, which I shall sink into the ground up to the brim, and then, putting a little mould at the bottom, fill it with water. I shall first have it painted thoroughly inside and out with a slate-coloured paint, to prevent it from rotting, and to make it hold water better. I shall plant flowers both in it and on the edge; the money-wort will be admitted. The pail arrived yesterday.

March 30.—I sat in the drawing-room while papa and mamma were at breakfast. The conversation was very interesting; it turned on the education of poor children, for mamma happened to be reading an article on the subject in some periodical work. Papa also took up the book, and read some of it aloud. It mentioned that poor children of about the ages of seven and eight had more vacancy and stupidity of mind than those of the higher ranks. Here Mr. Taylor remarked that it was shyness more than anything else. Papa did not think so exactly. "I do not think," said he, "that it is a natural want of intelligence, but because they are not drawn out by questions; they are not in the habit of being taught to apply what they know. Now, see how much more handy they are in some things than other children; a boy takes care of his younger brother, and does it very well, or takes charge of a horse, and many other things. But as to intellects, if a child asks any question, he is told to do something or other, and if he does not understand, then comes a great thump on the head, and the child is knocked down. I have myself seen more than once a woman calling to her children, who were running about the streets; she stood at the door armed with a horsewhip, and lashed each child as it ran screaming into the house."

April 8.—Mr. Taylor,* who is always very good-tempered to us, walked in the garden capping verses with me, and, after a hard-fought game of perhaps half an hour, he conquered me with a line ending in X, which rarely begins a word in English. I had, it is true, found one, but soon after he gave me another, which was the rhyme of his first one, and I was vanquished. The couplet was—

> "Taking especial care to fix
> The hour of parting, half-past six" (in the morning).

However, when I came indoors, I was sure that there was in "Paradise Lost" some line beginning with Xerxes, and Arabella found one, which I shall have in store the next time I cap verses with this terrific Mr. Taylor.

April 9.—A very agreeable visitor arrived—a Mr. Charles Shore (the entertaining gentleman I mentioned on March 29, 1832). He said a great deal about Sweden and Norway after dinner, some of which I will put down. He said that there was no such thing as a dissenter from the Church throughout those countries; that the higher classes were all staunch churchmen, but only in word, for many of them were never near a church in their life. "The apathy and indifference," he said, "that prevails everywhere appears quite astonishing to the active mind of an Englishman; it is like being in an exhausted receiver." The Jews are very intolerantly treated by the Government, for they are totally expelled from Norway, and confined to three towns in Sweden. Mr. Shore said when he heard this of Norway (the government of which is a republic, and Mr. Shore is a Tory), he thought it was a fine specimen of the tyranny which is always an accompaniment of a republic; but when he came to Norway he found that it was a regulation of the absolute Danish monarchy, when the Danes

* The late Sir Charles Taylor, a constant and well-known traveller in Norway.

possessed Norway, not of the present Government. At Copenhagen Jews abound, to the displeasure of the inhabitants. A gentleman of that town said to him, "Why, this one thing I do know of the Jews, that whenever the town do go back, the Jews they do go forward." The prime minister of Sweden, he said, is a thoroughly excellent and pious man; his name is Rosenblad, and his brother is a general officer. Tanning is not understood in Sweden. A gentleman of Mr. Shore's acquaintance went over to Sweden to set up that trade; he expects it to prove a very profitable business. His sister married a Swedish gentleman. Mr. Shore has travelled also in Denmark, Italy, Germany, Ireland, and Scotland, by having been in which last place he has given us a little piece of information. We had always thought that the three islands of Graveloch, introduced by Miss Martineau in her stories of Political Economy, were fictitious; but Mr. Shore says they do exist, and that he has seen them. They are not habitable; the largest is half a mile long and a quarter broad, they are surrounded by a very rough sea, and near them is a magnificent whirlpool, as large as the Maelstroom at Norway.

April 16.—Mamma began last Saturday to read to us the "Lord of the Isles," by Sir Walter Scott, which Mrs. Keal was so kind as to lend us. She reads it to us in the evening, after we have done our Greek and Latin with papa, and commonly finishes one canto at a time. Now, in describing the toilet of Edith, the heroine of the poem, Scott says—

> "Young Eva with meet reverence drew
> On the light foot the silken shoe."

This I somewhat disputed, because I did not think silk was used in Great Britain before the reign of Elizabeth. But papa said that silk was certainly known over Europe very much earlier than that; * however, as papa did not remem-

* By means of merchants to the Levant.

ber the date of introduction into England, he gave me leave to look for the article "Silk" in Chambers's Dictionary, a huge folio of two volumes. There I found, amidst a great quantity of information, that silk was invented (when I do not know) in the island of Cos; that as early as 555 A.D., two monks coming from India brought the trade to Constantinople, but that the incredulity of the people in believing that it could be the production of a worm materially hindered its advancement; that in 1130 Roger, King of Sicily, set up silk manufactories at Palermo and some other places, and that in the time of Louis XIII. they were set up in France. But, unluckily, all this, as papa said, was nothing to the purpose, because we wanted to know when silk was first introduced (not manufactured, for that it never was) in England. However, we concluded that in the time of Bruce and the Lorns, silk might be in use, at least among the rich.

April 18.—What we now take most notice of is the number of birds which frequent the garden. There are blackbirds and magpies, but very few sparrows; the robins are plentiful and very tame, and we to-day took great notice of a beautiful chaffinch very near us, which chirped continually. The chaffinch, of which there are a great many in the garden, has a red or orange breast, and wings barred with black and white. We are making friends with a water wagtail, which seems to have built its nest at the top of the house, or in the weeping ash before papa's library, for it sits there very much, and sometimes even pops itself just outside the window and looks into the room at papa, who, being fond of all animals, takes a great fancy to it. The wagtail flies very oddly, jerking up and down. It is very tame. I scattered some crumbs about when it was there; as soon as I had gone to a very short distance it came down to eat them.

April 20.—Mamma finished the "Lord of the Isles"

this evening, to our great delight. I like it very much, but it is extremely inferior to the "Lay of the Last Minstrel," the "Lady of the Lake," and "Rokeby;" I do not say "Marmion," because I have not read it. The name is not a good one; it ought to be called the "Maid of Lorn," for she is much more important in the story than Lord Ronald is. The characters are not in general well drawn, and the poem is full of careless and unpoetic passages. The story itself is awkward, and ought not to be extended to so long a space as three whole years. Neither is it very clever that both Ronald and Edith have other lovers, one apiece. All unhappy ladies are wont, by the common consent of poets, to let their hair stream towards the four corners of the compass, and I am sorry to say that Scott has also fallen into this fault. The having two ladies in a story is likely to make neither very interesting, and in this respect Isabel and Edith steal from each other. Ronald is by no means well drawn; Bruce is one of the most interesting persons in the whole poem, but his brother is not much so; Cormac Doil keeps up his character. The best part in the poem is the scene in the cabin (canto iv.). The dream and thoughts of poor Allan are very well described, and his death is pathetically told. Edith, in her disguise of a page, is very melancholy and much to be pitied; but it is rather unaccountable that Ronald should never have discovered her. It is very natural her springing suddenly on Isabel's neck when she heard her readiness to give up marrying Ronald. A little more, I think, should have been made of Edith's being discovered; Scott should not have let it pass off in the dark. The battle has some beautiful passages, and the immense appearance of the English army is excellently described. And Edith's forgetting herself and speaking in her agony of fear for Ronald, and the crowd mistaking it for a miracle, is extremely natural.

April 23.—Mamma took us across the cow-pasture to

Everton church. On the way, in a beautiful broken field, which was very wet and marshy at the bottom, grow vast quantities of the marsh marigold, a splendid gold-coloured flower, which is not really a marigold, but quite as large as that flower, and with a succulent stalk. It often grows in clumps at least a foot high, which are quite covered with the golden blossoms. With some difficulty I gathered a few, and brought them home to put in water.

April 26.—A very amusing conversation ensued after tea about the royal family, in the course of which some anecdotes were told. A story was told about Princess Charlotte, the daughter of George IV., who was extremely passionate when a child. She took a fancy to make a will, in which she bequeathed all her property to her sub-preceptor, to whom she gave it. He was foolish enough to keep the will; it was discovered, and he was dismissed. The upper preceptor, conceiving that the former had been unfairly sent off, refused to appoint any new sub-preceptor till the first had been provided for, and in the mean time himself performed the office of instructor. One day he entered the room and found her reviling and abusing one of her attendant ladies, in high wrath. He gave her a lecture, and moreover presented her with a book on the subject, which he charged her to read. A few days after, he caught her in a still greater fury, and using still worse language. So he said, "I am very sorry to find your Royal Highness thus. Your Royal Highness has not read the book I gave you." "You lie, my lord; I both read it and attended to it, otherwise I should have scratched her eyes out."

April 26.—There are a few very small gooseberries out; but this is still very late, for last year we had a gooseberry pudding on April 16.

May 1.—In the morning Henrietta brought me a little cottony spider's nest, which had probably been in the shape of a ball, but was now torn open. It was full of eggs, about half as big as those of the silkworm, and quite white; a few of them were broken, and very minute spiders came out; they were of a clear white colour, and soon died. I have seen such a nest as this, containing young spiders who ran about very briskly.

The *Penny Magazine* contains an ill-executed print of beavers, though the account of them is full and interesting; an engraving of the west front of Lincoln Cathedral; a description of Sicily, and of the gigantic chestnut tree of Mount Etna; the ruins of Netley Abbey; wars with wild beasts; the camphor-tree; Edinburgh Castle; the history of the small-pox; Richmond Castle; an excellent engraving of an ourang-outang; an account of railroads; the translation of a Chinese poem; and, above all, "two very spirited poems," author unknown, on the battles of Moncontour and Ivry, imagined to be songs of the Huguenots. The first was fought in the year 1569, in the reign of Charles IX., between the Huguenots and Catholics, the Duke of Anjou and Tavannes on one side, and Coligni on the other; the Huguenots were totally defeated. The second was fought in 1590, and was gained by Henry IV. over the Duke of Mayenne at the head of the league which opposed his accession. Of the two poems, I like that on Ivry the best; the other is the simplest, however. But, as papa says, the battle is made too chivalrous, just as it might be, at the very latest, in the time of Francis I. Besides this, I cannot help noticing that the Duke of Mayenne is called "the fiery duke," while really he was very slothful, sluggish, and gluttonous, and ruinously cautious.

May 2.—Another pupil arrived last night—the Earl of Desart, a boy fourteen years old, who lives in Ireland; his family name is Cuffe. He is thin and slightly made, with brown hair curling a little, blue eyes, and fair complexion, generally very rosy, but that is all I know about him.

May 3.—Richard contemplates buying a linnet and cage, much to my dissatisfaction; for it is miserable even to think of a bird, to which in a state of nature we must assign the range of at least a mile square, confined to less than the space of two feet; but to have it constantly before one's eyes is sadder still.

[On May 6 a journey was taken to Casterton, in Rutlandshire, of course by coach, and an account of so old-fashioned a proceeding may amuse.]

A post-chaise was hired to take us to Tempsford, which is three miles off, there to meet with the Regent coach, to go to Stamford. We had just come to that place [Tempsford], and were passing a cross-road leading into the high-road, when a coach drove past before us. Not doubting but that this was the Regent, we urged on the post-boy, and he drove on at a furious rate to overtake it. But when we had reached it we found that it went to York, and drove deliberately back to Tempsford, which we had left behind. Here we discovered that we had made more haste than good speed, and were three quarters of an hour too early. The post-boy was obliged to wait, lest there should be no places in the coach; and as the Wheat-sheaf Inn was a horrid little place, tainted with a vile smell of tobacco, we resolved to walk about the churchyard. The church is in general in the Perpendicular style, but there are four small Decorated windows in the porches.

The churchyard is grown all over with long grass and nettles. There were five pretty little calves in it. With one I made friendship, and gave him some mouthfuls of grass; the others were very timid, except a brown and white one, who ran after us bellowing.

The coach at length arrived, and we deemed ourselves very lucky in having the whole inside to ourselves. Extremely clean it was. We were accompanied part of the way by a hat, a dirty great-coat, two umbrellas, and a verbena, whose leaves we rubbed between our fingers, and found it very pleasant to smell. I think it was at Hilton that some one tossed into the coach, through the window, a nasty dirty coarse cloth, which rolled down my knee and fell on the floor. At the same place we saw a great fat fellow standing all the time we stopped at the inn, first with his mouth idiotically open, and afterwards with his thumb thrust into it, looking all the time a perfect image of stupidity.

May 7.—We came to Casterton about eight o'clock, having travelled from Stamford in grandpapa's carriage, which was sent on purpose to fetch us. I did not sleep last night till after eleven o'clock; however, I got up to-day at half-past four, and walked about the garden. The river is full of water, the dew was very thick on the grass, and there is a little frost. I took a short walk on the Great Casterton road, and had the pleasure not only of hearing the nightingale a long time, but also of seeing him all the while, only a few yards from me. He is a small bird, of a slight shape and a soft brown plumage, with a whitish ash-coloured breast and throat. He flitted about from bush to bush, and sometimes hid himself in the hedge; after a long pause he began again with a long, slow, loud note, something like "tweet, tweet." I never saw a nightingale before. This was about five o'clock in the morning. His song is extremely rich and varied, but the blackbird's is, in my opinion, sweeter.

There are two beautiful swans; one is sitting on six eggs in an open nest, which she has made on the other side of the river. Her husband takes care that nobody shall disturb her; he sails majestically up and down the water, watching, and will dart along as quick as lightning if he sees any one approaching, and he will make a great splashing too. The way to keep him off is to push him gently away with a broom or garden brush. Aunt Jane went into the boat to fill her watering-pot, and he immediately attacked her; he bit the brush, and tore up the grass in a rage. When he flies at any one he will bruise them black and blue; the strokes of his wings are like those of sticks.

May 9, *Thursday.*—After luncheon, Aunt Mary took me across the river in the boat to look for some flowers on the other side. She pushed the boat across while I held the broom. The swan was attending on his wife, but he immediately saw or heard us, for he splashed down upon us, spreading his wings terrifically. He was a moment too late, for we had landed when he reached the boat. . . .

Grandmamma showed me five miniatures; the two last were by far the most beautiful. One was of Aunt Charlotte when she was about two and twenty; it is sweetly pretty, and very like what she is now. The other was of Aunt Sarah, who died before mamma was married, and possessed the most extraordinary beauty, so that, as I have heard papa say, she created a sensation wherever she went. I must say I think her portrait exquisite. The hair is very dark, the complexion the finest conceivable, both for fairness and bright colour; the eyes are grey, the mouth a little too large, the shape of the face beautiful, and the whole countenance lovely. She stoops slightly, and wears a black silk dress. She died at the age of twenty-nine, and was as good as she was handsome.*

* The six eldest sisters of this family, whose surname was Twopeny, were, on account of their beauty, named by Sir Robert Grant (Lord Glenelg's brother) the "Splendid Shilling."

CHAPTER IV.

From May to Dec. 31, 1833.

May 16, *Thursday*.—I did wake at the proper time, or was woke by the children; and at five o'clock Louisa and I took an exquisite walk through the wood (Whitewood). We went very slowly, and at almost every step Louisa called out, and with justice, "Oh, wonders!" The nightingales were singing in great numbers; we saw two of them perched in the middle of a tall oak. There was also a blackcap hopping among some low bushes. . . . I went a good way across the heath, with a trowel, to the bogs to get flowers. What grows here chiefly is a cotton grass, which has a stalk about four inches high, tipped with a waving substance which envelops the seeds. It looks just like the cotton which is put into ink-glasses; when it is in great abundance, the place seems to be covered with snow. I took up several plants of the *Drosera rotundifolia*, or sundew; it is not yet in flower; the leaves are small and red, and covered with glutinous hairs, which catch flies in great numbers. I took up besides what I think is the *Pedicularis sylvatica*, a pretty pink flower; and, with some others, a most extraordinary plant, which looks like the Creeping cistus.* It runs along the ground in singular joints, which twist and creep in a singular manner, and are all covered with either very minute leaves or prickles. I brought these home, with Louisa's help, planted them in my gardens, and came in at half-past seven.

* Query, "cereus"?—Ed.

Mamma takes a walk in the wood every morning, to hear the nightingales and gather lilies of the valley, which are now extremely abundant, and when gathered scent almost half the house; besides which, they are very beautiful. I particularly admire the curl outwards of the blossom.

May 18, *Saturday*.—In the afternoon a lark, which Mackworth has long wished to buy, arrived. It seems to be full grown, and is almost twice as big as a sparrow, of a very elegant shape, and with a beautiful head. The colour is a mottled brown and black; the breast is whitish, with a cast of yellow. There are a few hairs at the origin of the beak, and he has a crest, which he commonly keeps lowered. He is very tame, and eats daisies out of the hand; he never seems frightened, but I pity him very much for being a captive.

May 19, *Sunday*.—Papa went to Cockayne Hatley. Between services Mr. Paroissien called, and, among other things, told us a curious fact in natural history respecting a fly-catching plant akin to the Venus' fly-trap. A philosopher—of Cambridge, I think—conceived the idea of feeding it with meat instead of flies. So he took two healthy plants of this sort, and kept them in the same place; but one was carefully deprived of every sort of animal nutriment, while the other, though kept from all flies and other insects, was supplied with very fine shreds of beef, put into the trap where the flies were caught. This one flourished, while the other languished and died.

May 20, *Monday*.—For some time in the morning there was a thick fog, but this afterwards went away, and it became clear and fine. Mackworth's lark is a very amusing bird; it is let out of its cage every day. The goldfinch, when let out at the same time, is unbearably impudent to him; he trots up to him, and eats his hempseed, and drinks his water, and pecks at his turf, which he is always provided with. The lark does not like this; he opens his mouth and screams, and sometimes drives off the goldfinch, who, however, comes again with the utmost assurance and impertinence, and has once or twice fought with and conquered the lark. These scenes are very amusing. Once, when Goldy was quite intolerable, the lark attacked him; but, being unluckily worsted, resolved on retaliation, ran off to the intruder's cage, and began greedily eating his canary seed. The goldfinch looked on very peaceably, being himself engaged in theft. I always take the part of the lark; it is quite droll to see him beaten by a bird as small again as himself.

May 21, *Tuesday.*—At about half-past six I went out alone into the wood. It is on one side very thick and entangled, full of briars and bushes; but on the right it is covered with grass, free from underwood, and filled with tall firs and a few other trees. I went into this part, and for, I should think, ten minutes watched a nightingale flitting about from tree to tree, and often perched on a tiny twig, so slender that it seemed unable to support it, and even shook. He was singing all the time.

Last night I sat up till half-past nine, partly in expectation of Arthur Malkin, whom we hoped to see this week, and partly because I had promised Richard and Lord Desart that I would stay to see the letting off of some fireworks which Mrs. Keal had sent him from London as a present for his birthday. . . . But I was several times ready to fall asleep, and I am determined I will never sit up so late again, though Lord Desart declares I assuredly will. I should like very much to disappoint him, and this night I went to bed at twenty minutes after seven, falsifying his prediction this night at least.

May 22, *Wednesday.*—. . . Mamma and papa went into the wood after our dinner, and when they had come in, Arthur arrived, a most welcome visitor. He had walked from Cambridge in four hours and five minutes, and was not tired.

This was about half-past four. I believe it was almost five o'clock when we had another very agreeable guest, Mr. Howard, whom we have long expected. But, unfortunately, he will only remain with us a day or two. However, Arthur is going to stay for a fortnight or three weeks.

Everybody walked about the garden after the parlour dinner. The weeping ash is almost in full leaf; the walnut is quite out, and most other trees. There are great feuds about the beauty of the weeping ash. Lord Desart infinitely prefers the common one, and Mr. Taylor joins him, even hating the weeping ash, which, however, Mr. Howard joins with mamma in liking, and calls the other cold looking. As for myself, I ought to like the first least, because it is a monster, and quite artificial; but then it is very rarely so large and handsome as ours is, and it droops so gracefully.

May 26.—Louisa, according to Lord Desart's desire, called him early by tapping at his door, on which the following dialogue took place:—

Lord D.—"Who?"

Louisa.—"Get up."

Lord D.—"What o'clock is it?"

Louisa.—"Five and twenty minutes to five."

Lord D.—"Oh dear me!" (*Stretches himself probably, certainly goes to sleep again, and does not wake till eight.*)

May 27, *Monday.*—Unhappily I did not wake till ten minutes to five, and consequently did not see so many birds as usual before breakfast. I wandered very far over the wood (Foxhill), and came to its termination on one side, where it is enclosed by a hedge, on the other side of which is a field and a deep clay ditch. All about here were immense quantities of bryony, of which there are two sorts, only one of which is a real bryony; the Latin name is the *Bryonia dioica.* It is a large plant, with tendrils, large rough leaves, and thick stalks; the flowers grow on long, slender, naked fruit-stalks, and are of a pretty striped green. The other is the *Tamus communis.* The stem is much slenderer, but full as long; the leaves are very full and glossy, and of a bluer green; the flowers are smaller and more numerous. This plant twines extraordinarily. Two or three roots generally grow in one patch; the stems shoot out and lay hold on other stems of bryony, till they are so twisted together that it would take days to disentangle only one. The tendrils curl remarkably, and seize even on hyacinths and dead wood. The first plant belongs to the class Triandria, monogynia; the other to Hexandria, monogynia; that is, according to the new arrangement of Thunberg and Withering. In the system of Linnæus they belong to Monœcia, pentandria, and Diœcia, pentandria, the imperfect classes, which are now mixed up with the others. These flowers are mixed with wild clematis, which is not yet in flower. I took one of the latter, and with great difficulty a piece of tamus, the difficulty being on three accounts: first, the twisting of the stems; secondly, the excessive hardness of the ground, which is a dry, cracked clay; thirdly, the great depth of the root, which is oval, white, juicy, rather woody, and as big as a small pullet's egg, sometimes as a full-sized hen's egg, perhaps even bigger.

May 28, *Tuesday.*—A visitor came yesterday, to stay for
16 two nights, a Mr. James Spedding, a friend of Arthur Malkin. He seems to be about thirty years old,* and is rather bald; he is not handsome, but has a very fine countenance and expression; he is rather florid and not tall. He has lately taken up drawing as an amusement; he takes likenesses admirably. Two of them I have seen; they are portraits of Arthur, and one of them is very like him. This one he finished here, and complained much of Arthur's impatience in sitting. He draws in chalk, and does not shade much. Mr. Spedding gave me some useful directions about my own drawing.

* This is a mistake; he is only twenty-two.

May 29.—. . . Another still more curious coincidence has taken place. I was reading in the "Architecture of 17
Birds" a fact that I never knew before, that tomtits with their beaks excavate holes in trees as a nest. Just at this moment Mackworth called out, "Oh, Emily, do you know, I saw to-day a tomtit hollowing a hole in a branch with his beak; he was quite topsy-turvy."

May 30, *Thursday*.—. . . A. and I found some curious caterpillars' nests on the walnut tree. There were only two sorts. One was done by a caterpillar an inch long, of a greenish white, without hairs, and not pretty. This creature rolls up part of a leaf and sews it down with cotton, in a kind of delicate web, or sometimes bends down the leaf in half, and spins some cotton across it just near the bend, so as to hold the two halves firm together; in this place it lies snug, probably about to become a chrysalis. The other sort is of the same colour, but only a quarter of an inch long. It forms its habitation by fastening the edges of two leaves together, quite flat, laid over one another, which, indeed, the other sometimes does. I gathered several leaves to see what butterflies they will produce.

June 1, *Saturday*.—At about half-past seven the whole party . . . took a most delightful walk across several successive fields sloping in a hill, at whose top runs a continued avenue of shady and beautiful lime trees. Arthur (who is an excellent leaper) and the gentlemen employed themselves in leaping over gates, hedges, and ditches, and got two or three falls on account of the slipperiness of the ground. . . . I found a plant of the *Solanum Dulcamara*, or woody nightshade, which is in bloom; . . . it is poisonous,* and Mr. Taylor, hearing this, chewed a leaf, and Lord Desart did the same with a flower, swallowing all the juice, to see if they were poisoned. Mr. Taylor was still more foolish, for

* The berries are so, but I do not know if the rest of the plant is.

he resolved to eat the belladonna, or deadly nightshade, of which every part is a deadly poison; it grows about the place where he lives.

June 2, *Sunday.*—In coming from church I found a caterpillar, a very handsome one. . . . As for the legs, I could not observe them, because the creature persisted in rolling itself up, and was teased when I tried to unroll them. Lord Desart would call this beautiful insect "very handsome *for a caterpillar*," and cannot bear caterpillars, because they give one a disagreeable idea and crawl disgustingly. I grant this may be true with *him;* perhaps he may have a physical infirmity which makes him dislike this order of creation. Mr. Taylor goes further; he called it a beast, and screamed and moaned when he allowed it to crawl on him. Sir George Baker alone duly appreciated its beauty without any malicious and insinuating remarks.

June 5, *Wednesday.*— . . . Before the parlour dinner, mamma saw a black-and-white wagtail pick up a great worm. Presently a grey one approached and quietly took it out of his mouth. Shortly after, another grey one came up for it, and a quarrel ensued, which ended in the original possessor regaining his property.

At seven o'clock I went out into the garden for a little while, and saw on a laurel tree in the laurel hedge a sweet little robin singing beautifully. On the same tree were a chaffinch and his wife, the former singing loudly and boldly, the latter looking on in mute approbation of her dear consort. At length she became wearied of doing nothing, and, resolving that her mate should alone adorn the tree, drove off the robin. He, poor fellow, flew off to another part of the laurel hedge, hoping to sing in quiet. There he found another chaffinch, probably leagued with the first; at all events, the next minute he attacked the unfortunate robin, who, in his flight, flew within a yard of the ground, and whisked by only a few inches from me. He took refuge among some thick branches, and looked much terrified. Meanwhile the two chaffinches kept answering each other from different trees.

June 7, *Friday*.—Mackworth, in returning from bathing, found a curious parasitical plant, the *Orobanche major*, or great broom-rape. It grows on the roots of plants, especially of the papilionaceous tribe. This one was growing on gorse. It is about ten inches high, without leaves, and having a thick, solid stem, over which are scattered dry scales about half an inch long. The stem is unbranched; at the top is a close spike of flowers, which are almost an inch in length, coarse and rough. The summit of the pistil is heart-shaped and yellow. The whole plant, flowers, stem, and scales, is of a purplish rusty brown. I went immediately and took up the plant. I do not know whether it will live, as I was of course obliged to break off its root from the root of the gorse. Its own root is whitish, tough, and woody.

June 8, *Saturday*.—The lark has now a confirmed hatred of the goldfinch, and screams if he even sees its cage. At the same time, he is more tame and gentle to us; he always walks under the table after breakfast to pick up the crumbs we have dropped, and eats out of our hand, especially when he is in his cage. When any one approaches he opens his beak very wide for a fly; if none is brought he looks sadly disappointed, for he loves flies. I suspect he does not like Mackworth, which is not wonderful, considering the teasing and frightening he has received from that quarter; for when M. attempted to give him a fly, he flew at, pecked him, and pursued him for two or three yards. He also attacked me, and tugged furiously at my finger; but as soon as M. was out of the room he became quiet, and ate gently out of my hand. He then walked into his cage, and grew very dainty; for he took a dislike to great flies, and pecked us if we brought them; but he eats little ones readily enough.

Nor would he (except once) be cheated by being presented with a bit of a large fly as a little fly.

We have been watching the birds a great deal to-day. I chiefly observed the redstart, which is very tame, and hops from tree to tree close to us. He is a most beautiful bird. The hen, which was the one I watched, has a grey back, with a purplish cast, a tail black above and red beneath, a deep black neck and throat; the crown of the head is white, the breast and the stomach red. She constantly utters a soft, sweet note, exactly like "hweet, hweet." The chaffinch—tiresome, aping bird!—imitated this, and very successfully, except that it was harsher. He took us in finely once. We likewise heard a singular noise, between a sneeze, a hiss, and the sound of a saw. It was evidently made by a bird, for when we examined the place whence it proceeded, I found only one twig, on which it must have perched, shaking up and down, while all the rest were quiet. Louisa afterwards ascertained that it was made by a little bird which I have seen before; it has a tail, which he wags frequently, and which is of a fiery red underneath. But, more than all this, Arabella's prying eyes discovered, fixed on a branch of a nut tree overhanging our gardens, or near it, a beautiful nest of a chaffinch, small, neat, and round, apparently formed of grey moss and twigs, lined with feathers. The hen was sitting on it, and allowed me to thrust my face within a foot of her before she would fly off. I shall take great care that she is not molested, and I shall pet her by daily feeding her with bread, and her little ones when they are hatched.

June 9.—. . . There is a great variety of songs in our garden: the loud, vain chirp of the chaffinch; the sweet, liquid warbling of the robin; the soft and mellow note of the blackbird; the cooing of the wood-pigeon; and, above all, the deep, rich, and varied song of the thrush, who will sing for above an hour together without intermission.

June 13, *Thursday.*—I have discovered why the lark

sometimes attacks me so violently. It is because I wear a different frock from what he has been accustomed to see me in. This shows a great deal of observation and intelligence.

June 14, *Friday.*—When I had done the work of planting my mulleins I came indoors and brought some flies to the lark; but he, instead of eating them, flew at me in wrath and bit me very hard. At length it occurred to me that this might be the consequence of my hands being dirty from gardening. I accordingly went up and washed them. When I came down the lark was all gentleness, and quietly ate my flies.

June 26.—. . . I, with Arabella and Mackworth, took a delightful walk down near the cow-pasture, through Lunnis's farm, amongst several fields, brooks, and thickets, all filled with herbs and flowers. We saw an immense number of mare's-tails of a prodigious size, above a yard in height sometimes, with a very thick stem, jointed and leafy (the leaves being like little stalks). The stem consists of two tubes, one within the other, and is either black or pale green. The young shoots, just coming up, are most curious-looking things. There are two sorts of *Hippuris* (mare's-tail). Withering and Galpine* only mention one; the other is, according to Rousseau, not much known. The first I am well acquainted with. It is very much smaller than this, which may possibly be only a large variety of it; but, then, I have never seen the two sorts growing together, and they are certainly very different, so I hope this is the rare kind. But, unfortunately, I know of no book which describes it, for Rousseau only just mentions its existence.

June 28.—. . . The lark is a most engaging and interesting little bird, though he has quite got over his ill temper, and never pecks; but he still will not eat from my

* And Sir E. Smith, too.

hand if I have got on a different frock. As for the goldfinch, he continues merry, happy, impudent, and affected, without any variation.

June 29.—. . . In the evening Mrs. Renouard related the following singular story:—

"A little girl was playing before the house, when a beggar-woman came up and begged. She had a baby in her arms, and the child was so delighted with it that she asked the woman if she would sell it to her. 'What will you give me for it, miss?' asked the woman. She replied, 'Half a crown,' which was all the money she had. The woman agreed; the half-crown was brought, and the child took the baby, carried it upstairs, and laid it on her bed. By-and-by she came scampering down to her mamma, calling out, 'Mamma! mamma! I have got a live doll! I long wanted to have one, but now I have got it.' Her mamma would not believe it, but the child persisted, and begged that the servant might be sent up to examine. This was done, and the baby was found lying on her bed. When asked how she had got it, she said she had bought it, and told her story. Her parents sent all over the town for the woman, but she had taken herself off. At first it was resolved to send the baby to be supported by the parish, but the girl, who was an only child, petitioned so hard against it that it was resolved to adopt the infant, who was a girl. It was accordingly brought up and educated, and on the death of the daughter, when grown up, she became heir to the property of her foster-parents.

This extraordinary story is certainly true, for the parties were known to Mrs. Renouard's grandmother.

July 6.—My poor little lark is very ill to-day; he will scarcely either move, eat, or drink, but sits shivering and panting. I suspect the cause is that I gave him a sow-thistle yesterday. I much fear that he will die; if he does we shall miss him very much, for he is a universal pet.

By the advice of the "Boy's Own Book" and Mrs. Keal, I 18
gave him a little saffron and liquorice in his water, besides three fat spiders, which he ate greedily.

July 8, *Monday.*—All of us continue to watch with great anxiety the condition of our favourite little lark. All yesterday he continued dull, and pretty much so to-day. But at six o'clock a decided improvement took place. His appetite had been before returning, but he now began to lift his head, and look about him, and he even began to plume, peck, and shake himself. Still he had no strength to stand actually up, and whenever he wished to move, toddled along with the help of his wings, though only for a moment. He drinks readily, and once tried to clean his beak, so that I have great hopes of him. Two or three times he crowed.

July 9, *Tuesday.*—The lark continues much the same. While I was cleaning out his cage I put him on the table beside mamma, and there he remained some time after, while I was shelling and bruising his hempseed; for Richard, when he went to Potton to-day, applied to Mr. Tebbut, his former master, about him. By his advice I feed him with a mess of the yolk of an egg, boiled very hard and chopped quite fine, mixed with bread crumbled, and bruised hempseed; he is also to drink toast-and-water the first day, plain water the next, and on the third plain water and saffron. (Mr. Tebbut decidedly attributes his illness to sowthistle.) While I was preparing his food the lark toddled up to observe my proceedings, and shortly after he walked on further still and tumbled himself down into my lap. There he sat quietly for almost half an hour, and greedily ate his food when given him. He retains his rancorous hatred of the goldfinch, for he screamed even when he flew over his cage.

July 10, *Wednesday.*—After seven o'clock in the evening mamma took a walk with us to the heath. Amongst the bogs I found several flowers. The bog pimpernel quite covers the ground, and makes a most beautiful appearance, with its elegant and delicate little blossoms. The cross-leaved heath also grows in great numbers, and has very beautiful rose-coloured flowers. But what I valued most was that rare plant, the asphodel, in Latin the *Narthecium ossifragum*, which I have before found in seed, but never in flower till now. It is a liliaceous plant, and is of the class Hexandria, monogynia. It grows on an upright, strong, unbranched stem, with a few narrow, doubled, sessile leaves, veined with red; the stem is likewise reddish. The flowers grow at the top, in something like a spike, with a coloured calyx in six long divisions (a rarity among liliaceous plants). The blossoms are very beautiful; they are nearly as large as those of the upright St. John's wort. The petals are yellow, tipped with red, and spreading out like a star; the stamens are bright yellow, beautifully fringed; the anthers are scarlet, and the pistil yellow; the buds are red and yellow. Besides these, I found the *Ranunculus flammula*, a ranunculus with yellow leaves, which is superior to everything else to be taken in cases where poison has been swallowed, which it is desirable to throw up instantly. The distilled juice is what is used. I gathered some more valerian in the wood, and found that it had not, as I supposed, perfect flowers on stameniferous plants, but sometimes produced four stamens instead of three. Still, however, on my first specimen there are a few perfect flowers, which is very remarkable.

July 11, *Thursday.*—My lark, though still ill and weak, continues to show his instinct, for he bit Mackworth's finger, which had a bandage on, and tried to pull off some goldbeater's skin from my thumb. He also has tried to fly a little.

July 15, *Monday.*—I am delighted to view the improvement in my lark's health. He is quite brisk and lively, and can crow, scream, and bask in the sun as before. He cannot yet, however, fly a long way, nor does he sing, but he will certainly recover. He has now been ill nine days. As for the goldfinch, he cannot fly at all, on account of his wounded wing, but he is as pert and conceited as ever.

July 18, *Thursday.*—Tuesday evening witnessed the first of those tea-parties under the shade of the ash which had been anticipated ever since December. We indeed spend our whole days in this hot weather out of doors as soon as the morning dew is off. On all these occasions the lark in his cage is brought out, and sits with us under the ash, and is most beautifully interesting and intelligent. He evidently likes company very much better than solitude, and is constantly chirping and crowing to bring people about him, still continuing his love for flies. When people put their mouths to his cage he kisses them; that is, he lays his beak on their lips, and even puts it into their mouths. We had a consultation yesterday as to the safety of allowing him a little run under the ash. It was urged that he knew us so well that, if he did escape, he would certainly return; that he never flies far in a room at least, but goes walking about (and here he would be engaged by picking up insects); that he would conceive himself to be bounded here as in a room, etc. But the danger of his escaping for ever, and the disappointment that would ensue, prevailed.

July 22.—The lark grows tamer and tamer every day; he runs up to people, and follows them about the room; he has even learnt to sit on people's hands and there eat flies. His manners are so interesting, engaging, and void of fear, that it is impossible not to love him.

I saw from my window to-day a little blue tomtit in the larch tree; it would suspend itself at the end of the feeblest twigs which hang perpendicularly, and there, head downwards, swing backwards and forwards, as the wind rocked the boughs.

July 23, *Tuesday.*—My lark is quite a companion to

me now in my room. He jumps on my hand, walks about the table and on my desk, examines my pencils, netting, and work, and is as familiar as possible. To-day R. was writing a letter; the lark placed himself on the paper, and every time the pen came down he pecked it, and curiously examined the stroke it made.

July 25, *Thursday.*—He has a great deal of curiosity; if anything drops from the table he trots up to examine it, and pulls about everything he sees. He has also a particular regard for a paint-brush of mine, which he makes a plaything of, tosses about, carries with him, pecks and bites.

July 28.—Mr. McLear has just obtained the appointment of Astronomer Royal at the Cape, and is going in about six weeks. He paid us to-day at dinner one of his last visits, though not his farewell one. I asked him some questions about the eclipse.

July 29, *Monday.*—A most sad misfortune has happened. The day being very hot, we as usual spent it under the weeping ash, and, as is customary with us, took the lark with us in his cage. We allowed him to come out on our knees to eat little crumbs of bread, and, as he always popped back again, we apprehended no danger. At length he came out with no object but to ascertain the extent of the weeping ash, and then walked beyond it to the gravel walk. This looked rather alarming. Papa went in for flies, and I for a piece of bread to entice him back again. When I returned I held out a crumb to him, expecting him to eat it. Instead of that, he spread his wings and took a prodigious flight over the trees and across the yard. A hue and cry was instantly raised. But everybody expected him back again, and for at least an hour the children good-naturedly employed themselves, under a broiling sun, in toiling over the garden with his cage and looking for him. We spied him several times, flying or singing, extremely happy; the first flight he has taken since he was born. I hope he will not get into dangers abroad. He is very much missed by everybody, but I fear he will not return. I hung his cage out of my window to attract him back, and sat up till ten o'clock to watch for him; but, alas! he never came, and I must make up my mind to bear the loss. It is the more disappointing, because his tameness was daily increasing, so that he would even sit on my lap, and always came when called by almost any one. My only consolation is that he will be happier at liberty than in a cage.

Aug. 1, *Thursday.*—Mrs. Steres has a young lark, very small, and only just fledged; on hearing of our loss she very good-naturedly gave it to me.

Aug. 5.—I paid a visit to Foxhill Wood, which I have not seen for a month or two. It is now most beautiful with flowers. The two sorts of enchanter's nightshade cover the ground by hundreds, and so do many other flowers; in two places, willow-herbs and meadow-sweets, taller than mamma, grow in such thick profusion as to look like forests, all in bloom, moreover, mixed with small shrubs and a tall sort of umbelliferous plant, which is crowned with a large head of snow-white blossoms. The hedge which I mentioned May 27 is now no longer covered with bryony, but with clematis, and very luxuriantly so, but only just coming into flower. After all, there is but a small part of this wood which can be walked in; it is chiefly filled as thick as possible with trees and bushes; and even the walkable part is now much overgrown with plants, especially the wild rose, added to numerous stumps of trees, and a very insecure footing on the rough and hard clay.

Aug. 6, *Tuesday.*—I am very sure that my present lark will be much more tame than even my other, because he is now so young. I let nobody feed him but myself; the consequence is that he knows me only, and will hardly eat if anybody else is present. He will eat out of my mouth as readily as possible; when I enter the room or pass near his cage, he flaps his wings, stands on tiptoe, trembles with impatience, opens his beak as wide as possible, and thrusts his head through the bars, in expectation of a piece of bread; when I give it to him his delight knows no bounds, and when he has done he pecks my face for more. I taught him to-day to jump on my hand. At the same time, a noise made by any one else frightens him extremely; and one evening he would not eat because somebody was reading in the room below.

Aug. 8, *Thursday.*—Mamma went to Potton to drink tea with Mrs. K., and was accompanied by Arabella and Mackworth. The rest of us had a most excellent game of play in Foxhill Wood. It was as follows:—We each had a piece of ground which served as our house, and we got our living by daily expeditions to procure food; this chiefly consisted of arum berries, nightshade berries, sorrel, enchanter's nightshade, wild raspberries, young shoots of plants, clematis, and thistle. Every one was to yield up one-third of his daily gains to a public magazine, which was kept for the support of the poor and infirm. We all tried to obtain a sufficient stock of provisions to enable us to live in ease, without being obliged to work. We ate only two meals, supper and breakfast; I both roasted and boiled mine. What we pretended to eat we really threw away. I cut down one or two angelicas, and out of the hollow stalks made several horns, which made a very loud noise; each was provided with one, and when in distress, or lost, blew it, and, being answered, found his way again.

Aug. 17, *Saturday.*— . . . What I prize most of all my discoveries this day is a most curious bees' nest. I found it at about the height of my waist from the ground, placed between the upright and slender stems of some young trees. It was about three parts as large as a wren's nest, which, indeed, I took it for, as it was composed of dead leaves, moss, and a very few feathers. But when I put my hand to take it away, I was startled by a loud hiss, and instantly ran indoors to report it. Everybody came out; the hiss was repeated, and it was conjectured that an owl had taken up his residence there. But this idea was speedily dispelled by the appearance of a bee, which came out and went in by a little entrance nearly under the nest. The bee was brown, black, and orange, something like a humble-bee. I think it is a carder-bee, though. If it is so, this is a most unusual situation for its nest, as it commonly builds on the ground, and with moss alone.

Sept. 17, *Tuesday.*—I attempted to kill one of those immense gnats which I mentioned,* by severing the head from the body; I had no sooner done this than, to my astonishment, the head, legs, and wings all flew off briskly together, leaving the decapitated trunk behind. This gnat, on near examination, is very beautiful and delicate.

Sept. 23.— . . . Lord Desart has a very large and noble Newfoundland dog, black and white. The head is entirely black, and has a strange protuberance at the back of it. He is very powerful and courageous, and very faithful to his master. He always goes with the gentlemen when they bathe, and makes himself quite troublesome by attempting to drag them or Richard from the water, under the apprehension that they are drowning. He was brought up to-day into mamma's room, for the second time, to amuse her. He is not fond of ladies, and, indeed, cares for few people besides Lord Desart. However, he received some bread and toast very graciously, and laid his paws very heavily, with a great bounce, on mamma's bed. He conducted himself very independently and unceremoniously, and by no means courts caresses.

Sept. 28, *Saturday.*—I found a honeysuckle leaf rolled up in a curious way by means of a gummy substance, and six or seven beautiful lady-birds comfortably lodged within

* In a former passage not extracted.—ED.

it. I suppose it was their nest. Mackworth discovered a wasp's nest in the wood; it was by a ditch under some clods of earth, and was a hole with two or three passages running underground, or at least what seemed two or three passages. A little twig was firmly fixed across the entrance, but this, of course, was the work of nature. A great multitude of wasps was going in and out. I did not, of course, see the greatest curiosity of all, the comb inside. The comb is a paper-like substance, made of very fine shavings of wood, which the wasp saws off with its mandibles, and reduces to paste. It is then made into a comb, with cells like that of a bee.

Oct. 25, *Friday.*— . . . A man brought to the door a great curiosity, a live stork, which he had caught near Gamlingay Lake, in a meadow. This bird is very rare in England. It is white all over, except some of the wing feathers, which are black; the neck is long; the beak is red, though in this specimen, which was probably a hen, it was a dingy colour; the eye is bright and very beautiful; the legs I could not see, except one foot, which was webbed; the wings are long, and the tail short. I did not measure
19 it, but Bewick says that it is three feet six inches long, and six feet broad, from tip to tip. It is a most noble-looking bird; it was very fierce, and thrust its beak through the basket in which it was kept.

Nov. 12.— . . . Trusty was taken into the library a day or two ago. While he was there caressing Lord Desart he suddenly espied a white plaster cast of the Dog of Alcibiades, which was standing over some book-shelves. Immediately, without taking notice of the other casts, or anything else, he leaped up, placed his fore-paws on the highest row of books, and stood looking earnestly at the figure; which showed, I think, a great deal of intelligence.

Nov. 18, *Monday.*—We had this night a nocturnal visit of no very pleasant kind. It was about half-past eleven, when I was awoke by a tremendous singing at the front door, in a voice of thunder. I sleep over the hall, and the singing seemed directly below me. In a minute or two the singing ceased, and a violent banging followed, on the front door, making it shake and rattle. I was terribly frightened, and naturally thought of thieves. I got out of bed, wrapped myself up in a quilt, and marched into mamma's room, which was next me, and where Charlotte, the maid, slept. I woke her, and persuaded her to go directly to find one of the men-servants, to discover the cause of this disturbance. She did so, and I remained listening to the blows on the door. In about five minutes papa came to the hall-door and called out, "Is anybody there?"

Three or four men answered, "Yes, sir."

"Where do you come from?"

"We come from Watford, sir."

"And, pray, is this the proper time to come to a gentleman's house, in the middle of the night?"

"We are travellers, sir, and we have lost our way, and we can't get a night's lodging anywhere, and we want a trifle, sir."

A little more passed between them, and soon after papa came up into my room. He opened the window, looked out, and said, "What are you doing there now?" They gave some explanation and petition, and papa said, "Pray, is it your practice to go about waking up all the gentlemen's houses at night? There is a sick person in the house, and here you are waking it up from one end to the other." They "hoped not," and papa ended by giving them a few pence, and telling them to take themselves off the premises. And so the adventure ended.

Dec. 31, *Tuesday.*—The weather is so mild that everything has been coming forward. The mulberry tree has been in bud ever since October; the syringa is even in leaf.

CHAPTER V.

From January to December, 1834.

[Age from fourteen to fifteen years old.]

Jan. 4.—The weather is windy and occasionally rainy, but not very cold, and everything, as I said before, remarkably forward. The snowdrops are in bud, and the daffodils and crown imperials are sprouting. I did not mention a certain great curiosity. A piece of hawthorn (may) in blossom, and with the leaves, was stuck on Christmas Day in Mr. Astell's pew. I saw a piece from the same bush, as I suppose, to-day. It was evidently not blackthorn; the blossom, the leaf, and even the hep of last year, all proved it to be the real white-thorn, or hawthorn, so no mistake was made in this particular. The same tree has been known to flower at Christmas several years ago. Withering mentions a singular tree of this kind, called the Glastonbury thorn; it is at Glastonbury, near Wells. It must be at least two hundred years old, and flowers twice a year: once at Christmas, and the second time, I suppose, in spring. The flowers are as big as a sixpence. I do not know whether it exists at present.

Jan. 10. . . . Mr. Cust, who called to-day, told us that they had twenty-four kinds of flowers in their garden at Cockayne Hatley, all in bloom already. This seemed very astonishing, so I looked in our garden, and counted eighteen sorts in flower: China rose, Indian rose, *Pyrus japonica*, hepatica, primrose, polyanthus, daisy, heath, polygala, *Cineraria purpurea*, gentianella, heart's-ease, auricula, snowdrop, American groundsel, stock, double and single, double wallflower, and laurustinus. I never knew such a forward spring before; but we have neither aconites nor crocuses, which I am rather surprised at. The aconite is really the winter-flowering hellebore. The real aconite is the monk's-hood, or wolf's-bane. The cineraria, by-the-by, is a greenhouse plant, so I should not have included it.

Jan. 15.—The birch is in full bud, and I think the larch is; so is almost every tree. I examined to-day the bark of different firs and pines. I found that of the spruce to consist of distinct layers, like pieces of wood laid one on the other, which I never noticed before.

Jan. 18, *Saturday.*—The oak, ash, filbert, and elder are in bud, and the wild honeysuckle is in leaf. I only hope we shall not suffer for this forwardness in the cold winds of March.

Feb. 1.—The garden-peas are half a foot high, and the sweet peas three times that height; the periwinkles are in flower; but, except the daisy, I have not yet met with any wild plant in blossom. . . . The birds appear to have been deceived by the mild weather, and to have taken it for spring; for actually a thrush, near Bedford, had a week ago hatched its brood, and a robin, too, has built its nest and laid eggs.

Feb. 13, *Thursday.*—I heard the blackbird for the first time, though it has been singing this month. The skylark has sung ascending ever since January 10, but continues to flock as it does in winter. Yesterday I saw a wryneck. This is a bird of passage, which commonly appears about the end of March, a few days before the cuckoo.

March 3, *Monday.*—It is curious to observe how every bird chooses a particular place to sing in. The thrush likes to be placed very high, commonly on a conspicuous branch. The blackbird is, in general, well hidden in a bush; the cuckoo always so. The nightingale warbles flitting from spray to spray, sometimes in very exposed places, as well as in thickly wooded ones. The blackcap I have heard too little to say much about it, but it seems to perch about ten or twelve feet high, and often flits about like the nightingale. The yellow-hammer sits in a hedge, pretty high up. The titmouse sings at intervals, hanging by his claws with his head downwards. It is very remarkable that there are no water-birds which sing.

Another thing to be observed in the habits of birds is in their nests. Every one knows that no two birds build nests exactly alike; but, in addition to this, almost every bird builds in a different situation. The fauvette builds generally in a hedge, but I once found a nest about fourteen feet from the ground, in a tree near the house. The robin builds carelessly in a bush or low tree, near the dwellings of men, and takes no pains to conceal his nest. The yellow-hammer builds on a hedge-bank; the chaffinch commonly on the branch of a holly, elder, or nut tree; the lark and wagtail always on the ground; the redstart in an old wall; the chimney swallow in chimneys; the house-martin under the eaves of houses; the sand-martin in sand rocks or high banks; the ox-eye and tomtit in holes of walls or trees; the thrush high up in trees, generally firs or larches; the blackbird well concealed in bushy places; the nightingale in banks; the ringdove usually at the top of tall trees; the rook, jay, and magpie much the same; the common sparrow almost anywhere, provided it is near a house.

March 13, *Thursday.*—I happened to be in the wood and on the heath at six this evening, that is to say at sunset, and I observed that the thrush, robin, yellow-hammer, and golden-crowned wren were all singing, and the blackbird, tomtit, linnet, and long-tailed titmouse chirping, and the ringdove cooing, at that late hour. The evening was beautifully calm, though cold and sunless.

March 17, *Monday.*—I have been much vexed to-day by hearing a new song without being able to find out certainly what bird made it.

What can this bird be? I know all the English songsters, except four or five, that have only one or two notes; three more that only sing at night; and lastly the tree-lark, titlark, woodlark, greater redpole, and garden warbler. It must certainly be one of these last five. It cannot be the tree-lark, because that bird sings ascending; nor the titlark, since that bird has not much variety, and mine has a great deal. As for the woodlark, it sings only on summer evenings. It must therefore be either the redpole or garden warbler.

March 25, *Tuesday.*—I discovered in my walk to-day a very pretty little spot, in a kind of hollow, below the cow-pasture and the other fields between Woodbury and Everton. It was a large orchard, on a high grassy island, surrounded by a piece of water, which is in most parts perfectly clear and bright, and about forty or fifty feet wide. On one side the channel is nearly dry, and filled with rushes. The banks are very high all round, on the outer side shaded with blackthorn and filbert; on the inner side they are thickly covered with dog's mercury, primroses, bluebells, a few cowslips, and splendid dark-blue violets. There are also very entangled thickets of thorns, brambles, and briars, and several tall ash-trees and willows. This spot is haunted by a great many different birds—blackbirds, missel-thrushes, rooks, carrion-crows, robins, wrens, fauvettes, long-tailed titmice, a handsome kite, and, above all, willow-wrens.

March 26, *Wednesday*. . . . I know by sight as many as thirty-one of the smaller birds, including all not bigger than the missel-thrush. They are the following:—Starling, missel-thrush, thrush, blackbird, nuthatch, creeper, green grosbeak, sparrow, goldfinch, chaffinch, spotted fly-catcher, skylark, the three wagtails, nightingale, redbreast, redstart, fauvette, blackcap, white-throat, willow-wren, golden-crested wren, common wren, ox-eye, tomtit, long-tailed tit, swallow, martin, sand-martin, swift; twenty-three of which frequent the garden.

April 15, *Tuesday.*—It has been for some time intended that I shall go to Casterton to learn dancing, and French at Stamford. This was the day fixed for my departure.

April 22, *Tuesday.*—I shall for the future be able to write very little in my journal, because my time is so much taken up with French and dancing. . . . As for the nightingales, I have been on the look-out for them ever since I came here. . . . I heard a few notes at noon on the 20th, and I was kept awake half the night by them, to my exceeding joy. The night was perfectly still and serene, the moon shining brightly, and the song of the nightingales sounded most exquisite. It seemed to come from the bushes near the river.

May 6, *Tuesday.*—Miss Hussey related a very curious story of some fowls, which she knows to be perfectly true. A turkey-cock, a common cock, and a pheasant were kept in the same farmyard. At length the turkey was sent away to another farm. After his departure, the cock and pheasant had a quarrel; the cock beat, and the pheasant disappeared. In a few days he returned, accompanied by the turkey. The two allies fell together on the cock and killed him.

May 27, *Tuesday.*—I have hardly time now either to observe the birds, or to enter in my journal my observations on them. I, however, attend as much to natural history as I can. I have found here a plant I never saw before, the *Campanula hybrida*, a small and very pretty flower, like the Venus's looking-glass. It grows in cornfields. It does not usually flower till August. I have also found a small sort of gromwell, a white flower.

June 3, *Tuesday.*—Miss Caroline sang to us a song called "The Lark." The music and singing were exceedingly pretty; the song itself I do not much like.

Woodbury, June 23.—I have seen the titlark for the first time. Several were singing yesterday evening on the heath. They rise into the air—whether from a tree or the ground, I cannot say—describe a semicircle in the air, and descend, singing all the time. Their song is not nearly equal either to that of the skylark or tree-lark; it consists chiefly of a loud "tit-tit-tit-tit." . . . There was a tea-party at the Astells'. Mamma, the gentlemen, and all of us went, so that, with the Clutterbucks, Paroissiens, and some others, we were twenty-five in number. We drank tea out of doors, while the gentlemen of the party were engaged at cricket; then followed archery and Les Graces, during which I contrived to keep close to Miss Caroline, and had a great deal of merry conversation with her, of which the following is a sample:—

Emily. I have a question to ask you. At balls and such places, what do people talk about? If they talk about neither sciences nor natural history, I shall set them down as thoroughly stupid.

Miss Car. Stupid! Oh dear me! let me see—they talk about neither sciences nor natural history.

Em. Stupid people! What do they talk about?

Miss Car. About? Oh, music.

Em. Music?

Miss Car. Yes, music.

Em. Well, music's allowable—very proper. What else?

Miss Car. Yes, they talk about music, and how hot the last party was, and which they shall go to next; and they talk scandal, and on the works of the day.

Em. Dear me! what foolish people! to talk about such absurd things! And do you really like to go to such places, Miss Caroline? Do you actually like it?

Miss Car. Yes, very much indeed (! ! !).

Em. Like it! How horrid! How can you like it? What a very great waste of your time, when you ought to be learning and improving your mind, to go to balls and talk nothing but nonsense! Where is the pleasure of it? Do you not think it a waste of time?

Miss Car. Yes, I confess it is; it is a corrupt habit, but when once you have got it, you can never get rid of it.

Em. That is horrible to think of. I hope I shall never get it! But if amusement is your object, why don't you study natural history? There's no amusement so great as that.

Miss Car. But I confess that I don't like natural history.

Em. Oh, how very wrong! You ought to like it.

Miss Car. But nobody taught me; when I was a child nobody took pains with me.

Em. Very true; then it is not so much your fault. But now, may I ask you, Miss Caroline, when you once begin in the season to go to parties, at what rate do you go? how many a week?

Miss Car. Oh, why—sometimes to three in a night.

Em. Three in one night! What a waste of life!

June 24, *Tuesday.*—The carrion-plant grows in Whitewood; we constantly smelt it, but have not hitherto looked for it; it is so difficult to find. However, this evening Mackworth brought it home in triumph. It is a species of fungus. The plant has a singular appearance; but the remarkable part is its odious smell, from which it gains its name. It is generally said to resemble carrion, but papa thinks it more like bad cheese; whatever it is like, it presently filled the whole house, and it was scarcely possible to go where it had been. We stowed it for the night in the garden.

From June 29 to the beginning of August I was ill of

a fever, or recovering from it, and I can therefore put nothing in my journal during that time, except from a few notes which mamma took for me.

August 7, *Thursday.*—One of my chief amusements while recovering from this fever has been to make a series of paintings, one for every month in the year, each representing a bird that sings in that month, in the centre of a wreath of flowers in blow in the same month. The flowers are from nature; the birds from Bewick, and from Mudie's "Birds," a book which I have just bought. I have finished 20
two wreaths—one for June, which consists of a goldfinch in a wreath of wild pink, agrimony, milkwort, bryony, wild rose, forget-me-not, and common ling; the other, for July, has a greenfinch, with harebells, red pimpernel, bog pimpernel, large blue geranium, heart's-ease, rest-harrow, and dodder. All the flowers are wild. I have begun a wreath for August, which will have a woodlark in the centre.

Aug. 8, *Friday.*—I gathered several beautiful flowers—rest-harrow, succory, mullein, and purple-spiked willow-herb, which is a most beautiful plant; it grows by water, and has tall spikes of purple flowers. It is no willow-herb in reality, but a *Lythrum*, and belongs to the class Dodecandria. I observe that succory and rest-harrow are always found together; they grow by roadsides, in a dry open soil.

Aug. 11, *Monday.*—We made another little expedition in the phaeton, but this was much further than to Bedford; it was to Ely, to see its fine cathedral. The day was intensely hot. We set off at half-past eight, and reached Cambridge at half-past twelve. . . . We left Cambridge, I think, at half-past five, and reached Ely at about eight. The road thither is through perfectly flat, uninteresting country, being, in fact, through the fens. The cathedral was in full view for many miles. When we arrived we put up at the Lamb Inn, which was close to the cathedral; and after we had had tea, we walked forth to view this magnificent building by moonlight. I have never before seen any cathedral; the largest churches I have seen are those of Stamford and Bury St. Edmund's, and therefore the impression made on me by Ely was very great. The west front is quite open, and this was what we saw this evening. The size of the edifice and the height of the western tower appeared to me immense, and the richness of the decorations exceeded everything I had ever seen or could conceive. I cannot conceive anything more imposing than a vast Gothic cathedral. I think our old English architecture has an infinitely nobler effect than the Grecian and Roman styles which are now so prevalent, and which are suited neither to our climate nor our manner of living.

Aug. 12, *Tuesday.*—I rose before five, and was employed till breakfast in sketching the west tower of the cathedral from my bedroom window. After breakfast we sallied forth. The west front consists of a great tower, originally flanked on both sides by what are called the north-west and south-west transepts, each terminating in two round towers, the whole in the Norman style, and as rich as possible. If this had remained as it was originally, it would have been, perhaps, the finest front in the world; but, unfortunately, the north-west transept has fallen down, an incongruous addition has been made to the great tower, and the Norman porch has been replaced by an Early English one, which, though exquisitely beautiful in itself, is out of place in a Norman front. This porch is forty feet long. The gateway is loaded with the richest ornaments, and the whole is as splendid as can be imagined. But I think the most imposing part of the cathedral is the view of the noble nave from the entrance.

This nave, except the windows of the aisles, is entirely Norman, of late character, and, consequently, much lighter than is usual in that style. The transepts are Norman, of much earlier date, and much more massive and heavy.

The most beautiful part of the interior of the church is, perhaps, the Decorated English lantern in the centre, which is of the most surpassing richness and elegance. Three arches of the choir are also Decorated English, with the triforium and clerestory windows above them; the rest is a splendid specimen of Early English. The east window in particular is, perhaps, unrivalled. The choir is much injured by a Perpendicular wainscoting all round, which forms a partition between it and the side aisles; and I think the screen and organ loft ought to be taken down, to give the whole effect of the vast interior of the cathedral. The side aisles of the choir are filled with monuments, some of Decorated character, and therefore very ancient, but the greater part are Perpendicular. They are terminated each by a chapel; that of the north aisle is Bishop Allcock's, that of the south Bishop West's. Both of these are splendid specimens of Perpendicular, and are loaded to profusion with the most gorgeous decorations, but are, unfortunately, much dilapidated. We then went in the Lady Chapel, now Trinity Church, an exceedingly rich specimen of the Decorated style, but in a dilapidated state, and injured also by the vile coats of paint with which it is quite covered. Lastly, we left the cathedral by the south transept, and wandered for some time amongst the curious old ruins on this side of it.

Sept. 3, *Wednesday.*—I was awake at a quarter past four, before sunrise, and I amused myself for an hour in watching the proceedings of the birds. It was dim twilight at this time, and the whole sky was of a cold blue grey, except where, in the east, there was a very faint blush of pink, which became gradually brighter and brighter, till it was a fiery crimson, and the whole east was tinged with a burning gold. When I got up, the cock was crowing, and at half-past four the little early robin was awake, though it was still almost dark, crying, "trrr-rrr," and in a short time he was singing sweetly. Then came the blackbirds, at twenty minutes to five. All I saw were hens. Five minutes after, a rook was flying over the paddock. At about five o'clock a thrush was sitting in the mulberry-tree, and then a tomtit began his little whispering note, and a flycatcher his "peek, peek." At a quarter-past five a swallow was singing. I saw no chaffinches; I suspect them to be very lazy. Chaffinches still continue to go in pairs. I see a great many hen blackbirds, but hardly any males. The nuthatch makes a great noise among the firs. I continue to see the golden-crested wren occasionally.

Sept. 6, *Saturday.*—The golden-crested wren seems to be pretty plentiful in the garden. I have more than once seen four or five together. This morning they flew into the larch, squeaking, and apparently quarrelling. I watched some of them for a considerable time pecking about the branches. At last, as I stood under the tree, I saw one, not two yards above my head, hanging from a twig, and it did actually sing, and that, too, very sweetly, though the song was excessively low and soft. Never did I hear it before. White of Selborne did not know that it sung—he said it had only somewhat of a note; Bewick says it is said to have a very melodious song; Mudie, that it sings early in the year, so that he at least knew it.

Sept. 8, *Monday.*— . . . I think it a rather curious property of a mulberry that, when it stains anything—a frock, for instance, as I have sometimes done—the pink part of the purple washes out easily, while a light blue remains, which one can hardly get rid of. . . . Miss Emma Paroissien told me a curious anecdote of a squirrel, which she saw in a nut tree, weighing a good nut and a bad nut, one in each paw, to try by the weight which was good, and the bad ones he invariably dropped, till he had formed a little heap of them at the bottom of the tree, which, when examined, was found to consist entirely of bad nuts.

Sept. 19, *Friday.*—This evening was most exquisitely calm and delightful; not a breath of wind stirred the leaves of a tree, and scarce a cloud was visible in the heavens, while the clear, silvery light of the moon contrasted beautifully with the dark shadows of the thick foliage. The bats were flying silently about in the twilight before the moon shone forth, and the wakeful robin had not yet ceased his sweet plaintive song, while at a distance in the wood sounded the deep hoot of the owl. The occasional falling of the rose-leaves, which looked as white as snow in the darkness, added much to the interest of the scene. I could not persuade myself to go to bed, but sat up a long time looking out of my window.

Sept. 26, *Friday.*—Amongst the plants which I brought from the bogs on Tuesday was one which had an upright, leafless, undivided stalk, with a pinky bunch of buds at the top. I could find no other specimen, and, as it was only in bud, I could not tell what it was. I gathered it, and this morning one of the buds expanded, and I was able to examine it, and found to my great joy that it was the *Menyanthus trifoliata*, or marsh buckbean, an uncommon plant, and one of the most beautiful of all English flowers. It has but a single, undivided stalk, which is thick, succulent, pinkish, or flesh coloured, and in my specimen rather serpentine. The leaves grow only at the root, and I could not find them. The flowers grow in a spike-like bunch at the top of the stem, each flower with a pink floral leaf at the base of the pedicle; the class is Pentandria Monogynia. The corolla of each flower is divided into five parts, so is the calyx. The flower is pure white above, pinky underneath; but its great beauty is that the petals are shaggy or feathery above, the featherings being pure white and as delicate as possible. The pistil is extremely short, and so hidden by the feathering that I could not examine it. The stamens are long, their filaments are pure white, and the anthers black and golden orange. The buds are pink. My specimen was about six inches high. It is impossible to conceive the beauty of this flower, and I am very proud to have found it.

Oct. 1, *Wednesday.*—The beautiful weather we have had of late still continues, without the slightest interruption. Every day is alike. The mornings are always very cold; the sunrise is usually bright and red; and sometimes there is a little mist, which, however, always clears up at half-past eight, or at nine. The rest of the day is uniformly warm and bright, with never a cloud to hide the sun; nor is there ever a breath of wind, so that it is often quite sultry and oppressive; yet the dews are so heavy that in many places we cannot walk on grass all the day through. Then in the evening it grows cooler, and the sun sets in a flood of crimson light. The nights are cold, clear, and starry, with seldom a cloud on the sky. The Milky Way is sometimes to be seen; the grass is quite white with dew.

* In the still noon of a sultry September day (such a September as we have had this year), when not a leaf is stirring, and almost every bird has retired from sight into the shadiest thickets, the appearance of the little solitary golden-crested wren, the only creature moving, seems to add singularly to the idea of quiet and silence. Its movements are unlike those of any other bird, except, indeed, the tomtit; but even this bird does not equal the lightness and airiness of the little wren. It flutters over the tenderest twigs and sprays like a butterfly, and quivers its tiny wings without the least sound, so that unless you see it you would not be aware of its presence. It is hardly like a bird; even the

* Two or three years after, this account of the golden-crested wren was expanded into an article which, with one or two others, appeared in the *Penny Magazine*. The editor of that periodical had, after her death, an idea of publishing her "Notes on Birds" in a separate work. —EDITOR.

little chirp that it occasionally emits bears more resemblance to that of an insect.

Oct. 6, *Monday.*—We continue to have the same weather; this is the tenth day without any interruption to its beauty. This morning has been foggy, but it is as sultry and oppressive as a day in July; but I cannot help thinking rain will soon come.

I have finished painting a wreath for September. It contains nine different sorts of flowers—the cross-leaved heath, the tormentilla, the milfoil, the golden-rod, a blue sort of scabious, the wild thyme, the pedicularis, the stinking horehound, and my beautiful buckbean. My specimen, after having been preserved ten days, is fading. It is very difficult to draw, on account of its extreme whiteness and its featherings. This wreath will have a woodlark in the centre; that for August, which I have finished, will have a swallow. In this one are seven kinds of flowers—the willow-herb, the lythrum, the nightshade, the rampions, the succory, the lesser centaury, and the pretty little lilac-coloured flower whose name I have forgotten.

I saw this afternoon vast flocks of greenfinches and chaffinches, twittering and *pink*ing, alighting on a field of stubble, and rising with a sound exactly like a rushing wind. Chaffinches mix a good deal with other birds.

I have not seen a single swallow or martin since October 2, when the swallows were in song.

Oct. 8, *Wednesday.*—What helps very much to give the appearance now of autumn is, that the swallows and, I believe, the martins are all completely gone. They had been gradually disappearing for about ten days before October 2, and after that day all had migrated. They added not a little to the liveliness of summer by their songs and graceful movements. They—that is, the chimney swallows—sing quite up to the time of their migration, a fact which seems unknown to White.

Oct. 22, *Wednesday.*— . . . I have got the *Geranium cicutarium* and *Robertianum*, or hemlock-leaved crane's-bill and herb Robert, two of the prettiest of our pretty native geraniums. The hemlock-leaved has very long awns, as they are called, to the seeds. These are long points, like thick needles, which have a very singular appearance. They have the curious property of twisting up like corkscrews in dry weather; in damp weather they are quite straight, so that they serve as a kind of barometer.

The little red pimpernel always closes up before rain; I have not observed that any other flowers do so.

Oct. 27, *Monday.*—A flock of wild geese flew over the gardens at a great height, so that we could hardly hear their cackling. They generally fly at the height of fifteen hundred or two thousand feet, and always in some regular form. The flock we saw to-day formed a kind of angular line, thus √, the short side being the foremost. Their leader was a little way in front, and was sometimes changed, as the followers were also occasionally. Their flight was remarkably steady; they went a little to the south of the west. They flew at a prodigious pace. Mr. Wells says they have been calculated to go at ninety miles an hour.

Mrs. Astell and Miss Harriet called this afternoon. Miss Harriet, finding that I noted down in my journal when she promised to begin Milton, desired me to note down to-day also that she had actually begun it, and has nearly finished the first book. This is, indeed, a wonderful occurrence, worthy of being noted down! I much doubt whether she will continue it, for she only began it to avoid being reproached for her neglect of it whenever she came to Woodbury, where, it must be confessed, she has hitherto met with nothing but reproofs on this account. However, I feel very much pleased with her now for three reasons —first, for beginning Milton; secondly, because she saw the flock of wild geese; thirdly, because she gathered the other day a nosegay of all the wild flowers she could find.

Captain Astell has gone abroad for his health, and Miss Harriet told me that the only specimen of natural history which he intends to bring home with him is a jar of potted frogs.

Nov. 11, *Tuesday.*—Most small birds now find their food on the ground—the robin, chaffinch, hedge-sparrow, and even the little wren. The wren makes the shrubberies resound with his harsh, jarring note; he sings also, but not very constantly. He always flies low; his flight is very peculiar, and resembles that of no other bird. He is now becoming familiar, haunts the house, and even perches on the window-ledge. The missel-thrush still haunts the garden, though not so abundantly.

Nov. 15, *Saturday.*—The birches are very richly tinted, and not at all bare. The mulberry is quite naked, and covered with brown buds; the Virginian creeper, the apples, and peaches are also in full bud. The robin and wren sing; the ox-eye and blue-tit still haunt the garden. Great flights of rooks, mixed with jackdaws, fly over it, and rest on their way in the tall trees. Fieldfares, blackbirds, thrushes, and chaffinches feed now on haws, of which there is a vast abundance in the hedges. The creeper still finds its food on the bark of trees. All the goldfinches and wagtails have left our garden; a very few of the latter are sometimes seen, uttering their usual cry, "chippeet." The golden wren has his two or three sharp whispering notes, but not his low squeak. He now haunts woods.

Dec. 1, *Monday.*—November is now finished, and actually—oh wonder of wonders!—we have not had a single fog during this foggy month. I doubt whether such a thing has ever before occurred in the memory of men. Moreover (except sometimes at night), we have had rain only four times, one of which was only a short shower; there has been one snow-shower, and two days only of hard wind. The weather in general has been warm, sunny, and delightful, with very few cold days, and always exceedingly dry. This day, the first of December, is beautifully bright, very warm (therm. 46°), but with a very high wind.

Dec. 3, *Wednesday.*—Mr. Tebbut, the hair-dresser and bird-fancier of Potton, was here to-day, and I obtained from him a good deal of interesting information about birds. He says that birds of all kinds, if taken from the nest at ten, or even six days old, and brought up where they can hear no bird sing, will sing their own natural song, but they may be taught any bird's song by being placed near it, except only the skylark, which, though it will readily learn another song, will always have a little of its own—a very curious fact. Bullfinches and linnets are the easiest to teach. My idea is that all birds sing from imitation, as they can be taught any song, but there are many facts for and against this notion. Mr. Tebbut has never known a bird dumb which had never heard a song. He says that there are snow-buntings to be seen in summer on Gamlingay heath, and that at Muggerhanger, seven miles off, aberdevines are not uncommon. At Gamlingay there are many rare and curious birds, among which are the reed-sparrow and kingfisher. The reed-sparrow, he says, does not sing, but has only a harsh cry. In this he agrees with Mudie, but both Bewick and White give it a soft song; Mudie says it has been confounded with other reed-birds, which sing sweetly. Mr. Tebbut has seen the nest; he says it is suspended among reeds. I shall try, if possible, to get a sight of them.

Dec. 10, *Wednesday.*—. . . Mrs. Clutterbuck showed me some splendid drawings by her father-in-law; they are sketches of scenes abroad and in England. Though not coloured, and only outlines in pencil, with scarce any shad-

ing, they display a very great talent for drawing, and the effect given by a few spirited strokes is quite remarkable. Though boldly, perhaps hastily executed, they are by no means too broad and coarse, but accurate and delicate. It is this style of drawing at which I aim, and I shall neglect shading almost entirely, for I see that in clever hands it is quite unnecessary in producing effect. I cannot bear what 21
the *Quarterly Journal of Education* calls the neat sampler-like style, practised by so many ladies.

Dec. 23.—There was no singing at nine o'clock (a.m.), but the wood was filled with the clear whispering chirps of tits and golden-crested wrens, who were flitting in numbers from tree to tree, and sometimes alighting on the ground. There were blue-tits, ox-eyes, long-tailed tits, cole-tits, and even the marsh-tit, which I never saw before. It is about the size of the cole-tit, with a black head and whitish cheeks, but no spot on the back of the neck; the wings are dusky, and the breast brownish white. Its cry and habits resemble those of other tits. I now know every kind of tit except the crested and bearded tit, which are very rare.

Skylarks and titlarks assemble in vast flocks, the former with their short subdued winter-warble. Mr. Keal told me to-day he has seen a white sparrow in Potton. Flights of jays, eight or ten at once, sometimes enter the garden to make war on their great enemy the missel-thrush. The creeper makes a pretty loud, shrill cry, several times repeated, as it flies from tree to tree.

Dec. 25, *Thursday.*—Christmas Day. . . . Going up into my room, I heard a nut-hatch uttering his deep loud cry, and I then heard a continued tapping or hammering on the boughs of an old pear tree before my window. I could not for some time see the bird; at last I discovered him flying to another tree. The nut-hatch, though clumsy and heavy in shape, is brisk and lively, and very active in creeping up the branches and boughs of trees, which he does like the creeper, but not so silently and timidly. His plumage is handsome—bluish grey above, and red orange beneath. He is a difficult bird to catch a sight of. I never saw him in a pine or fir, but often in oaks. He feeds as much on insects as on nuts, even when the latter are abundant.

CHAPTER VI.

From Feb. 10, *to July* 25, 1835.—*Woodbury, London, Rochester, Woodbury.*

Feb. 10, *Tuesday.*—. . . I shall study botany this year in a very different way from that which I have been accustomed to pursue, for I find that I have hitherto been a very superficial botanist, attending to little besides the classification, and not studying the habits, properties, and uses of plants, as I do the habits of birds. I might just as well call myself an ornithologist, if I knew only in what tribe to place a bird, as call myself at present a botanist.

Feb. 14, *Saturday.*—As we were sitting at dinner papa came into the room, and called me to look at a bird which he and mamma were watching from the library window, and did not know. I came directly, and saw the bird hopping on the path, between the weeping-ash and the shrubbery on the west side of the house. It was about the size of a starling, and carried itself something in the manner of a thrush. I was near enough to see the colours and its crest, and presently recognized it as that very rare bird, the waxen chatterer, or silk-tail, a German bird which occasionally comes to England, towards the end of winter, and feeds on berries and insects. It is very handsome, a kind of purplish reddish ash above, and grey and reddish orange below. The crest is long and silky, the face black, the wings irregularly barred with white. One of these birds was shot in Sussex not long ago. Very little is known of their habits. I shall watch this individual, if it stays in the garden. I already have observed that it hops, and comes to the ground to look for insects.

Feb. 17, *Tuesday.*—I have just tried to count the notes of the thrush. I listened to one singing before my window, and put down a mark for every different note. In less than two minutes I had got forty-six, including, not every single syllable, but every polysyllable, or cluster of notes; and I have not now exhausted all his notes. They are quite endless, and are multiplied by constantly varying the tone of each note.

Feb. 28, *Saturday.*—I have had for some time past a room to myself, which is a great pleasure to me. It is one which used to be called the lark-room; it looks east, over the east part of the garden, the paddock, and Whitewood. Immediately in front of it is the larch, which abounds in small birds; beyond is the shrubbery. I like it better than any room in the house.

March 4, *Wednesday.*—I have finished three chronological tables, which succeed one another in regular order. Each has five columns. The first column has the chronology of the Emperors of the West, succeeded by that of Italy in general; the second, the Emperors of the East till the taking of Constantinople; the third, Persia; the fourth, the caliphs; the fifth, miscellaneous, the latter part being the chronology of the Ottoman sultans. The making of these tables has been of immense use to me in teaching me general history and chronology. I intend to make one more, of the modern European nations. When I finish writing these tables, I glue on them an edging of pasteboard painted black.*

March 16, *Monday.*—. . . I ordered at Fraser's some time ago a folio book, of one hundred and twenty pages,

* These charts, eight in all, are still existing, and are marvels of execution.—ED.

ruled in a particular way, for me to take notes every day of what birds are in song. It came to-day, and cost eight and sixpence. Every page has ten columns perpendicularly, and above thirty horizontally. Of the perpendicular columns, the first is for the day of the month, the second for the weather, the rest for the birds' names. The horizontal columns, of course, contain the notes of every day. Every month will occupy two or three pages, except the depth of winter. I shall copy out into this book all my notes of birds' songs from last June up to this day, and then I shall continue my notes in the book itself.

March 27, *Friday*.—. . . We entered the orchard to-day, and as we were walking about it, a fox suddenly splashed into the moat, and, jumping out on the other side, ran off over the cow-pasture. A gentleman's house, in the reign of Elizabeth, stood on the ground now occupied by these moated fields and orchards.

April 13, *Monday*.—I began, after a long cessation, painting my flower-wreaths for every month; I drew an oxlip in a wreath for April.

April 14, *Tuesday*.—We may now expect any birds of passage. The cuckoo has been heard Sunday and Monday, and Mr. Ashton, one of the pupils, has seen two swallows this morning. I cannot believe, what I often hear said, that the birds return sooner in fine warm springs; for instinct must be a wonderful quality indeed, if it informs them, when at the equator, that it is fine weather in England! Besides, the instinct would be useless unless it informed them also whether the fine weather would continue.

April 16, *Thursday*.—. . . The study of natural history seems to me to be one which belongs to the nature of man, and is born with him. I shall never believe that an individual exists who could not have been taught to love it, if led to it early. This, I believe, is the only pursuit of which this can be said, for I am not quite certain that it is true of a literary taste. The study of natural history is perfectly inexhaustible. I believe that if I were chained for life to Woodbury, and never allowed to ramble from it more than three or four miles (the utmost limit of my walks), and excluded as I am, by its situation, from all the birds that haunt mountains, rocks, and the seaside (that is, haunting them peculiarly), and from most kinds that haunt all sorts of waters—I believe that even in this situation I should for ever be discovering something new.

April 25, *Saturday.*—I shall put down the substance of some explanations papa gave us to-day at our Greek lesson about the natural and artificial year. Every one knows that by dividing the year into 12 months of 28 or of 30 days, we make a year which is less than the solar year by some days, which accumulating, would in time bring the seasons wrong. The solar year consists of 365 days, 5 hours, 48 minutes, 57 seconds; but up to the time of Julius Cæsar the Roman year consisted only of 365 days, with an intercalary month every other year, to make the year correspond with the solar year. But this intercalary month did not make it correspond exactly, and the consequence was that in the time of Julius Cæsar the seasons came wrong, and what was really winter was called autumn. Cæsar put an end to the confusion by making one year of 15 months, and settling the year for the future at 366 days. But as the former year had been less than the real time of the earth's revolution round the sun, so this, though much nearer the truth, was more, and consequently in time the seasons again became wrong, the other way. Accordingly, in the year 1582, Pope Gregory XIII. corrected the error by throwing out of the year 11 overplus days, with a leap-year every fourth year, except every hundredth year, which alteration makes it so nearly right that the difference will hardly amount to a day in 7000 years. The Gregorian style was not adopted in England till 1752.

The Egyptians, according to Herodotus, divided the year into twelve months of thirty days, and every year added five days more, which made it very nearly the true solar year.

April 28, *Tuesday*.—. . . I begin to think that thrushes and blackbirds find out the cockchafer grub by hearing; for their manner of looking for them is not to apply the bill to the ground as if to smell, but to trot about, or stand still in a listening attitude, with the head high in the air, and then to dart off to the spot where they expect to find the creature.

May 9, *Saturday*.—This being a beautiful morning, mamma and I took a delightful walk through Whitewood at eight o'clock. The nightingales sung most sweetly; I think there were four of them. We watched one for a long time, which was perched in a naked oak very near us; he sat very calmly singing, without hopping or dancing about. We noticed that he makes his long "tweet" (designated by Coleridge, "One low piping note more sweet than all") without opening his beak at all, merely swelling his throat. Last night I heard three nightingales from my bedroom window, singing together—one in Whitewood, one in the fir plantation, one near the Greens' farm; three also were singing on the west side of the house, so that we have six nightingales within earshot every night.

The whole wood was echoing with songs. We heard the nightingale, cuckoo, blackcap, thrush, blackbird, willow-wren, golden wren, blue-tit, cole-tit, tree-lark, chaffinch, robin, wren, hedge-sparrow.

May 12, *Tuesday*.—I saw the interesting sight of a young bird fed by its parents. An old male blackbird and a young one descended on the lawn, just before the drawing-room windows. The old one began immediately to hunt for insects, the young one standing by quietly, continually opening his beak and making a little plaintive cry. At length the old one brought out a large cockchafer grub, the sight of which much delighted the young bird; the parent put it into his child's mouth, but it was tossed backwards and forwards two or three times before the young one finally gobbled it up. They then flew away together.

About half an hour after, I saw from my room another male blackbird with two young ones, for whom he was seeking food, and they watching his movements with the same impatient cry. I did not see the old one actually put the food in their mouths, but I was much surprised when he two or three times sang, though on the ground—I suppose to amuse the youngsters. On neither of these occasions did I see the hen. The young ones had a downy brown plumage, softer in tint than the hen's; their beaks were encircled by a pale yellow skin. They squatted in a very droll manner.

My usual walk now is to go through the lanes to Everton, descend the Tempsford hill to hear the tree-lark, reascend it, and return across the heath and through the wood. In passing the heath I go rather out of the way, through a very pretty part, enclosed by a high hedge; it is quite covered with gorse in full flower. Here I generally sit down for some time on the gorse, under the high gorse-bushes, telling stories to such of the children as are with me, according to my old practice, which I still continue. All round us stone-chats are flitting from twig to twig, making their clicking noise; ox-eyes are chirping, blackcaps and willow-wrens singing; all which, added to the delicious scent of the gorse and the perfect retirement of the place, make it quite delightful.

May 20.—I am actually writing this part of my journal in London. Last year, when Arthur Malkin and his wife visited us, they planned an expedition to London for mamma and me, who were to come and stay with them in their house in Welbeck Street. This day the plan was put in execution. We left Woodbury at ten o'clock, being driven in the phaeton to Biggleswade, and thence proceeded by chaise to London, where we arrived at about half-past five. It is a great delight to me to come to London. . . . The only time I ever saw London was in 1831, when we spent a night there on our way to the sea. . . .

For many miles before we arrived, the atmosphere was polluted with the smoke of the town and the vile smell of brickmaking. But over the town itself hung a dense cloud of smoke and fog which totally hid all but the nearest buildings. No view of it from a distance could be obtained, and there was no beauty in the surrounding country to set it off to advantage. The region for some miles round is neither country nor town; it consists of flat fields, with a few trees, thickly interspersed with those hideous creations, citizens' boxes. In short, nothing can be less beautiful, less imposing, less interesting, than the first sight of London, at least from the north road.

We avoided the City altogether, going by the New Road, through Regent's Park. I was altogether disappointed in the Park. I had expected at least to see fine timber. No such thing. The horrid atmosphere of London checks all vegetation. As far as I could see, there was not a tree in Regent's Park to compare with the greater part of those in Whitewood. Besides, the sky is smoky and dingy; there is no freshness in the air, nor the bloom of spring everywhere, as in the country. It has also a formal look; it is intersected with wide public roads, which are inclosed by hedges or railings. These roads were full of carriages, cabs, horsemen, and pedestrians, which are supposed to give so much liveliness to the scene; so they do, but I like a retired, unfrequented park much better.

On leaving Regent's Park we entered Portland Place. Here I was much struck with the grandeur of the buildings, surpassing anything I ever saw in the shape of private houses. If London had all been like this, it would have been a magnificent city. But I believe not many parts are so noble as this.

May 21, *Thursday.*—Though not in bed last night till ten o'clock, nor asleep till about eleven, I woke this morning at half-past five, and would have got up, but mamma kept me in bed till nearly six. I was surprised to see the sky blue, and the sun shining; in short, the air, at least above the houses, did not look less clear than out of London. Of course it must be infinitely dingier than this in winter, when there are so many more fires; and in the City, too, I suppose it is worse. . . . This evening we had a most pleasant little party—at least at tea, for all our visitors did not come to dinner. . . . The conversation at tea
22 turned partly on the Zoological Gardens, partly also on the horrid habit of smoking, which everybody, save Mr. Kemble, abhorred.

[Seven pages are here filled with the account of a visit to the Zoological Gardens.]

In conclusion I shall put down the opinions of two ladies of my acquaintance about the probable effect of seeing the Zoological Gardens.

"I think," says Mrs. Arthur Malkin, "that the most stupid person, the most indifferent to natural history, must be interested and pleased with the animals of the Zoological Gardens."

"I am sure," says Miss ——, "a visit to the Zoological Gardens is enough to CURE any one of natural history; the smell is so horrible,"—false,—"and it is so hot and fatiguing."

May 24, *Sunday.*— . . . In the afternoon we went to Vere Street Chapel. Here we had in the pulpit the most disgusting specimen of affectation, far beyond the reach of exaggeration and caricature. The preacher was a very young man, whose name we could not discover. His manner was such that it would not have been surprising if the whole congregation had burst into a laugh. He bowed; shook his head; sailed backwards and forwards; sank; rose; held one hand on his heart and stretched the other over the congregation, or clasped them both together; waved his handkerchief; closed his eyes; smiled sweetly; shook his voice; assumed a ludicrous sentimental tone, even when quoting a text; jogged his sermon up and down; leant over his cushion; grinned; sighed;—in short, did everything that he possibly could to make himself offensive and ridiculous. I never saw such a preposterous display in all my life, and Mrs. Malkin assured me it was very uncommon even in London.

May 25, *Monday.*— . . . In London all people go about three o'clock to make their morning calls; the consequence is that everybody is out at the same time, and it rarely happens that anybody is found at home, which the visitor knows very well. If by any rare chance they are at home, and wish not to be disturbed by visitors, they very coolly desire the servant to say, "Not at home"—a detestable practice; for, though its meaning is well understood by the visitor, it is not so by the servant, who is thus taught to lie. Besides, why not say they are engaged? which would be just as useful, and more honest.

I think much better of London now than when we first came, which was in very gloomy weather; and I admire many parts exceedingly. But still I am horrified at the mischief done by the smoke. Almost all the houses are blackened, the yards and back premises are covered with soot, the trunks of all the trees are black, all plants become dingy, clothes get tarnished by the smoke, the hands can hardly be kept clean, and in some winds great puffs of smoke enter the open windows. The extreme blackness and dinginess of the sparrows (which are numerous) is also worthy of note. I see jackdaws sometimes; they cannot be made blacker, but doubtless lose all their gloss, and I suppose their grey polls are darkened.

H

May 26, *Tuesday.*—. . . The concert began with a very fine symphony, which lasted a considerable time. Then came a duet between Rubini and Lablache; and then Miss Clara Novello came forward, and sang a little English song, "Marraton and Yarratilda." Miss Novello seems to be about nineteen years old, dark, and extremely pale, as all the others were, owing to the late hours they keep. She was simply dressed, and wore a bonnet and boa, while the audience were suffering from the great heat. She has an exceedingly sweet voice, but Mrs. A. M. says she wants skill and feeling. Next came a military concerto; then Grand Rondo, by Grisi. I shall not, however, go through all the parts of the concert, but I shall mention what I think of the different performers, beginning with the female singers after Miss Novello. Grisi is considered the first opera-singer in England. Her voice is exceedingly fine; I certainly liked it better than any other I heard. It is deep and very powerful; the upper notes, Mrs. M. says, are perfect, and her execution is wonderful. She is very handsome and finely formed.

Malibran, I think, is next to Grisi in point of excellence. Her voice is deeper and her lower notes are better than Grisi's, but her upper ones are not so good. Malibran has regular and handsome features, but not altogether a pleasing face; she is very dark, and her hair is jet black. She was encored in "Ah se estinto."

Mrs. Seguin has a good voice, but is very inferior to the others. She sang twice—once in a quartette with Grisi, Lablache, and Rubini, but her voice was quite drowned in Grisi's; the second time she sang a duet with her husband.

Lablache has a stupendous and very excellent voice; I was quite astonished to hear it. He is an immense man, elderly, with a large quantity of grey hair; he has a good-tempered brown face, and two bright black eyes. Rubini's voice is much less powerful, but I think equally good, as far as I can judge, not understanding music.

Parry is quite young and inexperienced, but has a very sweet voice, and promises, it is said, to excel all the other performers.

I shall only say that I was exceedingly delighted with the concert altogether, more especially as I never before heard anything of the kind; and this, says Mrs. A. M., was a very good one. It lasted till about half-past five.

May 28, *Thursday.*—. . . In the afternoon, at about four o'clock, we left London to spend a night at Highwood, the residence of Dr. Fitton. Dr. F. called for us at Welbeck Street, and brought us to Highwood in his carriage, the Malkins as well as ourselves. It was very delightful, after being shut up for a week in London, to come into the country; to see trees and flowers and fresh grass, to breathe fresh air, and to hear all my favourite birds singing again. Those that were in song about Highwood were the blackbird, the thrush, the blackcap, the robin, the wren, the willow-wren, the yellow wren, the chaffinch, the greenfinch, the hedge-sparrow, the lark, the yellow-hammer; twelve only. Highwood is a very pretty place, interesting from having belonged to the celebrated Wilberforce, whose portrait hangs in the dining-room; the furniture is as he left it. Dr. F. is a very scientific and agreeable man; he gave us a great deal of curious information about the wonderful discoveries of modern astronomers, particularly Herschel. He was also so kind as to give me what I have long wished for, and have been trying to make myself, an outline map of the world, showing all the physical features of the globe, without any names; he gave me also a little book on the geology of Hastings, written by himself.

June 3, *Wednesday.*—. . . Leaving the Colosseum, we returned to Welbeck Street, and, accompanied by Mrs. A. M., went to the Pantheon Bazaar, in Oxford Street.

As I never saw a bazaar before, it appeared to me quite splendid. There was one very large arched room, with a gallery round the top, and some other rooms above stairs, besides a conservatory below, containing a pretty fountain. We remained here a very long time, making some purchases. I bought a few things for the children at home—engravings for Richard and Arabella, a pencil-case for Louisa, and a six-inch ruler for Mackworth. As for myself, I was a long time fixing on anything—not because I wanted everything, but because I saw nothing which I wanted, for I never am plagued with the wish to buy everything I see. I should after all have gone away without making any purchase, but as grandmamma and Aunt Charlotte had very kindly given me some money to spend in London, and papa also, I thought I might as well buy something, as to-morrow we shall depart. So I got a box of chalks of different colours to draw with, and a pretty little glass bottle to put eau-de-Cologne in.

June 5, *Friday.*—. . . But now for the Dockyard, perhaps the most interesting and wonderful place I have seen since I left Woodbury. It extends along the bank of the Medway, and is nearly a mile in length. It contains ships of different kinds being built, and manufactories of all the different parts of vessels. We first went to look at the ships themselves; there are a great many now in the docks, chiefly war-ships of different sorts—many were ships of the line. Over each is built a shell or roof of timber, which is dotted all over with windows, and is supported by posts. The vessel, in this state, is, of course, without masts. We looked at these for a short time. One was but just begun, and had only the keel and the ribs. Another was a little more advanced, and had the naked ribs covered with planks running lengthwise. Another had been already launched, and was being quite completed; the masts were already fixed in, and all the decks and cabins were quite formed.

We went on board, and examined every part of it. It was a seventy-four-gun ship of the line; it was called a two-decker, because it had only two gun-decks, but it had in reality four decks, besides the hold. The poop makes a sort of fifth deck. The names of the decks are as follows:—the poop, the quarter-deck, the main-deck, the orlop deck, which last has no windows, and is the dreary habitation of the poor midshipmen. The captain's cabin is a very tolerable place, but all the cabins are so low. I was quite amazed at the prodigious size of the vessel; it is called the *Hercules*.

From the docks we went to the forge. This is an immense and lofty room, full of anvils, fires, furnaces, bellows, etc., and smiths at work. Here the anchors and other iron implements are made. We saw some men at work on the fluke of an anchor. A vast iron bar was heated red-hot, and then a piece was cut off. One man laid a chisel on it, drawing it along in the proper direction, and four others, each in turn, gave it a blow with a heavy hammer. When the chisel was too hot, the man ran and dipped it in cold water. When the piece was cut off, the bar, reduced to shape, was laid on several others of the same form, which were all to be welded together. We saw the process of welding two pieces of iron. They were laid in a fire, with their ends together; fuel was heaped over them, and they were heated red-hot. This place was intolerably hot, and we soon left it.

Next we went to the saw-mill. This is the most wonderful part of the whole dockyard. We first saw the steam-engine, which is of prodigious size and moves with a thundering noise. Of course the heat is intense. The saw-room is very spacious, and is filled with the most complicated machinery, all set in motion by the steam-engine. There was a single circular saw, about eighteen inches across, which revolved six hundred and fifty times in a minute, and cut great pieces of timber into some kind of shape; the timber was made to approach by machinery. But the larger saws were the most remarkable. These were fixed in rows along the middle of the room; they are perpendicular, and very tall. Six, eight, or any number of saws are fixed into one machine, the number being according to the number of planks into which a piece of timber is to be cut. The timber is dragged on by iron claws, which pull it forwards in the most curious way, and the saws cut it by jumping up and down with great noise and swiftness. I could have stayed here for hours watching the machinery, but, alas! we had only ten minutes to spare for it.

Thence we went to see the machine for dragging up the timber out of the pit in which it is kept to season, after being brought from the river, by an underground passage. This machinery is not so complex as the rest, and is easily understood. An iron boat is suspended by a chain which goes over a pulley; at the other end the timber is hooked, and the boat, being filled with water, descends into the pit. As it descends, the timber, of course, rises, and then by further machinery is made to travel into the saw-mill.

We could only give a few minutes to the turning-room, where everything is on the same gigantic scale. When we had seen this, mamma, being much tired, sat down to rest, while Cousin Edward took me to see the leaden pipes made. Unluckily they had left off working for the day, but we came just in time to see a sheet of lead cast. When we came in, a quantity of lead was boiling in a large copper, till it was sufficiently melted to be cast into shape, which took place a minute after we entered. Close to the copper is a cistern, and joined to this is the mould, a shallow reservoir, with a deep part at one end, separated by a little ledge. On the shallow part is a layer of smooth moist sand, leaving about three inches and a half between the sand and the top of the edge all round. Everything being ready, a little door in the side of the copper was opened, and out rushed a hissing stream of liquid lead into the reservoir below. When it was all out, it floated about in the cistern like quicksilver, with all the dross at the top. This a man skimmed off with two boards. The lead is then stirred about, and at the proper time it is put into the mould, which is effected as follows:— A chain is fastened to the edge of the cistern, passes over a beam in the roof, and is pulled by a wheel and axles on the floor; a man slowly turns the handle, the cistern is raised up, and out runs the liquid lead into the mould. Here it spreads equally, and when it begins to flow over into the hollow they stop. The lead settles, a man draws a board over it, and scrapes off the dross into the hollow. The lead is now pure, and looks like a sheet of quicksilver, but it presently cools, and congeals into a massive solid sheet three tons in weight. About five sheets are cast in a day.

June 6.—Our excursion to-day was to Cobham Hall, the seat of Lord Darnley. The woods and gardens are very beautiful, with dells and dingles prettier than anything I ever saw; they want nothing but water. The gardens are full of splendid flowers. There are whole thickets of laurels, rhododendrons, and magnolias; there are azaleas of a fine orange-colour which I never saw before; and in the greenhouses are several noble specimens of the magnificent *Cactus speciosissimus.* In the garden is a tame Demoiselle heron, which follows the gardener wherever he goes; it had a mate, after whose death it used to walk for hours before the windows of the orange-house, looking at itself in the glass.

June 8, *Monday.*—I picked up that most amusing book,
"German Popular Tales," and could not stop till I had 23
finished it. I read it once when I was five years old, and liked it very much. Cousin Susan showed me her microscope the other day, when I had not time to mention it. The microscope is a good-sized one, and requires a

strong light to show the objects. I saw in it the pollen, leaves, and petals of various plants. Their beauty is wonderful; they look like heaps of precious stones. The pollen of the grand scarlet poppy is particularly splendid. The petals of the pink and crimson geranium seem like rubies crowned with amethysts, and those of the spiderwort like a mass of amethysts.

Cousin Susan, who is very obliging and good-natured, has also given me two or three lessons in colouring flowers, by letting me see her do some.

June 11, *Thursday.*— . . . I am very glad to return at last to the quiet of Woodbury, much as I have liked this little excursion. We find everybody well, and the number of our bird pets somewhat increased. A cock bullfinch, shy as the species is, two days ago flew into the schoolroom; its head was bare of feathers, probably with fighting. Richard introduced him to his hen bullfinch; they live very amicably together. Mackworth is rearing a young blackbird, and Arabella and Louisa have two young chaffinches, which the mother feeds. A few days after we went to town, M. found a coal-tit's nest with six or seven young ones. He brought it to the house, and the mother came every day with food, which she brought every five minutes; she even forced her way into the cage in her anxiety to feed them. In about a fortnight the young ones were full-feathered, and flew away. The mother fed them only with small green caterpillars. The young ones had grown very tame, and perched on the heads, hands, and shoulders of the children.

June 19, *Friday.*—As my ear gets more practised in distinguishing the songs of birds, I am surprised to find how many little differences there are between the songs of different individuals, even of species which have unvarying songs, as the chaffinch and hedge-sparrow. I observe this mostly in the chaffinch and willow-wren. I am persuaded that, were my ear acute enough to discover it, I should find that no two individuals sang exactly alike. At present, I perceive that the chaffinches of Kent have a much softer and more liquid tone than any others I know, and even add two or three notes; those of Woodbury are very inferior performers, though they differ considerably from one another in point of excellence.

June 22, *Monday,*— . . . The hay is beginning to be cut everywhere. I noticed yesterday and to-day that in Mr. Astell's field, where the hay is cut, the redstarts collect and peck about on the ground, doubtless to find some insect which frequents hay. I have seen as many as three together, an unusual number in so shy and solitary a bird. L. has observed the same in our garden, where we are cutting the hay; a redstart, which frequents the garden and has built a nest and laid one egg, hops a great deal about the new-mown grass. I wish I was sufficiently an entomologist to know what food it finds there.

Mamma has bought a young jay, not quite fledged, which is to be her pet, and I have the care of him. His name is Cracow, a word which he will easily learn to say. He is kept in a large wicker cage in my room. L. had two young blackbirds. One died, but the other is alive and well, able to fly about and peck for himself. We call him Mottle. She takes him every day to the garden, and lets him run on the lawn, where he picks up ants for himself.

June 23, *Tuesday.*—Yesterday we put Mottle in Cracow's cage; they are very friendly, and jump on each other's backs. Mottle's screams for food woke me this morning before five. I immediately came and fed them, and found them very ravenous. Cracow is certainly in good health, and very promising. He opens his beak very wide and flaps his wings whenever I offer him a bit of meat. After breakfast (his I mean), he diligently plumed himself, and then sat sleepily on his perch. He is not near so sprightly and active as Mottle.

Jack, the jackdaw, is still alive, healthy, and happy. He lives under the weeping ash, where he has a little house to retire to when he thinks proper. He eats meat, bread, and potatoes, besides the insects he gets for himself. He is very fond of fine colours, and loves to carry in his beak petals of red or crimson flowers. He is rather ill-tempered, and soon takes offence. His favourite is papa, who is also very fond of him.

I shall now copy out into my journal a short set of notes which, in imitation of one in the *Penny Magazine*, I kept this spring of the progress of vegetation, and the appearances of birds and insects.

Jan. 3. Brimstone rarely seen.
14. Aconite and crocus bloom.
Skylark ascends.
29. Blackbird, thrush, blue-tit, sing.
Feb. 5. Scentless violet forms flower-buds at the root.
10. Honeysuckle in leaf.
Hazel covered with catkins.
24. Greenfinch chirps.
26. Bunting sings.
Mar. 2. Sweet violet blooms.
6. Golden wren sings.
13. Bees come out.
Brimstone abounds.
16. Coal-tit sings.
19. Primrose and ivy-leaved ranunculus bloom.
26. Nettle butterfly seen.
28. Thrush lays eggs.
April 1. Peacock and cabbage butterfly appear.
2. Willow-wren sings.
Glow-worm rarely shines.
6. Marsh marigold, cowslip, oxlip, bluebell, bullace, blackthorn, pear, bloom.
7. Ground-ivy blooms.
Blackcap sings.
Spotted orchis and wood anemone bloom.
9. Blackthorn and bullace in full flower.
10. Redstart returns.

April 13. Nuthatch whistles.
Germander speedwell blooms.
14. Swallow begins to appear.
Cuckoo heard.
20. Larch and hawthorn in leaf.
Nightingale returns.
22. Zephyr butterfly seen.
Birch looks green.
Leaf-buds of oak burst.
Horse-chestnut nearly in leaf.
Greater stitchwort blooms.
Tree-lark and swallow sing.
May 3. Leaf-buds of lime burst.
Crab in full flower.
Lily of the valley in bud.
6. Birch in leaf.
Hawthorn begins to bloom.
Pedicularis, tormentilla, *Geranium cicutarium*, bloom.
Redstart sings.
9. Cockchafer appears.
Yellow wren sings.
Leaf-buds of oak quite burst.
Jack-in-the-hedge in full flower.
14. Swift returns.
Bluebell in full flower.
Young starlings fledged.
16. *Sphinx apiformis* seen.
Orange-tip abounds.
Tree-creeper lays eggs.
22. Young coal-tits fledged.
June 5. Black woodpecker (very rare) lays eggs.
10. Young chaffinches and blackbirds fledged.

June 26, *Friday*.—Cracow is wonderfully restless and inquisitive, and loves running over the room and perching on everything he sees; he notices every sound, and sits in an attitude of extreme attention while the breakfast or dinner bells ring. When very hungry, his loud screams, the red interior of his open beak, and the violent flapping of his wings are quite ridiculous. He will plume himself for a quarter of an hour together.

June 29, *Monday.*—. . . I took Cracow out on the lawn to run about, and at last showed him to Jack, to see if they were likely to agree together in future. I put my hand above him to preserve him from danger, and thought him safe, especially when Jack, immediately running up, stood by his side without turning his head or beak to him. But I presently found this seeming indifference was only an artifice of Jack, for the malignant creature, swift as lightning, dashed his tremendous beak on poor Cracow's wing, and pulled him down on his back. The unhappy little bird sent forth the most piteous cries, while the would-be murderer darted back, uttering its own cry of wrath and ill-temper. I found that, with cruel instinct, he had fixed on the principal joint of the wing, and would certainly have broken it had I not been there; as it is, it is much hurt, and Cracow is dull and ill, but not, I think, in danger. I am afraid all hopes are at an end of his and Jack's living peaceably together. Jack is peculiarly ill-tempered. He in his early youth killed two small chickens, and made an attack also on L.'s young blackbird; he is fond, too, of biting people through their stockings.

Cracow is very good-tempered, and has a sweet expression. He is not ravenous, and does not eat as well as he did. I showed him a little pan of water; he drank some, and continually licked his beak after it with his tongue. He sometimes raises his crest; he pecks a good deal at nail-heads and the hay that gets entangled in his feet. When he is old enough to peck his food he may be allowed to drink freely.

As for Jack, his would-be murderer, he is himself the most extraordinary bird possible. His whims and caprices are without end, and are all unaccountable. When we first had him, his place of residence was on the east side of the house, before the breakfast-room; we then, finding that he picked the pinks to pieces, removed him to the west side, and placed his house underneath the weeping ash opposite the library. But the fanciful creature is always shifting his quarters from place to place. For some time he could never be induced to quit his house; then he took it into his head that when his food was brought he would come for it to the distance of a yard all round the cage, but beyond that he would not go. At present he has chosen to abandon his house and the ash altogether, and is comfortably in the midst of a flower-bed. He has marked for himself a boundary of a foot all round it, beyond which nothing can induce him to step. If a piece of bread is thrown to him, he will let the sparrows eat it before his eyes rather than go an inch too far for it. Sometimes he has a fancy of never stepping on grass, sometimes of never stepping on mould; sometimes he will sit for days together under one plant, or on the under bar of a seat in the garden. He has a great hatred to gloves, and is furious if any one strokes his head with one. He is fond of bright colours; and if scarlet-coloured petals are given him, seizes and carefully hoards them up. He eats bread and meat; his appetite is small; he is courageous and malignant, and evidently loves to inflict pain, which his great bill renders him very capable of doing. His wing being cut, he cannot fly, but he hops very fast.

July 11, *Saturday.*—A tabby moth, which M. caught for me yesterday, and which I set with pins and supposed quite dead, for not even the antennæ moved, actually laid eggs all last night, and continued it this morning, so that I suppose it was alive. The eggs are twelve or fourteen in number, small, hard, and white. I shall preserve them till next year, that they may hatch, for I believe the caterpillar is unknown to naturalists.

July 16, *Thursday.*— . . . Poor Cracow is in a lamentable condition, though not ill. Having, through weakness, lost the use of his legs, they have become, by lying under him, frightfully twisted and deformed, so that he will be probably a cripple for life. I cannot, however, bear the thought of killing him, he looks so gentle and mild. By Mr. Keal's advice I have straightened his legs as well as I can, and then bound them in adhesive plaster, which will perhaps do them good. I keep him always in a basket, because the more he moves the more he will hurt his wing.

July 20, *Monday.*—For two or three days I have observed a species of wasp come frequently into my room, and enter the keyhole of my dressing-table drawer, where it stayed a considerable time. This morning, I found two green caterpillars in the lock, each rolled up in a particular position, and both alive. It did not occur to me that there was any connection between their appearance and the visits of the wasp, and I was much puzzled to account for their being there. Soon after the wasp returned, bearing, to my surprise, one of these caterpillars amongst its feet; it carried it into the interior of the lock, and there spent some time in rolling it up into a ball, so that, though still alive, it had not the power of moving. I then discovered that it was the *Odynerus mucarius*, or mason-wasp, which always hoards up caterpillars in its nest for its progeny to eat; and I was greatly pleased at the opportunity of watching its curious habits. The caterpillars are all of the same sort; I do not know their name, but they are as follows in appearance:—length, about two-thirds of an inch; pale yellow-green; neck tinged with brown; head shining dark brown; a thread-like streak of a dark green runs along the back and along each side; the rings are thirteen; there are a few scattered hairs over the body.

Soon after disposing of this caterpillar, the wasp returned with a pellet of sand between her four feet, and carrying it into the lock, proceeded to form her nest. For about two hours I watched her proceedings, and noted the times of her returns and stays in the lock. During that time she made thirteen visits.

At ten minutes past ten o'clock she brought a pellet, and stayed three minutes disposing it properly.

At nineteen minutes past she brought another, and stayed sixteen minutes; half of which time she lay motionless in the lock, perhaps secreting saliva to knead up her next pellet.

At eleven o'clock she returned (always with a pellet); stayed one minute.

At four minutes past eleven she returned; stayed one minute.

At eight and a half minutes past eleven she returned; stayed a minute and a half.

At seventeen minutes past eleven she returned; stayed a minute and a half.

At thirty minutes past eleven she returned; stayed two minutes.

At twenty-five minutes to twelve she returned; stayed two minutes and a half.

At twenty minutes to twelve she returned; stayed four minutes.

At nine minutes to twelve she returned; stayed two minutes.

At four minutes to twelve she returned; stayed four minutes.

At four minutes past twelve she returned; stayed one minute.

At eight minutes past twelve she returned; stayed six minutes.

After this she was disturbed, and came no more, so that I am afraid she has deserted her nest. I have examined it as well as I can. She has much lessened the entrance (which is through the interior opening of the keyhole) by building it up with pellets of sand. Each pellet is about the size of a gooseberry seed. She dropped one by accident. I picked it up; it was not broken. I found it to consist entirely of moistened sand. This mason-wasp is smaller than the common wasp, differently coloured and shaped, of brighter hues, and with more black. Her strength must be great to carry a caterpillar as large as herself.

The servant, Ann, says that she has often found caterpillars in locks without knowing how they came there. This predilection for locks is curious, but quite explainable. It saves the insect the trouble of boring a hole several inches deep.

CHAPTER VII.

From July 21, 1835, *to April* 30, 1836.—*Woodbury.*

This afternoon, while mamma and I were sitting here, Mackworth called us to look at a humming-bird hawk-moth (*Macroglossa stellatarum—Sphingina Sessiidæ*). We came and watched it for some minutes, with much interest. It darted very rapidly, with a loud hum, from flower to flower, and as it came to each, without alighting, unfurled its long slender trunk and sucked the honey, itself suspended in the air, spreading out its tail and the white tufts on its sides. In the rapidity and yet steadiness of its movements, it is unlike any lepidopterous insect that I know. It did not seem at all disturbed by our presence, and even almost touched us at times.

July 22, *Wednesday.*—I was pleased at finding one or two moths. One was the brown-tail (*Porthesia auriflua—Bombycina Arctiadæ*). It is very pretty, of a snowy white, with very downy legs and body, the antennæ doubly fringed. The tail is a yellow brown. I brought it home alive and put it under a glass.

July 23, *Thursday.*—Mrs. Harvey very kindly asked mamma to bring us all some day to Ickwell, that she might take us to see Warden, Lord Ongley's place. . . . At five the whole party went to Warden, which is a mile and a half distant, to see the garden, which was laid out by Lord Ongley himself, and is a very curious place; in the opinion of most people very beautiful, but I do not myself like it much. The extent, I believe, is seven acres. It is full of little hills and mounds, covered with trees, shrubs, and flowers. Here and there are arbours shaded by ivy and clematis; in some places are little hollows surrounded by artificial rocks; in others are subterranean paths, besides railing, hedges, ponds, white tents, enclosures for birds, etc. Over the whole are scattered white statues and painted lamps, some on stands, others hanging from lofty arches which join the mounds. The principal object is the Swiss cottage, . . . which is surmounted by a "gilded pill," on which stands a dove of white stone. What I liked best was the conservatory. We entered a subterraneous passage, at the end of which is a little polygonal chamber, curtained all round with red and white, and carpeted with coloured sheepskin. The conservatory runs out from each side, at right angles with the passage, and has a glass roof rising above ground. . . .

The whole of this garden is in very bad taste, and much too artificial. The mounds and risings are not natural; the ornaments, such as the vases, statues, lamps, arches, etc., are altogether out of place. Even the Swiss cottage is ill-imagined, and the quantity of linen furniture in the arbours and tents looks ridiculous. In winter it must look most cheerless. In short, considering the thousands that have been laid out on it, it is surprising that so little has been made out of the garden.

July 24, *Friday*.—. . . Mr. Charles Astell caught two very pretty lizards, of different species, which I will describe. The largest looks four inches and a half long. The head is very like a snake's, flat, and covered with little plates of various shapes. The eyes are not disagreeably prominent, as in most lizards, but are very beautiful, being bright and expressive, hazel, with a black pupil. The general colour of the creature is green, scaly like a snake. Along the back runs an uninterrupted black line; the sides are dark, with a ridge of white dots just above and below them; the tail is half the length of the whole lizard, and consists of a great many joints or rings, fitting one into the other like those of the mare's-tail. Each joint is composed of many little pieces placed side by side, and it ends with a curious conical process. The legs are four, each with five toes, tipped with claws. Sometimes it raises itself up on its fore feet, resting on the tips of its claws. I cannot see the under part of its body. Its motion is a swift run. The expression of its face is thoughtful and intelligent.

July 25, *Saturday.*—My brown-tail moth, which last Wednesday I put under a glass, has laid several eggs, and wrapped them in fur, which she pulled off from her own downy tail.

[From July 27 to 30 is taken up with an account of a driving excursion to St. Albans, visiting Ampthill, Woburn Abbey, Dunstable Church, Luton. The description of parks, houses, and churches is very minute, but only two passages will be extracted.]

Dunstable Church.—"The west front has some noble Norman arches, the mouldings of which are exquisite for richness and variety, exceeding any of those at Ely. The whole surface of the front is worked in a pattern so very elegant, that, though I have sketched it regularly in my book, I cannot help putting it here.* There is a singular arch by the door, half of which is Norman, half Early English. The interior is not so striking; the nave is Norman, the rest mostly Perpendicular.

July 29, *Wednesday.*— . . . [The Abbey Church, St. Albans.] It is a very large building, exceeding in size most churches and many cathedrals, certainly Rochester. It has also possessed very remarkable beauty and magnificence, but is now in a miserable state of dilapidation. For two

* The pattern is copied in the margin, a frequent practice with her.—Ed.

years no church service has been performed in it, and a subscription has just been raised for repairing it sufficiently to keep it from falling altogether. If not only this were done, but if also money could be procured for the sole purpose of improving it, by taking down the numerous incongruous additions that have been made to it, it would be restored to something like its original beauty. If, further, the many parts of it now defaced and destroyed were faithfully restored, St. Albans Abbey Church would rank among the finest of our sacred edifices. Even now, though a patchwork of many unharmonizing styles, though ruined, imperfect, and clogged up with modern screens, it is very fine as a whole, and requires minute attention in its details, which are of singular excellence. The plan is uncommon in an English cathedral (such, in point of size, it may be considered), but very general in those of France. It consists of a nave, a central tower, transepts, a choir, a space behind the choir (called at St. Albans the presbytery), and, at the end, the Lady Chapel. The aisles of the choir are continued along the space behind it, which was originally entered through the aisle arches, and communicated by a door with the Lady Chapel; but at present these arches are blocked up with screens, and the way into the Lady Chapel is likewise closed. The screens of St. Albans, as well as everywhere else, are the bane of all effect. One, as usual, separates the choir from the nave, and the nave itself is divided across by another, which has neither use nor meaning. Not but that all these screens are in themselves very beautiful. I shall say more about them elsewhere.

August 9, *Sunday.*—In the evening I walked to the heath to see some poor people of the name of Betts, whom I sometimes teach a little. They are miserably poor, and live in a mud cottage, built by the man himself, and containing only two rooms for themselves and six children. The man can read, and is tolerably intelligent; the woman is deplorably ignorant, and knows nothing whatever of the doctrines of the Christian religion, so that she requires the very simplest instruction.

Another family, of the name of Barford, lives close by; these also I sometimes go to see. They are a very cleanly, industrious, worthy couple; they have just lost a daughter of a decline, whom I used to go and read to sometimes while still ill. She died July 20. I saw her corpse the next day; it was a very affecting and melancholy sight. It was the first I have seen. The deadly pale of the countenance, the whiteness of the lips, and the unmoving look give a dead body a very ghastly appearance.

August 19, *Wednesday.*—The removal of my cuckoo into the large dove-cage has made a sudden and remarkable change in his disposition and habits. All his gentleness, docility, and familiarity have disappeared. It is true he had already begun to display a revengeful temper by his hatred of a certain stick which I used, to drive him from the top of the bed, and which he always fought furiously whenever he saw it. But now he has become the most savage, proud, ferocious little bird that I ever beheld. He imagines that, instead of being a visitor in the cage, it was made on purpose for him; and he treats the rightful owners with great tyranny and contempt if they approach him, or examine his food; he strikes them with his wing, and often gives them a sharp peck, which they return. If I or any one else comes to the cage, he receives me with studied dislike, raises his wings, bristles up the feathers of his head, and glares ferociously; if a finger is shown to him, he flies at it, screams, hisses, flaps his wings, and bites very hard. The expression of his countenance is quite changed, and he looks ill-temper personified. As to his habits, his appetite is much diminished; he is not tumultuous to get his food, eats it deliberately, and is satisfied with three or four meals a day. He also shows what he never did before, some degree of timidity, and flutters about when the cage is opened from behind.

Five days ago I saw two young swallows sitting on the edge of a water-spout under the roof, where was probably their nest. The mother, meantime, was hawking for flies, and several times, in our presence, gave some to one of the young ones; this she did on the wing, by a quick and almost imperceptible motion. Papa called my attention to a very curious piece of instinct on her part. She hawked in circles, enlarging the circle every time, by which means she avoided the possibility of going again over the same ground.

Aug. 21, *Friday.*—. . . There is no end to the absurdities of the jackdaw; it would be in vain to attempt recounting them. I shall, however, mention one or two. If a piece of bread, thrown to him, should fall only a few inches without his usual range, he will let the sparrows eat it before his face rather than pass his bounds. But one day it happened that, a beautiful pied wagtail having come close to papa's window, papa wished to treat him to a piece, and accordingly flung one from the window, which fell several yards from Jack; but he, knowing that it was meant for the wagtail, took a sudden fancy that he would have it himself. So, with all possible haste, he hopped after it, and snapped it up before poor waggy could reach it.

Sept. 7, *Monday.*—It is very remarkable that the jackdaw has at last recovered altogether the use of his wings. He is now two years old, or nearly so; his wings were clipped in the first year, the primaries being, I should think, more than half cut off. At first he could not fly above a foot from the ground; by very slow degrees he became able to fly higher and higher, till this year he had a few weeks ago reached six or eight feet, though without being able to guide his flight. At length on Saturday, September 5, he astonished us all by taking a high, steady flight of twenty or thirty yards, and yesterday he was in full possession of his volatile powers, soaring over the garden at pleasure. What is interesting is, that now he can depart entirely if he chooses. He remains as tame as ever, coming at papa's call, eating out of his hand, giving his head to be stroked, and, oddest of all, when papa reproves him for ill-temper or rudeness, he quietly submits and shows every token of penitence. He retains his antipathies against particular people, whom he scolds and fights, and he walks quietly over the lawn as he used to do.

Sept. 9, *Wednesday.*—In the study of natural history it is particularly important not to come too hastily to conclusions, but to study facts from observation frequently and most carefully before any inference is drawn from them. I have always most particularly attended to this, but still it is provoking to find myself often making blunders from want of observing with sufficient carefulness at first.

What led me to these remarks is that I greatly suspect I was mistaken in attributing the sound "chick-check" to the marsh-tit, and I am pretty sure it is the chiff-chaff. . . .

As far as I have read, Virgil does not excel in drawing of character. Æneas is nothing but the pious Æneas, goddess-born, with broad shoulders, heaving a sigh from the bottom of his breast; and Achates is nothing at all but the faithful Achates. Dido is merely a magnificent queen, desperately in love with Æneas; and Ascanius is an affectionate little boy, and no more. There is something almost ludicrous in the trick solemnly proposed by Corœbus of assuming the arms of the slaughtered Greeks; and I can never get it out of my head that Anchises, in refusing to escape from Troy, really meant to be coaxed and persuaded into complying, that he might have both the merit of the intention of dying and the convenience of really living. . . .

I very greatly prefer Greek to Latin. The Greek is, in every respect, a finer language, far more copious, fuller of those little niceties and distinctions which form the beauty of a language, yet less artificial, particularly in the order of the words in a sentence, and fitter for more various styles and sorts of writing. The style of Herodotus is admirable; it has a complete resemblance to the style of the ancient English writers, as Sir Thomas North and the old chroniclers—a style I greatly prefer to the Latinized English now in use.

Sept. 10, *Thursday.*—I think I am now quite versed in the intimations of rain given by the swallows. The fact of a few merely flying low is a very uncertain sign indeed, and, similarly, a few flying very high is no pledge of the continuance of fine weather. What I observe of their conduct previous to rain is this: they fly about in great multitudes, with unusual swiftness, generally near the ground, or if they mount up for a little while, they suddenly descend again. Their attitudes are of every kind, turning and twisting, flying edgewise, throwing themselves almost on their backs; they hurry about in every direction; sometimes they nearly touch the ground, moving their wings much more than usual; they fly much under trees and by low shrubs; they are very fearless, and fly within a yard of you; they jerk backwards and forwards, from side to side, up and down; their whole conduct is altogether remarkable. I find that when they act thus, I may be quite sure, not merely that rain is very shortly coming, but hard and continued rain. There are multitudes both of swallows and martins to be seen now. . . .

The pied wagtail sings his little song very rarely; when he does, it is almost always an indication of speedy rain. The other day I heard the ringdove coo in a small shower, on a cold day. Had I time, I would devote myself to discovering the influence which the weather possesses on the songs and actions of birds, and I make no doubt I should find in them certain indications of the state of the weather. I should like constantly to have a barometer and thermometer in my possession for that purpose.

Sept. 16, *Wednesday.*—Papa has been setting up in the kitchen garden a meridian line, a contrivance which Uncle Richard told him of, for finding out with perfect accuracy the exact degree in which his watch gains or loses. It is a line of extremely fine wire, suspended from a south wall. At the end is a piece of lead, fastened, dipping into a cup of water to keep it steady. On the wall behind the line is a broad wooden peg, about an inch and a quarter in diameter. Papa took his watch to Bedford, and had it set exactly by real or mean time; then, having found by the almanac the difference that day between mean and apparent time, he knew at what time by his watch the sun ought to come to the meridian; and accordingly, observing the shadow of the line on the peg behind it, he marked the exact spot where it fell at the time pointed out by the almanac as apparent noon. Thus, for the future, observing the time when the sun's shadow again reaches the mark, and then calculating what o'clock it ought to be by his watch, papa can always find out whether his watch went regularly.

Sept. 18, *Friday.*—We finished the "Netherlands" this 24
evening. I have certainly gained a great deal of information from it, being before quite ignorant on the subject of the Netherlands, and I am very glad to have read it; but it certainly is a very ill-written work. On the government of the country, the origin of the States-General, their numbers, power, and constitution, the offices of stadtholder and pensionary—points on which I wish very much to be informed—it says absolutely nothing.

Sept. 23.— . . . The tameness of Jack [the jackdaw] is quite wonderful. He is now in every respect at liberty, and yet he is more familiar than ever. He pays visits to every room in the house, tapping at the window if it is shut, and if it is open he sits on the ledge or enters quite. The Chandlers, our tenants, finding him this morning among their filberts, brought him back to us, and our housemaid carried him in her hands into the library, which act did not alarm or offend him, but he sat quietly on a chair for four hours, and while papa was teaching the pupils, he began to prate, as if he wished to attract their attention. When luncheon came in, he flew to the table; and when papa carried him back, he returned, till he was fed and sent out of the room. After this, he was coming into the house all day, especially into mamma's dressing-room; and at last, at half-past seven in the evening, while we were sitting with fire and candles lighted and the shutters shut, a tapping was heard at the window. We opened it, and Jack entered. He sat for some time very solemnly on papa's wrist; he drank and ate when we brought him biscuit and water; and at last papa took him upstairs to mamma's dressing-room, for it was a very rainy night. He was placed on the back of a chair by the open window, and there he roosted all night. Early in the morning he began to prate, and then flew out.

Sept. 29, *Tuesday.*—I walked with papa to Tetworth to call on Mrs. Clutterbuck. Whenever papa and I walk or drive together, our conversation generally turns on two topics—first, on literary subjects connected with my studies; secondly, on imaginary tours through England and Europe, which we plan together. . . .

Sept. 30, *Wednesday.*—Papa drove Richard and me to Biggleswade. On our way there, I was extremely delighted to see, for the first time in my life, a live kingfisher. It was in a damp, willowy meadow, flying across a little brook. It was quite like a flying sapphire, with its splendid blue. It made no sound, and as we were in the phaeton I could not examine or watch it minutely; but I observed that its flight was straight, low, and steady.

Oct. 1, *Thursday.*—. . . I still continue always côrrect

in my predictions about weather. Yesterday, as we were returning from Biggleswade, papa remarked, "We are home just in time to escape the rain." It was then dull, damp, and cloudy; but having observed the actions of the swallows, I felt quite sure that it would not rain till next morning. I was quite right, and when I rose this morning I looked again at the swallows, and was sure it would rain in a short time, and very heavily. Accordingly, about an hour after, hard rain began, and continued till two o'clock.

Oct. 2, *Friday.*—As Richard and I were sitting in the library, beginning our lesson with papa, at about half-past six, a curious interruption occurred. The footman announced that Mr. Clutterbuck wished to speak with papa, who thereupon went and brought him into the library. Mr. Clutterbuck then informed papa of his errand. There is a notorious poacher about here, named Page, for whose arrest a reward of twenty pounds has been offered. The clerk of Everton was knocked down and injured the other day in the attempt. Mr. Clutterbuck and Mr. T. St. Quintin (the magistrate) sent for two Bow Street officers to take him up. He eluded them; but in the mean time two men committed a daring and impudent theft of two ducks at a farm close to our house, about two days ago. To-day they were arrested at Gamlingay by the Bow Street officers, handcuffed, and ready to be committed. Mr. Clutterbuck asked if he and Mr. T. St. Quintin could examine them in this house, on account of its being in the county of Cambridgeshire. He had brought the officers and prisoners along with him. Papa, of course, agreed. Just then entered Mr. T. St. Quintin and Mr. Foley, another gentleman who is visiting at Everton. The servants' hall was lighted up; pen, ink, wafers, and paper were provided. They adjourned thither; the policemen, prisoners, and witnesses were brought in; papa, Mr. Foley, R., M., and the five pupils were present as spectators; and the examination began.

It lasted about half an hour. The prisoners were fully committed and sent to Cambridge Gaol to await their trial at the next quarter sessions, which will be in less than a fortnight. Their names are Samuel Gilbert and John Baines. The Bow Street officers were named, one Goddard, the other Fletcher. The witnesses were three—our footman; Green, the owner of the ducks; and Larkins, the man who saw them steal them. One of the prisoners being asked if he had any questions to put, merely inquired of Larkins, in a drawling lingo, "Where did you ever see me catch a duck?"

Larkins (*in a similar tone*). "At the ould pond."

Gilbert. "Oh, did you?"

Mr. St. Quintin examined the men, and Mr. Clutterbuck acted as his clerk.*

Oct. 3, *Saturday.*—The Bow Street officers are still hovering about the county in disguise, in hopes of arresting Page himself. Papa met them to-day while riding; one was dressed like a gamekeeper, the other like a tinker. Papa knew them at once, and spoke, not knowing that they wished to be concealed.

Papa. "Well, what sort of success have you had?"

Officer (*in a low voice*). "None yet. We are going about in this disguise that it may not be known we are here." (*Aloud, as papa was going on*) "We'll take the letter for you, sir."

Papa. "Oh, thank you."

This was to blind a carter who was a little behind them, and might find them out.

Oct. 10, *Saturday.*—This was the first sunny day since

* It seems difficult *now* to believe that for this attempt to steal two ducklings, in which the thieves were interrupted and ran away, these poor young men, scarcely more than lads, were sentenced to seven years' transportation. The explanation probably was that they were believed to be poachers.—ED.

October 5, and in consequence, I suppose, eight or ten swallows made their appearance, hawking for flies very high in the air. This circumstance, a very common one, puzzles me more than any other concerning swallows. Not that I think it proves that they do not migrate; on the contrary, I think it tends to confirm the idea that they do, for if all remained behind, they would all come out on a fine day, instead of only a few stragglers. But whence come these few? They certainly have not left the kingdom; and where have they secreted themselves, or how subsisted, during their disappearance? There is no bird which procures food so openly, or whose haunts are so public, as the swallow; so that I cannot imagine how it can conceal itself for days, weeks, and even months—for swallows sometimes appear even in winter. As to its lying torpid, why does it ever wake up before the spring? or are any birds formed for so doing? *

Oct. 13, *Tuesday.*—Herodotus is full of stories which would make an excellent foundation for dramas and narrative poems, into which I long to turn them. As, for example, the misfortunes that befel Mycerinus, the conclusion of the history of Anysis and Sabacos, the vengeance taken by Nitocris for the murder of her brother, and the restoration of Helen to Menelaus—which latter, by the way, though I did not know it when I first thought of it myself, is already the subject of a tragedy of Euripides.

Jack has at last become really unbearable. It is impossible to frighten him or cure him of his mischievous propensities. He is for ever invading our rooms, especially mamma's, mine, Lord Desart's, and the library. During my absence from my room, he entered one day and stole

* It has been ascertained that young swallows, not yet fit for so long a flight, are often left behind, so that they either depart when their wings are stronger, or, more likely, perish ere long of hunger and cold.—ED.

from my desk my I.H.B. pencil, which is a great loss to me. Another [day] mamma found that he had been in her room by the following signs: her cap was on the floor, the covers were taken off two ink-glasses, and a little plate was pushed off a box on which it was placed. Another time he picked and spoiled the edges of her Prayer-book. In Lord D.'s room he tore to pieces the cover of a map; in Mr. Lushington's he threw down a looking-glass and overturned an ink-glass. In short, there is no end of his impudence. At the same time, he is so affectionate to papa that it is quite interesting to see. If papa opens the library window, Jack flies into the room from the other end of the garden. He will sit for an hour outside, pecking for admittance. He delights in being stroked and kissed by him. If papa is in the garden, Jack flies up to him and follows him about, and he never bites or hurts him. But so troublesome is his familiarity that, after many consultations, we had determined to get rid of him; to take him in a basket to a great distance, and there let him loose. However, it was considered so probable that he would either return to us or, on account of his tameness, get killed, that we resolved to clip one wing slightly, so as that it may grow in the spring. This was accordingly done, with great reluctance. Poor Jack, as soon as the operation was performed, finding himself unable to fly, went and hid himself in a dark nook, where he remained some hours, as if ashamed of his short wing. He now looks very sad and pensive, and is so meek that he lets anybody stroke him without biting them. It must be a great misery to him to lose the use of his wings a second time, after having had it for seven or eight weeks, especially as he delighted in soaring high in the air. He has grown quite a handsome bird, and has a purple gloss on his wings. We feed him three times a day with bread, meat, and potatoes, besides biscuit and such things at odd times. He is beyond doubt the nicest and most amusing pet we have had, and it is a great grief to us to treat him thus; but his mischievous disposition makes it quite unbearable.

Oct. 20, *Tuesday.*—At tea the conversation happened to turn on the subject of gipsies, who, it was incidentally mentioned in the *Quarterly Review*, are indisputably proved to have originally come from India. Papa was not aware that it had been so certainly proved, but he remembered many facts which make it very probable, and yet, alone, not at all certain. Their language is the circumstance on which the supposition chiefly rests. Papa's uncle, the late Lord Teignmouth, was convinced they come from India. He once made two gipsies tell him what words in their language they used to express several English words; these he took down as they spoke them, and at the same time employed his daughters to write them as they seemed to be spelt, according to the manner in which the gipsies pronounced them to their ears; and when the words were afterwards examined, Lord T. found that two-thirds were either pure Hindostanee, or a dialect of it. Another time, meeting a gipsy woman, he addressed her with a few Hindostanee words implying, "You are a great thief," to which she immediately replied, "I no great thief; I tell fortunes." But even these facts, papa says, are by no means conclusive, seeing that some of the Eastern languages are found to bear so close a resemblance to those of Europe that the Greek and Sanscrit are considered to be little more than dialects of the same language.

Oct. 22, *Thursday.*—We have been in great apprehension of Jack's life; he has been dull and sorrowful and shrinking from notice ever since the clipping of his wings, and has taken up his abode about the greenhouse. On Tuesday, as mamma and I were looking at him, he suddenly fell into fits, tumbled down, rolled about, flapped his wings, and struggled in agonies of pain. He remained a long time in this state. We gave him two pills of Morrison's, on which 25 he became literally sick, but still remained panting and convulsed to the end of the day. Yesterday morning we were surprised to find him as well as ever; but he had another and severer fit in the afternoon. We brought him in a basket of hay into the hall, and there he lay in great suffering, breathing with a frightful noise, so that we fully expected his death. We gave him another pill, and this morning he was again convalescent, and in no long time had quite recovered, except that he remains very low-spirited. Papa was very much vexed at the clipping of Jack's wing, and has never been near him since, not liking to see him unhappy; and I think Jack misses him. However, papa came to see him last night, and also this morning, and caressed him, to cheer and comfort him. I cannot imagine what was the matter with Jack. His illness had much the appearance of poison; I do not know whether he can now be suffering from the effects of some sips of goulard which he took a fortnight ago, when he came into Mr. Ashton's room.

Nov. 3, *Tuesday.*—I continue writing my tale of "Devereux" whenever I can find time, of which I spend but little in it. I never touch it before six o'clock tea, and seldom for more than half an hour, which is generally during the eight o'clock tea. I have now finished only three chapters, or forty pages, of nearly the size of my journal. A great deal of my time is occupied in teaching A., L., and M., whom I instruct together, on alternate days, in Greek,* Grecian history, and arithmetic. I also teach M., by himself, geography and French history. The

* A picture that lingers in the minds of survivors is that of her bending with her long ringlets over a slate on which she was carefully illustrating some of the complicated laws of Greek grammar, the mysteries of εἰ and ἐάν, and the particle ἄν, with the different moods, observing the while in a tone of pleasure, "I do think I shall be able to make you understand it."—Ed.

history which he reads to me is Mrs. Markham's, of 26
which I am very fond. For beginners it is unequalled; it is correct and unprejudiced, and the language is perfectly plain, easy, simple, and elegant. The narrative is made very interesting, and the conversations contain a great deal of curious and useful matter. The Grecian history I use with them is Malkin's. Arithmetic I teach them in the same way in which I learnt myself, by explaining the principles and reason of every operation.

Nov. 7, *Saturday.*—I am convinced that geography and history are among the most useful and interesting of studies. Besides what I study by myself, I learn a great deal by my teaching M.; it refreshes my memory, and confirms my knowledge on these subjects. Those who are not accustomed to teach have no idea the infinite advantage it is to the teacher.

Nov. 9, *Monday.*—. . . Papa mentioned a curious circumstance about cats, which he knew of himself, as it happened in his father's house. They had two cats, a male and female, called Chance and Chase. The latter, which was the male, was given away, and sent to a house about two miles off. Soon after Chance kittened. The day after, Chance disappeared, leaving her poor kittens to themselves. She was absent three days, during which papa and his sister preserved the kittens alive by pouring milk down their throats. In three days the mother returned, with her companion Chase, to find whom she must have passed through water, to which cats are so averse. It is, besides, a wonder how she could have discovered Chase's new abode. On her return, she again suckled her kittens, who all lived. . . . I must also mention here a very curious anecdote of a dog, though I am afraid that I cannot altogether vouch for the truth of it. A gentleman, fond of animals, had a pet dog, which his wife, who hated dogs, detested and banished whenever it entered the drawing-room. One day, as she was sitting there, the dog marched in, and lay down before the fire. The lady turned him out. The dog, supposing that she was afraid of his dirtying the room, brought a duster from the kitchen, deposited it on the rug, and lay down upon it. The brute of a woman ended by having him kicked out. She told it herself to the person from whom our informant, Miss Nowell, mamma's cousin, heard it; but the lady herself is also an acquaintance of mamma's.

Nov. 10, *Tuesday.*—Some time ago Mackworth bought a bottle of nitrous acid, which, on account of an accident which happened with it when he was using it to kill a moth, mamma caused to be put away. To-day he took it into his head to put a pin into the bottle, having before observed that a pin accidentally touching it caused it to bubble. The pin immediately began to dissolve, bubbling, smoking, and hissing; it was quickly destroyed, and the nitrous acid became of a beautiful green. This was a common brass pin tinned over. Two nails of cast iron were next put into the bottle, which were longer in melting, and finally changed the acid to yellow. Finally, by introducing a little lead, it became black. Spirits of wine made it effervesce like a saline draught, and soda and tartaric acid each separately produced the same effect.

Dec. 1, *Tuesday.*— . . . I long exceedingly to become thoroughly acquainted with every manufacture in England. I read carefully every account of any one which I can light upon, and I am much interested by those given by Babbage in his "Economy of Manufactures;" but, alas! we have very few books on this subject, and I doubt whether many exist. Besides, I am very desirous to see all the manufactures with my own eyes, and I should like to travel through Great Britain with that intent. I have seen none, except weaving and the manufactures in the dockyard at Chatham. It is astonishing how ignorant people are about the method of making the commonest things, and it quite vexes and mortifies me to look round the room and see scarce an article in it of the construction of which I have the least idea. I wish some one would write a book giving a minute account of all the English manufactures.

Dec. 5, *Saturday*.—. . . Mr. Legrice said that a little plant, whose name he had forgotten, has actually a small fibre corresponding to the heart in animals, to and from which the juice circulates. This has not been observed in any other vegetable, though it probably exists in all.

Dec. 19.—Papa began this evening to read to us the
"History of Protestantism in France." At a pause in the 27
reading, he made remarks to the following purpose:—"Now, we ought not, in reading these things (*i.e.* the persecutions sustained by the French Protestants), to consider of them only in this way—what a horrid Church the Roman Catholic must be to allow these things; it is *not* the Roman Catholic Church, but the spirit of intolerance that then prevailed, that produced it. One great cause of it among the Papists was the claim to infallibility of the Church of Rome; a Church that claimed to be infallible was likely to be a persecuting one. But the spirit was not confined to the Catholics; we find it also among the Protestants of those days, though they seldom had the power of gratifying it, and perhaps, also, not so much the will to do it; for the zealous Protestants were more intent on spreading their doctrine than on acquiring a spiritual ascendency. But it was the same spirit of persecution that made Calvin burn Servetus, and *he* did not believe in an infallible Church; it was the same spirit that made Cranmer burn the Anabaptists, and *he* did not believe the Church of England to be infallible. We are too apt to consider the Roman Catholics as looking on Protestantism in the same light with ourselves, as considering it true, and yet persecuting it. They did *not* consider it to be true; those of them who were sincere (and a great part of them were) believed it to

be the most abominable heresy that ever was heard of. It is something of the same kind of feeling that we have towards an atheist or a deist; we do not indeed wish to persecute or burn him, but we generally feel a dislike to him—we think that such a man deserves to be punished. Let us imagine what we ourselves should feel if, at the present day, a man was to preach openly the most atrocious, blasphemous, infamous doctrines, and then we shall have some idea of what the Roman Catholics felt towards the Protestants."

Dec. 20, *Sunday.*—Mamma having read to papa a little
28 sentence out of a book of Bishop Wilson's in her hand, papa said, "It certainly is not right, and yet somehow a precept of that kind impresses me much more if it comes from a person who, I think, attends to it himself. . . . But where we see the reasoning is good, it does not matter who wrote it. It is astonishing how much fallacy there is on this subject. If we are going to hear an argumentative speech in the House of Commons, how anxious we are to know the speaker's name! If we are going to read a book, how much impression the name of the author makes on us! And yet it ought to make no difference in our opinion of the reasoning of the book. . . . In matter of *testimony* where facts are to be stated, it may make all the difference in the world whether the man is accurate, or observing, or true; but in matter of *reasoning*, if that is good, it remains so, whoever wrote it, and it does not signify two straws whether it was written by a clever man or a fool, a rascal or a Christian."

Dec. 21, *Monday*—. . . A new *Quarterly Review* which came to-day contains among the advertisements the prospectus of a splendid French work, containing the engravings of ancient and modern coins and medals, of which a specimen is given. Without exaggeration, I think it is exquisitely beautiful; the appearance of being in relief is so perfect that, though I am well acquainted with this kind of engraving, I involuntarily drew my finger across it. In my opinion this is the highest point of perfection to which the art of engraving can attain; I cannot imagine it to be susceptible of improvement. It is described in Babbage's book.

Dec. 25, *Friday.*—Christmas Day. This day I enter on my seventeenth year. The first birthday which I recorded in a journal was my eleventh, and the first which I can distinctly remember, my fifth, since which time eleven years have passed away, and every one more quickly than the former, so that now the last anniversary of this day seems as if it was but yesterday. Very many things which happened to me a long, long time ago I remember so distinctly that I can hardly realize to myself that eight, nine, ten, or eleven years have passed since then. Every one finds that succeeding years fly quicker than the former ones, but I have no doubt that the degree in which this seems to happen depends a great deal on the circumstances of a person's being or not being continually employed. I do not myself remember in all my life (which I recollect as far back as the age of three) to have been one moment unemployed, or not knowing what to do with myself.

Dec. 26, *Saturday.*—. . . The frost has a beautiful appearance everywhere; everything is thickly covered with it. It has occasioned us a very melancholy loss; poor Jack was found this morning frozen to death on a flower-bed before the dining-room windows. He had always continued to live in the laurels, and refused to go into his little wooden house; his broken wing rendered him helpless, so that it is no great wonder that he died, nor perhaps should we regret it much, for he has never been happy since his wing was last cut. I think it not improbable that he was seized with a fit, and no one being at hand to give him medicine and take him in, he perished.

Dec. 31, *Thursday.*—Here we are at the end of 1835,

and now more than half the time for which papa took Woodbury is expired. Every successive year now becomes more interesting with reference to our future prospects, which are totally unfixed. When our lease is out, at the end of 1837, I wonder where our abode will be, for I think it very unlikely that we shall renew our lease. Whether we shall, in the course of 1838, be settled near Capetown, or in Van Diemen's Land, or in Canada, or whether we shall still be dwelling within the bounds of Great Britain, is altogether uncertain. Wherever it will be, I have one hope and one fear for the future—the hope that papa, whose strength and health, alas! are breaking down, may not continue the business of a tutor; the fear that we shall be no longer all living together, for Richard is growing up, and both he and Mackworth may then be put out in some profession or line of business.

CHAPTER VIII.

From Jan. 8 *to Oct.* 3, 1836.—*Woodbury, London, Hastings, Tunbridge Wells, Woodbury.*

Jan. 8, *Friday.*—Papa continually takes opportunities in common conversation to give us information on many subjects which we are not likely to find explained in books. To-day some questions which I asked at tea occasioned him to give us an account of copyhold and freehold estates, and the qualifications of individuals for voting for members of Parliament, as they now stand. By one of these papa has a vote for the county. Papa also said that the alterations produced by the late Parliamentary and municipal reforms are greater than any others within his recollection, and are therefore to be especially remembered. He explained to us the principal changes made thereby.

Jan. 9, *Saturday.*—Papa finished as much of the article "Boroughs" as has come out in the last monthly number of the *Penny Cyclopædia*; it unluckily concludes in the middle of the word "resolution" in a very interesting part. It will be a long time before we shall have the rest of it; but I have learnt a great deal from what has already been read.

Jan. 27, *Wednesday.*—A most beautiful day. All the birds were in motion. The coal-tit sang a little; the bunting, lark, and robin were in full song. The tits were all abroad, coursing each other, hunting for insects under the branches, and hopping about in the dead leaves at the roots of nut trees, all the while uttering their innumerable chirps. The ox-eyes were particularly busy; they are noisy and boisterous birds, and comparatively clumsy in their movements. They are, however, lively and very handsome, but I do not like them so well as the blue and coal tits. The blue-tit has the brightest colours of them all; his shape and movements are elegant, and his cries in general are not harsh, like those of the ox-eye. The coal-tit has a much more innocent and good-tempered look than his congeners (the ox-eye, indeed, has quite a fierce, malignant face), and, above all, he has so much more music in his voice. His chirps are all much sweeter, lower, and less jabbering, and he has a regular song which possesses at least great cheerfulness and a clear, merry tone.

Feb. 4, *Thursday.*—Amongst other amusements of my leisure hours, I am very fond of inventing plans of palaces and dwelling-houses on a large scale. These I first draw out in pencil on paper, and afterwards write minute descriptions of them, with the measurements, furniture, uses, etc., of all the apartments. One on which I am now employed is a magnificent stone palace, built round a court eight hundred feet square.

Feb. 11, *Thursday.*—Towards the end of dinner, the conversation turned—I forget how—upon executioners and the different modes of execution in Europe. It appears that the punishment of death is inflicted at Vienna by beheading with the sword; in Naples by hanging; at Venice, formerly at least, by drowning; in France, still by the guillotine; in Tuscany there are now no capital punishments. The office of executioner is everywhere held odious; nobody will associate with one. In some parts of Germany all the dead fowls are the perquisite of the executioner, and are left for him to come and take them; and, indeed, executioners are sometimes suspected of poisoning them to get the bodies. Executioners must be very accomplished artists, for great skill is required in the performance of their task. Mr. W. Spencer * told papa that once, when abroad, in a provincial town of France, he met a very pleasing and gentlemanly man, and conversed with him a good deal. Happening again to meet him at a *table d'hôte*, he was surprised to find that the stranger fought shy of him, and rebuffed him when he attempted to speak to him. As soon as they were alone together, "You do not perhaps know, sir," said the unknown, "that by speaking to me in public you are endangering your character. I have lost caste; I am, in fact, infamous; nobody associates with me. I am one of the most celebrated executioners in Europe; and if you were to be seen talking to me by any one who knew me, you would totally lose your own reputation."

Feb. 26, *Friday.*—Eliz. professes her intention of retrieving her lost character as a correspondent, forgetting that it is no one's power to lose that which he has never possessed; and she drops a hope that mamma will not allow us to pull her quite in pieces for her delinquencies. This hope has unfortunately reached us a little too late, for three or four days ago the children completely dissected her.

March 7, *Monday.*—I have been confined to the house, and partly to my bed, by a cough—a thing which I have not for many years had, except before my last fever. So that, unless I get out very soon, I am afraid that I shall miss the first singing birds of passage. I see from the windows that several crocuses are in blow. I am likely to miss the first violets and primroses also.

April 14, *Thursday.*—This is papa's forty-third birthday. I gave him a little chronological history of Naples and Sicily from the time of William of Hauteville to the present day. It has employed me several days in writing, and has been very useful to me in brushing up my knowledge of the

* The once well-known Hon. W. R. Spencer, "without exception," says Lockhart, "the most charming of companions."

history of this kingdom. Mr. Paroissien has very kindly made papa a present of a barometer of his own making. It is not particularly handsome, but extremely neat, and I should think a very accurate one. It is made of mahogany. Mr. P. put it together here, which occupied him about an hour. I find that the plates on which the signs of a barometer are written, and the dial-plate of clocks, are both made of plates of brass, covered with a silvery wash. Papa intends me to register the height of the barometer and thermometer, which are put up side by side in our hall, regularly twice every day, at eight in the morning and eight at night. This will, I hope, teach us to be weatherwise.

April 19, *Tuesday.*— . . . While we were at prayers this morning, and papa was reading out of the Bible, a chaffinch came and alighted on the ledge of the open window, and, while sitting there, sung his loud song four times over, being answered between each repetition by another at a distance. He almost drowned papa's voice.

April 30, *Saturday.*—I now conclude the fifth volume of my journal, which I have kept for six years, including a short diary during the year 1830. I find it such an useful practice, and so entertaining, that I am fully resolved to continue it all my life. It was first suggested to me by the possession of a small pocket-book, given me by a pupil when I was ten years old. I have ordered a sixth volume to be made by Fraser at Potton, and I shall have it on Monday, when I shall forthwith begin it. I have been long convinced that, as Abbot says in his "Young Christian," the use of the pen is amongst the most valuable means of improving the mind.

May 10, *Tuesday.*—I have been so unwell for many days with cold and rheumatism, that I am obliged strictly to keep the house, and partly my bed, so that I am quite unable to observe the birds, except a little from within the house. The weather is becoming very fine and warmer, though the winds are cold. I hope I shall be able next Sunday to see the eclipse.

May 20, *Friday*.—This is the eleventh day of uninterrupted hot summer-like days, and perhaps it is the last, for the barometer falls fearfully and the sky is stormy. The weather has during this period been really exquisite, and I have been unable to enjoy it owing to my fever, which continues in all its force. But even from within the house I can hear the excellent warbling of the birds, and I can see the rapid progress of vegetation, which now renders the view from the west windows quite enchanting. Nothing can equal the delightful beauty of the first tender green of spring.

May 24, *Tuesday*.—The weather is now again excessively cold; . . . we have fires all day, and I crouch over them, yet we are on the verge of June. The lilies of the valley are in full bloom, and the gardens and meadows are golden with buttercups. The weeping ash is beginning to be leafy, and the walnuts are covered with a brown-green foliage. What I principally admire is the great beauty of the white and pink lilacs, now in full bloom in the laurel hedge. The cow-pasture, too, looks very beautiful from the west windows, all covered as it is with golden furze and broom.

June 6, *Monday*.—To me, all this spring and part of the summer are quite lost, and it might almost as well have been continual winter. From the first day of March up to my illness, I have not been altogether out of the house more than sixteen different days, including going to church and a few drives, and some occasions on which I merely stepped out of the house for a few minutes; and during the whole year I have been in a state of very indifferent health, not to speak of this month of fever. So that I have been quite debarred this year from rising at four or five o'clock, and walking in the woods at will to watch the birds and hear their songs. I shall not now recover my strength for many weeks; and my mind, even to my memory, is equally enfeebled. The very slightest fever completely upsets all one's powers.

June 11, *Saturday*.—. . . I quite forgot to mention that I predicted the rain of June 2 on the preceding day, from hearing a thrush sing loudly, after a dead silence for a very long time during the drought. I have always found this a correct sign.

June 12, *Sunday*.—I was drawn out of doors for half an hour this evening and enjoyed it much; I came in stronger and better. . . . This morning the grand scarlet poppy blew. . . . Our roses are most splendid; the west side of the house is covered with them in the richest profusion, and one of the drawing-room windows is half hidden by them. The red roses [China] are also splendid, and reach as high up the house wall. Both species can be gathered from, and look in at, the second story.

I rose to-day an hour earlier than usual, *i.e.* at eleven o'clock. I am not strong enough yet to be up all day. This is the sixth Sunday on which I have not been able to go to church, that is, not since May 1. Indeed, if I could have gone, I should have seen, at least in the evening, what it is no loss to have missed seeing—a most shameful quarrel between two women for places, which delayed the service for full five minutes. A similar scene, I am told, took place last Sunday, when two girls actually fought and struck each other while the congregation were on their knees, and made a great hubbub till the clerk, with some difficulty, turned them out. Such conduct is really unexampled.

June 29, *Wednesday*.—I get stronger, but my cough gives way very slowly, and my pulse continues high and strong. There is certainly danger of my lungs becoming affected, but we trust that, if it please God, the sea will restore me to health and remove the possibility of consumption. I know, however, that I must prepare myself for the worst, and I am fully aware of papa's and mamma's anxiety about me.

[It was decided to take the invalid to Hastings for about two months.]

July 3, *Sunday.*—This is the last day we spend at Woodbury for these two months. The intense heat makes it impossible for me to get out till the evening, when we walked out and took a last view of our garden, which is quite blazing with flowers. I went to bed at half-past seven; while I was undressing Miss Harriet came to see me and bid me good-bye. The other Astells we saw yesterday. They have been all particularly kind to me during my long illness, furnishing me with books, and with strawberries, and everything I wanted, in the most friendly manner.

[*London.*]

July 5, *Tuesday.*—To-day was effected the chief object of our stay in town, the consultation with the physician. The choice of one was left to Arthur, who determined on Dr. James Clark. He was to come to Welbeck Street at four o'clock, but arrived an hour later. I went up to my bedroom, and mamma talked with him some time alone. She then called me down. Dr. James Clark is of middle height, rather thin, very dark, and of a grave and quiet demeanour, speaking very little. His aspect, however, is very pleasing and amiable. My illness has made me exceedingly nervous, and his presence agitated me greatly. I trembled all over, my heart throbbed, my pulse quickened, and the perspiration broke out from every pore. Dr. Clark examined me most minutely, tapped me, and tried his stethoscope on my chest, neck, back, side, shoulder. He said nothing about the result of his observations, but retired with mamma to another private conference. I, in the mean time, was left in a state of anxiety amounting almost to agony. I could by no means compose myself; the doctor's tapping had given me pain of the left side of my chest, and I had no small reason to apprehend the pulmonary disease had already begun. I prayed earnestly for submission to the Divine will, and that I might be prepared for death; I made up my mind that I was to be the victim of consumption.

At length mamma re-entered the room, and told me Dr. Clark's opinion, viz. that my lungs are by no means at present diseased, but that there is the greatest danger of it, unless extreme care be taken of me. This was much more than I had dared to hope, and I thanked God for it. . . .

This was an intensely hot day, exceeding all the preceding ones. A gentleman who had paid great attention to the weather says it is the hottest day we have had these twenty years. It is quite equal to the usual Calcutta heat; indeed, in all probability we feel it more because we do not provide against it. It is very fortunate for me that I do not suffer from heat now nearly so much as other people, and can bear more clothing. My rheumatic tendency also makes me avoid every breath of air.

July 6, *Hastings.*—Instead of being either broiled or baked, as we had been threatened, we found, on entering Hastings, that the temperature was delicious, and the sea-breezes very cool and invigorating. When we were established in the hotel, I lost all my fatigue, my cough was almost gone, and I felt both strong and well.

July 9.—. . . I forgot to mention yesterday that we saw walking on the Parade a singular-looking old gentleman, entirely in black, wearing over his coat a prodigious cape, which stuck out all round him; and on his head a very broad-brimmed, high-crowned straw hat. His clothes were all handsome, whence we supposed him rich. He was not tall; his gait and carriage were erect and firm. We found on inquiry that he was a rich old gentleman of eighty-five, who has suffered much affliction, having lost his wife and three of his children very lately, and it appears, too, that he is unkindly treated by some of his surviving relatives. His mind seems affected by grief and old age, and he is continually weeping over his troubles with a person who was formerly his servant.

July 12, *Tuesday.*—. . . The most notorious person in Hastings is a lady of great beauty, who is continually walking along the Parade in very gay habiliments, and excites considerable notice. We had heard a good deal of her, and this evening met her on the Parade. She is of a middling height, and very beautiful. . . . Nobody knows who she is; she gives herself out as the Honourable Mrs. Carr.

July 20, *Wednesday.*—In the books we get from the library there are frequently marginal notes, in pen and pencil, by different readers. In the "Memoirs of Marie
Antoinette" Madame Campan relates the horrid circum- 29
stances of the guards' heads stuck on pikes, and adds that they were curled and powdered by the barbarians. The English editor states in a note that this latter fact is untrue. But some Frenchman, I suppose, has written below, "Tout au contraire; j'ai vu la procession, et les deux têtes dont on parle étoient frisées et poudrées." . . .

Captain Hall says, "This interval (six weeks in America), 30
though short, had been so busy that it appeared very long." The commentator scrawls this stuff, "Generally speaking, any time spent busily appears to pass very rapidly, therefore our worthy writer must be naturally made of odd materials." I opine that the "odd materials" appear in the composition of this scribbler. Captain Hall is very right. When in such a space of time a great deal has been done and seen, especially in the way of travelling, it does really appear on retrospection exceedingly long. This I can testify from present experience, for when I look back on all that we have done and seen in the last fortnight, and particularly

my rapid improvement in health, I can hardly realize that this day three weeks I was a hundred and fourteen miles distant, at Woodbury, suffering from cough and extreme debility, hardly able to walk, and almost forbidden to speak. It seems to me as if it was many months ago. It is when the occupations are unvaried and regular that time seems to fly so quickly.

July 25, *Monday.*—. . . After tea, as it was a most delightful evening, I walked for a long time with papa and mamma on the Parade, which was much crowded. Here we passed and repassed twenty times "the pretty lady," as we call her, whom I mentioned July 12, and had opportunities of observing her face much more minutely than we ever had before, so that we admire her infinitely more. Mamma declares that she is lovelier than any person she ever beheld; for my part, I never saw a beauty that could be compared to her. She is exquisitely, perfectly beautiful; her features are all but faultless, the only defect being that her nose (though very well shaped) is a little too large. It is difficult to say what is her greatest beauty, whether it is her unrivalled complexion, her perfectly arched dark eyebrows, her large black eyes with their long lashes, or her exquisite mouth. I cannot conceive a lovelier face. She is short, and her face and limbs small. Her expression has something in it that pleases and something that displeases, though the former predominates. There is a softness and melancholy, and look of distress, which are touching, and make one pity her; but at times she has a kind of wandering stare which I do not like. That she is unhappy I cannot doubt; she never smiles and seldom speaks. But it is strange that she dresses in the richest and most showy clothes, as if she wanted to attract attention. This evening she wore a white muslin gown, a blue silk shawl, a white satin bonnet with broad crimson ribbons, and other rich articles of dress. Her child too, about two years old, an ugly little fright, had extravagantly rich clothes, its frock and tippet being of black velvet, bordered with swansdown. I forgot to add a swansdown boa to my description of the lady's dress. She looks scarcely twenty; her youngest child is in arms. I shall never forget her, nor do I expect ever to behold her equal in beauty.*

Aug. 17, *Wednesday.*—I finished reading the first volume 31
of Mrs. Trollope's very entertaining, prejudiced, and ill-natured work, "Domestic Manners of the Americans"—a subject on which she had no business to write at all, and, at all events, it was very unfair of her to describe the manners of the half-civilized back settlements as those of the whole nation; which she certainly does, though at the outset she pretends not to do so. . . .

A staymaker, by name Mrs. Howes, of No. 82, High Street, who works for mamma, gave her to-day a touching account of the many afflictions she had endured. She was daughter to a wealthy farmer, and in early life was waited on by servants and rode in her own carriage. Her father dissipated his property, and she afterwards fell into the greatest poverty, so that she has been three days together unable to afford a fire, and has had only a crust of bread to eat. Ten years ago she fell from an upper story, a height of fifteen feet, and by the fall dislocated her hip, broke three ribs, and broke one leg. From these injuries she was about two years in recovering. Then she had the typhus fever, and was not well for fifteen months. This was followed by small-pox, and this last winter she has had an inflammation of the lungs; so that now she is very thin and looks extremely ill. In one twelvemonth she has had seven deaths in her family, of which three were her children and two her parents. Last year she had an execution in her house, her landlord, himself much distressed for money,

* She proved to be a dancer in the *corps de ballet* of the Lyceum. —ED.

being able to wait no longer. She could easily have paid it all, but that the ladies for whom she worked would not pay their debts. There were no less than seven of these ladies in Wellington Square. Their unfortunate creditor went to them, represented her case, and begged relief, but got not a sixpence of her money; and the execution took place. Amongst other things her flowers, of which she had been particularly fond, were sold. One of these, a favourite fuchsia, worth seven shillings, a lady gave her a sovereign for, which was a great assistance to her in the distress she was now thrown into. After this she took another lodging, and by degrees began to prosper again in her profession. When the Duchess of Kent and the Princess Victoria were here, and all the tradespeople in the place sent presents to them, Mrs. Howes, having nothing else to offer, presented to the princess a pair of stays of blue silk, which cost her in making them fourteen pounds. She got nothing in return but a letter of thanks, which, however, did her some good, as it made her known; and now she writes on her cards "Appointed by their Royal Highnesses," etc., etc.

Aug. 18, *Thursday.*—The bathing women (for Louisa bathes in the sea every morning) told mamma a few particulars about the family at No. 36. It seems that there is a great mortality among them. As soon as they arrive at the age of twenty they die. The one whose hearse we saw was the fourth of them thus prematurely cut off, and one of them now is expected to have her turn—apparently the pale one, the elder of the two. What they die of we could not make out; probably consumption, though it seems to be a very rapid one. The one whom we distinguish as pretty does not seem to want cheerfulness; but the other looks melancholy, and I have never seen her smile. The boys, too, are pale and slightly made.

Aug. 28, *Sunday.*— . . . We went to bed trembling for the weather to-morrow, the important day of our journey.

The air was perfectly calm and clear; the sunset was a bright pale yellow. There were some large purple clouds blotching the south and west. The moon rose small and red; her orb hazy and ill-defined, which we thought a bad sign.

[On August 29 the travellers reached Tunbridge, and spent three nights there.]

Aug. 30, *Tuesday.*—The first thing I did after I was dressed, which was a little after eight o'clock, was to sally forth to procure a draught of new milk, resuming my old practice at Woodbury before I went to Hastings. It was a sweet morning, and I enjoyed the draught the more from having walked for it. The milkwoman, Mrs. Wait, lives near the mill, just five minutes' walk from the Miss Husseys' abode, in a brick house whose grandeur surprised me. I was shown into a little parlour, where a glass tumbler of rich foaming milk was brought me by Mrs. Wait herself, who looks as if she fully understood its nourishing qualities. On returning, I walked about my cousins' garden, exceedingly enjoying the dewy freshness of a country morning after having been confined in my morning walk for two months to the glare of a parade. It was quite delightful to me to hear once more the sweet songs of robin, wren, and swallow, and to be surrounded by flowers and trees not stunted by the sea air. . . . In driving through Tunbridge in this open carriage, I could observe much better than when in the coach what sort of place it is. It consists principally of a single street, almost a mile long, sufficiently wide, and for the greater part of the way sufficiently clean. It is an old town, and most of the houses have an antique look. One in particular I noticed, which had projecting stories and a cinquefoil moulding round the gable end; it would have been a good subject for Prout. The long street crosses the Medway, which even here is a very pretty little stream. It is bordered with willow-herbs and covered with yellow water-lilies; it winds through thick shady trees, from the midst of which peeps the grey old castle, shrouded in luxuriant ivy, and crowned with tufts of foliage.

At London.

Sept. 1, *Thursday.*—We are again at London, where we are to remain two nights, for the purpose of seeing Dr. James Clark again. We set off from Tunbridge at half-past ten o'clock in the Telegraph, a Tunbridge Wells coach. We were not so fortunate as to have the whole inside to ourselves, for we had two fellow-passengers, both ladies. One was about forty-five years old, in deep mourning, and evidently suffering both in mind and body. Her face was thin and ghastly, and, by her compressed lips and downcast eyes, she seemed to be struggling hard with tears. She spoke not a word the whole time, and noticed nothing that passed. The other was a jolly old woman, very fat, merry, and talkative, dressed up in gay silks, and wearing false flaxen hair. She bore in her countenance the trace of considerable beauty, and was fair and blue-eyed. We found her a very communicative and amusing travelling companion. Indeed, she gave utterance to a great deal more than we could hear or comprehend, owing to the rattling of the coach and the rapidity of her speech. She was a woman who knew the world, and led a gay life. She told us she lived seven miles from town, and had been staying with a friend at Tunbridge Wells. . . .

The Surrey side is by no means the worst part of London. The streets are, in general, very wide and pretty regular, and the houses not mean. We stopped a little while near the Elephant and Castle, and saw close to us, at the corner of two very broad streets, the Rockingham Arms, one of those pestilential gin-shops. It is a very fine large building, handsomely adorned with pilasters. Two ragged and sickly wretches, a man and woman, skulked out at a little door while I was looking. I make no doubt there was a pawn-broker's shop close by.

Sept. 2, *Friday.*—Dr. Clark spent nearly an hour in examining me, which he did with the greatest care and minuteness. He pronounces me much better in every respect, and finds my health more improved than he had expected. Indeed, I am scarcely like the same person, and I could perceive the greatest difference in my sensations when he tapped me with his hand. When he did it last time, it gave me great pain on the left side of my chest, but this time it gave me none. He observed that I was much fatter than when he saw me before. But he says that I still require as much care as ever, that it is extremely important to attend to my diet, that constant change of air by long drives is highly desirable, and, alas! that I must by no means remain during the winter in so cold a place as Woodbury. He recommends Torquay as the best place for me to go to, and says I ought to go in October. So that I am now going home to Woodbury for but a very short time.

Sept. 3, *Saturday.*—Papa having last week taken our places in the Bedford Times coach, we set off at two o'clock. For some time we flattered ourselves that we were to travel alone, but such happiness was not ours; for at the Peacock Inn, Islington, we took up a lady in green silk, who presently doffed her gloves in order to display a finger quite manacled with gaudy rings. She was a tall woman, with a brown face and large features. We found her uncommunicative. Not so a gentleman of great size, who to our annoyance came inside for one stage, and kept up a constantly noisy conversation, of which every other sentence was obscured by a loud unmeaning laugh. Who he was, I cannot tell; not her husband, though she was a married woman, by name Mrs. Taylor. She, it seems, had just returned from a trip to Boulogne, which she much enjoyed, except with regard to the society, the "three shilling people," who throng the place from London. I found it amusing to listen to their conversation; they rattled away at a prodigious rate. The gentleman showed us a watch, which he said had been the property of the great Duke of Marlborough. It was a curious and clumsy machine, but very handsome and richly wrought. . . .

At Woodbury.

We proceeded by coach only as far as Shefford, and then took a chaise direct for Woodbury, which is thirteen miles off. The evening was very calm and lovely. Close to Potton, on the Woodbury side of it, we were met by papa, who had been waiting for us some time. We were so happy to see him. He got up into the chaise, and had taken the trouble to bring us, in a little basket, some excellent figs and peaches from our own garden. It was now dark, and we did not reach Woodbury till after eight o'clock, and I must say I was very glad to see home again.

Sept. 9, *Friday.*—Mr. Astell called. Amongst other
32 things, papa and he conversed about the new Poor-law, which seems to be generally approved of throughout the country, although there is unfortunately a considerable opposition arising. It neither is, nor was, a party question. The Bill was passed by the Whig Government, but it owed much to the support of Sir Robert Peel and the Duke of Wellington, and was very popular in both Houses with all parties. Mr. Astell, for one, who is a high Tory, speaks of it with the highest approbation. He says it has already produced astonishing effects everywhere. In Gamlingay, for instance, the rates are already diminished two-thirds, and at Tempsford it is occasioning even a moral improvement in the population. If it goes on working thus, says Mr. Astell, there will, in a few years, be not a pauper in the country. This Bill is one of the most important political

changes which have been made within my recollection, amounting, as papa said, almost to a revolution among the labouring classes.

Sept. 12, *Monday.*—Intending to become very weather-wise, I am daily taking notes of the appearance of the sky at sunset, with, of course, the weather every day. I continue also noting down the barometer and thermometer twice a day, and I intend for the future to do it three times. That is, at half-past eight a.m., at one p.m., and at eight p.m.

Sept. 18, *Sunday.*—Some interesting conversation passed when papa was with us this evening; principally about Dr.
Arnold, of Rugby, Dr. Hampden, and Mr. Keble. Before 33
papa came in, mamma and Aunt Mary began about Dr. Arnold, who is a prodigious favourite of ours. Mamma highly extolled his sermons, and then expressed her opinion of himself, and said how, when he preached, the school was so quiet and attentive that a pin might be heard to fall. Hereupon Aunt Mary broke out, saying that Dr. Arnold was quite odious now; his character was quite gone down, and such had been his conduct to one of the boys, that numbers were now withdrawn from his school. He had acted, she said, quite brutally, and had struck the boy himself. Here followed a long argument, mamma strenuously maintaining the character of Dr. Arnold for perfect conscientiousness, disinterestedness, and earnest anxiety about his school; repeating what Mr. H. Reynolds told us, as coming from an exceedingly bigoted high Tory, that he almost lived on his knees, and what we heard from Mr. P. Payne, son to Sir Peter Payne, that, instead of recreating himself on Sunday, he spent that day in writing sermons for his boys. All this Aunt Mary could not deny, but kept her opinion about the business of young Marshall, though mamma reminded her it was but an *ex parte* statement; and also blamed his violence in politics, which certainly is to be regretted. Mamma recommended her to read his sermons. Aunt

Mary said that, by grandpapa's advice, she had begun the first volume; but not finding it interesting, she had left it off, and, having now a feeling against him, she did not intend to continue it. However, when mamma read to her one from his third volume (Sermon XIII.), she agreed that it was very excellent.

Having now got on the subject of party spirit and party violence, we came to Dr. Hampden. Here again mamma and Aunt Mary differed; and when papa came in, mamma called on papa to speak his opinion, which he did at some length. Mamma first asked whether, after all, his persecutors knew what his opinions really were.

Papa replied that they did not. Socinianism, he says, is a charge quite given up now; the utmost they can accuse him of is the making use of expressions which they do not approve of; and accordingly, in the bigoted Popish spirit now pervading the university, they think him fit for the faggot. That it was an indiscreet appointment, papa allows, for he before lay under some suspicion of heterodoxy; but still the whole business of his persecution, and the spirit in which it has been carried on, is a shame and a disgrace to Oxford. Nobody denies, not even his enemies, that he is a most worthy, pious, and amiable man. His writings papa has not seen; but whatever his opinions were, he has been treated in a most brutal and unchristian manner.

As to Dr. Arnold, and the affair of young Marshall, when papa heard that Dr. Arnold had been said to act brutally, he declared that no charge could possibly be more absurd or unfounded, and that none who knew him would venture to charge Dr. Arnold with any approach to brutality. The affair was this: that in the weekly examination one of the masters, by a mistake, accused Marshall of some fault which he had before committed, but of which he was not then guilty. The boy denied it, but was not believed, and was punished accordingly. It might have been an error of judgment in Dr. Arnold to take the word of the master, and not that of the boy; but it is what is invariably done. As to the punishment, the beating, knocking, etc. (which was inflicted, not by Dr. Arnold or by his ushers, but by one of the monitors), it might or might not have been wrong, but it is done a hundred thousand times in every public school. The statement of the father in the newspaper undoubtedly contains falsehoods, and the whole business has been taken up as a party matter.

Dr. Arnold has been calumniated and misrepresented by his enemies in the grossest manner. The *John Bull*, whose business it is to propagate lies, is not ashamed to assert that he says the very reverse of what he actually does say—giving the very words of the parodied quotation—and then to hold him up to execration, calling on all parents who regard the religion and morality of their children to avoid sending them to Rugby, the only school in the kingdom where religion is neglected. Now, at Eton, the only true religious instruction ever received from Dr. Keats was, that on Sunday evening they were called in for a quarter of an hour to hear a sermon of Blair's gabbled over, and at the same time the Greek and Latin exercises were given out for the next day. Yet *John Bull* takes no notice of this, and makes no appeal to parents about the religion of their children.

As another specimen of party spirit, no outcry is made against Keble for denying the Divine authority of the Christian Sabbath, although he notoriously and openly makes no distinction between it and week-days, and will play at cricket on Sunday evening;* but there is a vast commotion

* This, I find, is a mistake; the fact really is that Keble and his father encouraged noisy sports among the lower orders on Sunday evenings. [Apart from the unpleasant turn given by the words "noisy sports" and "lower orders," this is a very harmless fact. Keble, no doubt, thought cricket better for his parishioners than the alehouse.—Ed.]

when the same doctrine, in theory, is held by Whately, and others of that party, although he does not adopt it in practice, and considers a man of the Established Church conscientiously bound to keep it holy.

Such is the substance of the conversation, in which I took great interest.

Sept. 21, *Wednesday.*—In the evening came our long-expected pupil, Lord Ipswich. It is always a matter of anxiety, on the arrival of a pupil, to know what sort of a subject he will prove. There is nothing at all unfavourable in this young man's appearance, and we hear much that is good of him from his father and mother. He is tall, erect, and thin; very light haired; his eyes blue, and his complexion florid. Papa says he is very like his father, whom, as well as the Duke of Grafton, he has formerly seen.

Sept. 23, *Friday.*—I now really pride myself on my weather-wisdom. I can always, by observing the sunset, accurately predict the weather of the following day. I trust the sunset even more than the barometer.

The sunset this evening was the most glorious I ever beheld. As I have described it in my registering book, I shall say less about it here. At the moment the sun (an orb of gold) was setting, the western horizon was glowing with a fiery copper pink, sprinkled with small rich purple clouds of surpassing brilliance. But after he was quite set, the scene was far nobler. The whole western sky was one mass of various colours—red, lemon, orange, pink, lilac—melting together, and continually increasing in brightness. Then the light decreased in extent, and amalgamated more and more; the western horizon glowing like a furnace, till no colour remained but a belt of bloody scarlet, such as I have never seen before. This scarlet colour contrasted strangely and harshly with the intense dark purple of the distances; a contrast which, if seen in a painting, would be pronounced very ugly and unnatural. In the earlier part of it the eastern sky was blushing with curled and streaky clouds of a delicate pink, as if the sun was rising.

Even Mr. Wells was struck by it, and called out to Richard as he went by, "I say, Dickon, do come here, Dickon, and look at the sky! I never saw such an odd thing in my life!"

Richard. "It is most beautiful."

Mr. Wells. "Beautiful! I don't call that beautiful; why, it's a regular blood-colour." . . .

I do not expect to lose any more teeth; they have never ached before, and I attribute their goodness to the constant use of charcoal, of which I have the highest opinion. So has papa, who, having used charcoal daily ever since he was eight years old, never had toothache in his life, and never lost a tooth.

When suffering with the tooth which has just been drawn, I found great and instantaneous relief from a very simple remedy prescribed in *Chambers's Edinburgh Journal*, where I read it two years and a half ago. This is nothing but to put into the hollow of the tooth a wetted bit of cotton, dipped into an equal mixture of pounded alum and salt.

Sept. 24, *Saturday.*—Miss Pym, senior, and Miss Pym, junior, spent the day with us. The younger Miss Pym is about seventeen or eighteen years. She is an uncommonly pleasing and amiable girl; I should like to see much more of her than we have as yet done. She converses very agreeably. She told me some curious facts about the treatment of the scarlet fever. She and all her brothers and sisters, a family of nine, were taken ill together. They were attended by two doctors, who came on alternate days. One of the doctors was an old, the other a young, practitioner; the first preferred a warm, the other a cold, system of treatment. One-half of the family was under the hot, the other under the cold, doctor. The first were accordingly kept as hot as possible, covered with blankets, made to drink medicines to promote perspiration, and had their bed-curtains always drawn close round them. The others were treated in a perfectly different manner. The furniture of their beds was entirely taken down; the carpets were taken up; the furniture of their rooms all removed except two chairs; they had no fire in their rooms, although it was the depth of winter, had their windows constantly opened, were fed only on a little tea and bread-and-butter, and every evening were taken from their beds and made to stand in a tub, while cold water and vinegar were poured over their heads. Thus the two systems had a fair trial. The consequence was that those who were kept cool got well much the quickest, and were much less reduced, while those who were kept hot were in every respect the most ill.

While the Miss Pyms were with us, Sir Peter Payne and his daughters called. Sir P. is a remarkably healthy old man of seventy-five. He was naturally very delicate, and says he never knew what good health was till he was sixty years of age. He attributes his present good health and strength to his constant hard exercise and his great temperance. He never drinks anything but a single glass of wine in soda-water; he eats scarcely any meat, and lives principally on pudding.

Sept. 28.—We have just heard of a most melancholy event—the sudden death of the eldest Miss Cust, at the early age of nineteen. . . . I almost doubt if her poor mother will ever recover the blow.

Oct. 1, *Saturday.*—This day's newspaper (the *Evening Mail*) gives the real account of Mrs. Graham's frightful accident in the ascent in a balloon, which took place in the beginning of last August. We heard of it at Hastings from Mr. Henry Reynolds. How any one could survive such a fall I cannot imagine. She states that she fell nearly a thousand feet, and she was insensible for three weeks. We heard at Hastings that, though the ground on which she fell was hard, the impression of her body remained upon it. As for the Duke of Brunswick, he very quietly and safely stepped out when the car was on the ground, before she went up again. They had ascended four miles from the earth. It was at the duke's request that they went up so high. I cannot imagine a more frightful situation than hers when she was falling, for she was perfectly conscious, and fully expected death. The expansion of her silk pelisse, by lightening her fall, was what saved her.

I finished this evening all that I intend to do in the arrangement of the Penang ferns. It has been an intense labour. I have worked at it from morning till night, with scarce a moment's intermission, till I have been nearly knocked up. The ferns amount to many hundreds in number, and are of all sizes, from the length of four feet five inches to two inches. All that are not above two feet I have put into the portfolio ; but there are fifteen too long for that, which I am obliged to keep separate. Each fern I fasten in by sewing and gumming.

Oct. 2, *Sunday.*—Papa buried poor Miss Cust to-day. The funeral, he says, was conducted with perfect decorum. It is the first he has ever been present at in which there was nothing whatever to disgust him. After the ceremony, Mr. Cust informed papa that Lady Anna Maria (who had not been present) wished to see him. Papa accordingly was taken to the study, where he was soon after joined by Lady Anna Maria. She entered with a firm calm step, sat down, took papa's hand, and began to thank him, while the tears ran down her face ; yet there was no agitation, no sobbing—she was quite collected and resigned. She was, papa said, a beautiful specimen of Christian sorrow. She spoke to him a long time about her daughter, and was every now and then interrupted by tears. Her deep grief and calm resignation touched papa greatly, and he came home full of compassion and admiration for her, and a higher opinion of her even than he ever had before.

[It was decided that the invalid should spend the winter in Devonshire.]

Oct. 3, *Monday.*—This is my last day at Woodbury—my last morning, I should say; for we set off at eleven o'clock. I took a long farewell of house, garden, wood, heath, and every other object with which I am familiar. It was a direful morning; every object was obscured by rain, and all the country appeared to the least possible advantage, yet still I looked on it with great regret. But it was far more painful to part with papa and my brothers and sisters. Papa will come to Devonshire in December, so that I shall see him again in three months; but from the others I shall be parted for more than double that time.

[*London.*] . . . The sun was setting when we entered London, and I never saw this mighty metropolis to so much advantage, for the golden light of the dying orb illuminated it with splendour not its own, and gorgeously lighted up Regent's Park, green with the recent rain, and bordered with terrace upon terrace of noble buildings. No less did it improve the aspect of the environs, which I now pronounce to be very pretty; at least, beyond Highgate Arch, and partly within.

Still, in itself, I do not yet know of any entrance to London more overpoweringly striking than that over Westminster Bridge, which we crossed in coming from Tunbridge. But in every place it is impossible not to feel that London is a most astonishing city. It seems an endless maze of streets and buildings, spreading and increasing in every direction, and threatening to swallow up all that is left of country in the little county which contains it.

CHAPTER IX.

From Oct. 6 *to Dec.* 31, 1836. *At Exeter.*

[This volume opens with the coach journey of herself and her mother, from 8 a.m. to 6.30 p.m., from London to Salisbury, eighty-five miles, where they slept on their way to Exeter. On the first part of the journey—that is, as far as Salisbury—she observed that "there was a dense fog, which did not signify much, as there was very little to see or to hide" on the Salisbury road in general. But near Bagshot she notices heathy hills in many places, covered with open fir woods mixed with gorse.]

It has a peculiarly uninhabited, deserted appearance, which I like; not a house nor a human being to be seen, nothing but hill beyond hill to the horizon; often a high heathy hill rising on one side, and a valley covered with pine descending on the other. . . . About five miles from Bagshot the moors became more and more extensive, and very marshy, especially to the left; on the right there is a constant succession of hills.

Hartford Bridge, our next stage, is a long street. The country about is miserable, very flat and marshy, and thinly wooded. All the small timber is oak, all the larger elm. There are several plantations of oak of curious appearance. The young oaks are planted in long straight rows, eighteen or twenty feet apart, each oak growing out of a little mound one or two feet high, which being often covered with gorse in full flower, looks very pretty.

Forty miles from London all the country continues very flat, marshy, and dreary, the soil being gravelly in general. Somewhere hereabouts a railroad is being erected between London and Southampton; it is raised on a kind of mole. . . .

Lord Dudley's place is in this hideous region, one mile on the London side of Basingstoke, our fourth stage, at which we arrived at thirteen minutes to two. Here we dined. Now, I had a great horror of Basingstoke, because when papa and mamma went to Devonshire five years ago, they stopped here at a most horrid inn, and could get nothing to eat but putrid chops; the whole place, too, they described as filthy, abounding with bad smells. So that we rather dreaded dining here; but we were agreeably disappointed. I cannot deny that every street was flanked by two open drains nearly overflowing, nor that the horses marched to their stables through the same passage by which we walked to dinner, and that the only reason we smelt no bad smells might have been that we had no leisure so to do. But when we entered the dining-room, a large apartment, we discovered the following goodly apparitions: at the top a round of beef, at the bottom a fillet of veal, in the centre a ham, a chicken, potatoes, bread, and butter; the whole forming a capital cold dinner. Mamma and I, with a very good appetite, fell on the fowl. One of his wings was already gone; we took the other, and stripped him besides of his breast, and a portion of one leg. In about a quarter of an hour we were summoned back to the coach, and left Basingstoke greatly raised in our esteem. . . . Salisbury Cathedral I did not see. The coach put up at the White Hart, where we also quartered ourselves. After our long and uninteresting journey of eighty-five miles, we were thoroughly fatigued, and hastened to bed as soon as we could.

We had intended to travel from Salisbury to Exeter by

the Traveller, a coach which, we had learnt from Aunt Bell, started at nine in the morning, and got in at seven in the evening. But we heard from our fellow-traveller that this information was wrong; that it started at six and got in at ten, being thus sixteen hours on the road; that, besides being so exceedingly slow, it is a six inside, and stopped at every public-house on the road. These statements being corroborated at the inn, we gave up the Traveller altogether; and finding that there was no other day-coach, we resolved to go by the mail, which starts at five a.m. from Salisbury, and gets in at half-past two. Fortunately there is an auxiliary mail, which travels only from Salisbury to Exeter, so that we were able to secure our places that night, instead of waiting for the chance of the mail from London. This our fellow-traveller very kindly did for us, which saved us a good deal of trouble. The fare was £2 10*s.* each, not too much for eighty-seven miles in a mail. Having transacted all the necessary business, we drank tea, to our inexpressible satisfaction, in a very comfortable room, the floor of which was covered by an old Axminster carpet, which had once been very handsome. We then very quickly went to bed.

From Salisbury to Exeter.

Oct. 7, *Friday.*—We were called at four o'clock, to prepare for our very long journey. We dressed, of course, by candle-light, the first time I have done so for this twelvemonth. I was not primed for my journey by a good night, for I had been woke by the squeaking horn of a coach, the up Traveller, I suppose, and I did not altogether sleep three hours. As soon as we were dressed, we went downstairs, and stepped into the fly which was to take us to the Black Horse, the inn whence the mail starts. The fly was drawn by a pair of mules, but they might as well have been donkeys, for it was too dark to see them; they took us very well, however. We were in ample time for the mail, which was still waiting for the mail from London. We thought ourselves fortunate that they did not object to the quantity of luggage we took, which consisted of two trunks, a carpet-bag, a large deal box, and a small one. On getting in we found, to our great pleasure, that we had the whole inside to ourselves. It was an excellent coach, as mails usually are, very roomy, and so spruce and clean that it looked like a gentleman's carriage.

[The journey from Salisbury to Exeter is minutely described, as it was mostly through beautiful scenery, and, what to her curious eyes was a great attraction, "quite different, not merely in scenery, but in the aspect of all the towns and villages." Thus she describes it :]

In the first place, the roads are so pretty; they frequently wind between very high rocky banks, crowned with wood and beautifully festooned with ivy. Where there are not these banks, the hedges are adorned with red haws, hips, purple privet-berries, and blackberries—together with poppies, hawkweed, yarrow, and great ragwort, while beyond them the ground sometimes rises in broken hills, or sinks in little valleys, which are clothed sometimes with thick woods and groves, sometimes with orchards of moss-green apple trees covered with fruit, either of a pale green or a bright crimson. The towns and villages, too, have a peculiar character; being built of stone, they look, and are, much more ancient than those of Bedfordshire. The cottages have all a solid substantial look ; the grey stone with which they are built, the thatched roofs, the stone casements, and old square dripstones, give them a highly picturesque look. They are frequently covered, too, with China roses, Virginian creeper, clematis, and ivy, and are surrounded by lovely little gardens, filled with hollyhocks, dahlias, and many other plants in full blow. These gardens owe much of their beauty to the broken nature of the ground and the old stone walls, shaded with trees, which often intersect them. Out of one of these walls I saw a clear little fountain gushing, at which a girl was filling her pitcher. Now and then we passed an overshot mill, with its pretty little stream; and beautiful lanes continually branched off from the road, and wandered among woods tinged with the varied hues of autumn, the sycamore a bright scarlet, the oak and beech a rich brown, the larch and birch golden yellow, the spindle-wood a deep violet. Near one village, through which ran a stream, I saw one or two meadows strewed with what seemed to be hemp or flax drying. As we approached Crewkerne the country became more and more diversified with high round hills thickly clothed with wood. I was much struck with the beauty of one hilly meadow, through which ran two little winding streams, the banks of which were flowery, and so deep that the water ran four or five feet beneath the level of the meadow.

[Approaching Exeter, she says—]

The loveliest part of all is a few miles from Honiton. On the left rises a steep and beautiful hill, richly covered with heath and gorse in bloom, and crowned with thick woods; above that rises another hill, and above that another, so high and steep that we could only see their summits by stooping very low. On the right the ground descended abruptly into a deep valley, the sides of the hill being clothed with scattered woods, and sometimes shut out by the hedge. The whole valley, which is very extensive, is filled with groves; here and there a cottage, or a village, or a church tower, embosomed in trees. The opposite side of the valley is bordered with high hills, and the ends of it melt into distant woods of deep blue. This sort of scenery continued almost all the rest of the way. Beyond Honiton we continually saw lovely little pebbly streams wandering by the roadside, and shaded with trees. The road was bordered with tall beeches and oaks. I now began to notice the colour of the soil, as it appeared in the rocks and banks; it was a bright delicate vermilion, varying to brick-red and light crimson.

[She then gives an account of her arrival in Exeter; of the house, 7, Baring Crescent; the aunt, uncle, and cousin; of the first time of going to church for five months; and of her mother's departure after ten days.]

Oct. 13, *Thursday.*—About a year and a half ago, when grandmamma and Aunt Bell lived in Summerland Place, they all but witnessed a rather fearful coach accident. Summerland Place is at right angles with the London road, and the corner house, in which they lived, is close upon the very road. At that time, the road was divided into the upper and lower, which ran parallel, and at length joined, but the upper was for some distance six or eight feet higher than the lower. The lower ran close to my aunt's garden gate. Of course, in this situation, they always saw and heard the London coaches coming into the town. One calm moonlight night, as they were sitting together, they heard the Herald approaching at a furious rate, rattling along, and the guard's horn blowing as usual. They were listening to it, when all on a sudden these sounds stopped short, a single moment of silence ensued, then a heavy roll and a shout, and then all was quiet again. Uncle William exclaimed, "It's over!" and they all, in a terrible fright, rushed out into the road. There, to be sure, they found the Herald lying overturned on the lower road; the horses had kept their legs, but instead of running away, stood trembling with terror. It seems that the coachman, being quite drunk, had driven the coach over the bank, and through the railing, from the upper road to the lower. The guard, who saw what was about to happen, called out to him to pull up, but he was too drunk to do so. A young woman, who was sitting behind with the guard, asked him if she should jump down; he said no, she must keep fast where she was. He himself then jumped off safely, and over went the coach. The young woman fell off, and the coach fell on her; she was dreadfully hurt, and was carried insensible into the house. A poor sailor, too, was very severely injured; his ankle was dislocated, and his foot hung loose. The loss to him was very great from this accident, for he had with great difficulty come to Devonshire to go on board a ship which was to sail immediately. Of course he lost his passage. Nobody else, I believe, was hurt; the coachman, who deserved to have his neck broken, entirely escaped. Within five minutes of the accident a crowd of thieves and pickpockets assembled; at last the mob amounted to some hundreds, but I do not think anything was stolen. In about an hour the coach was raised up again by main force, and proceeded as before. Great pains were taken to hush up the affair; no examination or inquiry was made, it never even found its way into print, and I dare say our family know more about it than anybody else.

Oct. 17, *Monday.*—Mamma went away to-day, leaving me here for seven months, a hundred and seventy-one miles from home. But I think I shall be as happy here as I can anywhere away from home, for Aunt Bell is exceedingly kind, and I love my cousins very much. Mamma travels in the most convenient way possible, for papa's cousin, Bulkeley Praed, takes her to London in his own carriage.

Oct. 19, *Wednesday.*—We passed many rows of buildings in the most ugly, fantastical, nondescript style, a mixture of very barbarous Tudor English, with an approach to Grecian, and a great resemblance to Chinese. Most of the houses are painted or washed a glaring white.

Oct. 20, *Thursday.*—After, I am sorry to say, a very idle
week, I resolved to begin studying again. I took up 34
Morgan's "Arithmetic," and read over carefully some of the
earlier part. But I find my brain muddy and rusty with
disuse during my long illness, and I was quite fatigued in

a very short time. However, I shall practise study a little every day, and get myself into the way of it again.

Oct. 22, *Saturday.*—I took another walk with my uncle. We went up Castle Street and into the castle yard. Very little is left of the ancient castle of Exeter, except a bit of the wall, and a very picturesque ruin, of Norman date, covered with aged ivy, which looks as old as itself. The castle yard is a neatly kept area, bordered by tall elms; at one end is an ugly modern building, the sessions house, where my uncle told me that formerly, when the assize balls were held here, they used to dance over the heads of the prisoners, and in their very hearing. This barbarous custom is now disused. We ascended the rampart of the castle, and walked along the top of the wall. As soon as we had mounted, a most splendid view burst upon my sight through the lofty elms rising in front. The whole of Exeter lay outspread before us, and a wide extent of hilly and woody country on every side; we saw the river Exe winding along, and could trace its course down to the sea. I could even see Exmouth and its church situated at the mouth. I saw also the noble cathedral, the whole length of which was before me. It is certainly a glorious view, though unfortunately obscured to-day by a kind of hazy sunshine. I looked at it a long time with great delight; we then descended the rampart, and returned home by the beautiful walk of Northernhay. In Paris Street we stopped at the house of a man named Frost, a self-taught mechanic of wonderful genius, to see a very remarkable clock, constructed by an Exeter man two hundred years ago. It is a most singular piece of mechanism, having four [query, five ?] dial plates; the principal one shows the hour of the day or night, a small one above shows the month, another the day of the month, another the day of the week, another leap year. The clock has also a band of music, and various figures which act and move at the same time; also a moving panorama representing the course of the sun. The whole forms a very splendid and extraordinary work. It had long been out of repair, and Frost was the only man in Exeter who was able to reput it into order again. It is in the possession of an attorney, who, it is said, will not sell it for less than seven hundred pounds.

Oct. 28, *Friday.*—No less than five letters, from papa, mamma, Arabella, Louisa, and Mackworth. . . . Most of them speak of the poor Custs . . . "Lady Anna Maria," says Arabella, "Mr. Cust, and Lucy (now Miss Cust) have called; they all seemed so very unhappy that it was quite touching to see them, especially when they force a laugh or try to speak cheerfully; and you have no idea how ill and melancholy poor Lucy looked. She was as white as a sheet, her lips especially, and spoke in so low and sorrowful a voice as to be hardly audible; she was several times near bursting into tears, and altogether was the picture of distress and ill health."

Nov. 5.—Louisa writes: "Mackie has discovered a pair of large owls that take their pleasure in sitting alone in the laurel and holly hedge."

Nov. 8, *Tuesday.*—I was walking up and down the drawing-room, which I usually do for exercise when the
others are gone out, repeating my favourite poem, "Sir 35
Eustace Grey," when I heard, to my great surprise, the little squeak of a golden-crested wren. I instantly walked to the window, and looked out into the little front garden, where I beheld a pair of these beautiful little birds flitting about in the arbutus. While I was looking on, a black cat came stealing up slily, and put the golden wrens to flight.

Nov. 10.—A.'s letter is very amusing; she gives a very nice account of her studies and occupations. I am glad to find that Lord Ipswich seems to be as pleasant a pupil as any; indeed, more so—at least in his manners, which are very gentlemanly and unassuming.

Nov. 16, *Wednesday.*—We talked to-day about Mrs.
36 Siddons. Aunt Bell has met her at Bersted House, the place of Lord Arran, where she has dined when staying at Bersted Lodge with her aunts, Lady Mayo and Mrs. Smith. Lord A., an effeminate, profligate, ugly old man, with a withered leg, aspired to being a patron of the arts and sciences, and his house was always thronged by professors and amateurs of all [sorts]. One of these, whom my aunt recollects, was a Mr. Lodge, a musical performer; another was a Miss Wilkinson, a girl of sixteen or seventeen, who sang. Mrs. Siddons, too, was here. Now, she was an exceedingly proud woman, and was, of course, to be considered the queen of the party; but as there was not a woman in the house who did not by right rank above her, much manœuvring was employed to raise her above them. When Aunt Bell dined there, she was curious to see how this object would be effected. A little before the company was summoned to dinner, Mrs. Siddons vanished; and while they entered the dining-room at one door, behold, she was seen entering like a queen by herself at the other. She sometimes read Shakespeare to the party, on which occasions Lord A. always took care to have a scene ready, and was himself invariably prepared with tears and pocket-handkerchief. Lord A. was extremely unkind to his wife, who, when she died, declared that she was happy to depart from life, for she had always been miserable in it; yet she had no hope of a better world. She was a proud woman, but very gentle; she had a peculiarly dry way of saying witty and pointed things, which set all the company laughing, without moving a muscle of her own countenance. Lord A. had no children of his own; he had a nephew, of whom he took no notice, and he thought fit to bring up the children of his butler, to introduce them into the drawing-room, and admit them among his company. One of these was a girl named Mary Annie. Of the others,

one, who was lame and not presentable, he caused to be brought up as a chemist; and the two others, A—— and J——, he educated for the Church, and made his chaplains. Aunt Bell has seen them at his house. They were ordinary-looking youths, with not much of the look of gentlemen. J—— was impudent, liked his situation well enough, and, having something of a voice, would entertain the company with singing. But A——, who turned out a very excellent young man, felt his situation to be exceedingly painful, and lived a miserable life, by turns in the drawing-room and housekeeper's room, and well aware that he was treated with contempt by the company in the former, and turned into ridicule behind his back. He happened to be seated by Aunt Bell, who had previously made up her mind to take no notice of him; but seeing how unhappy he looked, she turned and spoke to him, upon which he gave a start of surprise and afterwards burst into tears. At first, their father, the butler, used to wait on his own sons, but this being thought rather preposterous, his office was changed to avoid it. Lord A. once gave mortal offence to the Duchess of Gloucester, by introducing these young P——s when she dined at his house, and endeavouring to place one of them by her, which she took good care to avoid. A living which had been promised to papa or my uncle was bestowed on one of them.

Nov. 26, *Saturday.*—My uncle does not know that we are reading "Ivanhoe," for we have said nothing about it to him; and after he had gone away this evening, A., P., and I fell into conversation about it and debated the propriety of giving it up. We were all very well inclined to do it, especially A., but we did not quite decide to do so. I confess I shall find it mortifying, and I cannot agree entirely with ——'s opinions, because he would entirely abolish all works of imagination. Now, why has our Maker given us imaginations, if they are never to be indulged? Besides, I am sure papa would not object, for he has occasionally read to us a novel himself, and I respect his opinion much more than ——'s or any one else's.

Dec. 4, *Sunday.*—Notwithstanding that I am aware I write too much already, I have not been able to resist the temptation of beginning a comedy, denominated "Breaking of Wild Colts," of which the scene and actors are in this house. The composing it is a great amusement to me.

Dec. 10, *Saturday.*—I should say, from all I know of Shakespeare, that his great merit lay, not in sketching individual characters, but in painting human nature in general, in displaying the different passions of the mind, and tracing its progress from one state to another. This I conceive to be the merit shown in the drawing of Macbeth. I do not know that there is much individuality of character in that tyrant, or that he acts differently from what most men in his circumstances would do; but nothing can excel the talent displayed in exhibiting the effect of those circumstances on the mind of man, and the natural transition from one kind of wickedness to another. And yet there is a certain sort of individuality in this play, after all; at least, so far as to show the different effects of ambition and murder on two different species of minds—on the weak and sensitive (comparatively so, I mean) of Macbeth, and on the strong, hard, and vigorous one of his wife. But as I have spoken on this subject before, I shall not enlarge upon it here.

Dec. 15, *Thursday.*—I feel now quite convinced that I must not exert my mind at all, compared at least with what I should like to do. I cannot read or write without a headache, and writing also gives me a pain in my chest, which I have not, indeed, been free from for some days. It is very painful to me deliberately to lay aside all my studies, and it seems to me that I shall some time hence look back with great regret on the year 1836, the seventeenth year of my life, thus apparently wasted, as far as study is concerned. Yet I ought not to entertain this feeling, for it is God's will. . . .

I always find it difficult to give way to fatigue or incapability of study, and if it was not for the reiterated lectures of all around me, I should not allow myself to be ill at all. I am told that I am not giving myself fair play; I am sorry that idleness is necessary to my doing so. A. and P. do not allow me to teach them as I used to do, which I exceedingly regret, as I cannot think it hurts me.

Dec. 16, *Friday.*—I wish I had leisure to commit to paper a hundredth part of the tales, poems, and dramas with which my brain is crammed. I have such splendid visions in my head that the idea of never realizing them with the pen is quite mortifying.

Dec. 18, *Sunday.*—It was a beautiful day, and there was another lovely sunset. I heard a wren singing, and it struck me for the first time that his song was very like Lieber Augustin.

My uncle read to us a part of Scott's "Essay on the Ten Commandments." Scott considers the Commandments as a summary of the Christian practice, containing, when properly understood, the whole of the Christian's duty. My uncle thinks the same. I cannot help differing. I do not think the Commandments have any interpretation but the literal one. Moses could not have meant them to imply more than the actual words, when he delivered them to the children of Israel. A spiritual interpretation was not according to the Mosaic plan, and they were meant not for us, but for the Israelites. We may use them, if we like, as texts from which to draw lessons of morality, but we ought not to think they were intended to teach us all that a Christian should do. It does not seem to me that Christ, in His sermon on the mount, is explaining the Commandments so much as showing the difference between the Mosaic, or moral, and the Christian, or spiritual code, and adding his own precepts to those already in force. Everybody acknowledges that Christ introduced a far purer and stricter system of morality; but how was that the case if He taught nothing that ought to have been new to the Jews, nothing but what they should have known and understood before? For, if the Commandments were intended to be spiritually understood, and if, as —— thinks, Christ blames the Jews for not so understanding them, it is plain that they ought and could have so understood them. It is manifest, too, that no turning, twisting, and straining of the Commandments can possibly extract from them even the heads or outlines of all a Christian's duty. There is no commandment to forbid lying, except with respect to our neighbour; there is no precept to inculcate humility, or forbid pride, or to teach the spirit of Christian charity, especially in the forgiveness of our enemies. And many things were allowed under the Jewish code which are not allowed to Christians.

Dec. 20, *Tuesday.*—We finished "Ivanhoe" yesterday. I think it is a splendid specimen of genius. . . . Except for the sake of that pathetic dialogue between Rowena and Rebecca, I would willingly part with the last chapter, and at all events the book should have finished when Rebecca leaves the room. Scott spoils his novels by finishing them so carefully with the future happiness of the hero and heroine. The death of the Templar is admirably conceived. To be sure, as Aunt Bell says, it was wrong of Ivanhoe to risk Rebecca's life on such a chance as his feeble and decaying strength; but then there is a moral grandeur in his confidence that Heaven would grant victory to the just cause.

This evening my uncle finished "King Henry VIII."

I must say I was mightily disappointed in it. Whether it is that I am not capable of understanding Shakespeare, and cannot distinguish his beauties, I do not know. . . . There is no effort in Shakespeare's works; he takes so little pains, that what is interesting, or noble, or sublime, or finely exhibiting the features of the mind, seems to drop from his pen by chance. One cannot help thinking that every play is executed with slovenly neglect, that he has done himself injustice, and that, if he pleased, he might have given to the world works which would throw into the shade all that he has actually written.

To be sure, this gives one a very exalted idea of his intellect, for even if the mere unavoidable overflowings of his genius excel the depths of other men's minds, how magnificent must have been the fountain of that genius whose very bubbles sparkle so beautifully! But to speak of "Henry VIII." in particular: Henry himself, Katharine, and Wolsey, though they display a degree of character, are not half so vigorously drawn as I had expected, or as I could, methinks, have done myself. The others are in general nonentities. The character of Cranmer exists more in Henry's language about him than in his own actions. Gardiner, as far as one sees of him, is accurately represented. But in general the characters do not figure sufficiently often to be made much of.*

* It may seem strange to say so, but do not these critiques, crude and shallow as of course they are, indicate, what she herself believed, that her talent would be for drama? What she sought in fiction, especially in dramatic fiction, was the exhibition of character, vigorous presentment of passion, with trust in general human nature, even to realism, and the sincere and bold portraiture of individualities. Her critical views, like those of the day, were frankly objective; she had always before her, for her standard, living human nature as she saw and understood it, and the subtler metaphysical depths escaped her. She shows this by the suggestion that his beauties, which she could not fail to perceive, "seem to drop from him by chance," and how

Dec. 25, *Sunday and Christmas Day.*—Yesterday I was sixteen years old, to-day I am seventeen; the sound of the words seem to effect a greater change than the actual space of time. I lay awake last night for a long time, kept awake by a little matter which has disturbed my equanimity and put me into a painful state of mind. I heard the midnight clock strike twelve; I counted every stroke, and when the last had sounded, I had completed my seventeenth year, and entered on another.

I look back on the year I have just finished with many mingled feelings, most of a painful nature. . . . When I have felt happy, I have also felt that something more was wanting to complete that happiness, and for that something I have ardently wished and longed. This feeling has always rankled within, with various degrees of intensity, sometimes so little acknowledged to myself (never to any-one else) that it has seemed no longer to exist, and for a time my life has glided on in calm and uninterrupted enjoyment. I remember that last year I had no outward impediment to happiness. All was prosperous around me, I could pursue unchecked all my favourite studies and amusements, and I grew more and more attached to the world and estranged from heaven. In this state I felt my danger. I felt as if no ordinary call could awaken me from my dream of happiness; I almost wished and prayed for affliction, if there were no other means of correction. And has not God answered this half-indulged wish? Has He not chastised me by withdrawing me from those things which chiefly formed the delight of my life? It is a

strikingly, though unconsciously, does she thereby pay tribute to his unrivalled genius! Indeed, her suggestion that he might, if he pleased, write works far beyond what he had already done but states the fact, for she had not then read "Hamlet," save as a child, nor "Othello" at all, which when she did instantly couched her hitherto dim-seeing eyes.—ED.

striking, an impressive circumstance, in which I cannot fail to see His fatherly hand.

There is completely a world within me, unknown, unexplored, by any but myself. I see well that my feelings, my qualities, my character, are understood by none else. I am not what I am supposed to be; I am liked and loved far more than I deserve. I hate—yes, I truly hate myself; for I see the depths of sin within me, which are hidden from all other eyes. No one ought ever to feel satisfied with himself, with his progress in holiness; but they may feel peace of mind; and much must I be changed before I can reach this state! Yet I have now many advantages, which I hope to improve. I have more leisure for serious thought; I have a dangerous illness hovering over my head to warn me; I am, by my removal to Devonshire, removed also from the temptations to some of my chief faults.

Dec. 26, *Monday.*—I frequently read and repeat poetry to A. and P. I cannot express how passionately I love poetry. It is in all my thoughts, sleeping and waking. All day long I have some line or passage running in my head; whenever I am by myself, or lying awake at night, it is my delight to repeat a poem; and when I open my eyes in the morning, the first thing which occurs to me is commonly a passage of poetry. Besides which, I frequently compose it myself, and have constant visions of new poems floating in my brain. I could not exist without poetry.

Dec. 31, *Saturday.*—This is the last day of the week, the last day of the month, and the last day of the year. It seems wonderful to think that the year 1836 should already have passed away, and it is awful too. Time flies each year on more rapid wings. I lay awake in bed this night, as well as on that preceding Christmas Day, and heard the clock strike twelve, the hour that parted two years of this world's existence. Stroke after stroke I counted with deep interest; each stroke seemed a bell tolling a dirge of the old year, its funeral knell. At last I went to sleep, and had a brilliant dream. I dreamed of a glorious moonlight night; the sky was of a dense blue, almost black, and there was a lunar rainbow, a phenomenon which I have never in reality beheld, and which in my dream I gazed at with wonder and delight. While gazing at the splendid vision, I woke to the cold reality of a frosty morning in January.

CHAPTER X.

From January 10 *to July* 17, 1837.—*Exeter, Sidmouth, Teignmouth, Picton, Marldon, Torquay, Exeter.*

[This chapter, whose opening finds Emily just past her seventeenth birthday, and therefore fairly entered upon womanhood, seems to furnish an opportunity for touching on some points which could not be looked for in the journal, or are not fully explained there. Some of the natural feelings of her age were now unfolded in her; she was no longer exclusively the student and the observer; she enjoyed the society and some of the lively amusements of the girls and young women around her. At the same time, we find—for the first time in her life—occasional tendencies to deep sadness.

But in the period contained in the next four volumes, we find two features of her character so developed as by degrees to throw her former tendencies into the shade. These were an ardent piety and a turn for passionate friendship. Neither of them tended much to her happiness. Her piety was self-reproachful, for she could not satisfy the claims which the severe creed she believed in made on her; her friendships—always for women somewhat older than herself, whom she revered as wiser and better than she, or for girls of her own age, whom she thought she could be of use to and raise to her own spiritual and intellectual level—were too devoted and absorbing for the peace of a mind linked with so weak a frame. Of the former kind of friendships we find here the first birth of the one that was henceforth almost to engross her heart, that for a most attractive family, and for one of them especially, whom she believed, not wrongly, to be the type of all but angelic goodness in woman's form, and towards whom she merged all her own powers and tendencies "to warn, to counsel and command," in childlike reverence and loverlike attachment. She was a sunflower, for ever turning to the sun. Her good sense corrected many exaggerations, many idealizations on other subjects, but this feeling remained unchanged to the last.

No girl, perhaps, ever had much insight into character, and her first judgments were no more divinations than any of those passed by youth and inexperience; but her instincts (to use a phrase somewhat unmeaning in this connection) in the end always clung to the worthy and let go the worthless.

During this summer season amidst romantic scenes and happy youthful companionship, there sprang up one special acquaintance in which her part was maintained with such a pure and quiet simplicity as made it appear scarcely to disturb the peaceful balance of her being. Yet one almost shrinks from recalling even the pretty incidents of this innocent love story, buried as they are under the ashes of years and the earth in which the actors have long reposed. Indeed, over all things like these the intense maiden modesty of her nature kept a seal; her heart was a shrine whose veil was never, or but a corner of it, lifted. What she had to reveal of actual incident was told only to her mother, and of her own feelings she never spoke even to her, except in a few slight words on her deathbed. For though more than once in her young life she had experienced admiration and something more, what feeling she had to give in return remains an enigma.

> "It was scarcely her time to love; beside
> Her life had many a hope and aim."

In truth, "her heart was as full as it could hold." The first love, and that which remained strongest to the last, was for her parents.

I will attempt no picture of her outward appearance, but only quote a friend who described her, at the age of eighteen, as "pretty, pretty Emily, like a flower, so bright and delicate." She was never, we think, known once to allude to her personal appearance. A younger sister, thinking to please her, told her of the admiration expressed for her by a young man at a first chance sight; she was silent, and then, in a changed, grave tone, said, "You ought not to have told me that."]

Jan. 10, *Tuesday.*—I read to Anna some of Scott's lesser poems, which are great favourites of mine, namely, "The Grey Brother," "The Wild Huntsman," "The Fire-King," "Helvellyn," and a part of "Glenfinlas." "Helvellyn" I think a most beautiful little poem, far superior to that of Wordsworth on the same subject. The third stanza is peculiarly sweet.*

"The Grey Brother" is a singular ballad; it is but a fragment, and the conclusion exceedingly disappoints one, especially as there is something very fearful and mysterious in the last stanza. "Glenfinlas" I hardly understand throughout, but I think it is one of the finest little poems that has ever been composed. It was Mr. Howard who first pointed it out to me, and recommended me to read it; and the same too of "Helvellyn," and many other poems which I am very fond of.

* The selection is very just. The third stanza begins with the charming lines—

"How long didst thou think that his silence was slumber?
When the wind waved his garment, how oft didst thou start?"

She is right, too, in preferring the poem to Wordsworth's, which is shambling and prosaic in comparison.—Ed.

Jan. 11, *Wednesday.*—I read to Anna "The Ancient Mariner," which is a prime favourite of mine. It is a most extraordinary poem, unlike any other that ever was written, singular in conception, and exquisite in execution.

The latter part of verse iv., in part vi.—

> "The air is cut away before
> And closes from behind,"

struck me as such a singular idea, that I actually started as I read it.

Jan. 15, *Sunday.*—We hear that this kind of attack, which they call an influenza, is extremely prevalent and fatal. The newspapers say that in London there are six hundred policemen and three hundred banking clerks all ill at once. This indeed may not be true, . . . indeed I feel inclined to strike off a cypher from each number. It is very fatal in Exeter. Mr. Tripp preached on the subject to-day, from the text Ps. iii. 1, and said he never knew death so busy as at present. There were nine burials in his parish last week. Mr. Trevillian, an old gentleman whose pew my cousins share in church, told them that he has now eight ill at his own house. The complaint seems to be spreading like the cholera five years ago. It is quite awful and melancholy.

Jan. 24, *Tuesday.*—The prevalence of the influenza, as it is called, being in reality the same low fever to which we at Woodbury are so subject, is really awful. There is scarce a family whom we know, either personally or by name, which has escaped, and in most of them the greater part of the individuals in each family are ill. It is raging too amongst the poor. Aunt Bell sadly wants an assistant to her servants, and cannot get one; all are ill. We hear of it from every quarter. The word "influenza" is in everybody's mouth; the streets are quite thinned; nobody is in spirits except Mrs. Halse, the person who sells Morrison's pills. She says their spread is quite wonderful, and that she hears that in Bath they are almost universal. So much the better; 'tis very good news. I do not understand why the complaint is called influenza. The name was coined about six years ago, but the complaint itself, I suppose, is as old as any other. 'Tis the common fourteen or twenty-one day fever, more or less violent. . . .

After dinner we walked to Exeter, to pay visits and do shopping, and were out for about an hour and three quarters. We first called at the Misses Lee's, No. 4, Upper Summerland; they were ill with influenza. Then at Miss Baring's, at 6, Lower Summerland; she was at home, but ill of the influenza. Thus, to our great joy, we escaped all four visits, and went straight on to call on Miss Wyatt in Lower Southernhay. Here we were admitted, but found Dr. Miller attending on her sister-in-law, Mrs. Wyatt, who is ill of the influenza. Then we went to the lodgings of Mr. Harrington to inquire for his sisters, and found them too ill.

Jan. 27, *Friday.*—Mr. Dornford dined on Wednesday at Dr. Miller's, where there was to be a large party, but almost every one sent excuses on account of being taken with the influenza, and Dr. Miller himself was obliged to rise from table in the middle of dinner and go to bed. It is said that sixty thousand are ill at Berlin. It is not infectious, but an epidemic.

Feb. 1, *Wednesday.*—I amused myself with sketching on paper a scene which I recollect in a dream some months ago. It was a very beautiful and poetic scene. I thought I had entered a long series of chambers hollowed out of the bosom of a massy rock. I passed from cave to cave, till I came to one which was handsomely furnished, in a dim twilight. At one end were two great Gothic windows cut in the rocky wall, without any glass or casement, but quite open, and reaching down to the floor. I stood at the window, and found that I was looking out into the open air. Before me spread the vast ocean, which came close up to my feet; there was not a wave or a ripple; the whole sea was perfectly calm, of a deep dazzling blue. Above were the heavens, of the same pure blue tint, without a cloud. The moon shone brightly, and steeped the whole scene in her silver light. Around one side of the sea stretched a long line of dark and lofty cliffs, continuing those out of which the cavern was hewn. This cavern communicated by a Gothic arch with another, which also had windows looking out upon the sea. The whole scene had the brilliancy and splendour of fairyland.

Feb. 7, *Tuesday.*—. . . High Street greatly rises in my estimation. I saw it to-day to particular advantage, as it was fine dry weather, and there was no market to cause a crowd. I now think it a decidedly striking street. It has none of the advantages of regular architectural beauty; it is crooked, and has not the least pretension to uniformity of building, but it is very long and sufficiently broad; the houses are mostly old and pretty lofty; it is full of gay and animated shops, and altogether has an extremely picturesque appearance. I particularly like the old houses, with their gable ends, projecting windows, and rich carved oaken mouldings. The old red-brick school, with its handsome Perpendicular windows, and one or two little churches, improve the appearance of the street; but the Guildhall, by projecting so much, spoils it; and the Fire Office with its Corinthian pillars is incongruous.

Feb. 14, *Tuesday.*—I am sighing, I am pining for the country. I miss, sadly miss, the deep retirement all around my distant home, my lonely walks in the meadows, copses, and orchard, the woods echoing with the songs of a hundred merry birds; far from the din of towns and cities, and out of the hateful sight of crowded streets, and carts and coaches, and ugly houses, red, white, and all manner of hideous colours. How I do detest towns, and love the peace and solitude of the country!

Feb. 21, *Tuesday.*—When I remember the delights of my country walks, the exquisite pleasure I enjoyed in watching the progress of nature in the opening year, and especially in listening to the merry and melodious songs of a thousand little birds, I cannot help bitterly regretting the necessity which binds me to the neighbourhood of a populous and noisy city for probably three quarters of a year. I hope, however, that I am not repining and discontented. . . .

Feb. 22, *Wednesday.*—It is about half-past ten o'clock in the morning, and while I am writing, the view from these windows is singularly beautiful. The range of hills is of an indistinct blue colour, very dark to the south, and dim and pale in the west and north. The city of Exeter, beneath, appears with extraordinary clearness; the noble cathedral stands out in fine relief—its form is perfectly distinct, every line is traced with exquisite delicacy and sharpness; over the whole scene is cast a brilliant sunlight, which illuminates every building under its influence. St. Sidwell's spire shines as white as snow. Behold! while I have been writing, the whole scene has clouded over, the rain is falling, the wind howling, and the beautiful landscape is mournfully obscured.

Feb. 26, *Sunday.*—. . . How thankful I ought to be for having so entirely escaped this awful epidemic (influenza)! I dare say (as Aunt Bell too says) that Dr. James Clark fully supposes me to be now dead and buried. He had directed me to write to him from Exeter if I became worse, or wanted any instructions from him. Five months have now passed, during which he has heard nothing of me; when I left him he considered me to have tubercles in my lungs, and he no doubt thinks that this influenza has finally carried me off. What would he say if he were to see me now, so much fatter, stronger, and less susceptible of cold?

March 3, *Friday*.—. . . From whatever cause, a great change has of late taken place in my tastes in one particular respect, viz. that I no longer feel the interest I once did in works of fiction. Of these I have read, or heard read, but a very few; and they used at one time to work up my feelings to a state of the highest excitement. I looked forward to the evening, when they were read, as the most delightful part of the day, and my brain was quite filled with pictures of the scenes therein represented. Now, all this is changed. For instance, we are now reading "The Bravo." I hear it with a calmness and indifference which I can scarcely realize to myself; the narrative makes no impression on my fancy; I never feel the slightest impatience to begin it, or reluctance to put it down. The same was the case when we were reading "The Waterwitch," and, to a certain degree, even "Ivanhoe," which quite amazes me. Perhaps if I had read them all to myself, they would have interested me more. I am reading to myself, however, "Gil
37 Blas," which interests me just as little, entertaining as it is. It can hardly be that my imagination is decaying, for my love and enjoyment of poetry is as vivid as ever; indeed, more so. Thus, I listened with greater pleasure to "Ion" than to "Ivanhoe." But "Ivanhoe" lost much of its beauty by being badly read. I do think, however, that this change in my taste is no bad thing; it gives me a greater enjoyment of soberer and more useful reading.

Another beautiful sunset. The sun was a glorious orb of fire, setting in a mantle of blue cloud. It was most beautiful to see him gradually lessening as he sunk behind the hills; his last lingering spark seemed to rest upon their summit like a crest of flame.

March 6, *Monday*.—. . . We hear that the country about Exeter is infested just now to a remarkable degree by desperate ruffians, who, armed with bludgeons, haunt the lanes and attack the passengers. Many robberies have been committed, and persons knocked down. The jails are filled with villains, and there have been discovered on the Black-Boy Road two caves where the thieves deposit their plunder.

March 7, *Tuesday.*—. . . A minute before we turned into it, I observed to Dickon, "Now, if I were in the country to-day, I should hear the golden-crested wren and chiff-chaff." We then entered the lane, and forthwith the song of the golden wren fell on my ear. I was quite delighted, and presently spied out the little songster, and two others flitting merrily about some trees close to a white gate at the entrance of the lane. I stood and listened to the joyous song of this beautiful little bird. How sweet and yet how minute are its notes! It has begun unusually early. I perceive that it sings in a different tone from the golden wren at Woodbury, and the notes themselves are slightly altered. The difference between the Exeter and Woodbury chaffinches is very decided. The different individuals of the Exeter chaffinches also vary; some hurry through their song in a slovenly way, leave out one or two notes, and run those at the end too much into each other. To-day, for the first time, I heard the coal-tit; several were singing, principally that variation of their song which sounds like "chee-ki, chee-ki," slowly repeated. The blackbird, hedge-sparrow, wren, and robin were also singing.

[Here follows a vivid picture of an illogical mind, a thing of which Emily had a keen and rather disdainful appreciation.]

March 11.—Alack! poor girl! she, as I knew before indeed, is utterly incapable of arguing or reasoning. She takes for granted the point in debate, she starts away from the point, she says a vast deal that is quite irrelevant to the subject, she constantly overlooks some little fact or circumstance which entirely alters the matter, and she talks a great deal of nonsense. There is a little casuistry, and a little that is plausible at first sight, but there is nothing that will bear close examination or general application. In short, there is no depth in what she says. Besides, her judgment (though she denies it) is evidently warped by prepossession; she treats the subject unfairly, looks at it through a distorted medium, and deceives herself.

March 31.—. . . The spring of 1833 was one of the happiest times I have ever enjoyed. . . .

I have often, with A., laughed at poets and poetasters prating so much about the pensive recollections called up by the moon, as, for instance, where Montgomery says—

> "The full moon's earliest glance,
> That brings unto the home-sick mind
> All we have loved and left behind!"

But I now think it very reasonable and true, for natural and intelligible reasons, which however, I suspect, have rarely occurred to the poets. The moon, the heavens, and all the heavenly bodies are the only objects which are common at once to all places (of course in one hemisphere), and which can be gazed on and admired at the same moment by absent and distant friends. That very same golden moon, which is gleaming at this moment before my eyes, I have often watched at Woodbury with equal delight, and at this moment, perhaps, is watched there with equal delight by my dear absent relatives. I cannot feel this with any other object. We breathe different air, we tread on different earth, we behold different features of terrestrial nature, we have different homes and different society; but there is one sun for both, one moon, one heavenly canopy; to both, all that is celestial is the same.

April 7, *Friday.*—. . . Just here I was attracted by the cry of a bird quite new to me; it was like the baaing of a lamb, and I instantly commenced a pursuit. I once or twice caught glimpses of it in the tops of high trees, and was able now and then to observe it flying. It seemed to be a slender bird, somewhat of the willow-wren shape, whitish beneath, with black about the head or throat; but in all these points I may be mistaken, for I could see it with great difficulty. From the sound of its cry, I should rather guess it to be a soft-billed bird. I tracked it from tree to tree, from hedge to hedge, from field to field; I crossed and recrossed lane, meadow, and stream, following it by the sound of its voice, sometimes far, sometimes near. The eager delight with which I engaged in the chase reminded me most strongly of past days, when, in full health and strength, I used to ramble for hours amongst the woods and fields of dear Woodbury, in unwearied search of some unknown warbler. Oh, how often have I engaged in this delightful occupation! I have not been able to enter on one of these bird-hunts for almost a twelvemonth, and oh, how forcibly did it recall recollections of home and of old times! Alas! I can never hope again for these enjoyments at Woodbury, which perhaps I may see no more. . . . I was a long time watching the sunset. There were no very striking colours, but the mixture of bright light with heavy masses of purple cloud was very fine. Over the hills, just behind the cathedral, there was a tract of sky which passed from an angry crimson to a kind of dull lurid red. It was continually diminished by the clouds slowly sinking down and burying it beneath their dark heavy pall, but as long as any of it lasted, the cathedral towers shot up into the red sky with uncommon grandeur. Towards the north, there was a very bright pure lemon-coloured light, on which the naked tops of the trees seemed pencilled out with exquisite clearness. But everything below the winding line which traced out the summits of the hills was melted into one undistinguished mass of misty blue; hillsides, city, cathedral (all but its turrets), were confounded in the same dim unvarying shade, where neither shape nor form could be discerned, so that one who knew not the place by day could not have guessed that in that long line of grey evening shades lay a great and populous town. The lights in the western sky had not yet faded away, when the lamps in Exeter began to be lit, and a few brilliant stars of fire seemed suddenly to start into existence from out of the mass of blue in the distance.

April 8, *Saturday.*—I observe more and more the difference in dialect between not only the songs of the chaffinches of Devonshire and Bedfordshire, but the different individual chaffinches of Devonshire alone. One which I heard to-day had a particularly fine variation; he greatly improved his song by the introduction of a clear, liquid, high note near the conclusion. I have not yet perceived that the same individual bird varies at all.

April 10, *Monday.*—. . . In the evening I took up Kirke
38 White's "Remains." . . . I can hardly make out whether I like his poetry or not. He has certainly a great mixture of the original and commonplace, and I must say he generally gives me the idea, not of a self-taught poet, but of one who had acquired to perfection the received language and everyday ideas of poetry. Kirke White was a youth of great genius, but I do not think his genius was equal to conceiving a poem in an original style, though he might be able afterwards to dress it up with an original invention. There is also in him a certain want of taste which makes it impossible for him to put out of hand any completely elegant little poem. Kirke White could not for his life have written Horace's ode, "Quis multa gracilis," etc.*

* We may be allowed here to allude to the justness of her poetical taste and power of judging for herself. A year or more before this, she had detected the merits of a then unrecognized genius, though she knew nothing more of him than the extracts given in an article of the *Quarterly Review* intended to turn him into ridicule. "Those lines,"

April 11, *Tuesday.*—I actually begin the eighth volume of my journal. It seems but the other day I began the first. I was writing it in the drawing-room of Brookhouse; papa, mamma, poor Miss Hall, Lady Malkin, and Sir Benjamin were in the room. Alas! such a party shall never meet again on earth. I well remember Benjamin peeping over me as I wrote, and then, taking up the volume, he read a passage aloud for the amusement of the party. I think I can now see his good-humoured face and hear his pleasant voice as he said, in reference to the part he had just read, "This is quite an insult; you have mentioned Arthur's being of the party at the inn, and you have quite forgotten me;" and I think I can hear the laugh which followed, as all declared that Ben was well punished for his curiosity, while I protested that it was by pure accident that I omitted his name, which he maliciously refused to believe.

The commencement and conclusion of every new volume in my journal always seems a kind of era to me. I expect the one I have now begun to be highly important; it will most probably settle me in Hampshire, and, perhaps, launch me into the nineteenth year of my life. I wonder where

she said, quoting the verses, "And through damp holts, new flushed with May, Ring sudden laughters of the jay," "I am *sure* are good." She praised also (though that too was laughed at) the image of the river, "which in the middle of the green salt sea Keeps its blue waters fresh for many a mile." I need not say that this unknown poet was Alfred Tennyson. At eighteen years old she became acquainted with the "Lay of Elena" in Taylor's "Philip Van Artevelde;" a younger sister, who had picked it out of a volume of that same *Review*, repeated it to her, and the scene was not to be forgotten by those who witnessed it. Already an invalid, she lay on a couch, listening glowingly to that "liquid lapse" of melody and feeling. Occasionally she whispered to herself, "Lovely! Music itself!" then, earnestly, with lifted head, "But, A., I never heard anything like it!" and finally, starting quite up, "The man ought to be canonized who wrote those verses!"—ED.

we shall all be when this volume is concluded; I wonder which of our family will be together, and whether either of my brothers will have entered on any profession or means of gaining a livelihood. But oh, how impossible is it to calculate on the future! . . .

My occupations this day were as follows:—I read the Bible, then worked, then wrote to Julia, then completed an index to the second volume of my journal, then began a note to Mrs. Arthur Malkin. Dinner came; after which I finished the note, wrote my journal, continued my drama, and sealed up the packet of letters which was to go to Lord Mayo. Then I spent some time in reading Kirke White's poems, and then read a chapter of Doddridge's
39 "Rise and Progress." After this, while evening was drawing on, I took up "Gil Blas Corrigé," which occupied me till we sat down to tea, at half-past seven. After tea, I took up my work, and continued it till prayer-time, while Aunt Bell read to us "The Pioneers." After prayers, I went up as usual to undress, came down in my dressing-gown, and sat by the fire, reading the Bible, and looking to see the psalm and hymns which came in turn for me to repeat that night. I then proceeded to curl my hair and go to bed, where, after having repeated a number of hymns and psalms, I fell into a painful train of retrospective thought, which kept me awake for some little time. I looked forward also to the happy time of my return to Woodbury, and I amused myself with watching the scenes which, according to custom, seemed to rise up before my eye. One of these was a deep and awful ravine, between two black stupendous cliffs, down which I seemed to be looking. The scene lasted but an instant, and then vanished. It did not return, and I endeavoured to recreate it by tracing it out with the pencil of memory, but this, of course, produced a far less vivid impression. Finally I fell asleep, and dreamed that I was listening to a duet played by Anna

and Phœbe towards the close of a still and beautiful summer's evening. . . .

Richard declares he saw a great many swallows or martins skimming over the river. It is very early for any species, and extraordinary in such weather as this. If possible, I will go to-morrow, and see them myself.

April 12, *Wednesday.*—In the evening, as I was sitting
by the fire, reading "Gil Blas Corrigé," enter Mr. Dornford. 40
I forget how it began, something led Mr. Dornford to speak of the state of his parish, and of the demoralizing effect of the old poor-laws, especially in destroying the feelings of gratitude and affection in the son towards the father, by taking the latter off the hands of the former, and placing him in the workhouse. He mentioned a frightful instance of this callous insensibility in a man of his parish, who, being very well off for his station in life, having a comfortable dwelling, a spare room, and a wife who had little to occupy her time, refused to support a respectable and kind-hearted old father, who was above eighty and bed-ridden, and allowed him to go to the workhouse. When there, he seldom came to see him, occasionally brought him a bit of meat, gave him no money, and said he could not spare him a blanket, when the poor old man was starving with cold. One day the father was being lifted out of bed by a woman not strong enough to do it, and he fell; she sent for his son to raise him up again, and he despatched one of his men to do it! Finally, the father died, and the son followed him to the grave, wept over him, and donned a smart suit of mourning. Mr. Dornford then enlarged a good deal on the horrible evils of the old system, and showed how, by its old provisions, it encouraged early marriages among the poor instead of checking them. He traced it back to the war, when the farmers, through the high price of corn, gaining immense wealth, considered themselves so raised above their servants and labourers, who used always to share

their meals with them, that they no longer admitted them to the same table with themselves, and the same familiarity as before, which drove them, some to the public-house, others to early marrying, for the sake of getting a comfortable home. Thus the number of poor was vastly increased, and the poor-rates increased in proportion, till in many places they actually exceeded the rent-roll, and became twenty-one or twenty-three shillings in the pound, so that persons have actually found it expedient to give up an estate in order to escape the poor-rates! Mr. Dornford then enlarged a good deal on the difference between the youth of the upper and lower classes, inasmuch as early marriages are checked, as they ought to be, in the former and encouraged in the latter. He then went on to speak of the horrid money-making propensities of small farmers, particularly those about his parish (Plymtree), in whom the desire of gain, being their one object, makes them frugal, sober, industrious, but completely narrows their minds, hardens their hearts, and shuts up all the avenues of charity, of which he gave me the most appalling instances. He says that the effect of the new poor-laws about Plymtree is on the whole good, though there are some tyrannical provisions which ought to be altered; but he says that we have been so long going wrong, that it is impossible to get back directly into the right road, and that much misery must be expected for some years. One evil is the arrangements about medical man, forcing the poor to go to some particular medical man, who may live perhaps eight miles off, and may not be at home when the patient comes, so that he loses an infinity of valuable time. . . .

We also had a long political conversation about Ireland, which is in a most wretched state. Mr. Dornford says that, humanly speaking, nothing can preserve Ireland from civil war but a change of ministry. That the present ministry are endeavouring to throw open the corporations to the

Catholics, on the ground that they are to the Protestants as five to one. That if this is done, the corporations will be filled with Catholics, and become centres of agitation throughout the country, with O'Connell, the master-fiend, at 41
their head. That, notwithstanding they are numerically inferior, yet such is the superiority of the Protestants in lands, in opulence, in education, and chivalric spirit, that if they and the Catholics were to fight it out among themselves, Mr. D. is of opinion the Protestants would conquer. He also stated sentiments about the Catholic Emancipation very different from papa's, which I gave December 19, 1832. . . . Mr. Dornford's style of conversation is peculiar, from its being so full of illustrations, sometimes very apt. I quite agree to one in particular, of which he made use this evening,—that a physician experimenting on his patients is like a pilot in the Pacific, who sounds, and thinks he is in deep water, and then unexpectedly comes on a coral reef. This is just what physicians do, so they need not wonder that their patients die.

April 17, *Monday.*—I am not of those who think the recollection of past pleasures agreeable; I am much more inclined, with Montgomery, 42

> "To wet with unseen tears
> Those graves of memory, where sleep
> The joys of former years;"

and while I write this, I feel a sadness at heart which is quite oppressive. Above all, the recollection of one enjoyment is intensely clear and intensely painful, and that enjoyment is the being able to get out into the open air in spring, or summer, after a long confinement with a fever. Twice have I known this at Woodbury, and the delight of it is heavenly. Willingly would I pay the penalty of another fever, for the sake of enjoying it once more. I seem even now to feel the bright sunshine of June; to breathe the soft and balmy air, fragrant with the bloom of summer; to gaze with delight on the garden blazing with ten thousand flowers; to tread, with slow and feeble, yet delighted feet, on the soft green turf; to see the verdurous meadows and cool leafy woods, to drink in the joyous songs of a hundred warblers. Oh, I seemed in paradise! Oh for those times to return! It is impossible for language to describe my sensations when I was first drawn out in a little garden chair on our lovely lawn, unable to walk, but my heart bounding with ecstasies at all I saw and heard and felt. Oh for summer! Oh for Woodbury! Oh for home, for the sweet scenes I know so well, for the dear companions whom I love so much! . . . Well, I am sure that, wherever my future life will be spent, Woodbury will always be with me "a grave, where sleep the joys of other years." Ten thousand associations and recollections will cluster round its name, like fragrant woodbine round an elm tree. And if I live in the most lovely spot on earth, my sweetest and most delightful remembrances of nature and the country will always be united with WOODBURY. And every brilliant summer day will always carry me back to the gardens, woods, and fields of WOODBURY. And, last, not least, wherever I meet with the friends whose society I have there enjoyed, I shall think again of dear WOODBURY.

April 20, *Thursday.*—. . . I have to give my opinion on Kirke White's poems, which I have finished. This, too, I must do shortly. They have greatly risen in my estimation. I think they display much feeling, and have often great force and spirit. Some passages struck me very much. I extremely like the touching lines beginning—

"'Do I not feel?' The doubt is keen as steel."

To my thinking, the most original idea in all that he has written is as follows:—

> "The lark has her gay song begun,
> She leaves her grassy nest,
> And soars till the unrisen sun
> Gleams on her speckled breast."

I never before met with this idea to express the great height to which the lark ascends, and I like it.

April 24, *Monday.*—. . . The truth is, I am always apt to see things in richer colours at first sight, and then, writing about them while my fancy is yet heated, I unintentionally exaggerate; and I believe I have done this with almost all the scenes I have described in my journal.

May 6, *Saturday.*—Mr. Dornford brought his phaeton at ten o'clock in the morning, and took Julia and me a delightful drive to Haldon, a very long and high hill, which runs along the left of the Exe between Exeter and Teignmouth. I must, alack! be very brief. . . . Above and before us the scenery was wilder than any I have seen. The rocky slope of Haldon is thickly covered with larches, pines, heath, and gorse, and as we rose towards the top, to our right stretched hill beyond hill of wild unbroken moorland.

May 16, *Tuesday.*—The thoughts of my pleasure on the coming morrow long drove sleep from my eyes, and I lay awake in excitement.

[A visit to her cousins at Teignmouth took place between May 17 and June 24.]

May 17.—Well, the wished-for morn is come at last. . . . Mr. Dornford came for us at half-past ten, and we set off in high delight. . . .

May 18 [*Teignmouth.*]—I have been exceedingly anxious ever since I came to see the Warrens, and this evening, to my great joy, Matilda Warren (commonly called Tilla) drank tea with us. My cousins tell me that what they told Matilda of me put her so in mind of a dear friend of hers called E. S., now no more, that it almost made her cry. Of this E. S. Julia gave me an account, extremely interesting, to-day; though where the resemblance to me lies I cannot say. . . .

[A visit to friends at Sidmouth, Bicton, Exmouth, Teignmouth, Torquay, and Marldon occupied the period between May 26 and June 24. On June 7 took place a picnic excursion to Bradley Woods, a merry young party who boated, scrambled, sketched and sang, recited poetry, and read aloud, and dreamed happy young dreams by the sunset and the moonlight. But that summer day, intensely as she enjoyed it, set the seal on the malady she was apparently recovering from. She caught cold, and from that time may be said never to have really rallied, though no one was aware of the fatal harm that had been done.]

June 1, *Thursday* [*Bicton*].—. . . I find William and Richard most delightful companions in walks. They are good, amiable, lively boys, thoroughly fond of scenery, and perfectly well-bred. It is pleasant to have a brother and cousin so civil, attentive, and good-naturedly ready to carry my sketch-book, help me over a stile, or do anything else which I could like them to do. . . .

Our excursion to-day was to Laderham Cove, which is about two miles and a quarter from Bicton, between the Otter and Sidmouth. . . . The descent to Laderham is down a steep little rocky lane, under a lofty cliff, which rises before you in a very striking manner. Having descended this, we found ourselves on the beach, in a magnificent cove, in the shape of a semicircle, entirely surrounded by the grandest rocks I have ever seen. They are red, and not merely perpendicular, but in many places overhanging; they are very rugged and craggy, hollowed by the waves into clefts and caverns, nearly bare, but adorned here and there with a few scattered tufts of grass, sea-pink, and gorse, and crowned at the top with straggling hedges. On each side of the entrance of the cove stands a very lofty isolated rock, washed by the waves; one of these overhangs its base considerably, and looks ready to fall; it is crested with gorse, grass, and stunted pines. I was quite astonished at the grandeur of the spot, and ran up to Miss H., who, with the composure of perfect indifference, sat quietly on the shingles, holding her parasol over her, and looking neither to right or left. "How grand, how magnificent this is!" I cried. "Ah," says she, with great nonchalance, looking round, "it's very pretty, isn't it?" I was thoroughly provoked and marched off.

June 5, *Monday* [*Teignmouth*].—In the evening, as we were taking a walk on the Den, we met Mr. Henry Warren, who frequently walks over from Torquay. He joined us, and walked up and down for some time, and afterwards spent half an hour with us at Spring Gardens. I was very much pleased with what I saw of him; he is decidedly a great improvement on the race of young men of the present day. He is a handsome young man of three and twenty, dark and sunburnt, with curly black hair, and puts me very much in mind of A. Malkin. He has a particularly open, good-tempered, pleasing countenance, most unaffected manners, and is quite gentlemanly (he has been at sea from the age of fourteen). He is naturally very shy, even to nervousness, but is nevertheless merry, good-humoured, and full of fun. It is arranged that he is to accompany us on Wednesday in an excursion we are going to make to Bradley Woods.

June 7, *Wednesday.*—. . . We went by water, and had a boat to ourselves. The Bradley Woods are a mile from Newton, which is seven miles up the Teign. . . . We had a sweet walk through Newton to Bradley Woods. . . . We first walked through lovely woods and lawns, between hills, and along the banks of hidden brooks murmuring in the shade, whose margins were profusely covered with stars of Bethlehem and bluebells. We came to a mill in a sweet spot, deep in a little valley between high rocky walls. . . .

As to giving a minute account of all that we did, that is impossible, for we were amongst these rocks and woods for six or seven hours. Some rambled one way, some another; several sketched, and we were all much dispersed. Nearly the first thing I did was to sit down on an edge of rock amongst the gorse, and sketch the profile of a bold rock and part of the valley. Mr. W. sat a little below me, and sketched the same part. . . . At last we voted that it was time to decamp. I first took a sketch of the two sailors who were lying down asleep on the grass, and then we rose, and having recalled Richard and Phœbe, who had gone exploring, we commenced our return to the watermill beneath the rock. Mr. Warren and I were before the rest; we walked on, conversing about Cooper's novels and other subjects. Phœbe afterwards joined us on the other side, and sketched the mill, which is an old and highly picturesque building, in a lovely situation. Mr. W. sketches very well, and in a free and spirited manner. The others, as usual, were scattered in all kinds of directions, some on the hill, some in the woods by the mill-stream. At last we all assembled in the mill, where we all refreshed ourselves, some with porter, others with excellent new milk, foaming from the cow. We then scattered again, and Mr. W. and R. took a scamper up a hill covered with gorse, in pursuit of a young kite. But notice that we were going to return to the boat was now given, and Mr. Warren, Anna, R., and I crossed the mill-stream, and proceeded on our walk back to Newton before the rest. A. and R. lagged behind, and we three went on together. Mr. W. and I had a great deal of very interesting conversation, chiefly about poetry and natural scenery, of both of which he is a great, admirer, so that we agreed very well in our tastes. He repeated to me a few bits from Byron and Shelley. On arriving at the passage-house we waited some time for the rest of the party, who were delayed by Paulina's tumbling into the mill-stream. I think it was a quarter to eight when we were all safe in the boat on our return. The sun set gloriously over the Tors, and the twilight added to the exquisite beauties of the river Teign. Mr. W. sat next me at the stern, and we talked almost all the way home, partly on the same topics as before, partly admiring the lovely scenery and beautiful heavens, partly about what Mr. W. had seen abroad. . . . So ended our excursion to Bradley Woods, which altogether gave me more pleasure than anything of the sort I ever enjoyed. I only wish A. had not suffered so from headache.

June 9, *Friday.*—. . . It happened this evening that all were in uncommonly high spirits during tea, and jokes flew round with wonderful rapidity. My aunt, having finished her tea, went to the piano, and played a waltz or two. Nothing would serve my cousins but wheeling away the tea-table and waltzing about the room; they made me join also, and showed me how to do it, and good fun it was. The windows were opened, the bell rung, the tea-things hurried off, and the candles sent for; and then the universal cry was for a dance. So my aunt played, and we all formed a quadrille. There were but seven of us, and only one gentleman among us, nevertheless we all enjoyed it excessively, and fun and laughter were incessant. From the quadrille we went to a country dance; then the *coquette* dance, which was capitally amusing; then A. and P. performed the *bouquet* dance, to exhibit before the rest of the company. The two latter are, I think, highly objectionable in public, though of course nothing could be more harmless among ourselves. At last dancing dropped off, and my cousins took to singing. The merriment did not cease; nothing would serve Miss Julia but she must make Anna play tunes for her to sing to. She set us in roars of laughter. She made Anna sing, "I cannot be a nun." After this, several other songs were sung, and it was half-past ten when we began to disperse. I then went up as usual and curled my hair with Anna and Phœbe, and we had plenty more fun. It was eleven o'clock when I went into my own room, but I sat up writing my journal, and was not in bed till near one.

June 19, *Monday* [*Marldon*].—It is after eleven o'clock. I am sitting up in my room, writing this when I ought to be in bed. The house is quite quiet. I hear no sound but the motion of my pen, the ticking of my watch, and the distant moaning of the wind, which sighs through the trees, and occasionally rattles the windows and howls in the chimney. Why, there are two persons talking outside my room! Now all is still again. Now I hear a dog barking. The wind increases, and sounds very dismal. Whose voice is that? Mrs. Gee's, I think. A door is shut, the voice ceases; I look out of the window. Dark and cloudy, moonless and starless; in the south I see a kind of stormy light, like a rent in a pall that hides the day beams; against this I see the tall trees waving their black and gloomy branches. The village lies beneath the hill in deep shadow, save that one glimmering light shines faintly through the obscurity of midnight. Oh, how dreary does it look abroad!

June 22, *Thursday.*—[A visit to Babbicombe.] Never have I seen the sea so beautifully clear as at Babbicombe. The most sparkling summer brook is not more pure and limpid; you cannot gaze on it without longing to taste the wave that seems to roll in liquid diamond. I could not resist it myself. I stooped, dipped in my hand, and sipped the water, salt and bitter as I knew it was. We clambered about the rocks a little, and began to disperse. I mounted an isolated rock which has a narrow ridge up to its summit, where there is room only for two. Mr. H. W. spread his handkerchief for me to sit on, and good-naturedly held my parasol over me while I sketched. . . .

We returned to Torquay. It was a sweet evening, and

I thoroughly enjoyed myself. Mr. W. and I were behind as before, Maria and R. going on much faster. We conversed as before on all kinds of subjects, and I was quite sorry when the journey was at an end. We went to tea, and after tea I sat a little while with dear Miss Warren. I had seen her already before we went to Babbicombe. I love her more and more; I think her almost perfection. It is difficult to stop my pen when once I begin to write of her. She talks to me in the sweetest manner, and likes very much to have me with her, which I feel to be particularly kind, as I am so much her inferior in everything, as well as much younger. Oh, if I were to take any human being as a pattern, it would be Miss W. How I wish I were as detached from earth and as prepared for heaven as she is. How I wish I could cause to my own family half the happiness she does to hers!

June 23, *Friday.*—. . . In the evening Mr. W. told us some very remarkable stories of apparitions and supernatural appearances, for the truth of which he could himself vouch. They interested me very much, and some made me shudder when he told them in the silence and darkness of evening. He himself, like most sailors, believes in apparitions, and no wonder, after he has personally known the following singular occurrence. He happened, during the middle of the night, from twelve to three o'clock, to be the officer placed over fifty or sixty men, who were employed on board an eighteen-gun brig off Port Mahon, which had been sunk, and was now, if I understood him right, being raised again. The men were very merry, and were doing their work to the sound of songs. At last Mr. W. sent down the carpenter, whose business it was at stated times to measure the depth of the water below. He went down with a light, and was absent so long that Mr. W. was alarmed, and sent down another man to look after him. The sailor was presently heard on deck calling from below for a light. In an instant a sudden silence and panic seized all, and Mr. W. descended into the hold with a lantern. Now, a vessel that has been sunk always turns quite black, so that, as may be supposed, its appearance was dismal enough, and in the midst of the gloom and darkness lay on his face the poor carpenter, looking like a dead body. He raised his head, and displayed a countenance of ghastly paleness. He stammered out something about having tumbled down and put out his light, tried to put a good face on it, and followed Mr. W. on deck. Mr. W. saw that something was the matter, and called him aside. "Now, tell me," said he, "what has happened to you?" "Oh, sir, I won't tell you; you will laugh at me." "Why, what is it? I won't laugh at you. Have you seen a ghost?" "No, sir, I've not seen a ghost; but, sir, I saw all my three sisters at the times they died, and to-night I have seen my mother." And it turned out afterwards that his mother did actually die at this very time.

Poor Miss Warren had passed a sleepless night, and her father was also very unwell; so Tilla and I agreed that it would be best for us not to stay another night. Mr. Henry Warren pressed and urged me to stay, said he could not think why we should go, and was extremely annoyed when I persisted; however, he resolved to accompany us to Teignmouth. The fly was ordered at half-past twelve; so I had a whole morning with Tilla. Mr. Warren showed me some capital sketches of his, and his log-book; he begged me to draw one of my sketches into a blank leaf of the latter as a memento of me. I did so, and while I was drawing it, he read to me some beautiful passages from "Childe Harold," a poem which I long to read if papa and mamma would allow it.

I went up to Miss Warren's room to take leave of her, and had a long delightful chat with this angelic young woman. Her affectionate manner to me gave me the most heartfelt pleasure. She was sitting up in bed, looking so sweet and lovely that I could not take my eyes off her. Her writing-case was before her, and she gave me a little pencil note to Phœbe. She made me sit on her bed, and kissed me many times, and was kinder to me than ever. Then, while she held my hand clasped in hers, her eyes full of tears, yet her countenance lighted up with a heavenly smile, she said, "My heart is in heaven, Emily; all my joy and happiness is there." Her countenance, her voice, and her manner were so earnest and sweet, that it quite overcame me. After a moment's pause, she said, "It seems strange that it should bring tears to my eyes, and yet you can understand the feeling that causes them." These were among the last words she spoke to me; again she kissed me, and I was obliged to hurry away. I cannot without tears think of the farewell I then took of Miss Warren; I look back on the happy conversations I have had with her, I recall her most sweet countenance and gentle voice, and I feel a melancholy presentiment that we shall meet no more on earth. Oh that we may hereafter meet in heaven! . . .

We entered the fly and left the place where I have spent the happiest hours I have passed for many months. Farewell, dear Torquay!

We took up Mr. Henry Warren into the fly at a little distance from Torquay, he having walked on before. I enjoyed conversing with him very much. He talked a great deal about his intended journey to Switzerland, which he means to begin next week. He was continually saying how he longed to have me with him, that we might climb the mountains and enjoy the lovely scenery together. He says that he shall be quite alone, with nobody to talk to who can understand his feelings. He means to correspond with Richard. "I must not write to *you*," he said to me, "so I shall write to your brother." He then begged me to write to him just three lines in a postscript to Richard's answers, saying he should value them so much; but this I am afraid I cannot do.

At Exeter.

June 25, *Sunday.*—Mr. W. came to breakfast and spent the day with us. After breakfast we went into the drawing-room, and I read to him several of Keble's hymns. . . .

June 26.—Mr. W. came to breakfast as before, and then he took a walk with us. . . . Here the two boys left us to do an errand in the town, and while waiting for them, Mr. W. and I ascended the castle wall, looked at the view of Exeter, and sat down under the trees, where we conversed for some time. He was not well, poor fellow, and at last resolved, which my aunt had wished him to do, to give up the tour to Dartmoor, and set off for Switzerland on Wednesday. In consequence of this change in his plans, I shall see him once more before he leaves England, as he will call at Baring Crescent on his way. He wishes me to send him every information on literary subjects, the names of books which I should wish him to read, and the best course of study for him to adopt. He also begged me to write out for him some of my favourite little poems which I know by heart, that he may learn them too.

June 28.—I am pining to be at Woodbury. It is now in all its beauty; the drawing-room is perfumed with the China roses, and the garden is in full bloom. Alas! I shall see Woodbury no more.

June 29.—I took a walk in the evening with Jane and Selina Molesworth. The lanes about Exeter, which I used to admire so much, have quite sunk in my estimation after those round Teignmouth and Marldon, for which I am quite sighing. It is hateful to have to walk through the horrid dusty streets and high-roads before I can get into anything like country; and even then it is not solitude, for all Exeter turns out every evening into the lanes and meadows. Richard received a letter from Mr. H. W., who says that he has postponed his journey to Switzerland, and wishes to set out to-morrow to the Dart with R., who is to meet him at the Teign bridge. R. is delighted at the idea of going. Matilda added a page to me.

June 30.—When we were coming from Teignmouth last Saturday, Mr. W. wished me very much to net him a silk purse. I promised to do so, if I had time before he went; but now finding that I shall not, having many other things to do, I purpose making him instead several marks for books, of coloured and gilt paper, which will be useful to him in his studies, and will not take me much time in making. Accordingly, I bought several sheets of fancy paper this evening, and shall set about the business to-morrow.

July 4, *Tuesday.*—My constant fatigue and weakness are quite distressing to me. About bed-time I generally feel brisker, but during the rest of the day the slightest thing is a painful exertion to me; I dread walking up-stairs. Both my mind and my body feel worn out and exhausted; my hands can with difficulty hold a book; and actually I am content on these beautiful summer mornings to sit quietly and stupidly at my needle, alone for any length of time, silent and scarcely thinking, unwilling even to repeat poetry. Besides, I am out of spirits; my mind continually turns involuntarily at all hours of day and night to Woodbury, Teignmouth, and Torquay, where those I love best dwell, and which I shall in all probability behold no more.

July 10, *Monday.*—I shall hurry over this day, not being in a humour to relate, except very briefly, the events and circumstances thereof; in fact, I had rather think of them than write them down.

As we were assembled in the drawing-room at four o'clock,

Mr. H. Warren was announced. He is going to leave England on Friday, and is now come to spend a night in Exeter, and take leave of us. I proposed to go and see the view on the Tiverton Road, to which he gladly assented. So he, Richard, and I walked to Exeter, took a fly, and drove along that beautiful road, returning by the ravine and the lovely Cowley Road. Mr. W. admired both exceedingly, but did not enjoy it, being unhappy and out of spirits, and, in fact, he was more employed in talking to me than in looking at the views. I imagine he speaks more confidentially to me than to any one else; he says he has told no one so much about himself, his feelings, views, and wishes. Indeed, I'm highly honoured; for all the times he has seen me do not when put together amount to a week.

[The next day came the parting; an extract from a letter follows.]

July 17, *Monday.*—A packet from Teignmouth—there was also a letter directed by Julia to Richard; it is written by Mr. W., and is evidently meant for both of us. He has neither dated it, directed it, begun or concluded it; he has written nothing but what I here copy out. "I might have spent another day with you, for Mr. Spencer only returned from Plymouth this morning; this I regret; but, as it must be, as the word 'good-bye' (which like a barrier has sprung up between us) has been spoken, I have to comfort myself with the flattering idea that I am *not* to be forgotten, that the ties of friendship that have been formed are not to be broken, that we are still to know each other. If you but knew the pleasure that this feeling gives me, you would forgive my rhodomontading on it.

"Next Saturday I sail in the yacht for Cherbourg, from which place I intend to steam to Rouen."

[And here the innocent idyll closes. There were some after meetings, but its further progress was stopped, with much suffering to at least one of the parties, and some painful correspondence, by paternal prudence. The preceding extracts, thus brought together, may give the idea that her journal and her mind were at that time wholly taken up with this love affair. But in fact those passages are everywhere interspersed with others which have been omitted, indicating an apparently equal interest in many other things, and filled most especially with her passionate love for Mary W.]

CHAPTER XI.

From July 18 *to Dec.* 27, 1837.—*Exeter, Loder's House, Bartley Lodge.*

July 18.—Well, all is settled. We do *not* go to Binderton, nor anywhere in Sussex, but to the New Forest. . . . A month, a month—and I shall once more embrace and kiss them all. I shall feel once more *at home*, a feeling I have not known for almost a twelvemonth. . . . I shall soon, I think, be sick of Devonshire, much as I have enjoyed myself here. . . . But I regret to find my health going back so much; I know how it will disappoint papa and mamma. . . . The effect of my cold at Bradley Woods (which certainly became a fever at Marldon), together with the heat of the weather and the state of my spirits (for I am anxious and unhappy on many accounts), will certainly account for some of it.

July 31.—The last day of July, which to me has flown very quickly, in so unvaried a manner has it been spent. During its course, one event interesting to us all has taken place, namely, the fixing on a new place of abode; and one event, or perhaps I should say circumstance, of consequence to me personally, which *may* be the beginning of what will affect my future lot in life.

This is the last letter I shall receive from Woodbury. Mamma thus describes their evening party: "We are all round the drawing-room table at nine o'clock in the evening. Papa and your sisters at their *foolish books* [*i.e.* books of amusement]: Mackie out, I suppose, after his moth-catching. The day has been the hottest we have had this year, the glass having been 82½° in the shade. The windows are both open, and the jessamine, that is now full of flowers, perfumes the room. The limes in flower perfume all the air around them. The children say it is delightfully snug."

Aug. 4.—I am highly amused now at seeing the strong and universal interest which is taken in the elections at present pending. The election for the county is the one now proceeding, the candidates being Mr. Parker and Sir J. Buller, Conservatives, and Mr. Bulteel, a Radical. The two first are likely to succeed, and their cause is warmly espoused in this house, especially by the two youths who are continually going to the castle yard to ascertain the state of the poll. . . . "Aunt," says R., as they are assembling at tea, "that abominable boy has been into the town, and I can't get him to tell me anything about it." "Why, how's that, Will?" "Why, he asked me when I was reading." "Well, if you did that, I think he was justified in not answering you." "No, but, aunt, just listen. I said, 'William, have you been in the town?' 'Yes.' 'Where have you been?' 'Elections.' 'And what did you see?' 'People.' And that's all he would tell me." "Oh," says my aunt, laughing, "if he told you *that*, he might as well have told you all, for it must have interrupted him full as much to say 'Yes,' 'Elections,' 'People.' But come, *I* have heard it all." . . .

It is a matter of concern to us that our cousin Lord Teignmouth, who stood for Marylebone, and was thought sure of success, has failed. Another cousin, Winthrop Praed, has just come in for Aylesbury, having withdrawn from Yarmouth. Both these are Conservatives.

Aug. 5, *Saturday*.— . . . On coming home, we were surprised to find our Parliamentary cousin whom I mentioned yesterday, Winthrop Praed,* who had come here to vote, together with his wife, to whom he has been married two years. . . . He is a very clever and very agreeable man . . . about thirty-five years old, as thin as a lath, and almost ghastly in countenance; his pallid forehead, haggard features, and the quick glances of his bright blue eyes are all indications, I fear, of fatal disease. He seems, alas! sinking into a consumption which his Parliamentary exertions are too likely to hurry forward, if indeed he be not in one already. The profile of Winthrop's face is very like that of Lord Byron, and at times there is a sort of wildness in his look, but the usual expression of his countenance is remarkably sweet.

Aug. 7, *Monday.*—This day took place the chairing of the two newly elected members for South Devon, Sir John Yarde Buller and Montague Edmund Parker, for I should have mentioned that on Saturday, Bulteel, the Radical, finding he had no chance of success, withdrew from the contest; and we now hear that the excitement, exertion, and disappointment have made him dangerously ill; nay, it is even reported that he is in a state of derangement. Our party went to see the chairing from Winthrop's apartments in the New London Inn. . . .

We were there at eleven o'clock, wearing the proper colours, pink and blue, which we exhibited in the shape of a pink carnation and blue convolvulus. The chairing did not begin till after twelve. I call it *chairing*, but I should properly have said *horsing*, for at Exeter the members, instead of being chaired, ride round the city in a long procession of horsemen. On this occasion the horsemen assembled first in a dense crowd before the New London Inn, threw themselves into a sort of order, and rode to the castle, where they marshalled, and then the procession

* Winthrop Mackworth Praed, the distinguished poet and politician, was her father's first cousin.

began. Every window was crowded with heads and gay with banners, the street and area were thronged with spectators, and the repeated hurrahs gave notice of their approach long before they appeared. It was a fine spectacle, though not equal to what I had expected. First came a band; then a long line of men carrying boughs of oak, and flags of pink and blue with mottoes of gold; then the herald, a portly man in a sky-blue dress, with a brass helmet and bearing a bugle; then the procession of horsemen, which seemed almost endless. The members were distinguished by their bare heads, their repeated bows and looks of satisfaction. . . .

When the procession had passed, all our party went back to Baring Crescent, except me, Mrs. W. Praed having kindly offered to take me with her to hear the speeches after the election dinner. . . . We three sat down in the inn to a quiet dinner; presently some one tapped at the door. It was Mr. Parker, come to call Winthrop to the dinner, where every one was waiting. So away they went. When we had dined, Lady Frances Stephens and her daughter, Miss Bentinck, friends of the Praeds, came to offer us tickets of admission to the orchestra, where we were to look down on the electors, and to tell us that it was time to come and secure good places. So away we went. We ascended the orchestra, where we had two front places which Lady Frances had kept for us. It was a fine sight, four hundred electors seated at four long tables; the wine and dessert were just being brought in. . . . I shall not assume the office of the newspaper, and detail all the proceedings which took place. I presume they were all much as usual. The chairman gave the toasts, accompanying each with a pompous and prosy speech. As the whole was a scene quite new to me, I was much amused to see the whole body of electors rise at every toast, wave their glasses in the air, and with united voice fill the whole room with hurrahs. I think the most thundering cheers of all were received by the toast "Church and State," and next, perhaps, "The Duke of Wellington." Mr. Taylor, of Bishop's Teignton, a very young man, returned thanks for the "Army" in a speech not worth hearing, which indeed may be said of all that I heard spoken, with one exception, which I shall presently mention. Sir John Buller's speech was perfectly commonplace, and his delivery very bad—a kind of measured, unvaried sing-song. Mr. Parker's was evidently learnt by heart, and was delivered in a solemn, funereal, hesitating voice, in the manner of an ill-preached sermon. Nevertheless both were much clapped, especially when the electors were informed that they had shown their independence, and had made their own choice.

At last was given "Winthrop Praed." Immediately followed shouts of "Praed! Praed!" and a long loud hurrah. Then "Sir Robert Peel and the Conservative Members of the House of Commons," a toast Mrs. Praed and I had been anxiously expecting, as it was the signal for Winthrop to speak, and we knew he would far outshine all the rest.

He rose when the hurrahs had ended. During the preceding time he had been sitting silent, grave, and thoughtful; to my eyes there was even a shade of melancholy across his pale and interesting countenance, as if he had secret forebodings of the result of the unseen malady within him, that malady which is so often the accompaniment of fine genius and deep feeling. But when he had risen and begun to speak, the pensive look was gone, and was succeeded by a union of intellect and animation; his eyes lighted up, and, as he kindled, flashed round him with bright and rapid glances.

His speech was long and excellent, and his delivery ready, natural, and graceful. Both matter and manner were as different from those of the other orators as light from darkness. Sir John Buller's was full of awkward pauses between numbers of sentences; Winthrop's was spoken with perfect ease and fluency. Mr. Parker's was learnt by heart; much of Winthrop's must have been quite unpremeditated, as it referred to what he had just heard uttered. In short, it was quite a treat to hear him, and so the electors thought; they listened far more attentively than they had previously done, and continually gave the most hearty and universal cheers. In Winthrop's speech alone there was point and wit, which frequently produced loud laughter. He wound up very cleverly, and finally sat down amid roars of deafening applause. . . .

Aug. 11, *Friday.*—I must just add a few lines to say that I have taken up the paper, and that Winthrop's speech is most incorrectly reported. I was quite provoked to see it. The mistakes made are ridiculous; all the point and wit are destroyed, and the whole is shamefully abridged. No one would think it a good speech from this edition of it.

I was much amused to read of "the glorious phalanx of ladies who graced the orchestra, whose bright eyes and sweet smiles, from behind the Old English heart of oak, told far more than words how deeply they felt the success of the Conservative cause." Now, I was one of this glorious phalanx, and I think it would be more correct, at least in some instances, to say that their broad grins and hearty laughter showed the high entertainment they derived from the scene. I am sure this was my case.

Aug. 15, *Tuesday. Loder's House, Bridport.*—Uncle Paul, like papa, takes pupils; and his vacation being ended, one came back this morning, for which I am very sorry. He is a Mr. Carden,* of Irish family, and is a very

* Well known afterwards for the attempted abduction of Miss Arbuthnot.

handsome youth, of pleasing appearance; but I understand that he is by no means an agreeable inmate.

From Bridport to Cadnam.

Aug. 21, *Monday.*—. . . The last stage before Southampton is Stoney Cross, eleven miles from that place. Here we put on lanterns, for it was between eight and nine o'clock, and a thick cloudy night. Soon after, the welcome sound of a drag-chain rattling beneath us fell on my ear, and, to my great delight, we descended into deep dark, uninterrupted forest, the road seeming pierced through dense wood. The lateness of the hour prevented my distinguishing much; the trees each successively gleamed with a frosty white, as they came within the area of the light cast from the lanterns, and then each passed rapidly away into the thickening mass of gloom behind. I saw that there must be "interminglings mild of light and shade," though at present the shade was that of night, and the light only the rapidly moving illumination of the lantern and the sparks of fire which streamed brilliantly from the drag-chain as it struck the stones on the road. I was greatly delighted. "At last," thought I, "we have really reached the New Forest." We continued to travel through thick wood till we reached Cadnam, a village about a mile from Bartley Lodge. A little beyond Cadnam, on the roadside, stands a public-house, called the Coach and Horses. Here it was arranged that papa should meet us. The coach stopped; my heart beat quick with expectation. Through the darkness I distinguished two individuals. I knew one of them, who approached the coach-door. I held out my hand; it was seized by dear papa, and I was happy.

At Bartley Lodge.

Yes, at our new home, at that home to which I have looked forward with so many various feelings. But I must tell how we came there. While the footman, William, remained behind with Richard, looking after the luggage, for which he had brought a cart, papa took me under his arm and led me to the house. The coach had stopped at four cross-ways; down one of these, to the right, we went. It seemed pierced through a dense mass of foliage, and the darkness prevented me from distinguishing the glades. In a few minutes we turned out of the road into a path on the left, which took us into deep shade, where we groped about amongst the trees, and even papa lost his way. Presently we came to a gate, and emerged from the dark forest into an open park, where we could see our way sufficiently. We followed a straight carriage road, which led up a slight ascent, and seemed to terminate in a cluster of wood. It was too dim for me to distinguish more. A bright light appeared before us; it was that of a lantern held by our old well-known servant, Mary, to guide our way. She had advanced a little way from the house, and met us joyfully. I could still hardly see where we were going; we passed through a little gate and shrubbery, and came by the back way into the kitchen. Mamma and the children had been waiting here, and looking out for us for half an hour or three-quarters, and at last, in despair, had retired into the drawing-room. Thither papa led me. . . . I shall not describe the evening. It was all joy and happiness. How much we had to tell and to hear; how many questions each had to ask and to answer! I did not this evening see anything of our new house, except the drawing-room, mamma's bedroom, and my own. The first is a large lofty room, twenty-four feet long. I like it better than that at Woodbury. It has a pretty light paper, a very handsome, old-fashioned, carved chimney-piece, and two windows. Mamma's room is just the same size; mine I quite love. It is at the back of the house, and has two windows looking out into the garden and forest beyond. Mary, our servant, had taken pains to fit it up nicely for me, and hang up my chronological charts all round, which was a very pleasing bit of attention in her. When I went up to bed, mamma accompanied me.

Aug. 22.—All went down to prayers before I was dressed; when I descended, I saw a group of happy smiling faces assembled round the breakfast table, a sight to which I had long been unaccustomed.

In a shrubbery round the little wicket-gate I saw a yew tree. I stopped before it and remarked to my sisters who were with me, "I hope the golden-crested wrens will build here; it is just the place for them." I had scarcely uttered the words when I suddenly perceived, suspended from a bough, the elegant nest of the very bird of which I had been speaking. "Why, here's the nest!" I exclaimed in amazement. The young were flown; I broke off the bough and carried my prize into the house.

Sept. 11, *Monday.*—. . . And now I will do what I have long waited to do—describe my room, my dear little room, the possession of which is a true delight to me. I call it my lion's den. It is quite my property, and I feel completely independent in it; I can spend here whatever time I like, sit up in it when all the house are gone to bed and suppose me gone too, and can arrange its contents as I think proper. Everything in it is my own, and everything which is my own is in it.

To begin: it is at one end of the long passage in the second story; its aspect is north-east, looking into the garden; its dimensions are near eighteen feet by twelve feet four inches, and it has two windows with white curtains. On one of the long sides is a four-posted bedstead, hung with moreen; opposite to which is the fireplace, which has a handsome carved chimney-piece. On one side of the bed, near the windows, is a cupboard with five shelves, opposite to which is the washhand-stand; on the other side of it, between it and the door, is a bonnet-press. The dressing-table is between the windows, and at the opposite end of the room are a mahogany chest of drawers and a painted bookcase of five shelves. Before the fireplace stands a little mahogany table, at which I am now writing. The room contains three chairs.

And now I must describe the ornaments of the walls, which consist of various engravings, likenesses, and charts drawn up by myself, altogether fifty-eight in number, quite covering the paper-hangings, against which I have fastened them with pins. The engravings are views, groups of figures, heads, birds, and beasts, etc., besides a framed one of Potton Church over the chimney-piece. The likenesses are shades, cut in full length, representing Grandmamma Shore, my uncle, Aunt D., Aunt B., papa, and William. The charts are tables of chronology, and a set of arguments against dissipation, all fastened to the wall with tin-tacks.

In one window is a chair, in the other a little chest of drawers of chestnut-wood, holding my collection of insects. Between the bed and the cupboard are pegs to hang up cloaks, etc. The cupboard contains, on the first shelf, stuffed birds and large birds eggs; on the second, the nests of the baya and golden-crested wren; on the third, drawing-books, scrap-books, manuscripts, etc.; on the fourth, map-books. On the chimney-piece stand bottles of lavender and eau-de-Cologne, a little writing-box, the bronze-mounted thermometer which Anna gave me, a bag, and a morocco case.

On the table there is nothing just now but my rosewood desk, at which I am writing, a china candlestick, and a drawing-book. Near it is a deal box containing dresses. The bookcase contains the greater part of my library of one hundred and twenty-eight volumes, besides five of my own works bound up. On the top shelf stand also a work-box, a pen-box, a paint-box, and a botanical tin case.

Between the fireplace and bookcase stand against the wall a bonnet-box, a drawing-frame, and a "System of Birds" glued on a board.

Between the bookcase and chest of drawers stands a little cabinet or portable cupboard of two shelves—one filled with letters; the other containing shells, a palette, bottles of gold and silver dust, chalks for drawing, ornamental baskets, locks of hair, etc.

On this cabinet stands a deal box filled with birds' eggs. On the chest of drawers are placed a great portfolio filled with Penang ferns and mosses, a portfolio of my drawings and drawing-paper, a portfolio of maps, a little black leather portfolio containing various miscellaneous articles, my registering book of birds' songs, and two bound volumes of the Diffusion Society Maps.

Between the drawers and the door is a trunk of dresses. On the bonnet-press is a box of minerals and other curiosities, and on the box my large old mahogany desk, and on the desk a work-basket.

And so ends the description of my room, the appearance of which is somewhat grotesque and singular. I like it all the better in consequence.

Sept. 15.—[In a ramble through the glades an adder was killed by the youngest boy.]

Sept. 16, *Saturday.*—I did not ride, but took a stroll with papa about the garden and grounds. Papa took me to the stables, which I had not seen. As soon as we had opened the door, to our great amazement, Mackworth presented himself, and, walking up, exhibited the skin of his viper stretched on a stick. We burst into a fit of laughter. It is quite entertaining to see the silent absorbing interest of that boy in his own pursuits in natural history and natural philosophy. He has not a spark of vaunting or bragging; he killed and carried home this viper without a word of exultation or self-congratulation, as if it had been a matter of indifference to him, yet it has been in his mind ever since. The first thing I saw on coming into the drawing-room in the morning was a pencil sketch he had taken of the animal, and his copy-book to-day contained an account of it.

Sept. 18, *Monday.*—In looking back on the beginning of my illness, I feel sure that one of the principal causes of it was overworking my mind with too hard study, which is no uncommon cause of consumption. For many months before I was actually ill, I tasked my intellectual powers to the utmost. My mind never relaxed, never unbent; even in those hours meant for relaxation, I was still engaged in acquiring knowledge and storing my memory. While dressing, I learnt by heart chapters of the Bible, and repeated them when I walked out, and when I lay in bed; I read Gibbon when I curled my hair at night; at meals my mind was still bent on its improvement, and turned to arithmetic, history, and geography. This system I pursued voluntarily with the most unwearied assiduity, disregarding the increasing delicacy of my health, and the symptoms that it was giving way.

Sept. 26.—I am going to turn author. I am writing some articles for the *Penny Magazine*, which I shall first send to Arthur for his inspection. I shall explain to him, with mamma's high approval, and consult him about it, my plan of publishing a book entitled "Extracts from a Naturalist's Journal." I want to know if the market for such works is overstocked.

Sept. 30, *Saturday.*—. . . My packet to Arthur consists of a letter to him, and a sketch of Ugbrook, and some articles for the *Penny Magazine.* The articles are on "The Golden-crested Wren," "Account of a Young Cuckoo," two anecdotes in natural history, and my "Epitaph on a Goldfinch killed by a Cat." The sketch is meant as a specimen; I want to publish in the *Penny Magazine* a series of views of Devonshire scenery, with short notices of each, and this is to be one, if approved.

Oct. 1, *Sunday.*—. . . My cough is gradually returning with the approach of winter, more than it did last year. My short breath and palpitations of the heart on moving or lying down are very annoying; my heart beats so loud at night that it is like the ticking of a clock. I am subject, too, to pains in the chest and side; and altogether I am very weak and out of health. I feel as if I should never recover the strength of body and unwearied vigour and activity of mind I once possessed. God's will be done, it is meant for the best, though so early in life, when I have but just quitted childhood; it is a painful prospect, and a severe trial both in endurance and anticipation.

Oct. 2, *Monday.*—I am installed housekeeper; mamma has given the whole of the household accounts into my keeping. I am glad of it; it will greatly assist mamma, and will be of much service to me. I am highly pleased at the idea of making myself of use in some way, now that I cannot do it by teaching my brothers and sisters.

Oct. 5, *Thursday.*—I began regularly to-day the plan of study I intend to pursue for some time. The books I am reading are, "Sketches of Venetian History," "India," in
43 the "Modern Traveller," and the "History of the United
44 States" in Lardner's Cabinet Cyclopædia. In the morning, I am up but a short time before breakfast, and am employed in my room in reading the Bible till prayer-time. After breakfast, while my own room is being put to rights, I sit in the drawing-room, employed with the "United States." I first draw out (from the book) a short chronological abridgment of my preceding day's lesson; then I read a fresh portion, of course with maps. Then I go and sit in mamma's room, painting one or two maps, by way of relaxing my mind sufficiently. Then I go to my own room, and study chronology. This I do by

means of my tables of comparative chronology; I carefully read through a portion of one, and then learn by heart all the dates I think it necessary to remember. This occupies me for some time. Then I take up the Venetian History, doing the same as with that of the United States. I then take up the "India." As yet I have not got further than the geography, natural history, etc., so I do not yet abridge it. In these readings of history, I make great use both of my chronological tables and of the Society maps, which I take in. All this occupies me till about two or three o'clock; till tea at eight, I am employed in taking exercise, in desultory reading, in lying down, and in accidental occupations. After tea I read, in the "Biographie Universelle," the life or lives of one or more 45
distinguished individuals mentioned in my English studies of the day, which both keeps up my knowledge of French, and impresses the history more strongly on my memory.

In addition to this, I learn by heart, or rather keep up what I have already learnt, from the New Testament. This I do while I am curling my hair in the morning.

I do not know whether I shall be strong enough to pursue this system of study very long, particularly as my health seems getting worse. Mamma is afraid of my overworking my mind again; still I cannot bear the idea of living, even in sickness, without systematically acquiring knowledge. So I shall devote myself at present to making myself mistress of history, chronology, and geography; the study of languages, mathematics, arithmetic, and the sciences of mechanics, etc., I must leave till I am quite restored to health.

Oct. 7, *Saturday.*—. . . It is no small delight to me
to possess the works of Massinger and Ford. They are 46
amongst the most celebrated of our admirable old English dramatists; Massinger is often considered inferior to none but Shakespeare. They are very little read in modern

times, and I shall have great pleasure in exploring their unknown or forgotten beauties.

Oct. 12, *Thursday.*—. . . I rode on my pony, accompanied only by papa. We explored some lovely glades on the right of the Lyndhurst road, between the road to Mistead and our common. There was nothing to be seen that had life, but the wild deer or an occasional jay, and no sound to be heard but the cries of blue-tits and the whisper of the golden-crested wren. Sometimes on the little open common we fall in with peasants loading a waggon with fern, or a girl carrying a bundle of faggots on her head, and driving home a few cows to be milked, the tinkling of the cow-bell sounding through the arches of the trees.

Oct. 15, *Sunday.*—The first fine Sunday since we have been at Bartley Lodge; but I, of course, could not go to church. Being unable to walk, I sat out of doors for an hour or two in the afternoon, in a little sheltered spot in front of the house, before the eastern wing, which recedes a few feet back. It is a very small piece of grass, between rhododendrons on one side, and laurustinus on the other, with the wall of the house covered with jessamines behind. In front is the park and forest; so that altogether it is a sweet little spot, and I enjoyed sitting here very much. It was a calm, delicious day, the forest bathed in sunlight, the sky a pure pale blue. On my left, close to the wall of the house, is an oak grey with lichens; here I watched the merry ox-eyes flitting from twig to twig, and tapping them with head downwards; and the handsome nuthatch, with his loud clear whistle, running up the boughs like a mouse, and hammering at them with all the concentrated force of his powerful body. In the herbage of the park, I heard the mingled tinkling warble of a dozen goldfinches; the sweet song of the robin sounded from tree to tree. From the forest arose a few melodious notes of the thrush, and the loud laugh of the green woodpecker. A pied wagtail with his cheerful "chippeet" alighted on the roof of the house above me; a lark flew across the park, uttering his pretty plaintive cry. In the garden, the scream of the jay and the chattering of jackdaws completed the gay, though not always melodious, concert.

Oct. 25, *Wednesday.*—It is a great satisfaction to me to find myself daily making a very visible progress in my present studies. I have just finished the first volumes of the Venetian and American histories, abridging each as I go on. With neither of these histories have I been previously acquainted, so that the reading of both adds greatly to my stock of knowledge. I am particularly pleased at the insight the former gives me into the different and complex annals of the great families and principalities of Northern Italy, such as the Carrara of Padua, the della Scala of Verona, and the Visconti of Milan, of whom I before knew little but the name. Really there is hardly any pleasure equal to that of acquiring knowledge. And yet, at the same time, every step we make in the path of learning opens to us so vast a number of endless vistas and newer tracks (just as in our forest rambles), that it quite discourages one. It is hopeless to think of exhausting all the stores of knowledge. In chronology, too, I am making great progress. I really think my memory is improving, which at my age is more than I could expect.

Oct. 26, *Thursday.*—I took up Shakespeare this evening, and read parts of "Hamlet." This is my favourite play; I do admire it most thoroughly. The whole interest, indeed, is swallowed up in Hamlet, but how deep, how absorbing is that interest! His profound melancholy, the struggles and conflicting passions in his noble mind, his painful sense of his own want of resolution, unite in forming one of the grandest conceptions and creations of even Shakespeare's mighty genius. There is no character in any of his plays (at least of those which I have read, and I know all the best except "Othello") which displays such a splendid depth of talent. Nor am I acquainted with anything in the range of the drama so intensely pathetic as the character of Hamlet.

Nov. 2.—Winthrop and Mrs. Praed came to-day, as we had hoped, and we enjoyed their visit very much. Poor Winthrop looks exceedingly delicate; he is so pale and thin that he seems as if a breath would blow him away. . . . He was, as usual, very agreeable, and I like his wife as much as ever.

Nov. 6, *Monday.*—. . . From dinner to tea I was busily occupied in studying those parts of Keightly's "Outlines of History" (Lardner's Cyclopædia), of Russell's "Modern Europe," and of Muller's "Universal History," which relate to the times of Charles VIII., Louis XIII., and Francis I. of France, the Popes Alexander VI., Julius XII., and Leo X., Maximilian I. and Charles V., of Germany, which I have reached in the Venetian History; being of the opinion that to read the history of the same period in different books is an excellent way of impressing it on one's memory.

Nov. 7, *Tuesday.*—. . . I have finished learning from my four charts of general history down to the present time; they are complete in themselves, and begin with ancient history. The first chart contain the histories of the Jews, Greece, Rome, Egypt, and Syria, in comparative columns, to the Christian era; the second, the Roman emperors, those of the East and West, Persia, the caliphs, and miscellaneous history; the third, Italy, the emperors of the East (succeeded, where they end, by Greece), Persia, the caliphs (succeeded by Poland), miscellaneous history, and the Ottomans.

The number of dates out of all these, which I have learnt by heart, amounts to three hundred and sixty-five, and I dare say that I shall add to it continually, besides beginning another set of charts.

Nov. 8, *Wednesday.*—Finding myself stronger, I am resolved to begin again the study of languages. I rather think I shall study Greek one week and Latin another. I began to-day with Greek, and spent about half an hour on it, which is the utmost I shall give to either that or Latin at present. My intention is to resume Herodotus, of which I have already read three books, pursue it regularly through, and, besides, read alternately a speech of Demosthenes and a Greek play. As my time is now so much more occupied, I only read the Indian History every other day.

Nov. 9, *Thursday.*—A horrible accident, accompanied by fearful loss of life, has occurred at Southampton. A rocket, amongst the fireworks on the 5th November, set fire to an oil and turpentine warehouse on the water-side. Nobody was in it; but a number of respectable tradesmen and others rushed to the spot and attempted to save the property, when a large quantity of turpentine within blew up, burying the poor men under the ruins of the building. It is supposed that as many as thirty suffered this fate; several have been dug out, mostly dead, but some few still alive. . . .

Nov. 11, *Saturday.*—. . . I find Herodotus (as I can read it quite easily) so very entertaining. It is as easy to me, pretty nearly, as French, only that I have every now and then to look out a word in the dictionary; and when once I take it up, I find it difficult to lay it down again. Demosthenes is much harder work, and requires close attention.

Nov. 14, *Tuesday.*—. . . This reading of lives is very laborious, and always leaves me thoroughly fatigued. Papa and mamma are both afraid that I am overtasking my brain again. But what shall I do? It is so delightful to be at all able to study again, and I have so much lost time to make up for, that I really cannot restrain myself. Sometimes I am quite disheartened at the huge mountain of knowledge which I have to climb, and feel myself like an ant at the foot of the Andes. Still it is encouraging to see what can be done by exertion and industry, and I am gratified to find myself making a very visible progress every day. I now generally spend the last half-hour or twenty minutes before tea in reading Shakespeare, being then so tired with my matter-of-fact studies as to require some relaxation in the way of works of imagination. I am at present engaged with the "Tempest."

Nov. 15, *Wednesday.*—I have begun to teach geography to Mackworth regularly on the following plan :—I give him the name of some town, as Jerusalem; he is to examine the maps, and find out every town of note on the same degree of latitude; the next day he is to tell me them, and give an account of their situation, and everything he can find in books about their history, natural productions, etc. This is, I think, a useful and entertaining way of learning geography.

Nov. 17, *Friday.*—. . . I usually repeat a chapter from the Bible by heart while I am dressing in the morning, and a chart of genealogy (from about seventy to a hundred dates) while undressing at night.

Nov. 23, *Thursday.*—During this week I have been reading "Romeo and Juliet" to mamma and the three young ones, who all enjoy it exceedingly. . . . I am always obliged, for health's sake, to limit myself in the use of the pen, so I shall only add that, to my mind, one of the most touching parts of the whole play—touching from its exquisite yet solemn simplicity—is that short speech of Friar Lawrence to Juliet, when she wakes in the tomb and finds Romeo dead.

Nov. 25, *Saturday.*—. . . We took another drive to Romsey, where I have not yet been, and I enjoyed it very much. The cottages hereabouts are remarkably pretty and picturesque; the eaves of the roofs project, and are supported by slender columns of the trunks of firs, so as to form little rustic verandahs; the porches are formed in the same way, and are adorned with creeping plants. The entrance into Romsey is strikingly beautiful; indeed, it excels that of any other town I know, except Torquay, and perhaps Hastings, which places have the advantage of the sea. From the top of a steep hill you look down on the old dark-red town lying beneath you, with its noble cathedral-like church towering above every other building, and a rich extent of distant wooded country behind; to our right and left were beautiful green sweeping hills with little dells between them, and their sides and summits mantled with thick woods, now of course nearly naked. The appearance of the distant country from behind the waving outlines of these hills is very fine. We drove down into Romsey by a road bordered with elms, and crossed at the entrance of the town by the pretty little river Test, on whose wooded banks, in a sweet situation, is Lord Palmerston's place. Romsey is a neat old town of some size; the most singular feature in it is a little narrow stream or aqueduct, bricked in, very clear and very rapid, which flows for perhaps half a mile along the side of the principal street, turning two mills on its way, and falls into the Test. It runs close to the houses all the way, and is crossed by little bridges, much in the manner of the stream at Budleigh Salterton. Its clearness is remarkable; every stone at the bottom can be distinctly seen. In most parts I think it cannot be more than two yards across, though it sometimes dilates. . . .

With the single exception of St. Albans, this is beyond comparison the most magnificent country church I have anywhere seen. The size is considerable, and the plan that of a cathedral, with transepts, and side aisles to both nave and choir, and, moreover, a space behind the choir, as in French cathedrals. Nearly the whole church is in the Norman style of architecture, and Norman of very rich character, far surpassing the interior of Ely, or anything at Dunstable. The beauty of the capitals is remarkable. There are some interesting specimens of transition from one style to another, especially in the nave, which is chiefly Early English, Norman arches having been hewn into pointed ones in a very curious manner. The western window is a very fine specimen of plain Early English three tall lancets with deep mouldings, like those at Jesus Chapel, Cambridge. The font is a curious piece of old stonework, which we had not time to examine. There are some Decorated windows, and a beautiful Decorated arch over an old monument; there are several other old monuments and brasses, and many details of various kinds deserving minute attention; but unfortunately we had only a few minutes to spare.

Nov. 27, *Monday.*—. . . I finished "Timon of Athens." I am ill qualified, I know, to pass any opinion on the matter, but if I were to give one, I should say that it was not the work of Shakespeare. Not but that I admire it exceedingly, and think it a noble play, but it seems to me that the style and language are not those of the author of "Hamlet." The poetical descriptions, many of which are exceedingly beautiful, seem to me to be written differently; the choice of words, the construction of the sentences, the cast of ideas, are peculiar; the tone of the dialogues between Timon and Apemantus, in particular, is not like that which pervades most of Shakespeare's scenes. . . .

I think dramatic writing one of the highest efforts of human genius. To excel in it, one must not merely think what it is likely that the characters would do and say in the situation in which they are placed—we must think what we ourselves should do in those situations,—no, rather, we should throw our whole soul into the character we are depicting, and make it, as it were, our own, so as to feel ourselves, naturally and deeply, every passion which racks his soul, and be able to express it by expressing our own unstudied sensations at the moment. How strange it seems, then, that the dramatist, who must thus be personifying himself, should be able, by so doing, to personify so many various and conflicting characters, and to paint passions which in the natural state of his own mind he may have never felt! He must as it were multiply his own character, and create new feelings in himself; all which requires a mind which soars infinitely above the common level.

Nov. 28, *Tuesday.*—I received a letter from dearest Eliz. . . . I do not remember the time when she was unknown to me; she was a dear friend of papa and mamma before I was born. . . . Sometimes it appears but the other day that I saw her last and kissed her last; sometimes, that I kissed her and laughed and talked with her years before she went away; sometimes ages, a lifetime, a separate existence, appear to have passed since then. I can hardly realize it. Indeed, it is now a different existence; life seems changed to me, young as I am, since I parted with Eliz.; one of its chief features is blotted out of the landscape. My heart aches when I think of those past pleasant days, and as I now write this my eyes are almost blinded with tears. So I will think of it, if I can, no more just now. Farewell, my kind, most beloved friend Eliz.

Dec. 5, *Tuesday.*—The unusual interruption of visitors prevented me from attending to all my studies to-day. But when I went up to bed I could not resist the temptation of taking up my favourite Herodotus, and I sat up reading him till after eleven o'clock. I have now nearly finished the fourth book; it is the most entertaining work I ever read.

Dec. 6, *Wednesday.*—I have at last finished the "Thirty 47
Years' Correspondence of Knox and Jebb." I was beginning to get rather tired of it; the second volume is far less interesting than the first. . . . Both had an exceeding

dislike to the Bible Society, their reasons seeming to be that it receives the support of all denominations of religion indiscriminately, and that it publishes the Bible without comment, neither of which appears to me to be any objection. They had a dislike, however, to the whole Evangelical party. By the way, I have a great horror of this division of Christians into two parties. . . . In Devonshire the two parties will not even speak to each other; they each profess to hate the other, and avoid them as serpents; even my cousins say, "If you find that any persons have prayer-meetings, they are of the *professing* party—avoid them!" I cannot bear that prayer-meetings, or the Bible Society, or anything else should be made a test of party. I abhor tests.

Dec. 11, *Monday.*—. . . The sensation created through half the south of England by the late catastrophe at Southampton is really extraordinary, and amounts to a mania. Subscriptions for the survivors and the destitute families have been received from Winchester, Oxford, London, and many other places. Above £4000 have been collected, which is more than is wanted, and is a great pity; for these are not the only objects deserving of charity, and such extravagant aid to these will render it difficult to give adequate assistance to others.

Dec. 12, *Tuesday.*—. . . The little village of Cadnam is celebrated for its oak, which is said to put forth leaves on Christmas Day. This, called the Cadnam Oak, is described in the *Saturday Magazine*. It is a small half-withered tree, with part of the trunk gone, and only one bough left; it stands on a rising ground close to the road, on the banks of a rill, with a vigorous young tree by it, just as represented in the *Saturday Magazine*. We have been talking about this tree lately, and resolving to examine it at Christmas, for it appears that about that time it really does shoot forth. This evening Mr. Trower, who had visited it in his walk with Henry Mallet, brought me two little twigs from it, which he had found with great difficulty high up in the tree. One of these twigs has two young leaves perfectly formed, and the other one smaller ones. The largest leaf is about two inches long. Both twigs are covered with little brown buds, but this is the case also with all trees at this time of year. It is almost a fortnight before the reputed time of sprouting. . . . Even though the oaks and beeches are bare, there is still great variety in the foliage—the contrast of brown woods in the foreground, blue woods in the distance, and, close to the roads, of bright green hollies with scarlet berries, ivy round the naked stems of the oaks, moss on those of the beeches, and hawthorns hung with festoons of ivy and thick grey lichens.

Dec. 15, *Friday.*—Well, it is of no use to go on always struggling with weakness and incapability of exertion. I cannot hold out for ever; and now I begin to feel thoroughly ill. I am afraid I must relax.

Dec. 16, *Saturday.*—I have now concluded my batch of writings for the *Penny Magazine*, and I find it no small relief to be rid for the present of the cares of authorship! I do not think I could have gone on with it much longer, in my present state of health, especially as I am now suffering from pain in the side. How ridiculous that, at the age of seventeen, I should have anything to do with the cares of authorship! It makes me laugh. The articles I have just finished are, "Account of the Willow-wren," "A Tame Squirrel," and "Anecdotes of Dogs."

Dec. 18, *Monday.*—. . . Being as usual wakeful at night,
I could do nothing but think of Matilda and her arrival 48
to-morrow, when a striking couplet of Cowley's, which I have always admired, darted forcibly into my mind—

> "Hope, thou bold taster of delight,
> Which, whilst thou shouldst but taste, devour'st it quite!"

Dec. 21.—Tilla and I fell into a long theological discussion about regeneration, the new birth, and the use of baptism, points on which we disagree . . . It was very foolish of us to enter into the controversy, for we were neither of us qualified to decide on so deep a question. We certainly did not succeed in convincing one another, and ended by ascertaining that, after all, we agreed in loving each other very dearly.

Dec. 24, *Sunday.*—. . . When I was with her (Tilla) in her room at night, she showed me some little pencil notes of E. S.—the only relic she has of that sweet and lovely girl. I read them, small and insignificant as they are in themselves, with the deepest interest; and I could not repress my tears when Tilla again talked about her now sainted friend. I never heard of any one like her; I do not suppose another E. S. ever existed. It is strange I should enter so much into the story of one so utterly unknown to me; and yet I do, as strongly as if she had been my friend too. I seem to have the image of her before me with the distinctness of reality.

. . . The clock had done striking, I jumped up, and stood an instant, saying, "It has struck twelve, and I am eighteen years old." . . .

Dec. 25, *Monday, Christmas Day.*—And am I really eighteen years old? Am I no longer a child, and are so many of the years allotted to me for intellectual and spiritual improvement already past? How quickly they have flown! How appalling is the progress of time, and the approach of eternity! To me, that eternity is perhaps not far distant; let me improve life to the utmost while it is yet mine, and if my span on earth must indeed be short, may it yet be long enough to fit me for an endless existence in the presence of my God.

Dec. 26, *Tuesday.*—Papa spent the evening in finishing to us "Othello." What shall I say of this wonderful, wonderful, most wonderful work? To criticize it were absurd, to attempt an elaborate investigation of its merits were hopeless. The only way in which I can praise it is by speaking of its effects on us all. It harrowed our feelings to a degree I never saw equalled amongst us, and produced an emotion which even astonished ourselves. . . . We could not speak, even to thank papa, or to express our opinion of the play. Neither shall I attempt to do so now, except to say briefly that I think it a work none has or ever can equal; it is the most glorious effort of human genius, and as much surpasses any expectations that can be formed of it, as it interests you intensely while you hear it, and astonishes you with its almost miraculous display of mental power when it is concluded, and you think it over. When I went up to Tilla's room, I found her still with eyes full of tears; she threw her arms round my neck, and said, "Oh, Emily, I wish Shakespeare did not write so beautifully, or I wish your father did not read so beautifully, or I wish I were not a fool!"

Dec. 27, *Wednesday.*—We had this evening a little party. . . . And now, if I chose, I could pen an amusing and ludicrous account of the evening, and hold up to ridicule several of those who formed the party; shall I, or shall I not? I think not, though such subjects would give variety to my journal, and make it far more entertaining to write. It is no little amusement to me to watch and study characters, manners, and faces in my own mind; but to put all these observations to paper would occupy some time, and be very unsafe. And what is the good of representing in a ridiculous light the errors or follies of our acquaintance, or noticing them at all, except to avoid them and profit by the example?

Dec. 29, *Friday.*—I have been peeping, almost for the first time, into the celebrated "Pickwick Papers." My brothers and sisters, and even papa and mamma, who read them with the keenest relish, have long revelled in them, and admire their wit and talent exceedingly. There seems no doubt that they are exquisitely faithful delineations of real life, and also that they have as little coarseness as the nature of the subject will allow; indeed, their talent is unquestioned, except when the author attempts the pathetic. Still I cannot make up my mind to go through them all; a little of them is quite enough to satisfy me.

CHAPTER XII.

From Jan. 3 to June 28, 1838.—*Bartley Lodge, Worthing, Bevis Mount, Jersey.*

Jan. 3, *Wednesday.*—We took Tilla for the first time among the glades in the depth of the Forest. She and I mounted the ponies and proceeded at foot's pace, accompanied by papa and Arabella walking. We went to Minsted by our favourite forest walk. On emerging from the Forest to the foot of Minstead Hill, we did not enter the village, but turned to the right, re-entered the Forest, and went nearly to the keeper's lodge; then turned into the Forest at our right, and passed through a long succession of lovely and solitary glades and commons, till we came into our own common on the Lyndhurst road. . . . In one part we were stopped by a stream, which was dry in summer, but is now very full, deep, and rapid, and runs bubbling and sparkling along through its lovely banks, rugged and winding, fringed with trees and shrubs. The Forest is now filled with streams like this, and most beautiful they are. We followed its course a long time, looking for a place to cross, and hesitating at many spots, for fear my pony should lie down in the water; at last, while papa was looking out for another ford at a distance, Tilla and I encouraged one another, and splashed through, shouting with laughter.

. . . Of all these, by far the most interesting to me was the number for last month of the *Penny Magazine*, which I have been longing to see, for I knew it was to contain my articles. I seized it, but before I had opened it, papa, also in great glee, took it into his own hands, and looked into it while I poured out the tea. My brothers and sisters, too, and even Tilla, were all watching anxiously, and I believe all were delighted to see in the title-page the words, "Account of a Young Cuckoo," and "The Golden-Crested Wren." My feelings were very odd at this moment; I can hardly explain them. So I am actually in print, have actually begun my career as an authoress! I say career, for I fully hope to follow it up. And I have begun it, too, at the age of seventeen, for though I am now eighteen, my birthday had not taken place when these little articles were published. It seems to me very odd. Three articles of mine are now in print—those which I have mentioned, and two anecdotes, and I shall soon see some more. At night, when I went into Tilla's room, she very coolly said, "Emily, if you ever become a very clever woman, and distinguish yourself, I shall certainly write your life, and this night shall enter into it!" "Oh, Tilla!" I said, shouting with laughter, "what a ludicrous idea! That's taking it for granted that I am to die first!" "But I may write your life while you are alive, may I not? I am determined to do it."

Jan. 19, *Friday.*—. . . When I had got into bed, I lay awake for some time, watching the snug appearance of the chamber. The chintz curtains of the windows and bed, the firelight dancing on the ceiling, the prints over the chimney-piece and on all the walls—all looked the picture of comfort. The fireplace is opposite my bed, so I watched the smoke going up the chimney, illuminated by an occasional spark, and sometimes an aspiring flame. It is particularly pleasant to lie awake musing when the room is cheerfully lighted with the fire, and I did so to-night with indescribable enjoyment, thinking of—of—all sorts of things, wise and foolish, grave and gay.

Jan. 27, *Saturday.*—. . So that on the whole I think

I have crammed a good deal of fresh information into my pate to-day, and it is very encouraging for me to know that without any trouble I shall retain nearly all of it. Nevertheless, as often happens with me, in the middle of my reading, the conviction of the utter hopelessness of ever learning a millionth part of all I ought to learn, and of the littleness of what I have already learnt, suddenly darted into my mind so forcibly, that it cast a gloom over me, and, in a melancholy and desponding fit, I felt for a time inclined to give up altogether the gigantic task of acquiring knowledge, and I seriously debated whether I should not do so. But the thought that by cultivating my mind I might render myself some day useful to others finally decided the question; otherwise, had only my own gratification been concerned, I doubt whether I might not have come to a different determination. And this is no new story with me; my despondency at times is almost overpowering.

Jan. 28, *Sunday.*—. . . I also learnt by heart, by reading once over, all that I did not know perfectly of my favourite poem, Spenser's "Hymn of Heavenly Love." I remember the delight I felt when I first dived into Spenser's treasures. I was barely twelve years old, and my attention was first led to him by meeting a few verses of this hymn quoted in
Bowdler's "Selections." I think I relished it as much even 49
then as I do now; the greediness with which I devoured "Mother Hubbard's Tale" and some of his Eclogues. I really think it hardly possible for a child to delight more in poetry than I always did; at the age of ten I could say every syllable of Montgomery's "Wanderer of Switzerland," a poem in six parts; and at twelve I knew almost the
whole of "Rokeby," though I had made no attempt at 50
learning it. It would be very interesting to me to look back and trace the progress of my fondness for poetry, and the gradual change of my taste; I think I could do this in some measure, and I shall try it some day.

Jan. 29, *Monday.*—. . . After luncheon I took Tilla's likeness, while Arabella read to her the second volume of "Devereux." It is very disagreeable to hear one's own work, and "Devereux" in particular sinks amazingly thereby in my estimation. I am quite ashamed of such a trumpery tale; my next, if I ever write another, shall be better, I hope. The style is absurdly florid, and the language of some of the characters is too sentimental.

51 . . . Papa has met Blanco White at Oxford, and describes him as a light-haired, light-complexioned, singularly ugly man, and till he speaks not pleasing, but in conversation highly agreeable. His friends are all devotedly fond of him. How melancholy and how strange that a man like him should not merely have fallen, but relapsed, into Socinian errors! Papa read to us his touching letter to Charles Butler on the subject of Æneas Macdonald's brutal speech. Tilla listened attentively, and when it was ended, remarked, "I do not envy the feelings of Butler when he read that letter."

[Here comes a story of grief, the news of the death of a beloved friend.]

Feb. 2, *Friday.*—How could papa bear it as he did! It is wonderful, for I believe he has lost in Benjamin more than all of us have. It is a loss nothing can replace —nothing, nothing. We have talked of little else all day; our thoughts are—— Oh dear, I cannot write, I cannot compose my ideas. I ought to have taken example from the extraordinary firmness and self-possession of my poor father, but I could not. I wept till I was weary with weeping, and till night, ever and anon my tears burst forth, and would flow. I went to bed, and thought, as I extinguished my candle and found myself in darkness and silence, "We have one friend less in the world."

Feb. 3, *Saturday.*—. . . When we returned to mamma's room, I was struck with the silence—only papa was speaking, and he said, in a tone that quivered, and [with] a look of unutterable misery, "As for me, there were one or two people in the world whom I cared about, and now I have lost one who was more than a brother to me, and whom nothing can ever replace."

Feb. 22, *Thursday.*—. . . I finished the "Fair Maid of 52
Perth." Dwining is overdone; he is too intensely wicked, too exquisitely horrible, for possibility. He is the portrait of a fiend, not a mortal. One cannot enter into or remotely imagine his feelings, and therefore one does not watch his villainy with that sort of interest one usually feels in the progress of crime.

The Duckworths are going to town in about a week. We shall miss them much, for they are the only neighbours we like, and we do like them extremely.

Feb. 26, *Monday.*—. . . The "Adventures of a Younger 53
Son" is a very amusing book. It is hardly a novel, but a slightly connected series of rambling adventures, with descriptions of scenery, and sketches of savage nations in various parts of Asia, threaded together on a very slender string of story. What amuses me exceedingly is that in the plan, the style of many parts, some of the incidents, and especially the character of the hero, it bears a most striking resemblance to my own tale "Devereux." In reading many parts I could hardly believe that I had not myself written them. There is more of story and of character in mine, but mine is much shorter, though I doubt whether it will be when finished. Were I ever to publish "Devereux" nobody would believe that it was not a grossly servile imitation of the "Adventures of a Younger Son."

Feb. 27, *Tuesday.*—For the last few days we have received the *Morning Herald* or *Morning Post* from Lord Teignmouth, to acquaint us with his progress in the election for Marylebone now going forward.

March 3.—The post brought papa a letter and two newspapers; these last we instantly opened and eagerly examined, but they only gave us the state of the poll down to three o'clock. While we were trying to find it, it was perceived that the letter, which had been thrown down disregarded, was from Charlotte Shore, Lord Teignmouth's sister. It was not franked. "Then that settles it," said papa; "he's not elected." Mamma broke the seal; there were but two lines: "My dear Tom, all's well; Charles is member for Marylebone." Then came delight and exultation. We are highly pleased, though Lord Teignmouth's politics are not exactly ours, as he is a Conservative—a very moderate and liberal one, however. But what is of most importance is that he is a man of the highest principle and the strictest honour and integrity. So now papa has two first cousins in the House of Commons.

March 4.—A letter from Lord Teignmouth; it was his first frank, and in a few hurried words announced the triumph of the Conservative cause.

March 5, *Monday.*—A letter from Henry Warren, dated Poole, informing us that he hoped to see us *to-day!* which surprised us not a little. . . . He made his appearance at the hall door about two o'clock, wrapped up in a great-coat which rather disguised his handsome face. I hardly knew whether to be glad or sorry. To see him, hear him, and talk to him did most forcibly remind me of past times and old scenes in Devonshire, when I little thought I should see him here. I was much pleased at being able to introduce him to mamma and my sisters. I was also very glad that he made a favourable impression on all, as indeed he does everywhere, and no wonder. For some other reasons, his coming rather annoys me, and very much surprises me too. But let that pass; he is a very pleasant guest, and his company, during the couple of days he proposes to spend here, will be agreeable to all.

March 6, *Tuesday*.—Our conversation at dinner turned to the New Forest roads, and thence to Calcutta roads, the country about Calcutta (where Mr. Warren has been), tigers, tiger-hunts, Indian affairs, Indian trade, the East India Company, and the slave-trade, on which a great deal of very interesting conversation passed between papa and Mr. Warren.

March 7, *Wednesday*.—Mr. Henry Warren left us early this morning, returning to Poole and to the revenue cutter, on board which he had accepted the situation of first mate. He has spent most of his time since in cruising off the British coast. This led him into our neighbourhood, by bringing him to Poole.

March 12, *Monday*.—. . . There was a sort of fairy beauty in the scenery of the lovely Forest; the blue sky glowed through the delicate embroidered veil of the leafless sprays with extraordinary lustre. The lights and shades, the variety of tints and distances, the purity of the atmosphere, I have never seen surpassed. My heart quite bounded with delight, as we roved from one glade to another, and every minute discovered new beauties in each. We very soon got into a succession of glades and thickets quite new to us, although so close to the house, and we ran about shouting to each other, sometimes plunging in a shady hollow; sometimes standing on a grassy ride or terrace, and looking down on commons gleaming with sunshine and embedded in wood; sometimes following the course of a little rugged, winding stream, now dark in shadow, now sparkling in the sunbeams; sometimes looking down long bright vistas, varied with endless forms of fantastic foliage. Numbers of pretty yellow butterflies were flying about in all directions; the deer were grazing in the heathy openings or half hidden among the trees; the deep calm was interrupted only by the coal-tits answering one another, the "clear joyous notes" of the ox-eye, the soft warble of the robin, and the occasional songs of thrush, hedge-sparrow, and chaffinch.

March 17, *Saturday*.— . . . At dinner, talking of the weather, and late and early seasons, led to the hawthorn, thence very naturally to Glastonbury, thence to the body of King Arthur there deposited. Then a long talk about King Arthur and the authorities for his existence. Then the body of Edward I. in Westminster Abbey. Then Shakespeare's dust at Stratford-on-Avon. This suggested Warwick and its castle, and lastly followed a long conversation about Battle Abbey and the Websters.

March 29, *Thursday*.— . . . On returning I stepped into the garden, and took a peep at the little family with which my rabbits (whom I have named Vincent and Wowski) have presented me. There I saw them, wrapped up in such a quantity of fur that I think Wowski must have half stripped herself in behalf of her young ones. A singular instinct of nature.

54 *April* 3, *Tuesday*.— . . . I finished Racine's "Esther," which I have been reading at odd times. I do not think it possesses much merit besides elegance; there is neither character, passion, nor incident. Only compare it with the last drama I have read, Massinger's "Duke of Milan"! How powerful the latter, how tame the former!

April 9, *Monday*.—I finished "Britannicus," and, for that school of dramatic writing (which it is not fair to compare with the English), I pronounce it a beautiful play. Some passages in it, especially that between Nero and Barrhus, Act iv. scene 3, I admire very much. But the French and English drama are so totally different, and I so infinitely prefer the latter, that I am hardly a competent judge of Racine. His elegance, his harmonious versification, etc., are merits, but they are not the kind of merit for which I have been accustomed to look. A reader of Shakespeare and Massinger, who admires their painting of character, their knowledge of human nature, their unstudied eloquence, their copiousness of incidents, and who is familiar with their wildness, irregularities, rough diction, and disregard of rhythm, is not likely to be much enchanted with a writer who is exactly the reverse of all this, and whose beauties are quite of the opposite kind.

Having finished this, I took a rather different kind of book with me into the garden, the *Penny Cyclopædia*, and sat 55
reading it under the laurel hedge. I fixed on the article "France," and read the portions entitled "Its History" and the "State of France before the Revolution," which last interested me very much. I had not before a distinct idea of the enormous oppressions and grievances of which the French had reason to complain. . . .

The hawthorns are beginning to show their leaves; the park is in some parts carpeted with wood-anemones, primroses, and ivy-leaved ranunculus; the forest filled with butterflies; bats fly in the twilight, the gnats buzz at night, the woodpecker laughs loud and long, swallows are beginning to appear—welcome, welcome, these signs of coming spring! I only wish now to hear the sweet liquid notes of the willow-wren, and the clear, joyous echoing cry of the little chiff-chaff. And when I look upwards, instead of my glance being stopped by a thick leafy screen, I gaze at the deep blue sky through the embroidered veil of the delicate tracery of naked sprays which still reminds me that we have but just escaped from winter.

I have been for some days so busy with the needle that I have not had much time to devote to study. However, I have managed to read in the *Cyclopædia* to-day the lives of the great Elector of Brandenburg and all the Kings of Prussia up to the present one; to look over again the history of Este; and to continue the life of Napoleon. Being very much fatigued with my walk, I was obliged to lie down, and while on my bed I read, or rather skimmed, the reigns of Louis XIII., XIV., and XV. in Eyre Evan
Crowe's "History of France," for the sake of getting a good 56

general view of those times. I also continued exercising myself in dates, and learning new ones.

April 12, *Thursday.*—Mackworth * finished reading with me the first vol. of the "Siècle de Louis XIV." It is an interesting history, and written in an easy, sprightly style.

[On April 14 she went with a younger sister to Worthing to pay a long-looked-for visit to her beloved friends the Warrens. Here she stayed till May 17, then paid a five days' visit at Bevis Mount, near Southampton.]

Worthing, April 15, *Easter Sunday.*—The weather prevented my going to church, and I had some long delightful conversations with Mary. She is truly an enchanting being, and converses most beautifully; it is a privilege to hear her, and to watch her changing, lovely countenance, full of the expression of intellect and goodness, is quite an engrossing pleasure. On whatever she talks, she talks well; her grace of manner, felicity of language, and extreme softness add a charm to the originality of her thoughts and the beauty of her ideas and feelings. But especially the one thing needful is the great engrossing business of her life, the study and delight of her mind. Oh, I wish I had a little time, only to mention the subjects on which we talked, and then all her valuable observations would remain fixed in my mind. But as it is, I am sure I shall forget very few.

16*th, Monday.*—And now at last I have seen the three cousins. . . . We had expected them to dinner to-day, and were anxiously waiting for their arrival. Mary had told us how excessively shy they were, how frightened and silent they would be, and we had had no end of fun and merriment beforehand. Mary said she would put three chairs for them in a row, and would ask them how long they meant to be shy, for that I would minute them, and speak

* A boy of twelve years old.

to them at the end of that time. At last they came; we rushed laughing to the window, and watched the carriage-ful pouring into the house. We shook hands with them, and then they all walked silently to the window in dreadful confusion, turning their backs upon everybody else; I stood amazed and bewildered, Mary laughing heartily. We made an attempt to unbend them, by taking them to our room to prepare for dinner; it was all in vain—we could hardly extract a sentence from them. The face of affairs improved, however, by-and-by, thanks to Mary, who is the life and soul of everything. . . . It is very ludicrous for these girls to be afraid of us, for we are but pigmies compared with them; they are great tall girls whom I am frightened to look at.

April 21, *Saturday.*—. . . I shall always have the image in my mind of the happy smiling circle round the table or the fire; I shall still seem to hold dear Mary's hand in mine, to watch the play of her speaking features, to hear her sweet and changing tones; I shall remember her cap with its long lace strings in the morning, and a black ringlet straying over each cheek, and her crimson shawl and gauze handkerchief, and in the evening her beautifully formed head, undisguised by a cap, and adorned with the long clustering curls, which once grew there; her white throat, and the ample folds of her many coloured Grecian scarf—these are pictures I shall always see.

May 5, *Saturday.*—. . . Oh, it was delicious. It was the first evening walk I have had for seven or eight months, and it seemed to me like paradise. There was just breeze enough to temper the heat of the descending sun; the sky was cloudless, the birds singing joyously, the air scented with wallflowers and primroses; the shrubs were tinted with the fresh green foliage of May. And oh, the soft, soft, cool green turf! I ran about it as if I was still a child; I stooped down and pressed it with my hand; I quite loved it, for it reminded me of spring and Woodbury. I rushed about hither and thither, unable to control my delight; I took off my bonnet, and stood still to let the air blow through my hair and cool my face. I almost felt as if I were once more in the enjoyment of health and strength, in the woods and meadows of my own dear Woodbury. Mary, too, could not resist the temptation of sitting down on the shady grass. I think she was as happy as I was.

May 8, *Tuesday.*—. . . While we were conversing, out ran A., saying that a box had come for me from Bartley by coach, with some Greek words written on the direction card. I went in to see, and was mightily amused to find that, by way of sending me news that my last letter had arrived, without breaking the post-office regulation which forbids sending letters in parcels, papa had written on the outside the short Greek sentence, *ἐξέστι σοὶ μένειν ὅσον σοὶ ἂν δοκῇ χρόνον* ("It is permitted you to stay as long as you think right").

[Description of Cowdray Park.] *May* 15, *Tuesday.*— . . . Deep dells and dingles, filled with the thickest and most varied foliage, winding paths round wooded hills covered with flowers, ascents and descents, views of the rich and hilly distant country now and then bursting through breaks in the thickest, peeps of the little Arun wandering amongst the meadows at our feet, ornamental shrubberies, and wild natural luxuriance of vegetation, cool green shade and chequered light, and the clear sky appearing far, far above through the "delicate leafy veil," spread over us by ancient and lofty trees,—oh, how all these varied beauties made my heart bound with joy! And the brilliant freshness of the young fresh foliage, and the blended songs of blackcap, golden wren, and yellow wren—how I longed for some one to share the delight I felt in drinking in their melody! There was no one who could do so, and I wished for mamma, the only person on earth who can quite enter into my feelings on hearing the warbling of these summer birds.

. . . We got out of the carriage and clambered about the gorse and heath, mounting the highest ridges to see all that was to be seen. As I stood looking—could I believe my ears?—a few notes of the nightingale rose up from the woods below. I listened again; I heard the "swift jug-jug," and, unable to control my delight, sprang up into the air. I had not heard the nightingale (by reason of illness) since 1835, and its sound set my heart throbbing famously.

May 17, *Thursday.*—. . . Alas, the day of departure from dear, happy Worthing! What a dreamlike year will this have been to me! I had a restless, wakeful night; my thoughts were too busy for sleep, and I rose early, to pen a few lines of my journal, and to finish packing. After breakfast I snatched a few minutes' conversation with Mary; the tears fell fast from my eyes as we talked of parting. H. W. was long before he made his appearance; when he entered the drawing-room, I had on my bonnet. His manner was sad and thoughtful; I was anxious to read his face, but dared not look up and meet his eyes. We sat a little while in the drawing-room, waiting for the coach. I had the honour of being the one topic of conversation, for nothing was said but to exhort and command me, with threats and entreaties, to take care of myself, and not to fancy I was strong and overwork myself either in mind or body. I mocked at their preaching, declaring it was nonsense to make me an invalid, and that I could do like other people. I am not quite sure whether this is quite honest, but this I know, that, small as my strength is, I think it is all I shall ever have, and I may as well use it to its full extent. I hate being invalided.

[A visit to a grand house followed, from which we extract a few lines.]

May 17, *Thursday.*—Oh, what a contrast to the quiet,

comfortable little (comparatively) house at Worthing is this great, grand mansion, with its huge rooms, spacious halls, long pillared passages, and endless doors and windows. Our bedroom here would hold three of those at Park Crescent, and the bed is the great-grandfather of all beds. To my great comfort, none of the family were visible on our arrival, and we went up into our room to dress for dinner. We kept dinner waiting, and at last crept down to the big library. There we found assembled the whole awful party of strangers and demi-strangers. . . . The evening passed on. Mrs. —— is most kind. . . . Of course I cannot expect any of that affectionate cordiality on which I lived at Worthing, but I miss it most painfully. The tears came often into my eyes. I am chilled at thus emerging from amongst friends who loved me so dearly, to plunge into a circle of strangers who care for me not at all. Meantime I was half dead with fatigue, and had no kind Mary to place me on the sofa, where I dared not in this grand house place myself. At last they discovered that I was "tired," and hurried me off to bed.

[Ease came after a time and some enjoyment, but she was homesick. On May 21 she returned to Bartley Lodge.]

I must not forget that the first sound that met my ear as we drove through the first park gate was the "jug-jug" of a nightingale close to us, and my heart bounded with delight. . . . I very soon got mamma into her room, alone, and there I gave her the whole history.

[A visit to Jersey took place from May 25 to June 27.]

. . . I must not forget that I took one short last walk round the garden, gave one look at the crimson buds of the rhododendrons and the young foliage of our four favourite oaks, and then re-entered the house with a feeling of regret for all that I was going to leave. When it was twilight, I went into the drawing-room, which was empty; I sat in solitude at the open window, and listened earnestly to the hurrying notes of a nightingale in the Forest. And as I listened and looked, oh, how melancholy I felt! how I longed and longed to enjoy those sweet notes a little longer! For three years I have been entirely debarred from hearing them, and now I have only been able to catch a few passing sounds before they are again silenced by summer. Oh, if I could but have spent May in the Forest!

May 30, *Wednesday* [*Jersey, St. Helier's*].—. . . We sat down under a seat under a shady bank, and overlooked the beautiful bay and crowded town below. While here, my ear was caught by a song quite new to me. I listened and listened. It was a rich and varied note, with an occasional resemblance to parts of the linnet's and blackcap's, and I could not conceive by what bird it was uttered. I commenced a search for it, and after staring up amongst the tops of the trees for some time, I spied the bird in a small sycamore, and I feel almost sure it was the blue-throated robin, which in England is exceedingly rare, and I had never before seen. I could distinguish, at all events, its small head, red breast, and blue round the head and throat. I am quite rejoiced at having added this very uncommon bird to those I know.

May 31, *Thursday.*—From what I have seen of it, I think I should not like the society of St. Helier's at all. It is split into two furious parties, the professedly religious and those not so, who have no intercourse whatever with each other, and, I suppose, hate each other cordially. There are also tests and badges of parties, which I abhor of all things, and if one of the religious party were in any one point to neglect one of these, all Jersey would be in uproar. And all the conversation, all the ideas, of the religious party, seem to me to be pervaded throughout with the essential spirit of gossip and scandal. Everything that everybody does, bad or indifferent, but seldom good, is talked about everywhere, exaggerated, misrepresented, and commented on by all parties. People are continually calling here, and from not one have I heard anything but the most frivolous gossip.

June 1, *Friday.*—. . . I stooped and drank the salt water, for I love everything connected with the sea. Its sight, sound, smell, even taste, all have charms for me—of association, at all events. I longed to run and jump about among the rocks, and on the shingles below. . . .

June 2, *Saturday.*—. . . The most foreign-looking objects are the stone cottages and the pretty picturesque wells by the wayside, arched over with rough stone, and often fringed with fern and flowers and ivy. All the scenery is very pretty, but on a very tiny scale; the hills and valleys are often lovely, but always diminutive, and the grey rocks that sometimes peep out from furze and heath are but imitations of rocks. There is an abundance of rich wood, but none of anything like fine timber; we passed the largest tree in the island, a beautiful and picturesque old ilex. Orchards, now in full bloom, are everywhere to be seen. The lanes are sweetly pretty; they are Devonshire lanes in miniature.

June 6, *Wednesday.*—Every five minutes some little lane opens into the road; these lanes are the celebrated Jersey lanes, which are so innumerable and so endlessly complicated. They are extremely narrow, often scarcely broad enough for a wheel-barrow, and look like long hollow tunnels cut through the trees, winding away from the eye. I should like to ramble amongst them, they look so tempting. On either side of our road lay rich wooded country, but little hill, and no sea, for we were quite in the interior.

June 8.—It was just this time last year, yesterday twelve months, that I was at the picnic I enjoyed so much at Bradley Woods, on the river Teign. Oh, I should like to live that day once more! How very happy was I then, and how clearly do I still remember everything that happened!

June 9, *Saturday.*—We sat down on seats overlooking

the beautiful bay, Ellen looking sweetly pretty, with her little slight figure, long ringlets of rich brown, and beautifully pure white complexion, just tinged with the most delicate pink. She is a sweet little creature. . . .

June 13, *Wednesday.*—. . . How comes it that an occurrence taking place before us often seems perfectly familiar, as if we had known it all long ago? Mary told me a singular instance of this which had happened to herself and her brother Henry. He had returned home after a long absence; it was a summer's evening, and they took a walk together. They turned down a lane with which Henry was unacquainted; at the end of it was a felled trunk of a tree, on which they sat down conversing on various subjects. At last H. suddenly clapped his hand on Mary's mouth, and said, "Stop! I will tell you every word you are going to say." He told her, and then added that the whole walk had seemed perfectly familiar to him—everything they had each said, that very lane, that very trunk, till his heart went pit-a-pat with amazement and perplexity. Again, a scene which we have seen in early infancy, before the days of recollection, will remain in the mind, distinct, but not understood, till in after years it is seen and recognized. Mary says that she was for some years haunted by a scene representing high grey rocks, covered with flowers and foliage, especially mountain-ashes with red berries, all painted with perfect distinctness; but whether it was a real scene, or a creation of the fancy, she could not tell; till, long after, when grown up, she visited Tunbridge Wells, and recognized it in the High Rocks. She had been at Tunbridge Wells when two or three years old, and this spot had dwelt in her mind, though she had no recollection whatever of that period.

The same thing happened to me. I was haunted by a drawing-room with three windows; the arrangement of the room, the door, the furniture—I saw them all distinctly. I saw myself entering, and Richard, then a year or two old, sitting on a footstool, playing with one of my dolls. When eight years old, I went to Bury St. Edmunds, which I had left when three years old, and recognized the room in Mrs. Hall's house, Northgate Street.

June 16, *Saturday.*—. . . When we emerged from these, we saw—let me see, I have a vision of cottages and farm-houses, with their picturesque arched stone wells. These we passed, and began to descend a steep road with high wooded banks. Suddenly we entered a very beautiful green valley, narrow, deep, long, and winding, at every turn the hills which enclose it varying their shape. Little narrow gorges filled with wood run down into it between the hills, and at the bottom are wild yellow flags and orchises. This is St. Mary's Valley, which is about a mile in length. It is one of the sweetest little valleys I have seen anywhere, but it is all in miniature, so that, as we drove through it, it gave me the idea of fairyland, and then I could not help wondering that fairyland should not merely seem so lovely, but so striking. At the last turning of the valley the sea burst on us, and we entered Grève de Lecq, another of the little rocky coves of Jersey, which I am so fond of.

. . . St. Peter's Valley, which I would on no account have missed. It is much larger than St. Mary's, being near two miles in length; of much the same character, only that it is heathy on one side, and wooded on the other. It is very winding, so that every ten minutes it appears in an entirely new aspect, with its knolls, and jutting rocks, and woods, and other little dells running down into it; here and there is an overshot watermill, or a picturesque stone cottage. It increases in beauty the whole way, and I hardly know what part I saw with the most delight. It would be more easy to give Miss N——'s opinion. During the morning's drive her taste had led her to give her principal attention to the bathing-machines, hollow-backed cows, and staring new houses; and in St. Peter's Valley I heard no exclamations of rapture till we suddenly spied a potato-ground deforming the pretty side of a wooded hill. This was "delightful! Oh, quite delightful! really it gave one double pleasure!"

June 23, *Saturday.*—. . . The drive home was by a prettier road, through St. Lawrence's Valley. I do greatly admire the Jersey farmhouses; they are large old stone buildings, frequently covered with vines, and almost always have those pretty, picturesque stone wells, which I am so fond of, arched behind and square in front, with a stone trough before it for the cattle. They are usually covered with grass, mosses, and stonecrops, sometimes with vines, and, when in the hedge-banks, with fern and ivy. These wells, the vines on the cottages, the hedgerow chestnuts, and the gay-coloured tunics of the peasants, are decidedly the most foreign-looking objects in Jersey.

June 27, *Wednesday.*—. . . And so ends our visit to Jersey. How quickly it has flown! It seems in the retrospect as short in space as last night's dream. I have enjoyed it, and I have also been very unhappy. . . . When or where shall I meet again those from whom I am just parted? Not, I think, in Jersey. . . I watched for a long time the receding and lovely shores of Jersey; the bays of St. Aubin's, St. Brelade's, and St. Owen, successively passed away from sight, and in the mean time the islands of Sark, Herm, Jethou, and Guernsey came to view on the other side. I could see how completely Sark is shut in by a wall of rugged grey rocks, almost perpendicular. The sea was rough, and rolled in waves of a dull leaden or inky hue. . . . Alderney by degrees came in sight, and as the others had not yet vanished, we saw all six islands at once, together with a part of the French coast.

The weather constantly became more and more gloomy, the waves blacker and rougher, the horizon more dark and hazy, so that the islands were scarcely distinguishable. . . . Alderney and France were still in view when we passed the Caskets, a remarkable pile of bare rocks far out at sea, crowned with lighthouses. These, too, passed away into the distance, and for a long time there was no land visible but the faint shadow of Alderney in the mist and rain. Finally, this too vanished, and I was delighted to find myself on the wide waste of waters, entirely out of sight of land.

I was determined to see the sun set in the sea. I found that the whole heaven was covered with clouds, except a broad belt of clear yellow light along the western horizon. Into that the sun was going to descend. I saw his orb, blazing with gold, emerge gradually from the clouds and descend through a sky whose tints became every moment more glorious. Every little speck and cloud was gilded almost too bright to look upon. It began to rain, but we could not lose so grand a sight, and stood under an umbrella, with the heavy drops pattering around us. The sea, which near the vessel was an inky black, became towards the horizon a rich lilac, speckled with the deepest violet; but both colours were interrupted by the long narrowing path of light which was traced across the waters. Each black wave, as it rolled past the vessel, as soon as it reached that bright path, became crowned with golden lustre; but all the ocean on the other side of the steamer was grey, dark, and misty. Happening to turn my head, I saw on the opposite side of the heavens a rainbow, resting on the waters. I never before saw a rainbow at sea. We remained on our seats under an awning, and when it was near eleven o'clock, and we were tired of sitting, we curled ourselves up in our cloaks at opposite ends of the seats, and composed ourselves to sleep.

June 28, *Thursday.*—I have not often passed a more sleepless night. If I ever did drop asleep, I woke directly to ask what lights they were watching, and to beg the stewardess to call me as soon as we were near the Needles. This she did before one o'clock. Unfortunately, there was no moon, but I could distinguish the outlines of three masses of rocks, similar in shape to the prints I had often seen of them. I then returned to my couch, and was more successful in my endeavours after sleep.

When I next woke, it was nearly three o'clock. We had almost reached the Southampton pier, and the various vessels were reflected with beautiful distinctness in the calm, motionless water, silvered with the softened light that precedes the dawn.

CHAPTER XIII.

July 1 *to December* 28, 1838.—*Bartley Lodge, London, Ship "David Lyon," Madeira.*

July 1, *Sunday.*—. . . I have been addicted of late to growing faint after breakfast. I do not much mind it myself, only that it alarms papa and mamma. Poor papa is so anxious about me, that one would think every cough I utter is my death-knell.

I suppose I am never to be strong again. It is nearly three months since I have walked into the Forest, and now I am always left behind when others go out. This evening I could almost have cried when I saw mamma, Aunt Charlotte, Cousin Susan, and the four children set forth joyously to ramble in some of the loveliest glades, and poor I was obliged to content myself with the dull drawing-room. It was a sweet, still summer's evening, such as is proper for the enjoyment of the Forest, and I would have given worlds to have gone too. However, I had a partner in misery, poor papa, who is at present equally unable to walk. So we remained quietly conversing at home, and certainly I enjoyed it very much. I grew envious again of the strong party, when they returned at nearly nine o'clock, extolling the beauties they had seen, and bringing in a handful of butterfly orchises, whose delicious fragrance scented all the room, and recalled me to those long-past days when I used to gather them at Woodbury.

July 2, *Monday*.—. . . I remained peaceably in the house till six o'clock, when, though not very strong, I determined at last to attempt a ramble in the Forest. So I set forth with Louisa, Mackworth, and a camp-stool. We were out nearly two hours, and I have seldom enjoyed a ramble much more. We walked first into Mary's Glade, and there sat down. I was in raptures. I never before saw the Forest in its early summer garb. The only drawback was the scanty foliage of the poor ravaged oaks, but the beeches are in all their glory. Thence we went into Tilla's Glade, which is beyond comparison the prettiest immediately round Bartley Lodge. I had not seen it since it was clothed with foliage, and it looked ten times lovelier than ever. The view down over the wood-locked heath below is quite park-like, and has a graceful, ornamental appearance, that seems scarcely to belong to the wildness of primitive forest. Here we sat in the shade, looking down a vista of sunlight. The turf on which we sat was as soft and green and smooth as an artificial lawn; but what are become, as Cousin Susan says, of last year's dead leaves? It was enamelled with a thousand flowers, and every clump of moss and heath was covered with blossoms. From this spot we rambled to Papa's Parlour, and then from glade to glade and path to path with no particular object, chatting, admiring groups of trees, shady vistas, or sunny openings, listening to golden wrens, gathering flowers, and occasionally sitting down in some spot scented with the butterfly orchis. Then we crossed the branch Cadnam road, and, descending through thick fern and heath into dense wood, reached Papa's Terrace, along whose green, flowery ridge we walked, looking down into the verdurous hollow at our feet. Our last halting-place was under a large oak on the edge of the wood, looking over our favourite common, where the pretty deer were grazing in large herds. All these places were new to me since the appearance of foliage;

and I had never before seen the carpet of tormentil, pedicularis, bog-pimpernel, yellow loosestrife, blue milk-wort, eyebright, bedstraw, yellow-rattle, and many others whose names I do not know, mixed with taller foxglove, butterfly orchis, and various heaths, some in crimson spikes, others in pale rose-coloured clusters of bell-shaped blossoms. Mackie was in high spirits, and so happy! now lying on the green turf, now running amongst the thickets and gathering flowers for me, now cutting fern-stalks and showing me the oak tree, now watching the pale green moths that flitted about, now telling me about stag-beetles, red-deer, and buck's antlers, now asking me questions about Mary and Tilla. We returned through Mary's Glade; it was nearly eight o'clock, and the contrasted lights and shades of the beginning of our walk had melted into the softened hue of evening twilight. The park is full of flowers, particularly the meadow-lychnis; M. tells me that a short time ago it was quite blue with the pretty milkwort.

We came to tea this evening with our curls adorned with wild flowers we had gathered in the Forest.

July 3, *Tuesday*.—. . . Now for my reading. First, I read through an amusing play of Massinger's, "The Emperor of the East." Then I took Foster's "Essays." Papa has been telling me he thinks my reading too much confined to mere historical matter-of-fact books, and recommends me to diversify my studies with books on moral and didactic subjects, such as Foster's "Essays," and the "Natural History of Enthusiasm." Accordingly I mean to read them both, and then dive into Butler's
57 "Analogy." I was thinking over, as I lay in bed, what plan I had better now pursue in my studies, for I had come to a pause in them before I went to Worthing. I have resolved to have the following books in hand at once: "The History of India," Foster's "Essays," and Mrs. Somer-
58 ville's "Connexion," either all on the same or on alternate

days. Geography will accompany the first, chronology I shall pursue as before. But oh! languages! how shall I manage that? I must keep up French by the reading of Lamartine. Italian I have begun, and must continue by a vigorous effort and application for a few weeks, to the exclusion most likely of any other, unless I finish "Medea" to keep up Greek, and the "Æneid" to keep up Latin. And in due time I must begin German, which I am sighing for, and which my sisters are already learning. I am afraid I cannot make time for a sixth language, or I should learn Spanish also.

Then I must continue drawing, and teach myself to colour; then there are all the necessary duties of needle-work, household affairs, etc. Well, I think it quite time to be quietly at home again, or my youth will have slipped away before I have acquired any knowledge.

But to return to Foster's "Essays," which I began this morning. I presently got deeply interested in them, read three letters, and laid down the book thinking it one of the most delightful I had ever seen. Many new ideas, the truth of which I immediately perceived, were suggested to my mind; many, which had before struck me, I found repeated; and many, which had floated vaguely and indeterminately amongst my crude notions, I saw put into words, to my very great satisfaction.

July 6, *Friday.*—The eleventh volume of my journal, begun, like the two last, at Bartley Lodge, our lovely home in the Forest, but where it will end I know not.

I always consider this a memorable day to me, being the anniversary of that on which, two years ago, I went to Hastings with the faint hope of its benefiting my health, at a time when I felt dying. Yet it has pleased Heaven to prolong my life up to the present time, as so far to restore my health that with care it may not be materially shortened. Even this, indeed, I sometimes doubt in my secret soul; for though I am not steadily going back, yet I do not go forward in the progress to strength.

My cough, however, is materially better to-day. I even joined the rest of the party for half an hour in drinking tea at seven o'clock at Beechwood, in the garden too, which we found very pleasant. I had not seen the Duckworths for some months. They were very kind to me, as, indeed, they always are to us all. It is but a step from our house, so I walked back by myself half the way, and as I slowly sauntered up the park to the house, I gathered a few flowers to botanize, an amusement I have long neglected. By the time I had ascertained the names of two very common plants—the *Prunella vulgaris*, or self-heal, and the *Lathyrus pratensis*, or tare everlasting, *alias* yellow vetchling—it was too dark for me to examine any more. So I threw myself back in the comfortable beehive chair, and indulged myself in pleasing reveries, much of them audible if any one had listened, for I cannot conquer the habit of talking and laughing aloud when by myself. My thoughts then turned to this day two years. I remembered Hastings; I remembered how I hailed its blue sea, and how the first breath of the salt air revived my languid and sinking frame.

My mind not being capable, under the influence of a blister and a second nearly sleepless night, of any very exalted studies, I again revelled in my favourite old dramatists. I read two plays of Ford's, and have now gone through them all, except one which I do not mean to read. The two are "The Sun's Darling" and "The Witch of Edmonton." The first is not so much of a play as a masque; it is amusing and lively, has no dramatic merit, but many sweet bits of poetry. The "Witch," etc., I like exceedingly, though it has many faults and absurdities; in particular, the nonsense of the merely comic parts, and the unmingled, uninteresting villainy in the character of Frank, for his penitence in the end is too quiet and unnatural to please. But I think many of the pathetic scenes are quite beautiful. Susan is a lovely character, conceived in an utterly different spirit from Ford's other heroines, and calculated to rouse all our gentler sympathies. The scenes between her and Frank in Act II. Sc. 2, and Act III. Sc. 2, are, to my thinking, among the best in Ford's plays. There is much fine poetry in this drama, especially where the witch is introduced. See her opening speech in Act V. Sc. 1.

I next opened the "Beauties of Beaumont and Fletcher," 59
and lighted on some noble passages, which made me regret bitterly that the plays in which they occur cannot be read; that the gifted dramatists should have done themselves such injustice as to render it impossible for the reading public in general to admire, according to their deserts, works strewn with such inimitable beauties.

I finished Foster's first essay, "On a Man's writing Memoirs of himself," and it has given me much subject for thought and self-examination. In point of fact, this journal of mine, which I have continued for seven years, beginning at the early age of eleven, is much the sort of memoir Foster describes. I am sure it is a memoir of my character, and the changes and progress of my mind—its views, tastes, and feelings. But I am conscious that, at the same time, it is far, far from being as complete as with this end it ought to be. Till the last three years, I meant it for little more than a journal of occurrences, deeds, occupations—not of the private state of my mind; consequently it has till lately been a journal meant neither merely for myself nor for any one intimate friend. I allowed most of my friends to see it. Still, even in this state, it could not fail to show many great changes in my mind and ideas, but more those of the head than the heart. For two or three years my journal has altered its character, and since this it is that it has become to me a valuable index of my mind, and has been the record of faults and follies which have made my cheek burn on the re-perusal. I have poured out my feelings into these later pages; I have written them on the impulse of the moment, as well as from the coolness of calm deliberation. I have written much that I would show only to a very few, and much that I would on no account submit to any human eye. Still, even now, I cannot entirely divest myself of an uncomfortable notion that the whole may some future day, when I am in my grave, be read by some individual, and this notion has, even without my being often aware of it, cramped me, I am sure. I have by no means confessed myself in my journal; I have not opened my whole heart; I do not write my feelings and thoughts for the inspection of another—Heaven forbid!—but I imagine the vague fear I have above mentioned has grown into a sort of unconscious habit, instinctively limiting the extent of my confidence in ink and paper, so that the *secret chamber of the heart*, of which Foster speaks so strikingly, does not find in my pen a key to unlock it.

I would this were the case, for it would be very profitable to myself, and might be the means of changing my character, which greatly needs it. I cannot do so in this journal, for its existence is well known; neither would I lock it up entirely from my family and particular friends, for the parts which I leave open afford them so much entertainment that I should not like to withdraw it. Besides, a last and remote consideration, but one which, absurd almost as it is, I choose to take into consideration, should it hereafter happen that I should be married and the mother of a family, I think that much of these records of my own early life may be very interesting and instructive to *them*.

I think, then, though it is with difficulty I am quite resolved on it, this is what I will do. I will continue this journal on my present plan, but I will commence and steadily continue another, into which I shall pour *all* the secret feelings of my heart; my sins, my weaknesses, my progress towards goodness, or, if unhappily necessary, an occasional relapse or decline,—things known only to my conscience and my God—shall all be carefully and daily recorded there. Yes! I will endeavour to do so unshrinkingly. I know the task will be most painful and humiliating, I know I shall seem to be cutting across every sinew of my self-esteem with a blade of caustic; but do it I must. May God give me grace to persevere, and to do it honestly; for if either of these two requisites be wanting, it will be useless. Let me do it, feeling certain that it will never be seen by human eye, and let me take effectual means that this shall be the case.

July 9, *Monday.*—. . . To-day we turned off from the Ringwood road some time before that to Boldrewood, and pursued a grassy track in a new direction, which papa has lately discovered and explored. . . . At last, when on an elevated open spot, covered with heath, gorse, and foxgloves, we suddenly plunged from the open light of day into the soft twilight of one of the most beautiful woods I ever saw. It consists chiefly of tall old beeches, and is a kind of terrace, the steep shaded slopes of which are crimsoned with splendid foxgloves, and through the thick foliage of the foreground, dark and dusky with its denseness, we caught, every now and then, peeps and glimpses of the distant blue woods, gleaming in sunshine. . . . We lingered in this beautiful grove for some time, then returned to the wild open heath, and drove down a long, steep, difficult descent, a little to the right, till we plunged into another wood, in a hollow at the bottom. We left the carriage and wandered about. As in the other, it was radiant with the natural jewellery of foxgloves and sunbeams.

July 14, *Saturday.*—Here is a query, which I shall be

able to answer decidedly at the end of this volume, most likely before. What is indicated by all these symptoms—this constant shortness of breath, this most harassing hard cough, this perpetual expectoration, now tinged with blood, this quick pulse, this painfully craving appetite, which a very little satisfies even to disgust, these restless, feverish nights, continual palpitations of the heart, and deep, circumscribed flushes? Is it consumption really come at last, after so many threatenings? I am not taken by surprise, for I have had it steadily, almost daily, in view for two years, and have always known that my lungs were delicate. I feel no uneasiness on the subject, even if my ideas (I cannot call them fears) prove right. It must be my business to prepare for another world; may God give me grace to do so!

July 15, *Sunday.*—. . . I read this afternoon (besides the Lesson for the day) 1 Sam. xvi., and I cannot understand why, in ver. 18, David is described as a mighty, valiant man of war, at a time when he was but a stripling who took care of sheep—as is mentioned, too, in the next chapter.

It is nearly eight o'clock, and I have been alone for the last hour, for all the rest (how I envy them!) are gone to enjoy a walk in the Forest. . . . Eight o'clock! Little grey clouds tinged with pink are floating across the south-west sky. All the Forest in shadow. . . . Oh, here they come—merry voices—not like mine, for it is a great effort to me to speak at all, and often difficult to utter a few words audibly.

July 16, *Monday.*—. . . I amused myself in bed with some of Scott's lesser poems, and, reading the "Poacher" for the first time, was surprised to find that the scene is laid in the New Forest, and that Malwood is even mentioned by name. But I take leave to doubt whether Scott knew anything of the scenery by personal inspection, or he would not have talked of a sea of birches and copses of hazel! I do not believe a hazel is to be seen throughout the whole extent of the New Forest, and sure am I that it is only in some parts you can find, here and there, a straggling birch. It is dangerous to attempt describing country you have not seen.

It is painful, however, to be the object of such constant care and anxiety to my parents, especially my poor father, who has harassment enough in his wearing profession without my (innocently) adding to it. It is impossible to describe how he watches me, and how, without being fidgety, he catches at any glimpse of my being better. I am sure there never was such an affectionate father.

July 18, *Wednesday.*—. . . I must not forget that in the lovely bit of forest I mentioned there is a stream, choked with trees and spotted with yellow water-lilies, around which the ground is boggy, and completely covered with a profusion of a low shrubby plant which I never saw before. Papa gathered me a bit, and I found it to be very sweet-scented, though out of flower. I brought it home, with the rather hopeless intention of ascertaining its name. 60
Oddly enough, I remembered that in Crabbe's "Birth of Flattery," which I read the other day, there occurs the line—

> "Gale from the bog shall yield Arabian balm,"

with a note to explain that this was a plant called "Myrica gale." Somehow I thought this might by chance be my plant, so I looked for the name in the index to Withering, and found that the description exactly agreed, except that, as it was out of bloom, I could not examine the flower. I make no doubt it is the same. In English it is called sweet gale, sweet willow, or Dutch myrtle.

[From February, 1838, to the present date, July 20, the journal is very largely occupied with the return to England, after six years' absence, of the very oldest and dearest friend that the writer had. But this return was under such melancholy circumstances, and the expressions of love, pain, and pity, during the expectation and at the reunion, are almost monotonous, and so mixed up with morbid depression from the poor journalist's own sinking health, that it has been thought better to omit the whole of this subject (which takes up pages on pages), save a passing word or two.]

July 20, *Friday.*—The dream is over, the long dream of absence (how short it now appears!), and Eliz. is restored to us at last. Alas! how little we all thought that this would be the awakening!

July 23.—Our favourite, Mr. Howard, arrived late at night, after most of the house were gone to bed.

July 24, *Tuesday.*—Mr. Howard made his appearance when everybody had done breakfast. I was very glad to see him, which I have not done for two years. He has just the same amiable, thoughtful countenance, and the most simple, pleasing, unaffected manner as ever. He has just been at court, and says that the queen is a pretty, pleasing girl, and very graceful.

While papa and Mr. Howard went in the afternoon to call on the Paultons, on the Romsey road, another party of us took a lounge in the Forest, amidst the glades near Minstead. I rode the pony; mamma, Eliz., Arthur, and my sisters walked. I enjoyed it very much, and my spirits were all the better for it. Arthur enters delightfully into the beauties of the Forest, and so indeed does Mr. Howard.

This ramble, I fear, has occasioned me a loss I feel bitterly—the little cross of Gibraltar rock given me by Mary Warren, the only keepsake of her I have. I missed it just after dinner from the chain at which I wear it. I searched vainly for it over the house. I have not an ornament I could not better spare, and it has saddened me all the evening.

What share the weakness of my bodily health has in it I cannot exactly say, but I feel myself sinking into a gloom and melancholy I cannot describe. I have a sort of hermit-like, misanthropic feeling. I fly to my own room as much as possible. I am quite pining for entire quiet. I have more constant depression of spirits than I have ever known before, and seem to have lost all interest in my occupations. I feel almost as if I shall soon have done with this world, as if my studying days were quite over, and as if I had no longer any interest in the busy scenes of life. In this mood, all other circumstances touch me and harass me much more than ever, especially the state of my father's health, and all he is continually undergoing from the toils and anxieties of his wearying profession.

I am much pleased to see the good effects the presence of Arthur and Mr. Howard have on papa; he delights to show them the Forest, as well as to converse with them, which he does as with brothers, for I think we have no two friends with whom we are on such intimate terms. Papa is roused and animated by them, and the exercise he takes with them improves his health.

July 25, *Wednesday.*—The first thing that I was saluted with in the morning was my recovered Gibraltar rock cross. . . . The bustle in the house distracts me; I enjoy one thing, and that is to listen to the conversation of papa, Arthur, and Mr. Howard.

July 26, *Thursday.*—. . . We passed a very merry evening. Mr. Howard was much amused in looking over the old pencil likenesses of the old pupils which I used to take when a child, and the conversations in which he and others figured. I made Mr. Howard read aloud, for the edification and very great amusement of the company, Arabella's imitation of Wordsworth. . . . We hear that Mr. Howard wrote to Mr. Stanley that the happiest part of his life was spent at Brook House.

July 27, *Friday.*—Mr. Howard, I am sorry to say, leaves us to-morrow, to stay two days at ——. He says he has enjoyed his visit here very much; he has certainly seemed to do so; he is perfectly at home, and talks and looks just as he used to do.

July 28, *Saturday.*—. . . In the afternoon we all sallied forth into the Forest, taking the little pony-carriage, which carried, at different times, mamma, Eliz., and me, at foot-pace. . . . This was Mr. Howard's last walk with us; immediately on our return papa drove him to ——, whither he had delayed going till the last moment possible. And so ends one of the pleasantest weeks (except to me) that we have ever had; the three friends who are the very dearest we have all in the house together, a circumstance which never happened to us before.

July 29, *Sunday.*—. . . Mr. Howard called on us this evening after church. I doubt whether he much enjoys his visit at ——.

July 30, *Monday.*—. . . I was delighted to-day with Medea's soliloquy when meditating the death of her children. It is one of the most pathetic pieces of dramatic poetry I know; equal to anything in Shakespeare.

Aug. 6, *Monday.*—It is odd, when Eliz. talks of India, to hear her so often mention her friend Mrs. Trevelyan, for this is actually Mrs. Charles Trevelyan, sister-in-law of Mr. Otto and all the other Trevelyans who are such dear friends of my cousin's. I have heard of her and her wonderful memory, and how she can repeat Pollok's "Course of
61 Time" all through.

Aug. 10, *Friday.*—Oh, Mary! you are still to me something like a fairy dream, too beautiful to be real—a being so pure, so perfect, so lovely, even here so angelically fascinating, that I can hardly believe heaven can add a charm to her; and yet I can actually feel and know that she loves me amongst those she loves most dearly. This is the strangest part of all, and the most painful; for very painful is my shame to think I am so different from what she thinks me to be.

It so happens that all my friends are older than myself. This is just as I like, for I feel it is my disposition to cling to another, and look up to her for her affection. I should feel crushed, not injured, by an unkind word.

Aug. 12, *Sunday.*—. . . I believe mamma was frightened to-day by my difficulty of breathing; I breathe three times to her once. Meantime what I crave most is *quiet.* QUIET! QUIET!

Mackie caught a very fine snake in the Forest, which he means to keep and tame. He brought it to me as I was lying down, and let it glide about the bed. It is a beautiful creature. And when lying down in the evening, I had another rather remarkable visitor. I heard a murmur of voices at the door. It opened; enter Arabella, saying, "Yes, here she is;" then Louisa; then Gertrude, laughing; then papa, carrying in both arms an ENORMOUS cat, which George Duckworth had brought to show us. It is fifteen years old, quite deaf, and having once been tabby, is grey with age. Really I never saw such a huge creature. Papa was quite delighted with it.

Aug. 13, *Monday.*—. . . Eliz. has given me a chain made of her beautiful rich brown hair before she left England. I have generally worn a pretty little chain of *bought* hair, and when people have asked me "whose hair is that?" I have been mortified at being obliged to answer, "Nobody's." *Now,* when asked the same question, I shall be able to say it is the hair of my best and dearest friend.

Aug. 14, *Tuesday.*—I spent some hours of the afternoon and evening in the garden, sitting in an easy chair on the grass with desk and book. Eliz. joined me, reading Vathek. We were silent companions, except when we paused at half-past five to regale ourselves with coffee. At last I closed my book and looked around me. It was after seven o'clock; perfect calmness reigned around, not a leaf of the four great oaks was stirring, the air had a slight moisture of coolness, the sky above was pale, unclouded, and of liquid clearness, while through the trees at one end of the garden flashed a few rays from the western sky, denoting a brilliant sunset. "Let us go round and look at the sun," said Eliz. We rose; she gave me her arm, and we walked to the front of the house. The exquisitely-clear outline of the trees traced on the glowing and painted skies behind, the various distances of the thick Forest, each mass softened into a different shade of blue or grey—all formed a scene of quiet beauty, which filled me with such deep delight that my limbs felt stronger, my step more elastic. I thought I could have walked anywhere and to any distance. We walked up and down the gravel path for some time, conversing and drinking the loveliness above and all around. The thought crossed me once or twice, "Will this be the last evening walk I shall ever take?" I was so revived, so brightened up this evening, that it was like a lucid interval, perhaps the last in a long illness.

Aug. 15, *Wednesday.*—Mamma and the children stopped at Beechwood for an hour during their evening walk, and came home loaded with flowers which Mr. Duckworth had kindly sent me. I am quite grateful for the interest they take in me, and the constant kind attentions they are always showing me, now sending me fruit, now flowers, or offering to take me a drive, and a hundred little things I cannot name. Indeed, their kindness to us all is remarkable; from the first they have thrown off all ceremony, but the *delicacy* with which they do us all these kindnesses is most remarkable. Mrs. Duckworth is one of the most pleasing women I know—a union, rather uncommon, of very pensive and very quiet manners, with great warmth and kindness of feeling in *appearance* as well as reality. Mr. Duckworth is as pleasing in his way. . . .

Aug. 22, *Wednesday.*—Mackworth mentioned an odd circumstance about a wasp which he was going to kill by smashing it under a little pen-tray. The wasp, seeing itself confined only by the leg, which was squeezed between the window and the tray, proceeded to set itself at liberty by biting its leg off.

Aug. 24, *Friday.*— . . . The inscription which I have
written (*i.e.* am going to write) on the other side of the 62
page was composed by Mr. Macaulay for poor Benjamin's monument,* and an admirable inscription it is. There is not a word in it which is not strictly true, as papa says; and there is not a single quality mentioned for which he was not eminently distinguished, above perhaps any other being I know. And it is difficult to say which of them shone forth most, and was most obvious to sight, unless perhaps his most unruffled temper.

* Inscription on a tablet erected in the Cathedral, Calcutta—

"This monument
Is sacred to the memory
of
SIR BENJAMIN HEATH MALKIN, KNT.,
One of the Judges of the Supreme Court of Judicature.
A man eminently distinguished
By his literary and scientific attainments,
By his professional learning and ability,
By the clearness and accuracy of his intellect,
By diligence, by patience, by firmness, by love of truth,
By public spirit, ardent and disinterested,
Yet always under the guidance of discretion,
By rigid uprightness,
By unostentatious piety,
By the serenity of his temper,
And by the benevolence of his heart.
T. B. M.
Dec. 7, 1837. "Born Sept. 29, 1797. Died Oct. 21, 1837."

Aug. 27, *Monday.*—. . . The Duckworths called for mamma and me at two o'clock, with two carriages, to take us with them to see Embley—a gentleman's place near Romsey. The party consisted of [ten people]. Embley
63 belongs to Mr. Nightingale. The great beauty of the place consists in the approach to the house, a drive of three miles through most beautiful deep shrubberies and plantations; part of the way the road is bordered by splendid rhododendrons. There are rich extensive peeps of the distant Forest through breaks in the foliage; the ground is rich with fern and heath, and under the woods with ivy. The house is an old brick building in the Elizabethan style, now undergoing repair. There are some formal gardens with a very long gravel walk, which Mr. Duckworth says is so like the style of Louis XIV., that one always imagines people with hoops walking in it.

Aug. 31, *Friday.*—My chronological tables and French history were my chief occupation. I am quite passionately fond of history; I believe I could almost devote myself to it, to the exclusion of nearly every other study. I have already acquired a great huge mass of it, and every day adds a very substantial portion. I read the life of Sobieski. I must remember the battle of Choczim, fought 1673.

Papa and mamma dined with the Duckworths, and we were left to drink tea by ourselves. We had a very merry evening, notwithstanding the absence of mamma, who is to me quite sunshine; I am generally altogether dull and gloomy without her. She is not yet home. What a brilliantly bright moon is before me!

"As fixed as if it grew
In its own cloudless, starless lake of blue."

So now we quite bid adieu to all that looks like summer. —Oh, what a sweet, serene farewell! The evening is so calm that I believe I could almost hear the rose-leaves falling.

Sept. 2, *Sunday.*—I read Jeremy Taylor's second 64
sermon on "The Flesh and the Spirit." I think he here, as is not uncommon, states rather unfairly the anxiety of men to acquire gold, which he represents as for its own sake entirely; whereas he should not have overlooked the fact that gold is valuable and coveted, not for itself, but for the very great advantages to be gained by it—influence, power, rank, the gratification of luxury, the means of benefiting ourselves and others, etc. Now, it is all these things, not the mere word "gold," which he should in fairness have put as the counterpoise to the benefits of religion. But altogether the sermon is very admirable and eloquent.

Sept. 8, *Saturday.*—I am exulting over the completion of two charts of chronology; the one, which I mentioned yesterday, of two pasteboard sheets, I have revised, glued and nailed to the wall of my room; the other, of Este, Savoy, and Brandenburg, on one sheet, I finished this evening, but have not nailed up. I have been working at it most indefatigably and laboriously, spite of weakness and fatigue. I spent nine hours to-day on these tables, being resolved to finish them, which was not done till after ten at night. I did nothing else all day, except a little of the Greek revolution at odd times, and two pages of the life of Washington.

Some of our party again drank tea with the delightful Duckworths. . . . Nothing can exceed their kindness to us, especially to me as an invalid. "I wish you could find something for us to do for you," said Mr. Duckworth on going away; and this feeling seems to be the key to everything he does. . . . I am sure Christian benevolence is a family quality. . . . We never meet the Duckworths without having sensible and interesting conversation; we have few acquaintance here of whom we can say the same. They are every way suited to us, and most fortunate are we in having such valuable friends.

Sept. 11, *Tuesday.*—Mrs. Duckworth called for me in

the carriage at three o'clock, and I had a delightful drive. . . . It was the very perfection of an autumn day—calm, cloudless, hot, yet with a cool clearness in the air. . . . We halted on a very elevated spot, before a pond or "tarn;" cattle were grazing round it, or standing still in it, reflected in the quiet water; on the further bank were a herd of deer just on the brow of the hill, with the blue country beyond. The whole formed a scene of delicious repose; it seemed as if Nature held her breath.

[On Sept. 12 the invalid went with her mother to spend a fortnight at Southsea.]

Sept. 16, *Sunday.*—Oh, how beautiful was the scene! The water like a pure glassy mirror; the ships distinctly reflected, their long masts tapering to an infinite length. Then came the Ryde steamer, polluting the pure air with its abominable tail of smoke, and disturbing the stillness with the thumping of its paddles,—like a shopkeeper's apprentice, tramping along and smoking his pipe. . . .

65 In Watts' "World to Come" I lighted on a notable piece of blundering, in the answer to an objection against the existence of a separate state, "How comes death to be so often called in Scripture a sleep, if the soul wakes all the while?" To which Watts replies, "Why is the repose of man every night called sleep, since the soul wakes, as appears by a thousand dreams?"—as if the word "sleep" had a meaning independent of the repose of man; as if it ever meant anything before it meant that repose! Why, sleep is an arbitrary term, not applied to the "repose" from any peculiar significancy or applicableness. The word was created for the thing—it did not exist first; and death, when called a sleep, is compared to the thing, and not the word. The proper answer should have been that this circumstance about the soul is only another circumstance of analogy between death and sleep, or something of that kind.

[*A visit to the "Britannia" frigate at Portsmouth.*]

Sept. 17, *Monday.*—. . . . What an astonishing triumph of art is this immense fabric, this floating city! I do not think the grandest palace, the noblest cathedral, ranks so high amongst the most wonderful works of men as a first-rate line of battle ship; and, to me, the spectacle had all the overpowering charm of novelty. But I am not going to give any account of the *Britannia*, as mine must be necessarily imperfect, will be no help to my memory, and can in no wise, except in its imperfection, differ from ready-made printed histories. It is hard to say what I most admired, or what most astonished me; perhaps it was the enormous bulk of the spare-masts and yards which lay on the deck. But, indeed, all was astonishing; the perfect order that reigned everywhere; the ingenious contrivances for accommodating everybody and everything, even to a cow, sheep, and poultry; the storeroom and armoury, where tools, weapons, etc., are arranged in symmetrical figures on the walls; the huge chain-cables, the vastness of the masts and bowsprit penetrating the lower decks, the immense capstan, the supply of fresh water in the hold, the—but really I do not know where to stop in enumerating all that struck me. The number of decks, too, struck me; I thought we should never have got to the bottom. The highest part of the ship is the poop; then the quarter-deck and forecastle, where there are no guns. Below are three gun-decks, to wit, the main deck, middle deck, and lower deck; below this last is the cock-pit, where the little middies sleep in the dark; below that, the hold. So that there are seven stages from the highest to the lowest part of the ship's hull. By-the-by, nothing gave me so impressive an idea of the gigantic size of the ship as looking down over the stern and seeing the enormous depth below. I was surprised that so much space could be spared for the state-rooms, which are really very comfortable; and the stern-walks pleased me much.

[On Sept. 20 they left "ugly, amusing Southsea" for Brighton, on a visit to a friend, Miss Benyon.]

Sept. 25, *Tuesday.*—. . . Now I have seen the Custs. Mamma called there early, and I joined her at once, in a fly which had taken Miss Thompson to a bath. They are at 153, Marine Parade. The first thing I saw was Reginald's head at the window; the next instant the door opened, and Lady Anna Maria and Lucy greeted me with the most affectionate cordiality, kissed and welcomed me with hearty kindness. It was a true delight to me to see them once more, after more than two years of separation. I know hardly any friends I should have had more pleasure in meeting thus. But, alas! one is wanting since I saw them last; and in poor Lady Anna Maria's pallid face and altered manner I could too easily read the effects of that bitter loss. All the briskness, the liveliness, the *brusquerie* of which some complained, are quite gone; she has softened beautifully, but all her natural frankness and thoroughly sincere cordiality remain. There is an equal improvement in Lucy—a beautiful, graceful, most striking-looking girl, who formerly had a slight *hauteur* or air of superiority which somewhat spoilt the amiableness of her appearance. Now she is not only beautiful, but lovely—gentle, mild, engaging, both in countenance, voice, and manner. Nothing can exceed the kindness to me both of Lady Anna Maria and Lucy,* and afterwards of Mr. Cust when he entered. They promise to call on us as soon as they can, and wish us to spend a morning with them. Unluckily we are almost at opposite ends of the town. . . .

To Lucy I have feelings of warmer friendship than I

* "Lucy" died some three or four years after the writer of these lines, and on her death-bed, after speaking of her sister, to whom she should soon be reunited, she said, "And I shall see Emily again."

ever had before. . . . Her exquisitely fair complexion, light hair, blue eyes, fine features, noble figure, and air of dignity and rank would unite to form no bad representative of Rowena. . . . She is a clever as well as amiable girl; I believe a truly good one too.

Oct. 5, *Friday.*—Mr. Wishaw, still wishing to take me
a drive, yesterday sent "his compliments, and wished to
know at what hour he should call for Miss Shore the next
day." This kind offer we accepted; named half-past two,
and dined to-day at one. At the appointed time he and
his chariot appeared, and we had a drive of nearly two
hours, which I found very pleasant, for he is a very agreeable man. He is very infirm with age, is nearly blind, has
a cork leg; and now and then a momentary wandering or
absence seems to indicate something like the incipient
decay of mental vigour. Nevertheless, he retains his con-
versational powers and his remarkable memory; his information is extensive, and his manners pleasing and benevolent.
He is rather deaf, and my weak lungs rendered the effort
of making myself always intelligible rather fatiguing; however, I exerted myself, and got all out of him that I could.
He told me, amongst other things, an interesting circumstance respecting Mrs. Marcett's "Conversations on Chemistry," which, being read by the bookbinder to whom it 66
was sent, struck him so much that it turned his attention to
that science; he studied it deeply, and is now the eminent
Mr. Faraday.

[*Return to Bartley Lodge.*]

Oct. 11, *Thursday.*—. . . I found in my room, when I
returned to it, two books which I had ordered before I left
Bartley—Vertot's "Révolutions de Suède," in two little 67
vols.; and Dunham's "History of the Germanic Empire,"
in three vols. of Lardner's Cyclopædia. I looked over the
latter; it seems to be much less a history of mere events

than of the constitution, laws, and manners. This, if well done, must be very interesting.

Oct. 13, *Saturday.*—. . . I read an article on "Domestic Service," which is signed "H.M." * I was very much interested by it. . . . Surely it is the most absurd idea to attach the notion of favour to the mistress's performance of her part of the contract, and to teach the servant that she owes gratitude for the same. Gratitude, forsooth! Why, what should we be without servants? We should be much worse off without them than they without us. The hardships to which we universally subject our servants on certain points have long been a matter of reflection in my own mind, and on some of them I had come to the same conclusion as the reviewer. But I think he a little exaggerates the jealousy and ill will existing between the two parties; at least, I do not think it is universally so strong. And there are certainly instances of perfect confidence and friendliness between mistress and servant, as I very well know.

Oct. 14, *Sunday.*—. . . I read Knox's essay on the opinion of the Church of England respecting baptism. I wish, if possible, to be able to form some opinion respecting this most difficult subject; and I shall read whatever comes in my way relating to it. I see that papa does not like discussing the matter, so I shall think it over to myself. As yet, I confess I cannot see more in the ceremony than a sign of the infant's being admitted into the outward and visible Church of Christ. For what is meant by the regeneration at baptism, by those who suppose (as John Knox does) that the child is *spiritually* regenerated? I suppose the new birth spoken of in John iii. But, then, does not this necessitate the new birth taking place twice in that immense majority of cases in which the individual grows to years of discretion without any trace of the Christian principle supposed to be implanted at baptism? For in

* By Harriet Martineau.

all these cases a complete and entire change must take place in the heart before the individual can be changed. Now, this I take to be the *new birth.* If it is not—if baptism be the new birth—why,. then all have been born again, and what is the use of the very strong impressions to imply that we *must* be born again in order to be saved? And is there no term in the Scripture to express that great necessary change from sinfulness to holiness in after-years?

Oct. 23, *Tuesday.*—. . . Our thoughts are now turned more seriously than ever to emigration. Papa really wishes, if he can manage to raise the money, to go out next year. . . .

Oct. 30, *Tuesday.*—Still Australia, Australia—nothing but Australia! nothing else engrosses our thoughts from morning till night. Our plans and prospects there are the constant subject of discussion; the only difficulty is the want of money, and this we hope to find means to raise. . . .

But oh! it will almost break my heart to leave England; to leave my native country and all my friends, for ever! It is dreadful; but I know too well that it must be, and that objecting is equally absurd and wrong.

Oct. 31, *Wednesday.*—. . . I then read several lives of Russian sovereigns. Being determined to discover some book where I might find the missing links in my chart of chronology, I examined every work I thought would help me, and at last, to my great joy, found in one of the "Companions to the Almanac" a complete table of Russian Czars. I am very glad I did not find it till I had gone through all the useful toil of reading, comparing, and examining, which is far enough from labour lost.

Nov. 2, *Friday.*—. . . Herodotus, history, and chronology are at present my only studies, and, with needlework, almost my only occupations. This sort of health deprives me of all energy, all strength, and I can study nothing fatiguing. I am longing to read Nichol's astronomical book which Mrs. Duckworth has lent me, but do not feel able. I wonder at myself; I am such a different creature from what I was three years ago. Since then I have lost the blessing of health—now, I believe, for ever.

Nov. 4, *Sunday.*—. . . The Edward Twopenys come to-morrow for a few days; then immediately come Arthur and Marianne; then shall Mary come, or I shall never see her more.

Nov. 6, *Tuesday.*—I have just heard it, but I know nothing more yet—the difficulties are found to be too great, and we cannot go to Australia. . . .

I have now heard of another plan suggested by Edward. . . . He proposes to us to go out to Madeira. The climate would, in all likelihood, restore papa's health, which is breaking fast; living must be much cheaper there, and papa would take two little boys as pupils. . . . Probably there would be in Madeira an ample field for a tutor like papa. Papa might also engage there in some literary work, which would just suit his taste, and perhaps be very successful.

Nov. 7, *Wednesday.*—. . . Journalizing has lost its interest with me. I am dreary, dispirited, and ill. . . .

The only occupation I pursue with any interest is that of increasing my knowledge of chronology. I have in the last few days learnt perfectly a hundred dates.

Nov. 8, *Thursday.*—I began Nichol's book on the "Solar System."

Nov. 14, *Wednesday.*—. . . I, meantime, was up in the clouds, ay, and beyond them, amongst the fixed stars and
68 the most distant nebulæ the telescope has discovered. I was beginning Nichol's "Architecture of the Heavens," and could not put it down till I had read nearly a third of the book. Astonishment, delight, admiration, almost overpowered my imagination and thoughts; if I enjoyed the other book, I devoured this.

Nov. 16, *Friday.*— . . . I devoured all the rest of Nichol's "Architecture of the Heavens," and laid it down with feelings of astonishment and delight, which I cannot describe. What wonderful views does astronomy give us of the immense extent, variety, and harmony of creation; and above all, of the infinite mind of its Creator! Can any astronomer be an atheist? It is not possible. I have no words to express the intense eagerness with which I followed, step after step, the demonstration of each amazing truth, and saw the beautiful (I can use no other epithet) ingenuity with which Herschel and La Place have discovered proofs of their wondrous theories.

Nov. 18, *Sunday.*— . . . A letter from Mr. Astell relieves one anxiety, by announcing that he can now actually give Richard his writership, and that he must be examined in January. . . . It is a Bengal writership.

Nov. 22, *Thursday.*—Another alteration has been made in our plans, suggested, I believe, by Arthur, and which has many great advantages. It is that mamma should take Louisa and me to Madeira *immediately*, before the rest of the party. The principal reason is my health, which every week is becoming of consequence as winter draws on. . . . The plan is an excellent one, though I confess my eyes filled when I heard it. Another parting and separation! Besides, it renders it nearly impossible now for me to expect to see dear Mary. However, the thing being settled, I sat down and wrote to tell her the state of things, and to wish her farewell if she could not come. I did not think it right to *press* her, on her father's account. . . .

Since we go so soon, I must quickly begin my farewell letters. I must write to Miss Kenyon, to my cousins, and Lucy Cust. I never expect to see any of them again; for, even if it were not our intention to settle in Madeira, I do not think I shall live to return to England. My cough seems fixed to my lungs.

Nov. 25, *Sunday.*—This is the last Sunday I shall spend in England. Letters this morning inform us the *David Lyon*, 460-ton West Indiaman, will sail from the London Docks next Wednesday. . . . As the ship unfortunately does not call off Portsmouth, we must go to town on Tuesday morning. . . . The Malkins kindly insist on our occupying their house at 21, Wimpole Street.

Nov. 26, *Monday.*—. . . The post brought me at last a franked packet from Worthing. It held a letter of introduction from Archdeacon Webber to the Rev. Cyril Page, a letter from Henry Warren to mamma, a note from Tilla, and a closely written letter from Mary. It is a most affectionate letter, and I was quite overcome; I burst into an agony of tears. I can see her no more—now I know it; and I can hardly endure the thought. Her father has had a return of the inward bleeding, and she could not venture to leave him, or she would have come immediately on the receipt of my letter of last Monday. . . .

When dinner was over, and the dessert was laid on the table, we drew round the fire, and formed a grave and saddened group. Papa produced a little black bottle of forty-year-old Constantia, and we all drank, in a most melancholy manner, to another such meeting in Madeira, while I believe each felt in their hearts that it would never be. . . . That awful packing! it seemed as if it would never be done; and certainly it never would, but for our kind, kind friends. Most of the house were up half the night; mamma was not in bed, I believe, till long after two.

Nov. 27, *Tuesday.*—. . . I was up at half-past five, when papa followed the servant who came to light my fire, and asked how I was. He had actually been sitting up all night, writing letters. . . . We were too hurried to be melancholy; we had not time to let our thoughts dwell on parting. When I had swallowed some breakfast without any appetite, I went up to my room for the last time, to finish my wrapping up. I looked round it—all my books and charts and prints the same as ever; it did not seem as if I was bidding it adieu for the last time. . . . Arthur accompanied us in the fly to Southampton, to see us safely into the coach. We went—we bid adieu for ever to Bartley Lodge, and to the lovely New Forest, which, as if in compliment to us, still retains its tinted foliage. The sudden, hurried manner of departure seems to have numbed and hardened my feelings, and they would not flow. It was all the better; for instead of the agony of grief I had anticipated, I could not shed a tear. I took leave of all calmly, and though when I kissed dear, dear Marianne, perhaps for the last time, the tears came into my eyes, yet they did not fall, and it was a very quiet sorrow. Marianne's pale, sad face was the last thing I saw at the window as the fly drove off, and hurried us away from scenes we loved so much.

At London.

I never before entered London after day had closed, and was perfectly surprised at the superb effect of the gas-lights in every street and shop, the long rows of glittering lamps, and, above all, the concentrated mass of starry lights seen across the Park, which had the effect of enchantment. The coachman was accommodating, and agreed to set us down at our destination. It was six o'clock when we arrived at 21, Wimpole Street, where we found a fire ready in the drawing-room, and all ready comfortably to receive us. I found waiting for me a kind letter from my dearest Mary, containing a little myrtle-leaf, which she tells me to keep till we meet again. She talks of the possibility of our meeting in Madeira. We sat down to a snug dinner, and during the evening had a conclave of friends. First came Mr. and Mrs. Keal to wish us adieu. Next, our grave, excellent cousin, Lord Teignmouth, whom mamma congratulated on his approaching marriage with a Miss Caroline Brown, said to be "a prize both in mind and person." I had a good deal of talk with him about Norway, and he informed me that Inglis' book, which enchanted me so much, is not much to be depended on. Then came in our most kind cousin, Edward Twopeny, with his friend Captain Jones, who, though personally unknown to us, has been our friend during all the Madeira business. . . . He is a blunt, downright sailor, all kindness, good temper, and honesty, with a rugged sun-burnt face, and rough grizzled head. . . . Oh, with what kind friends are we surrounded!

I have never been in London at this time of year before, and am disgusted at the fog, smoke, darkness, and most uncleanly atmosphere.

Nov. 29, *Thursday.*— . . . All is for the best, and I am sure this has been most strikingly the case with us; everything even which we regretted having afterwards turned out for our advantage. As, for instance, this delay of the ship's sailing, which annoyed us at first, has been productive of the most essential good. Richard breakfasted with Mr. John Shore, and brought us a table of the Portuguese duties on imports in Madeira, which perhaps has half saved us from ruin. They are absolutely immense, inconceivably so. We knew that the duties were high, and that the Portuguese custom-house officers are very apt to seize all *new* articles of British manufacture; but it now appears that the duties themselves are so enormously high as to amount, in many cases, to prohibition. Every article of every description, without exception, if not used, pays duty. All dresses, for instance, not made up, pay duty; and if they *are* made up, if they have not been worn, the duty is four times the value of the original article!

. . . So many encouraging circumstances and the kindness of so many friends have quite cheered dear mamma;

her spirits revive, and she feels much happier and more composed, which rejoices me much.

Dec. 1, *Saturday.*—. . . We certainly are rich in friends, even amongst those who know but little of us.

Dec. 2, *Sunday.*—. . . It is now a little after eight, our last evening together, our last evening in England. This time to-morrow we shall have bidden Richard a long farewell. We are all round the table writing, but we cannot help continually alluding to our novel circumstances; and we have all agreed that this last week, in Wimpole Street, has been a most happy one. Especially to Richard, who has seen much more of us than he has done for a long time; and besides, has had great amusement in going about London, making calls and seeing sights. We leave him rich in friends; he has kind and warm invitations from Lord Teignmouth, John Shore, George Shore, Miss Duckworth, Mrs. Duckworth, Miss Pym, and many others, besides all our relations; so that he will have plenty of homes during his Haileybury holidays.

Dec. 3, *Monday.*—We were up at half-past six, breakfasted at a quarter to eight, packed up our few remaining things, and were ready when the hackney coach came at a quarter to nine. Captain Jones arrived not long after, and we were all packed in, and started for the West India Docks.

It was a very fine morning, and our drive through the city was on the whole pleasant enough; there was neither crowd nor impediment, and we were amused by seeing public buildings with which we were unacquainted, such as Christ's Hospital, the India House, Newgate, and others. . . . Our luggage being put into the boat first, we followed, and in two minutes were alongside of the vessel.

Aboard the "David Lyon."

Richard first scrambled up the side of the ship by a rope-ladder; then mamma, I, and Louisa were by turns hoisted up in a kind of chair, and swung upon deck. We were immediately sent into the cabins, to be out of the way. . . .

However, in course of time, Captain Jones took us all by turns up to the quarter-deck, and I was much amused with seeing the tiller-ropes that move the rudder, the binnacle where the compasses are, the coops where the unfortunate ducks and fowls are kept for our benefit, the vegetables suspended on ropes, etc. . . . The air was cool and very refreshing to me, after having tasted none of it for some weeks except what I could snatch from coach-windows.

Soon after this we were introduced to the captain, who had just come on board. . . .

Captain Jones soon after walked into the dining-cabin where we were sitting, and said, "Mrs. Shore, here is a gentleman who declares he knows you." With these words he produced Mr. Barrett,* who was going as far as Gravesend, and who, as we were before aware, had known, or at least had met, mamma when she was a girl at Casterton. He shook hands with us most cordially, and very much pleased us with his frank, good-natured countenance. He resembles the portrait of Porson; and we all stared when Captain Jones said, "Now, would you believe it, he had the assurance to tell me the other day that he was turned fifty?" In fact, he looks little more than thirty.

. . . We heard that we were near Gravesend, and that the temporary passengers must immediately prepare to enter a boat.

. . . This was the summons to part with dear, dear Richard, and it was a very bitter parting. I will hurry it over. I have nothing to mention but floods of tears, a few broken expressions of heartfelt grief, and a last long earnest gaze through the stern-windows, following the boat to shore till it was lost among the shipping. . . . We did not sit down

* This gentleman was the father of Mrs. Barrett Browning.

to indulge our grief, but proceeded to divert our thoughts by occupation. I must not forget our parting with our kind, excellent, valuable friend Captain Jones, who has really been to us like a brother, so that we felt comparatively friendless when we had lost him too. He called hastily for Richard, then walked up to us, and finding us drowned in tears, he made the parting as short as possible. He shook hands warmly with us. Mamma attempted to express her gratitude to him. "God bless you, ma'am!" he said; "God's with you, be sure!" and so he hurried away.

I had observed about the ship, and at dinner, a seaman-like man whom I concluded to be the mate, and to whose appearance I took an exceeding aversion. . . . He has a small active figure, which on deck is always darting agilely about, but in the cabin has a sort of angry erect stiffness, varied by an occasional fierce short movement of the head, when giving an order or seeking for anything. His face is thin, and of that scarlet look which so speakingly indicates an addiction to spirituous liquors. Everything in his face, which has almost the expression of a demon, tells of a temper the most furious and passionate that can be imagined. I never saw so horrible a countenance—it was revolting; and yet, with a common inconsistency, I could not help continually looking at him while he sat opposite me at tea, bolt upright, stiff, and silent. His small, quick, bloodshot grey eyes, rolling about continually, their whites glaring hideously amidst the crimson of his face; his sharp features, close curled hair, short red whiskers, and firm compressed mouth, whose thin lips when he is busy on deck seem constantly opened to emit fury, and ever quivering with suppressed or muttered rage, all formed a picture truly terrible to behold. I thought he must be a most unhappy as well as fierce-tempered man.

. . . We retired to our cabins at about half-past nine; watched, as we undressed, the brigs and schooners that floated past our stern-windows, their white sails gleaming in the moonlight; listened to the rush of waters whenever a steamer hurried by; and at last scrambled into our little cots, and fell asleep amidst a silence so great that we could almost fancy ourselves in the depths of our beloved Forest. And so ends our first day on board the *David Lyon.*

Dec. 4, *Tuesday.*—. . . I saw for the first time a ship in mourning, *i.e.* with a stripe of blue paint. There was a whole fleet of fishing-boats at anchor, and we were much amused with seeing the fishermen dragging up their nets full of small fishes, looking like bags of silver. . . .

After dinner the gentlemen did not let us retire—indeed, there was no warm room to retire to—so we three ladies merely betook ourselves to the sofa and stove, while they sat over their wine. The conversation was kept up entirely between Captain Selby and Mr. Houghton. The mate sat stiff, determined, and sinister at the bottom of the table; the heavy man (who I think is the pilot) sat grave and silent, and Mr. Cross seemed too shy to talk. The captain and Mr. Houghton fell upon politics, and discussed the aristocracy *in toto* and individually, to the great amusement of mamma and me in our dark corner. At length Mr. Houghton came and seated himself by us, and talked to mamma. I got up at last from the sofa, and followed mamma from the hot room to our cool cabin, where we looked out of the window, saw that all was dark and gloomy, and returned with our work-boxes, with which we went to the table. We entered into a long conversation about Madeira and the West Indies, the climate and its victims; thence to the slaves, the Baptist missionaries, the mischief they are declared to have done and to be doing; then to the subject of Dissent and Dissenters in general, the reasons and causes of it; the state of the Church, the former neglect and present zeal of its ministers, the violence of party spirit and faction, the differences of religious opinions, the low state of religion in the upper classes—subjects which I should not have expected to discuss with a West Indian captain and a Madeira merchant! The good captain was amusingly vehement about the neglect of the clergy, and the consequent spread of Dissent, and I think, with the best intentions, went a little out of his depth.

Dec. 7, *Friday.*—. . . Again I saw Ryde and its half-mile of pier; again the pretty terraces of Cowes, to behold which Louisa and I rose from a lesson in Portuguese pronunciation which Mr. H. was giving us. On we went through a narrow channel, bounded on one side by the island, on the other by the Shingles, which the tide rendered just visible. The coast of Wight became more bold and bare, with dark-coloured heathy hills terminating in rock; and at length Yarmouth, with its church and houses, appeared through the little side window as if in a picture-frame. The last object on the Hampshire coast was Hurst Castle, on a low sandy slip of land. When we had passed it, it grew dusk, and, just faintly discerned through the misty twilight, the Needles began to appear ahead. We were most anxious to reach these before dark, and were delighted when point behind point of land rapidly came in sight as the breeze drove us through the narrow channel. At length, before night had closed in, all the Needles stood out clearly and distinctly before us—low, massy white rocks, rising abruptly out of the smooth dark sea, in a line running out from the rocky island, whose highest peak immediately above was crowned with a lighthouse. I now alternately looked out of the stern-windows to see the receding lights of Hurst Castle, and out of the side window of the dining-cabin to watch the Needles as they too seemed to glide past. At last it was only from the stern that anything at all could be seen, and that anything was only a dim outline of chalky cliff with a pale light on its summit, and the brilliant double lights of Hurst Castle, like twin sisters on the horizon. That outline of hazy cliff was the last I saw of British shore, perhaps the last I shall see for ever. It rapidly became still dimmer, then disappeared, but the pale light still gleamed above, now apparently in the sky, and the double fires below were not yet sunk into the waters. At length all was gone, and I could see nothing from the stern-windows but the heavens above spangled with glittering frosty stars, and an unbroken expanse of dark purple sea, slightly undulating, on which our ship left two bright tracks of foam behind her.

Dec. 8, *Saturday.*—. . . While we were sitting after dinner, I looked out of the little side window, and saw a bright double light on the horizon. This was the light on the Lizard Point, the last glimpse of Old England. It long continued steadily in sight, then it seemed occasionally to dip into the water, then by degrees it only emerged now and then as the vessel rolled, and at last it wholly disappeared. And so farewell to my native land, perhaps for ever.

Dec. 9, *Sunday.*—. . . I continue to be an excellent sailor, and enjoy myself thoroughly on board. My cough is almost gone, and I never wake up feverish and throbbing as I did in England. Really I shall hardly be an invalid when I reach Madeira. I already perceive a difference of temperature. It must, however, be an unusually warm December, or we could not, as we have done ever since we came on board, have dressed every morning with open windows. We sit with windows open all the morning. The days are lengthening now at each end, and mamma's watch is half an hour faster than the time in this latitude.

The captain is highly amusing, with his honesty, his good temper, his eagerness in conversation, his vehemence in politics, his abundance of anecdote, his love of a joke, and withal his very strong Northumbrian dialect. I think he must be about fifty years old, and is rather grey already. He bade me listen this evening to the sound of the waves breaking against the ship's side with a loud splashing sound.

"That," he says, "is our music at sea; I call it harp and piano together. I like it better than any other music." Which is because it is a sign that the wind is exactly aft.

Dec. 10, *Monday.*—. . . When the sun shines, the hues of the train left by a ship in her wake are very beautiful—blue and purple, and emerald green, mingled with masses of ice and spar, together with the snowy heaps of foam. And when night comes, I am never tired of watching the luminous sparks.

Dec. 12, *Wednesday.*—. . . Sat laughing and talking and watching the sailors at their occupations. Two of these particularly attracted our attention. One was the man I sketched at the wheel, whom we have often noticed since, for he has a very uncommon appearance. He has a short thick figure, but his face is like that of an antique statue, the features chiselled with almost Grecian perfection, and the profile in particular quite beautiful. The sickly, melancholy, unchanging expression of his sallow face, the strong contrast of jetty eyebrows over eyes of a light though not staring blue, the lips that even when he speaks seem never to open, the quiet unvarying cast of his whole demeanour, his seeming unconsciousness of ever meeting your eye,—all give this man a singular appearance. The other whom we noticed is remarkable only for being extremely handsome, but in quite a different style; his eyes are merry, his complexion is fair and very bright, and his fine features have a frank, quick, good-natured expression. He was at the wheel this evening; and his face and person were set off to great advantage by his picturesque dress—broad-brimmed sailor's hat and blue shirt—and the attentive eye required by his occupation. We observed also several others of the sailors, and I wished that I could know the history of each individual, and be able to judge how far his expression indicated his character.

. . . I could not refrain from running out once or twice

to look at the starry heavens. It was a magnificent, glorious sight, and to me the more striking from its novelty, for I have not before seen the dark blue heavens set with ten thousand gems, and arched with the pale milky way, through the sharp black tracery of ropes and spars, and the broad shadowy sheets of canvas, scarcely swelling in the soft breeze. I hope to be able to venture on a longer gaze some future night upon this most beautiful, most wonderful of created scenes.

Dec. 14, *Friday.*— . . . From eleven or twelve till dinner, and for some time after dinner, it is our custom to sit on deck, now and then taking a turn by ourselves when we can, with the gentlemen when we must. This evening was, if possible, more delicious than ever. I had rushed from the cabin in a state of high excitement, being raised to a towering passion by one of many conversations between Captain S. and Mr. H. on the subject of slavery. They take a pleasure in descanting on the former happy state of the slaves and the evil of emancipation, on the false views entertained in England on the subject, on the fact that slavery is a mere name, and other like nonsense; so that at last I could not help bursting forth, for my heart was thumping like a steam-engine, and I felt my lips and face quivering as if they were alive and in a passion too.

. . . When we sat down we each took up a book, but Mr. Houghton, who had been much amused at my fury after dinner, resumed the subject. Down went the books, and we entered into an argument, which became at last so stormy that I suddenly stopped short, with a positive assertion that I would never speak to him again about it. Louisa now joined us; we indulged ourselves in hearty laughter, and then looked leisurely at the glowing sky, from which I had hardly once removed my eyes.

. . . So very calm is it to-night, that there is hardly a

flake of foam in the ship's wake, hardly a ripple is to be heard, and a luminous spark only now and then appears. The vessel seems to be walking in her sleep, hardly conscious of her progress—and, indeed, there is not much to be conscious of.

Dec. 15, *Saturday.*—. . . A remark of Captain Selby about the widespread fame of Barclay and Perkins led to a conversation between him and Mr. Houghton about the great breweries and brewers and their combinations, then about the bakers, then the farmers, and the raising the price of corn in scarcities, and the wealth acquired by corn speculations. This led to a conversation about the old and the new poor-laws, the reduction of the rates, and the ruin they were causing. Mamma made a remark about the advantage of small allotments to labourers, upon which Captain Selby said that there was not a greater curse to the country than the enclosing open commons, which were such a blessing to the poor people, who can thereby support a cow, a donkey, etc. Mr. Houghton opposed this and asserted that these lands, when brought into cultivation, are a source of much greater profit to the community in general. Captain Selby grew very warm, and with his amusing vehemence of manner contended that it would be an incalculable loss to the poor man if he could have no place to walk on but the highway, etc.; in the midst of which eloquence Louisa and I marched out to the deck, and were soon followed by mamma.

. . . I never before saw a real golden light. In England we read of it, we hear of it, we talk of it, but never see it. I saw it to-night. The west was steeped in molten gold, every little cloud became a distinct mass of gold, the sea beneath the sun blazed with gold, everywhere was shed a liquid, spotless, golden light. . . .

Meantime the sea became a sheet of white—a strange contrast to its coloured and shaded girdle! Here and there a stormy petrel skimmed over its waveless surface, where it was distinctly reflected. And this was all of life that met our eye, besides our own little solitary world. Never did I feel so strongly how utterly alone we are. We have not seen a sail for three days; we are alone on a vast, calm, silent ocean, whose depth none but its Creator knows, and there is not a breeze to fill our sails, now flapping idly from the masts. There was an enjoyment so intense as to be almost painful, in watching the coming darkness and seeing the hues of the heaven gradually fading, except in the west, where the lake of gold had become a lake of fire. The sea looked almost like a sheet of glass, and reflected in long paths the purple clouds, the intervals of pale transparent green, the red west, and all the shades of colour around. The red west was burning still when star after star burst imperceptibly to sight, and the shadows of night had fallen on the broad white sails. Oh! I longed to sit all night watching the increasing beauty of the heavens and the ocean. But I am an invalid. I had already extorted several permissions to remain a few minutes longer, and at last my petitions were no longer attended to. Mr. Houghton took me down from the poop. I went to the cabin and sat down to my journal. I have a great deal more to write of to-day; but this volume is unluckily ended.

Dec. 18, *Tuesday.*—. . . At some distance to the right lies (for we are still becalmed) Madeira. During the morning we could hardly distinguish it, it was only a shade on the horizon, but as the sun went down it took a distinct form. So exactly, however, did it now resemble a solid bank of cloud, and so much higher was it than we expected, that we could hardly believe Mr. Houghton when he assured us that it was the island itself. He said he had never seen it so clear, for its summit is commonly covered with cloud. There, however, it was, with its peaks and promontories, growing more and more clearly defined as the sun became less dazzling, and forming a long mountain mass, far grander and more lofty than I had any notion it would appear at this distance. So that I was not at all disappointed, as Captain S. says visitors usually are.

. . . Again we had a sunset of the purest liquid gold; the whole western sky was melted into gold, and against it rested the noble outline of Madeira, traced out clear and purple on its glowing surface. When the evening air sent me back to the cabins, and I had taken off my shawl and bonnet, I sat down in the stern-window by myself for half an hour, watching the calm and lovely scene. The new moon had just appeared a little above where the sun had set; I could see her dusky orb within the little ring of gold—" a single star was at her side;" below was Madeira, and a belt of purple clouds, and the calm dark sea, that hardly rippled in the dark shadow of the ship's stern. The moon slowly sank, first through the cloud, in which she shone out like a jewel set in ebony, and then she dipped her horn into the ocean. When she had quite vanished, I looked up into the spotless sky; as if by magic it was now bedewed with ten thousand glittering stars. Below, whenever the heaving sea moved the ship a little, the phosphoric sparks gushed out; but they were few, for we continued on the same spot.

Dec. 19, *Wednesday.*— . . . Once and for all let me add that every night the moon, stars, and the red light of sunset glow together in the heavens of these delicious latitudes. But I think all yield to the starry sky when the sunlight has faded and the moon has set. Oh! the beauties of a starry sky are unknown, unguessed, in England. Such is the purity of this atmosphere that a veil seems taken from before the eye, a thousand stars seem added to the heavenly host, and each shines with redoubled glory. As for Orion, in England we only see his shadow. I could not have imagined the magnificence of this constellation as seen in these southern latitudes.

Dec. 20, *Thursday.*—. . . The sun set behind Madeira. Lorenzo Point, with its scattered rocks, and the blue Desertas, were clearly traced out in the red glow. A deep shadow lay on Porto Santo, which during the day had been beautifully distinct, with the finest variety of tints—rocks, black chasms, mountain-peaks, all painted on the blue sky. There was rain behind us, and for the second time a rainbow dipped its colours in the sea, without our having felt the shower.

Dec. 21, *Friday.*— . . . The sun had not yet risen, but I could see from my little window that we were sailing past the noble coast of Madeira, and that the little white town of Santa Cruz was visible. . . . The morn had risen in glowing beauty, and through an atmosphere that no English summer can equal, we looked on the magnificent pile of rugged mountains that rose abruptly out of the deep ocean, and pierced the clouds with their summits. And this was Madeira. We sailed slowly along, and so had ample leisure to gaze on every peak and cliff, on every changing point of view, on the varying lights and shades and tints. I believe we were about a mile from the shore, but it looked only a hundred yards. The soil, where not hidden by herbage and low vegetation, is a deep red; but the crags are dark and bare and bold, and many a steep black ravine yawned amidst the mountains at every elevation. By degrees, as we approached Funchal, houses began to appear, dotting the mountain-side. I now found that the novelty to me of mountain scenery had a curious effect on my ideas. I could not realize it; so that though Madeira is ten times as high as most hills I have seen, my imagination was rather struck with the littleness of the houses than with the vast height of the mountains which made them look so little. The Mount Church was pointed out to us, and not far from it the house of Mr. Webster Gordon, both in splendid situations half-way up the mountain.

At eight o'clock we went in to breakfast. Yes, we were actually, on the shortest day in the year, lounging about the deck before breakfast, seeking shade from the heat of the morning sun, while the thermometer, not exposed to its rays, rose to 72°. Such is Madeira weather. Meanwhile Funchal came in sight. After breakfast we went to watch it again. I can hardly imagine any town more magnificently situated than Funchal. It is built of white stone, and the houses are thickly crowded one upon another up the mountain-side; but, though so large as to contain thirty thousand inhabitants, it is so diminutive amidst the grandeur of the surrounding scenery as to look like a small scattered heap of white pebbles at the foot of a huge hill. There it lay, basking in the full blaze of the southern sun, and seemed as if it would be parched up for want of shade; but as we drew nearer we could distinguish the green foliage of the gardens. We now proceeded to finish our packing in a great hurry.

At Funchal.

It was about half-past twelve when the boat touched the shore, and was dragged up the black shingles by the bare-legged, copper-coloured Portuguese. Everything round us wore a strange and foreign appearance—the dark complexions and costumes of the Portuguese, the sound of a strange language jabbered on every side, the odd-looking boats, the numbers of horses and absence of wheeled carriages, the houses with their high turrets, and above all, the grand mountain. . . . We began scrambling up the beach, and I was actually able to walk all the way to the Houghtons' house. It is not above five minutes' distance from the shore, but the streets are steep and fatiguing. We passed through the Public Walk, which is planted with trees, and by the gates of the cathedral. In a very narrow street we stopped at the door of Messrs. Houghton and Burnett. We entered a small dark stone hall, which contained some empty casks, and a flight of very prison-like stone stairs. The rest of the party walked up first, and two Portuguese men-servants carried me up in a chair, so that I was landed without fatigue in a very handsome suite of rooms. . . .

When we came to the dining-room they threw open the Venetian blinds, and with delighted astonishment we looked down on a garden crowded with the richest green foliage, which, amidst the blaze of Madeira sunlight in December, looked as refreshing as a cool wood in an English July. I do not think any garden was ever so charming in my eyes, it was so surprising and unexpected. It was a story below us, so we looked down on a carpet of vines covering the trellis-work that shaded the walks—vines still in leaf, though they began to show symptoms of autumnal brown. Orange trees, five and twenty feet in height, loaded with golden fruit, light bamboos, bananas with their broad-fringed leaves, thick leafy coffee trees, forming an impenetrable and evergreen shade, camellias of enormous size, china roses still in bloom—all combined in a completely foreign picture different from anything I ever saw.

Dec. 23, *Sunday.*—. . . Our first Sunday in Madeira. Mamma and L. went to the English church, which I did not attempt to do; indeed, I was too languid to exert myself much any way. Towards the evening it was proposed to me to go into the garden; I did so, and was much pleased with it. The only way is through the kitchen premises, down flights of damp stone steps, and under stone archways; for everything in Funchal is stone, even to the huge kitchen fireplace, which is formed of immense slabs of stone in a long row. The garden is much neglected at present; still it is a sweet spot, and delightfully fragrant. It is partly laid out in walks covered with trellis-work, which is supported by stone pillars; the trellis is covered with vines, and the pillars are festooned with the thickest luxuriance of creepers. The garden is so entirely shut in, and sunk so low down amongst high mossy hedges, and so covered with the shade of its own foliage, that plants do not flourish well in it; and a little streamlet which runs all around, with a murmur which is heard in every part, helps to make it very damp and cool. Even now there are numerous flowers, especially the beautiful scarlet salvia, which almost dazzles one.

Dec. 24, *Monday.*—It is useless to make any remarks on the weather, every day is alike clear, bright, and warm; if any difference is perceptible, it is that it becomes finer the nearer we are to Christmas. Every morning, when we meet in the breakfast-room, we stand out in the balcony admiring the orange trees in the garden below, and the unclouded sunshine all around. We are not yet accustomed to the foreign appearance presented by everything that meets our eyes. But there is a sound which to me brings back England at once, and that is the sweet song of the robin, which I hear from the windows every day. I have also seen a chaffinch.

I quite forgot to mention yesterday that we made an excursion up to the turret, whither Mr. H. escorted us. It is six stories from the ground, and I made the ascent with much difficulty. But all the toil was well repaid when we reached the top, and from a little square chamber, with a window on every side, and a balcony all round, we looked out on one of the finest views I have seen. Funchal, with its gardens and turrets, the sea, with the shipping and the blue Desertas, and the magnificent rocky mountain on three sides of us, rent into ravines and sprinkled with lovely villas, composed the picture. The town is picturesque from its foreign appearance, but it must be confessed that, though of stone, the houses are without exception mean and shabby in exterior.

The balcony was filled with enormous pumpkins, drying in the sun; these are the principal food of the Portuguese servants. I have not mentioned guavas amongst the new fruit to which we have been introduced: they look like apples, but contain a sweet red pulp, full of hard seeds, which I believe are very unwholesome. We had a dish of *milho* at breakfast; this is made of Indian corn, and baked or fried in slices, which are like a very light pleasant pudding; it is eaten with sugar. While we were at luncheon to-day, arrived a common Portuguese present at Christmas, to wit, a tray of various sweet cakes made by the nuns, who seem to be cake-makers and confectioners-general to the whole island.

. . . The English place of interment, to which we next went, is at some little distance from the church. I should say places of interment, one belonging to the residents, one to the visitors. We first went into the former—a small gloomy spot, with straight walks and rows of cypress, enclosed with walls which are covered with half-effaced inscriptions; the stone coffin-shaped tombstones are overgrown with grass and straggling flowering-plants. Thence we went to the other burying-ground, which is much larger, and has all the appearance of a beautiful garden, with winding walks enclosed between the thickest hedges of geranium, four or five feet high, and so solid and massy that they appear quite different plants from the stunted and (comparatively) leafless specimens we see in England. . . . It was with a melancholy feeling that I gazed round this silent cemetery, where so many early blossoms, nipped by a colder climate, were mouldering away; so many, who had come too late to recover, and either perished here far away from all their kindred, or faded under the eyes of anxious friends, who had vainly hoped to see them revive again.

I felt, too, as I looked at the crowded tombs, that my own might, not long hence, be amongst them. "And here shall I be laid at last," I thought. It is the first time any such idea has crossed my mind in any burial-ground. What greatly enhances the melancholy appearance of this one, is the circumstance that almost all the inscriptions are partly, some entirely effaced; that is, the paint or ink has disappeared, whether owing to the dampness of climate or to bad execution, I do not know.

Dec. 25, *Tuesday* (*Christmas Day*).—And my nineteenth birthday. Why, it seems but the other day that I entered my teens, and now I am almost out of them. For some years past every birthday has been almost an unexpected addition to my life, so precarious has my health long been. Now that I am at last in this warm delightful climate, it is perhaps less unlikely that I shall see another. . . .

After mamma had gone out, to return calls, Mr. and Miss Freeman also paid us a visit. They did not stay long, but seem to be most pleasing people; indeed, from all we hear, we conclude them everything that is amiable and good. They are both young, brother and sister, recent visitors at Funchal like ourselves, come for Mr. Freeman's health. I found myself capable of taking a short walk this evening with Miss Rogers and little Marion, and greatly did I enjoy the same. The air was so deliciously clear and pure and warm that it was superior to anything I have felt in England, and seemed to me the very perfection of climate. We went to the fruit-market, which is in a spacious enclosure, paved, clean, and planted round with tall sycamores, whose leaves have only begun to change colour. The fruit is displayed in sheds or booths of wood; there is a great abundance of pumpkins, oranges, guavas, apples, tomatoes, and filberts. The market is partly surrounded with stone benches, on which I sat to rest in the shade, enjoying the view of the mountains with the evening lights upon their summits. From the market we proceeded to the seashore, crossing the St. John's river by a wooden bridge, and then immediately descending to the beach. Here I sat for some time on one of the great stones which I suppose are brought down by torrents. It was a sweet evening, and I was in the midst of beauty. Before me was the glassy sea, on which lay a frigate, a schooner, and some other vessels at anchor, and the unlucky *Transit*, preparing to depart, and receiving the visits of some Portuguese boats. To the right was the precipitous Loo Rock, crowned by a fort. To the left, over a low ridge, I could see some of the turrets and white houses of Funchal, with its ugly cathedral tower, the mountain-side sprinkled with villas, and the red rocky coast, abruptly terminating, with the Desertas seen dimly through a mist. Behind me also rose the mountains, with little clouds passing over them, and dipping into the ravines. There was a general air of calm and peace over the whole scene; no sound to be heard save the ripple of the retiring tide among the shingles. No one besides ourselves was near, except an invalid gentleman and two or three Portuguese boys, who seemed amused with watching us. The sky was clear and almost cloudless; the air, even when the sun was setting, was as soft as balm.

Dec. 27, *Thursday*.—. . . In the evening we made an excursion to see a house a little out of town, accompanied by Dr. Nichols, Mr. Vasconcellos Houghton, and Miss Rogers. It is called Quinta de Fayal, and is about two miles, or rather more, from Joaõ Tavera Street, in which we are. . . . Funchal is decidedly a picturesque town, especially along the banks of the little river, with the overhanging wooden stories, the balconies half broken down and filled with geraniums, and the trellises covered with vines. The narrow streets look very gloomy; the lower story of every house is always appropriated to stores and offices, and the iron gratings and dingy stone casements have exactly the air of a prison, an effect not diminished by the listless faces that crowd the heavy and half-ruinous balconies of the next story. The silence is remarkable; the hum of voices and the ringing of the church bells are the only sounds; no wheels, no footsteps, for the thin slippers commonly worn glide motionless over the strong pavement. I cannot imagine how the inhabitants have so much time to stare out of their houses at the passers-by; even from the most miserable cabin the heads of men and women, almost in rags, are always peering lazily forth. They seem as if they had nothing to do. I am surprised, too, at the hot glaring colours worn on holidays by Portuguese women; scarlet shawls and pink bonnets are great favourites.

As we ascended, a noble view was of course forming beneath us, and increasing in extent at every step. This I shall describe as it was when we reached the summit. Meantime, as we went higher, we passed garden after garden, and other pieces of open ground, all filled with Madeira vegetation, which, though seen at the worst season, impressed us with a high idea of its luxuriance. Abundance of vine-trellises, and stone verandahs covered not only with vines, but with another luxuriant creeper, the grenadilla; geraniums growing like weeds; peach trees already in blossom; bananas; in one garden a solitary palm, and everywhere the wildest profusion of prickly pear, growing as a weed, and to a size which quite astonished us, who are used to see it cherished and yet stunted in greenhouses. The roots and stems of many enormous plants are solid, woody, and as large as those of laurel trees, while the leaves are almost as large as docks. It has a handsome flower, not yet in bloom; the fruit is a favourite food of the Portuguese. Another plant, or rather shrub, of a remarkably bright green, was pointed out to us as a poison to fleas, which, from our personal experience, I should suppose must make it very valuable in Madeira. We heard everywhere the loud bubbling of little streams directed through the gardens, and some welled out of the wall, or ran along the roadside. The road, like the streets, is paved with round stones, and the pony, accustomed to the work and rough-shod, scrambled up the very steep ascent with surprising agility and sureness of foot.

Dec. 28, *Friday.*— . . . The sound of wheels astonished our ears to-day; they were those of a phaeton, of which there are two or three in Funchal, though but seldom used. If wheels were common on these rough pavements, Funchal would be the noisiest town in the world.

Dec. 29, *Saturday.*— . . . We made an excursion to-day to the celebrated convent. The convent is a huge and lofty building, close to the English church, which lies humbly at its feet. We alighted at the gates of a kind of hall, and waited a little while for our nun, who was to conduct us over the place. I looked with great curiosity at this, the first nun I have seen. Formerly, I have been accustomed to associate with the idea of a nun, iron gratings, attenuation, and melancholy, with a proper share of youth and comeliness. These impressions were entirely effaced by the first glimpse of Maria Clara. She is a short, fat, jolly old woman of about fifty-five, with a round, wrinkled, most good-humoured face, well adorned with very perceptible black moustaches. Nothing can exceed the happiness of her countenance, the heartiness of her manner; nothing can be less romantic than her cordial shakes of the hand, the garrulity of her tongue, and the liveliness of her laugh.

. . . The convent is very ancient (for Madeira), having been begun seven years after the island was discovered; and the long straggling passages, with their floors of teal-plank, so hard that every nail has had a place cut for it, and so durable that they have never been renewed, bear every mark of antiquity. The cells are generally in rows on each side of a passage, separated from it by an old wooden partition, but there are also many grouped about in all kinds of corners and projections. Maria Clara first took us to see hers. Most assuredly it did by no means answer to my idea of a cell; there was not even an iron grating. I should rather call it a very comfortable, airy, cheerful bedroom. It is narrow, but long, sufficiently well furnished, with two windows, opening on a balcony, and commanding a delightful view of the mountains, the sea, and, what is of more consequence to Maria Clara, of the neighbouring houses, for the nuns are the greatest gossips in the town. . . . On a little table in the window lay a tray containing a number of kisses; such is the English name (I forget the Portuguese) for a little sugar-roll, something like barley-sugar, which the nuns make and present to their guests wrapped up in white paper. It was odd enough to see Maria Clara's cell filled with people, gentlemen as well as ladies, laughing and talking without restraint, and she herself laughing and talking as merrily as any. . . . Every cell has at one end a kind of little canopy against the wall, generally containing a gaily dressed saint, or virgin, or infant Christ in the smartest of all possible cradles, and under it is a little table covered with all kinds of toys and knick-knacks, the work of the nuns, very tastefully arranged, such as cakes, sweetmeats, the celebrated feather-flowers, and the prettiest little models of churches or palaces, made of glittering materials; with these are mixed abundance of fruit, chiefly oranges, and innumerable flowers of every scent and hue.

. . . The convent was thronged with visitors, perhaps as many as two hundred, but it is so large that we never saw more than a small party at once. No cell was so crowded as that of the well-known Maria Clementina, which seemed a general point of attraction. My curiosity to see this far-famed nun was now gratified. I saw her several times, and watched her narrowly to obtain an exact notion of her appearance. She seems now about seven and thirty, is far superior in personal attractions to the other nuns, and has the remains of some beauty; but how she could ever have risen into celebrity on that score, I cannot conceive. . . . Her countenance was smiling and pleasant, but I thought not that of a mind at ease; there seemed lurking unhappiness beneath the surface, and there was a slight compression in her lips, which might have been affectation, but appeared to me to express a part of the same state of feeling. She really is, I believe, unhappy, and it is no wonder, for her former misconduct has given her a bad name in the convent, and the nuns avoid her; perhaps, too, they are a little jealous of her superior popularity. . . . The general kitchen of the convent is a small place to cook a dinner for fifty nuns; but, then, that dinner is only bean-broth. Each has a daily allowance of broth and bread. But let it not be supposed that they are nourished on such fare as this; they give it away to the poor, and concoct for themselves in their own private kitchens every sort of dainty; for every nun has one, two, or three kitchens of her own, and servants besides. We visited one of these, and saw some capital cakes and sweetmeats in preparation. I must not forget to observe that we espied a very well-used pack of cards in the kitchen of the convent, whereat Maria Clara laughed heartily, and said that the servants played. But it is very well known that this amusement is not confined to them.

We went through many pillared galleries and cloisters, looking into the little gardens, which are small paved courts delightfully crowded with the thickest flowering trees and shrubs, orange, lemon, hibiscus, roses, daturas, and very many whose names I do not know, the finest mixture of bright flowers and leaves. But I must not omit the singular changeable rose, which is not really a rose, except that the flower resembles it. It is a curiously shaped tree of small size, with large blossoms, which are red one day and white the next. There are numerous creepers, too, and small flowering plants of every kind; the profusion in which they grow is amazing. In the stone walls of the galleries are many little fountains, which are almost hidden by the delicate green ferns and mosses that grow luxuriantly over and around them. Little chapels too, surrounded with foliage, stand on the edge of the courts, with steps leading down to them; nothing can look more cool and refreshing.

Our drawing-room here is about twenty-eight feet long, the walls whitewashed, which is usual; the floor covered with matting, which is a luxury. It is furnished with three tables, a sofa, twelve cushioned chairs, a cane great-chair, a very comfortable easy-chair, which can be made into a sofa, two footstools, a music-waggon, and two sets of bookcases with cupboards. This is an extraordinary quantity of furniture for Funchal. It opens into a dining-room, which opens into a smaller room with a stove and large cupboards for glass, china, etc. Beyond this is my bedroom, which is very large, with a window at each end. Its entire furniture consists of a white-curtained bed, a deal table, a looking-glass, a chest of drawers, a fixed cupboard or wardrobe, two chairs, a small corner washhand-stand scantily provided, and three little strips of carpet round the bed; the walls bare, whitewashed, dismal—all so unlike my dear snug little room at Bartley, which I shall never again inhabit.

CHAPTER XIV.

From Jan. 3 to May 27, 1839.—Madeira.

Jan. 3, Thursday.—. . . . With much toil and labour we at last finished unpacking and putting away everything that we have brought with us, and thus we are in a state of greater comfort. But now comes a novelty. We are obliged, from the known thievish character of Portuguese servants, to lock up everything—a thing we never did in England. I have shortened this business by always locking my room when I leave it. It is most unpleasant to live in this continual distrust, and to be assured that after all we shall certainly be cheated more or less.

Jan. 4, Friday.—We spent the last half-hour of delay in a trip to the Esplanade. . . . Two or three gloomy little streets brought us to the side of the ribeira. Here we paused in extreme admiration ; the sea on one side, and the mighty mountain on the other, with its deep ravines, its nearer and more distant summits, varied more beautifully with light and shade from the rays of the sun sinking to its rest, than any scenery I have hitherto beheld. Full half of the mountain was bathed in a rich crimson glow, such a crimson glow as is never seen in England, while the other half was in dark shadow, except where the loftier ridges were tipped with the sunbeams, which, as the sun dropped rapidly, shifted from summit to summit, and glided up the hillside, almost with the play of the Aurora Borealis. At the same ducted. The Miss Pages, three in number, were sitting here, studying from a Portuguese master. The summer-house is nearly open at the sides, at least they are full of windows without sashes, so that there is little to obstruct the view; it is entered by a walk covered with vines, and the garden is full of flowers, the walls are covered with white jessamine and heliotropes, the latter growing with extraordinary luxuriance, to the height of eight or ten feet, and mantled with its fragrant blossoms. We sat for some time in the cool delightful summer-house, and enjoyed our visit greatly. The Miss Pages are very nice girls, persons that one feels at ease with directly. They kindly pressed us to come any morning and sit with them; I am sure no temptation is wanting to make us accept of the invitation. We begged we might not interrupt their Portuguese lesson, so they went on one at a time, while one talked to Mamma, and one to Louisa, and I sketched as much of the mountain as could be seen through one vine-clad window. I must observe by the way that no object on the mountain-side is more conspicuous than the Mount Church, a large and striking building of white stone, with two towers. We never look up at it, without thinking "how magnificent must be the view from thence!" Mr. Webster Gordon's immense country-place is at the same exalted elevation.—The eldest Miss Page, for whose health they came out, is a delicate looking girl, fair and blue-eyed; she was subject to bad coughs, and her brother, taking the alarm, declared that a winter in Madeira would set her up for life; in my opinion judging very prudently. It too often happens that this salutary measure is deferred till it is much too late, whereas at an earlier stage it might have answered. This last seems to be the case with Miss Page. She declares indeed that she will not allow herself ever to have been an invalid. We staid with them about half an hour, drank some wine and water which they brought us, and being rested and refreshed, returned home, much pleased with our visit, and bringing some flowers which Miss Elizabeth Page had gathered for me.

Soon after we re-entered the house, the Miss Tellis's called. The youngest sat mute, being unable to speak English; the elder, who seems to be decidedly a clever girl, talks it very readily, though now and then with a little

time, the Loo Rock rose clear and black against the blazing west, and the two Desertas were distinctly painted on the opposite sky. We did not stand looking, but crossed the ribeira, and entered the gate of the Esplanade, from whence we beheld the same delightful scene. This noble walk has but one defect, the want of turf, so that, as it is not even hard and levelled, the feet move with much discomfort over small loose stones. The place will soon be a complete geranium garden. When the trees are grown so as to afford a thick shade, which will be the case in a year or two, I should think that its equal would not be found in any place in the world. A walk of such magnificent dimensions, close to the sea, almost in the midst of so large a city, and surrounded by the splendid mountains of Madeira, their surface, as well as the face of the sky, ever varying with the play of sunlight and clouds of divers colours,—what other public promenade in the universe can boast of such manifold attractions? The low stone passage or parapet, scarce four feet high, which surrounds it, rises very little above the stony beach outside, and is here and there cut into seats, on which we rested ourselves. Nobody was there except a few Portuguese and English fops, smoking in groups, or swaggering up and down in solitude with an odious cigar. Mamma and I did not stay long, for we had not gazed many minutes on the crimson mountains before it all faded into a soft and quiet grey; it changed beneath our look, and we could see the daylight hurrying from the earth.

Jan. 5, *Saturday.*—. . . Mrs. P—— made her first call to-day. She is a sweetly pretty little creature, fair and delicate, has clear bright eyes, arched with the prettiest little pencilled eyebrows, a most pretty little straight nose, and a little affected lisp to set off all her other little prettinesses.

Jan. 6, *Sunday.*—. . . In the afternoon, being stronger than usual, I took a walk with mamma and L., longer than any since I have been in Madeira, and almost a country walk. We first went to the Esplanade, or, according to its more correct though ridiculous name, the Praça Academica. We did not stay here long, as I was seized with a sudden fancy of exploring the neighbourhood of the ribeira close by, up which none of us have yet walked. Thither, accordingly, we bent our steps. Every moment, as we followed the course of the stream, we seemed to approach nearer the mountains, and the deep ravine from which it flows—or rather flowed, for there is no water now in the channel, except close to the sea. A low stone parapet, cut into seats here and there, runs along the edge, and on these seats we now and then sat down.

As we proceeded, the country rapidly opened before us, and at last we reached a spacious amphitheatre, in the shape of a crescent, beautifully inclosed by the stream on the straight side, and the mountains curving round the other, picturesque houses at the base, and rising one over the other in terraces, with gardens, and vine-trellises supported on rows of stone pillars. Houses and vine-trellises bordered the other side of the ribeira, and before us it entered the deep ravine. This open space struck us as peculiarly beautiful; part of it was even covered with turf, which reminded us of England. But nothing could be more unlike England than every other surrounding object—the mingled bananas, orange-trees, vines, and flowers, which half embosomed every house; the rocky terraces, the towering mountain, the stony bed of the torrent, the groups of swarthy Portuguese lounging in the balconies, or gathered round a clear fountain gushing from the wall into a stone basin. We sat here for some time, looking back now and then at the pure blue sea, which began to narrow between the town and the mountain. It was a long walk for me, and mamma urged me to turn back. I confess I was very weary, but the scenery was so noble that I was tempted on, and could not persuade myself to stop. In a short time we reached the extremity of the open space, and turned round the corner of the rock, where there was only a narrow rugged path between the mountain and the ribeira.

Here we were at last truly in the country, and the mouth of that grand ravine which forms the most conspicuous object from Funchal. Opposite to us, on the other side, rose a nearly precipitous rock, covered with prickly pear, the commonest weed in Madeira, and fringed with bananas. A little stream poured down from the brink through the foliage, in a fall of fifteen or twenty feet, making a loud and pleasant murmur, which sounded most delicious in mamma's ears, as she is passionately fond of streams. Immediately above us, a little stone-built cottage was perched like a nest on the mountain-side, in the midst of foliage, with steps leading up to it, and a tiny rivulet dropping from the rock above, and sparkling in the setting sunbeams. We descended into the dry bed of the ribeira, which is filled with stones of all sizes and fragments of rock. On one of these I sat and rested, while mamma and L. wandered on a little further. The banks were covered with weeds, amongst them a profusion of the wild English furnitory. The ravine continued winding far away among the mountains; through the opening by which we had entered, there was one little peep of the still sea, and a single vessel floating on its surface. The song of the robin came across the ribeira; the little cascade was murmuring in my ears; all else was still, till a merry party of Portuguese boys, black-eyed, pale-faced, slender lads, came jumping and leaping from stone to stone along the dry channel. The sun was sinking, and we hastened homewards for fear of being benighted. We went by a rather different way, crossing the ribeira by a bridge a little above the Rua das Portas Novas. Here we met that stately gentleman Mr. ——, leading a little son by each hand. He condescendingly took off his hat, and half inclined his head with a majestic

"Your most obedient, Madam;" graciously paused to chat a minute, and parted with us without degrading himself by shaking hands.

Continuing our way, we came to Mr. Holloway's boarding-house, which is in a most lovely situation. The approach is by a paved walk entirely bordered with high hedges of luxuriant roses. The gate stood open, and we could not resist the temptation of walking in a little way. The owner of the boarding-house, a Portuguese, who speaks English, seeing us retreating when he appeared, followed, and very civilly invited us into his garden. We went up to the house-door by a flight of steps quite mantled with creepers, and leading to an open stone area before the door, railed round and adjoining to a little elevated garden full of flowers. The house commands a delightful view of the sea. Trellises covered with vines, pumpkins, roses, and white jessamine; shrubs of hibiscus covered with crimson blossoms, and complete hedges of heliotrope six or seven feet high; with bananas, orange-trees, and sugar-canes, covering the waste ground beyond, combined to form the usual foreign appearance presented by houses in Funchal. The Portuguese desired a girl—his daughter, I imagine—to gather us a nosegay, which she did with right good will, and we returned home loaded with flowery spoils.

Jan. 7, *Monday.*—. . . Mr. Phelps called; while he was in the room the bells of the Carmo Church opposite our window suddenly began to ring. "There's the sacrament going by," said Mr. Phelps; so we got up to look, for it was a sight quite new to us. A procession of men in scarlet gowns, carrying silver maces, and a canopy over the vicar, who bore the host, passed under the window; the bells rang as long as they were in sight, and every one dropped on his knees while they went by. They were going to visit a dying person.

Jan. 8, *Tuesday.*—Being determined to secure a walk

to-day, we set off between eleven and twelve. The thermometer at sunrise had been only 51½° out-of-doors, which is wonderfully low for Madeira, but by the time we were out-of-doors the temperature was like that of June. We could not endure the sun without parasols, and carefully sought out the shady side of the street. We went to another ribeira,* the one we cross in going to the Rua di Joaõ Tavera; I wish I knew their names.

We walked slowly along its side, up a continued but good ascent, and every now and then sat down to rest, and enjoy the very picturesque town scenery of Funchal, for I could not walk nearly far enough to get out into the country. The street by the ribeira is very broad, clean, paved, and planted with trees, amongst which are some beautiful weeping willows still in full leaf. All the ribeiras have a low stone parapet on each side, which is interrupted here and there by a steep flight of stone steps, for the washerwomen to go down and wash their linen in the bed of the torrent, where now only a scanty stream runs along, replenished by numerous little fountains gushing out of their sides, and, I suppose, coming through the town from the hills. We watched the washerwomen that filled the channel of the ribeira, which is about twenty or thirty feet deep, and when we saw them rubbing the linen on the great stones, did not wonder that it soon wore out. The sides of the ribeira are generally walled up with stone, on which, wherever a little stream runs down, a verdure of ferns and mosses springs. The banks are everywhere overhung with shrubs and flowers and creepers, from the houses and gardens on the opposite side. On our side the houses are at a considerable distance, leaving ample walking space. Narrow irregular streets diverge, and the mountain towers above all, appearing at every gap, through stone trellises covered with vines, and roofs mantled with the pumpkin.

* Ribeira di Santa Luzia.

The houses and gardens rise terrace above terrace up the mountains in the most picturesque manner, amidst the richest luxuriance of orange-trees, bananas, fig-trees, sugar-canes, and roses, with here and there a palm-tree or bamboo. I cannot describe the beauty of the vegetation; I say the same things over and over again in every walk, because the same things always strike me anew. I still cannot help noticing the dress of the common people—the handkerchiefs tied round the heads of the women, and the odd little carapousas* on those of the men. The carapousa is usually purple, lined with red, and is so small that I wonder it does not fall off. The only sort of vehicle used in Funchal, the wooden tray or sledge, drawn by a yoke of oxen, is constantly to be met, and, as the oxen wear bells, constantly to be heard. All the oxen are small, red, and something like the Devonshire breed.

. . . There is no one of all our Madeira acquaintance I like so much as Miss Freeman; she is a sweet creature, mild, gentle, thoughtful almost to sadness of expression, yet with no coldness of manner, but a soft engaging kindness; she is pleasing at the very first, but rather to be called very winning than very attractive. I cannot imagine anything gentler than she is; I feel that I should soon love her very much. She is in deep mourning for a sister, who died of consumption only two days after her brother and herself left England. He, poor young man, is, I should fear, far gone in the same disease, and his sister to-day says he is worse. His voice is almost gone, and often he can hardly make himself heard; but, although he is very thin, there is nothing in his appearance to indicate his fatal malady, except the bright glassy look of his blue eyes. He is as good and amiable as his sweet sister; I believe mamma is more struck with him, and I with her. Both of them seem entirely made up of goodness.

* Carapuça.—ED.

Jan. 9, *Wednesday.*—. . . The Freemans told us that they had brought their horse and man for me to take a ride; for which I was very thankful to them, not being able to walk much to-day. They took their leave immediately, and I prepared to ride, putting on a riding-skirt with which Miss F. kindly furnished me. Mamma accompanied me on foot. . . . As we returned home through Funchal another way, we were much struck with the lofty appearance of the mountains when we saw them through the narrow streets. We passed under the fort, which stands on a rock grey with prickly pear. The narrowness of the streets is a great advantage, as it makes them quite cool and shady, and produces pleasant currents of air. I am also quite reconciled to the sharp pavement, without which I think no horse would keep his footing. The Rua da Carreira seems to be one of the principal streets of Funchal; it is really handsome, spite of the irregularity of the building, for there are no two houses alike in Funchal, and certainly it is marvellously clean. It is easy to see where a stream ran down the middle; it is now covered over, with a perforated stone here and there, and gratings which lift up. The shops of Funchal are mean dark holes; nothing is displayed at the windows, and the name of the owner, instead of being placed conspicuously above the door, is written in insignificant characters on a small board hung out on a stick a few feet from the ground. The commonest notice on these boards is "Pao Vinho Bom," often abridged into "P. V. B."

. . . This is the fifth nosegay we have had given us in two days, and we have filled three finger-glasses with them, besides three wine-glasses of violets. They consist of various sorts of roses, camellia, japonicas, jessamine, hibiscus, orange-flower, lemon-flowers, salvia, geranium, heliotrope, bachelor's-buttons, arum, some flowers whose names we do not know, and a blossom of the datura, one of the most graceful of flowers, and very fragrant in the night-time. What a nosegay for January! I should add that almost all of these are finer than they would ever be found in England, and that they grow here like weeds.

Jan. 10, *Thursday.*—. . . Mr. V——, according to an agreement made yesterday, called for mamma and L—— at seven this morning, and they all took a walk. It was a sweet morning, and they came back to breakfast enchanted with what they had seen. They had been up one of the ribeiras, far up into the ravine, and L——, with Mr. V——'s help, had scrambled up the mountain-side, covered with wild myrtle. I sighed to think how impossible it was for me ever to see these wild rocky spots, where neither horse nor palanquin could travel. But I had my turn of delight afterwards, for kind Miss F. sent me their horse again, and I had a ride through the most beautiful scenery I have yet beheld. . . .

I came at length to where the path divided. On the left is a sweet villa, shaded with thick trees; on the right I slightly ascended, till I reached the gates of a grand quinta, called the Palmeira, if I understood my attendant rightly. We then passed along by a narrow path under its walls for a considerable way. Never did I see so magnificent a place as this Palmeira. The grounds must be immense; it seems to stand on a pile of precipitous rocks, or rather they surround it with a mighty rampart, beneath which my path wound for some part of its great circuit. The house being within, I saw nothing of it, but I saw that the rocks were crowned completely with trees of various kinds, which also partly clothe their sides, mixed with fern, mosses, ivy, and flowers, especially the prickly pear, which grows on every rock. The appearance of the place is something like an enchanted fairy-land. At length I came to a sudden turn, where beauty which I cannot describe burst upon me. I was immediately under the rocky wall, which now formed one side of a narrow ravine, through which a clear rapid rivulet rushed from behind, and falling in an irregular cascade foamed away down the steep hill to Funchal; the hill on the other side of the ravine is some way beyond, fringed with wood, and the view through the ravine in front is closed up with the distant mountain and the Mount Church. Behind lie Funchal and the sea. Turning to the left, I and my guide crossed the stream by a little bridge, and continued to go through a series of narrow roads between walls and gardens, and under vine-trellises. I had made a complete circuit of a great part of Funchal, ascended the mountain on the west, ridden along its front, and descended again towards its western side. I passed by Mr. Lowe's (the clergyman's) house, which is in a lovely situation. Indeed, there is hardly a house on any height in or round Funchal whose situation is not more or less beautiful. Finally, I came home along the ribeira with the willow-trees, entering much above the turn to Rose Cottage, where the rock rises precipitously on the other side.

Few towns are supplied with a number of such noble walks as these by the ribeiras of Funchal; they are broad, airy, shaded with trees, level for a long way, and pass through most picturesque scenery. I prefer them to the Praça Academica.

Jan. 11, *Friday.*— . . . Soon after breakfast Mr. Freeman called. "Have you perceived," he said, "that it is a *leste*, which is the same as the African sirocco? This is the wind in which invalids are always well, and the weather is perfectly to be depended on as long as it lasts, so that it must be taken advantage of for expeditions, for it is as warm up in the mountains as it is down here." And then, with his usual kindness, he offered me his horse again, having just finished his own ride, and suggested to me that I might go up to the Mount Church, the distance to which is three miles, and two thousand feet. I embraced the idea with delight. . . .

I enjoyed the ride thoroughly, and as for the scenery,

I never saw anything like it, for hitherto I have hardly been any way out of Funchal. We went up the Mount Road, part of which I had ridden yesterday in my way to the Levada. From this it is a continued ascent up to the church, slightly winding, partly between garden walls, partly between natural rocky banks. It is useless to expatiate on the beauties of these gardens, their corridors of vines and coffee plants, their walls and verandahs covered with splendid geraniums, scarlet salvias, and roses, their hedges of luxuriant fuchsia, their mantles of ivy. As I proceeded upwards, the hedge-banks became crowned with walnut-trees, and clothed with myrtles, aloes, broom, ivy, brambles, geraniums, laurel, stonecrops, and many other plants, both native and Madeirense. A turn to the left, not far below the church, brought me suddenly to the brink of a precipice overlooking a great ravine, that spreads out gradually as it reaches Funchal. On the right were the garden walls of the thickly wooded quintas of Mr. Stoddart and Mr. Phelps; on the left was the abrupt undefended precipice, nearly perpendicular, and perhaps four hundred feet in height. The road is broad, almost level, and shaded with walnuts and ash-trees, and a large evergreen tree, something like the ilex; the sides and bottom of the ravine are scattered with all kinds of trees, and some parts very thickly; and a mountain torrent, tumbling down in little cascades, foams along the bottom with a loud noise; the whole scene was more grand and beautiful than anything I have seen. I do not think I have ever looked down so deep a descent in inland scenery. I looked over the whole ravine, every tree and shrub below me diminished by the distance into low bushes, while above still towered the lofty mountains. The road continued along the brink for about ten minutes, when I turned to the right, and entered a shady road immediately under the mound on which the church stands. The banks were covered with violets and periwinkles, and crowned with chestnuts, walnuts, and the same dark evergreen. Winding round, I at length alighted from the horse on a walled platform at the foot of the church. Sixty-eight steps from this lead up to the door. I mounted them, and after gasping for breath for some time, leisurely examined the noble view beneath. Funchal is almost hidden by the interposing hill; all around is the magnificence of mountain scenery, and such an extent of dazzling sea as I have never beheld.

Jan. 13, *Sunday.*—While they went to church in the morning, I was as usual left alone, and I sank into a long melancholy reverie on subjects which *will* intrude themselves whenever I am alone, now that the busy excitement of our voyage and arrival is over. In leaving England I left so much that was dear to me. In Madeira I may possess content, and, indeed, as far as preservation from real misfortune and affliction goes, I ought to esteem myself happy; but all the *enjoyment* of happiness is gone, and cannot return. I knew I should feel it so, and the time is come now in which I feel it heavily. I shall not see any more the two or three dear friends I left in England, nor any of the other kind familiar faces I used to see with pleasure. I am torn away from all old associations, from everything like a home. . . . There is nothing in Madeira which is dear to me; the land, the people, are new and unknown and strange. Nay, it makes no little difference to me that in every room of the house I look round on strange furniture, which belongs to another, instead of our own, which I remember from earliest childhood. At Woodbury, and even at Bartley Lodge, almost every object was familiar to me. Madeira I admire with intense admiration, but she is to me as a beautiful stranger; England I knew, and loved fondly. Oh, there are moments when visions start up before me of sweet well-known spots —woods where the anemone and bluebell grow; streams shaded with ash-trees and hawthorn, where I have wandered alone in early spring mornings, on violets and primroses and grass drenched with dew, myself the happiest of the happy, listening to the songs of the birds, and shaking over me a shower of bright drops as I gathered the branches of the willow or bullace; lanes, too, carpeted with green turf, and sloping meadows covered with broom and marsh-marigold;—all these, and other spots full of a thousand sweet recollections, the sad ones for the time forgotten, will picture themselves so vividly to my mind that my eyes will fill with bitter tears. . . . But, indeed, year after year has stripped me of enjoyment, even before I left England. The loss of health and strength has altogether deprived me of the active amusements, the rambles and observations of nature, in which I so much delighted, and has continually checked me in my studies, in which I delighted as much. . . . And there are other causes, mental ones, which prevent my enjoying things as I once did; but they are partly my own fault, and partly what I share in common with others. Oh, how many happy hours, which seem to me but as yesterday, start up in contrast with the present! . . . I live it all over again, and I cannot avoid weeping. There is no language to describe the sharp pain of past and regretted happiness. I was much happier as a child than I am now, or ever shall be, and if I were not now with mamma, I should sink into an incurable melancholy. . . . Oh, how bitter it is to part with friends, and expect to see them no more! Faces I yearn to see haunt my pillow and surround my chair.—No more——

I was led into these thoughts by a verse in Keble's hymn for to-day, about "the willow" and "the moist and reedy grass." A word will kindle up a long train of associations. I was immediately transported to the banks of the pretty little Guash, and surrounded by the silence and stillness and dewy brightness of a May morning. All my feelings of affection are left in England. I could with happiness and enjoyment live in Madeira for even two or three years, if I could feel that I should then return to the same home I left. But this can never be; we have no home left in England, no spot which expects to see us again. Nay, more; we have no *home* anywhere, and if we do make one it will probably be in Madeira.

Jan. 14, *Monday.*—Housekeeping here is a very different thing from what it is in England; it is necessary to be constantly overlooking the servants, for they cannot be trusted to prepare things carefully themselves. It is mine or mamma's regular morning business to boil, or see boiled, the coffee for breakfast, to get the *milho* prepared, to see that the milk and butter are properly disposed of, and, in short, to overlook every arrangement. All this is unpleasant enough to our English habits; but we hope in time to drill our servants into more regular ways of business. Maria is an extremely quick and teachable girl. We had a dish of excellent green pease at dinner; this on the fourteenth of January!

Jan. 15, *Tuesday.*—At last we have had the satisfaction of eating at breakfast butter made with our own fair hands, not by any servant's, for we see that Manuel knows nothing about the matter. According to the instructions of the Burnetts and Houghtons, we have begun to take in two bottles of milk every day. We took in two bottles on Sunday, and scalded the milk; at the same time the H.'s man, Antonio, took in two bottles for us also, and scalded them to compare with ours. On Monday morning we skimmed ours, and found the cream equal to Antonio's, which he sent down to us. We then scalded the milk left by Antonio the second time, and scalded also two fresh bottles; the milk of our yesterday's scalding we were obliged to keep for breakfast. This morning we skimmed both, and mixed the four different creams together, taking for breakfast the milk which had been skimmed twice, and scalding again what had been skimmed once. I then began making the butter, by stirring the cream in a basin with a wooden spoon. Mamma relieved me at times, but I began and ended it, and finally washed and made it up; so that when I turned out about three quarters of a pound of beautiful butter, I felt quite proud of my work. The whole business occupied about twenty or five and twenty minutes; but we shall be quicker another time, as we fully mean to continue the plan. The scalding is a Devonshire art, and I should think no one in Funchal does it but ourselves and the Burnetts, who are partly of Devonshire origin.

Jan. 17, *Thursday.*—. . . The manners of Portuguese servants (without their intending any disrespect) are such as would be pronounced very free-and-easy in England. Manuel, when he brings in what he has brought, will stay in the room to discuss its merits, which he will lean over the table to do; he loses no opportunity of prating, and when he wants to insist on doing a thing he tries to force the spoon or plate out of our hands, saying most respectfully, "If de please, ma'am—if de please, ma'am," one of his few English phrases. He also laughs whenever he thinks fit, especially if he thinks he has got the better of me in an argument about the *troco* (change), in which he is especially stupid. Everything with him is "bit-naff," whether it be really a bit and a half, or two bits, or half a bit. He also begins every sentence with "ere's de," his deformed version of "here's the," and this without any meaning whatsoever.

Jan. 18, *Friday.*—. . . I rode in quite a different direction this time, to the east of Funchal, directing the man to take me to the Ribeira de St. Gonzalez. The road lies quite along the edge of the cliffs, so that I enjoyed to my heart's content the sound and sight of the waves breaking on the black rocks below. I went up and down, rising gradually to some height, Funchal, as usual, lying beneath me. The rocks are everywhere overgrown with prickly pear, and sprinkled with peach and fig-trees, the former going out of blossom, the latter already in leaf. Many of the vines still retain the fresh green foliage of last summer. I remarked a rosebush covered with the brightest crimson blossoms, overhanging the edge of the cliff. When I began my ride the morning mists on the mountains were tinted with the colours of the rainbow, which is often the case here.

. . . The beautiful scarlet geranium takes root in the clefts of the rocks, and mantles the banks of the ribeira almost down to the bottom of its channel with its luxuriance of blossom. The road crosses the ribeira by a stone bridge of one lofty arch, and ascends steeply on the opposite side. I ascended nearly all the rest of my ride, which I continued some considerable way further, still nearly along the edge of the mountain.

. . . As I rode back the view over Funchal was noble, and the expanse of sea immense. It was a delight to be entirely in the country; all around was solitary and silent, and the road was only trodden occasionally by peasants bearing cans of milk. I saw a few quintas above me. In one place I rode close to a parapet about two feet high, which was the only protection from an abrupt precipice, perhaps seven or eight hundred feet deep—so steep that I could see nothing over the parapet but sea; in fact, a single start of the horse might have thrown me clear over down the whole descent. I should have been a little nervous here, if I did not know how quiet the horse was.

. . . I found to my horror that I had kept Mr. Freeman's horse above two hours, and it was now one o'clock. I have felt compunction for it all day, and shall not be easy till I can apologize in person.

Jan. 19, *Saturday.*—. . . Miss Telles came this morning and gave us another lesson in Portuguese. . . . She told us a great deal about the English residents in Madeira, who, she says, have most of them risen from the condition of small clerks and shopkeepers; . . . and then, having very quickly made their money, they packed off their children, says Miss T., to be educated in England. These now assume great airs, look down on the Portuguese, and will not associate with them, which, she says, once made her think they must be the finest people in the world, but, when she came to England, she soon found the absurdity of their pretensions. . . .

All the residents speak an infamously bad Portuguese, as is natural, if they will not condescend to associate with the Portuguese gentry. It seems that no Portuguese lady is ever allowed, by the custom of the country, to walk anywhere by herself, whether she be married or unmarried, which I should think a very disagreeable restraint. Indeed, till lately even two ladies could not walk together without a father or brother. . . .

One ought to become very brazen after a season in Funchal, for nowhere is one so incessantly gazed on, and even stared full in the face. Wherever one goes, spectators lounging in balconies, and people on horse or foot, passing or meeting one in the street, always indulge themselves with a determined look. This staring habit is a principal amusement of the idle Portuguese, and I suppose the English are the most curiously examined. I am accustomed to it now, but I was obliged to turn away my head to laugh the other evening, when Louisa and I were sitting down in the Praça, and a moustached Portuguese fidalgo, who was pacing up and down with an oratorical friend, regularly gave me a good stare every time he passed, which might be about fifteen times. Another habit which amuses the visitor in Funchal is that of bowing to every lady whom a gentleman meets ; this has happened to us often, but not universally, owing, I believe, to the English gentlemen neglecting this civility to the Portuguese ladies—which is no wonder, for the Portuguese ladies are not in any respect easily distinguishable from their servants. The lower orders show a remarkable courtesy to each other; they never meet without taking off their hats or carapousas [*carapuças*]. They do the same whenever they pass a church or a priest.

Jan. 21, *Monday.*—. . . We have long had a great curiosity to taste the sugar-cane, which is very plentiful now; every boy in the street is sucking a piece. . . . The cane is somewhat curved, about an inch and a half in diameter, and extremely heavy; it is divided into joints, each from two or three inches to half a foot in length. The way to taste it is to cut off a joint and peel off the thick woody rind; there remains a firm white pith, which does not look very inviting, but when you cut it into slips and bite it, it almost melts into sweet juice.

Jan. 22, *Tuesday.*—. . . "Senhor Padre" called in the afternoon, and we had a very pleasant conversation with him. I was very glad when he at last began about the horse, apologizing for not having sent it for some days, as it gave me an opportunity of expressing my contrition for keeping it so long the other day. He would not hear of any excuse whatever, but said he wished I had been strong enough to keep it two hours longer. I shall never be tired of saying how delightfully amiable and good Mr. F. appears to be; goodness shines in every feature, and is heard in every word. There is an uncommon sweetness in his countenance, the expression of Christian benevolence and Christian peace.

Jan. 24, *Thursday.*—Miss Freeman seems to be about three or four and twenty years of age. I have never yet chanced to see her out of her bonnet, and have no idea how she would look without it. She has a tall, slight, graceful figure, and a pale face surrounded with light clustering curls; large blue eyes, rather too prominent, but of a most gentle expression; and a sweet mouth, which bespeaks at once her amiable disposition. Her voice is soft and slow; her whole manner expresses a mildness and benevolence and goodness far beyond what is usually met with. I believe she is naturally shy and diffident; actually, when she was first introduced to me at the Burnetts', though it was only to me, as mamma was out, Mrs. Burnett told me she was quite nervous, and unlike herself.

Jan. 25, *Friday.*—We were sitting at breakfast when there came a furious long rap at the door. As we were wondering what it could be, and agreeing that it was very like a Houghton rap, entered our friend Mr. Vasconcellos, who had good-naturedly left his breakfast to tell us that the *Vernon* was come in, and to bring a kind offer from Mr. George of going to it in a boat, to see if by chance papa is on board. I cannot express our delight, for though we do not expect papa by the *Vernon*, we may now expect the *Dart* in a day or two, as it is much the fastest sailer. The *Vernon* has had an excellent passage.

On the strength of this information, and this being one of our butter-making days, I proceeded to put in execution a plan on which I had set my heart, to wit, to make a little butter entirely myself for papa, who has a peculiar fancy for pure home-made butter. Accordingly, while mamma was at work on the larger portion, I had a little cream in a small basin to myself, and quickly produced and completed some much better butter than my honoured mother's, which I shall triumphantly display at table on papa's arrival.

Mr. Cross called again—it was after dinner this time, and I felt very cordial, though he interrupted me in "Old Mortality." The packet and *Vernon* were, of course, the principal topics of conversation, as they are with every one. We are now talking of the *Dart* all day, wishing, hoping, fearing, doubting, and I have even ventured to imagine myself this time to-morrow (8 p.m.) listening to papa or talking to A. What if to-morrow's morning sun should show us the *Dart?* has been our frequent remark.

Jan. 26, *Saturday.*—. . . I woke after a night spent in very vivid and natural dreams of the arrival of the *Dart*, and our meeting with papa. Whether they will be realized to-day, I cannot yet tell. Every knock at the door makes our hearts flutter; we think it may be Mr. Vas. coming to tell us of the arrival of the *Dart.* It is as yet very early. There is snow on the mountains to-day, and very strange it looks, contrasted with the verdurous gardens below, although the thermometer is not higher than 61°, which is cold compared to what it has been.

Down rushes mamma from the turret. "There is a large vessel coming in full sail!" Up rush I. A brig!—the *Dart!* the *Dart!* it must be! I feel ten times as strong!

I came downstairs. Mamma is at the Phelpses', and comes back saying that it is not the *Dart*, but a king's ship, and that the *Dart* will not be in, says Mr. Phelps, for a week. I am sadly disappointed.

Jan. 28, *Monday.*—. . . I have been looking at some illustrations of scenery in Syria and about Constantinople, published in parts, and lent us by the Phelpses. I have no words to express my admiration; it really makes me sad to reflect that I can never see these magnificent and beautiful scenes. To travel in the Holy Land has ever been my first and favourite wish—long, long have I even half expected that it would be some day gratified; but now I begin to give it up, and to discover that it is but a baseless daydream—a discovery which every succeeding year compels me to make with respect to the fondest hopes and wishes of my heart. . . .

Mine has not been an eventful life, yet for a long time past every year has been rife with what would have utterly astonished me could I have foreseen it all. What strange thing may fill its future pages? It is hardly less than three months since I dreamed of nothing less than living in Madeira. At this moment I care little where I shall be next; a continual sensation of disgust and dissatisfaction with myself gives me a frequent indifference to *my own* fate in particular; and then again my dreamy wishes return with double force.

Jan. 29, *Tuesday.*—The joyful day is come at last! But not the joyful hour; patience is now wanted more than ever. My hand shakes, I can hardly write. Morning rose as usual without the *Dart*, and as usual shower and sunshine followed each other. A good part of the morning was spent in making an extra quantity of butter, and I again made a little roll expressly for papa. When this business was over, I, much tired, sat down to rest, while mamma stepped over to the Phelpses'. Soon after, a long rap at the door announced our good-natured friend Miss Telles, who came to give us another Portuguese lesson. But we had hardly sat down before a messenger from the P——s' announced that the *Dart* was in sight! We rushed up to the turret and saw her plainly. Notwithstanding our joy and perturbation, we thought it best to continue our lesson, which we did, though we made it but a short one. Mamma soon returned, and Mr. Vas. shortly appeared to bring the news. But we hear that, as the wind is against her, and Captain D. not so skilful as her natural commander Captain O., she may be some hours before she can come in; perhaps not even to-day. . . .

Time went on, and as the Phelpses are just opposite, we conversed with them across the street, and asked them when the passengers would land. At last Mr. Phelps, who had been watching from his turret, told us that in five minutes the boat would be on shore, and that it was but a ten minutes' walk to the house. It was then a quarter to five, and I went and posted myself at the end window of the drawing-room to watch for their coming. Presently a little pencil-note came from kind Mr. Freeman to tell us that papa had actually arrived in the *Dart*—the first certain intelligence we had had. I resolutely sat at the window for more than three quarters of an hour, alternately looking at the clock opposite, and at the corner of the street where they would first appear. I was rewarded for my perseverance, for I was the first to exclaim, "Here they are!" Down flew mamma and Louisa, and in a minute or two up came the whole party, without Mr. Burnett, who had brought them here. Oh, it was a joyful meeting! I hardly know what we first asked, or said, or told, and though we sat up talking till half-past eleven, neither party had exhausted all their news.

. . . Papa has brought us much interesting intelligence, which I have not time to write. But the most important and joyful news of all is that Richard has passed his examination most honourably. There were thirty-one candidates, of whom seven were plucked; and R. was in the first class, consisting of three, whose merits were so equal that they cannot give the preference to any, so that R. has none above him. . . .

The kindness of the Duckworths has been beyond all praise. We owe more to them than we can ever be sufficiently thankful for. And, indeed, all our friends have laid us under the greatest obligations to them.

Jan. 30, *Wednesday.*—. . . Papa walked with mamma to Holloway's boarding-house to call on Mr. Charles Park, an invalid youth residing there, and afterwards to the Praça Academica, and came back perfectly enchanted with the beauty of what he had seen. He declares Madeira far surpasses his expectations. Also papa is well satisfied with our accommodation here, and with Madeira eating and drinking, and likes the *milho* particularly. To my great joy he is highly pleased with *my* butter. We are much amused with the astonishment of Arabella and Mackworth at all the novel objects which meet their view, and it gratifies our vanity to sport our Portuguese before them, in talking to the servants.

Jan. 31, *Thursday.*—. . . A succession of visitors called, chiefly on account of papa. They began with our favourite Mr. Freeman, whom papa likes very much indeed. He and papa talked about the Oxford Tracts, and the parties to which they have given rise, which have actually found their way even to Madeira, Mr. Lowe being a strong partisan, and Mr. Page something of the same kind.

Feb. 1, *Friday.*—. . . We had not quite finished butter-making when Mr. Charles Park called. He is a lad of fifteen, in very melancholy circumstances, and particularly recommended to our attention by the Duckworths. His brothers and sisters have been dropping off in consumption one after another; he himself anticipates the same fate. His father is dead, and his mother, who is in very narrow circumstances, is only just able to send him out to Madeira, where he is all alone, in delicate health, and suffering great depression of spirits. We in consequence feel much interested in him, and wish to show him every kindness in our power. He is a shy, modest boy, very gentle in his manners, and looks pale and sickly. He, however, tells us that he is much better since he has been in Madeira, and has escaped his usual spring cough.

Feb. 2, *Saturday.*—. . . Such a housekeeper am I become, that I was employed all the morning in reboiling some English preserves, while papa and mamma were paying visits and otherwise engaged. The Stoddarts and a Dr. Alexander Brown called before dinner, and afterwards Mrs. Burnett and Mr. Houghton. Mr. H. talks of going again to America for a year or two. He expatiated to me as usual on his sanguine disposition, his fatalism, and his happy life, and assured me that it was very foolish to marry.

Feb. 7, *Thursday.*—. . . We had invited young Charles Park to join our early dinner, meaning to make him at home with us; and he came, but unluckily a long succession of visitors beset us, as usual, half the day. . . .

A loud firing in the town, from the Loo Rock apparently, now attracted our attention; we all rushed up into the turret, but could see nothing, and then everybody went to the esplanade to discover the cause. It was supposed that a ship which sailed to-day had neglected to clear the custom-house.

Feb. 9, *Saturday.*—. . . There is a great courtesy in the lower orders of Portuguese, even to each other; they never meet without taking off their carapousas, and I never hear them address each other in rough rude language. They generally uncover to the English, and I always receive bows in my rides beyond the town.

Feb. 10, *Sunday.*—. . . Our room is always supplied with flowers, thanks to our friends. It took me some time to arrange them all this morning, for they filled seven glasses and jars, and I counted no less than thirty-three different species. Everybody went to church, and I was left alone. I cannot describe the sadness and depression under which I suffered all the morning. I felt quite sick at heart, and languor of body added to the dejection of my mind. A gloomy hue seemed to tinge everything in this world. I thought it impossible I could ever be happy; I saw nothing for me to enjoy either in the present or future. I felt that I could willingly die, and almost wished that this long illness might indeed soon terminate in my release from earth. And yet when evening came, and I was again in the midst of our family circle, this feeling of melancholy left me, and I was surprised to find myself so reconciled to life.

Feb. 11, *Monday.*—. . . I ended my ride, as on Friday, at the Freemans'. They overtook me as I was going there, having just been at our house. I went in with them; Mr. Freeman stayed a few minutes only, and then I had a delightful hour with my favourite Miss F., who looked lovelier than ever to-day, and was so warm and affectionate in her manner to me that I felt my heart open to her still more. Our conversation, as usual, turned presently to religious topics. Miss Freeman began by referring to the subject of learning by heart parts of Scripture, which we had before talked about, and she proposed that we should each set about learning the same portion. We chose Ps. lxxxvi., and after that, chapters xiii. to xvii. of St. John. We then conversed about various portions of the Bible, which led us to speak of studying the original languages, and other topics. "I regret so much now," said Miss Freeman, "that at one time I thought I ought to read no books but religious books, or at least to take a strong interest in nothing but religion. So, when I was reading Rollin, as soon as I became interested in it, I shut up the book, and did not take it up till an hour or two; and then, if I felt the interest return, I went to practice." "But do not you think that was a mistake?" said I. "A mistake? Oh, a very great one," she answered. "I think," added I, "that it must be our duty to cultivate our intellects, as they are given to us." "I thought so too, but that it was to be only a duty, not an enjoyment or pleasure," replied Miss Freeman. "And how long did you go on with this way of thinking?" "About two years," she said; "and then my illness came." She paused a little, and then gave me a very interesting account of herself. She had always, she said, been considered as an amiable child, and was attentive to her outward religious duties, but was not more than this, till suddenly the sense of her sinfulness and neglect of heavenly things burst upon her in an overwhelming manner, and she became completely miserable. "I got hold of Doddridge," she said; "do you know it?" I assented, and she went on. "It is a very discouraging book, and I read it incessantly. I was always sent to bed at a certain time, and after my governess had come to see that I was on the point of going to bed, I used to sit up for a long time reading and reading, till I became so puzzled and perplexed that I burst into floods of tears, and could read no more; and then I went to bed completely wretched, and woke next morning in the same state. I thought I never should be a Christian, that it was impossible I ever could be." "But had you no one," I asked, "to talk to?" "No; no one," said she. "Mamma was always extremely kind, but she never talked to us about religion; she was a religious person herself, and she used to hear us our Catechism, and made us go to church regularly, and gave us religious story-books to read; but she never talked to us on the subject for fear of teaching us to talk what we did not feel, to become hypocritical. So, though she was as kind as possible, and I loved her devotedly, I could not talk to her about this. And I was, besides, very reserved; I could not have said what I felt to any one. Do you know that kind of reserve?" "Oh yes, indeed I do!" said I; "I feel it almost as strongly as you say you did." "It is much to be regretted," she continued; "one loses a great deal." After a short digression she continued her narrative. She remained for some time in this distressing state, and got entangled in all sorts of intricacies and perplexities and errors, till her long illness came, which she considers as the greatest mercy to her. She said that when she was ill she had a great longing to live, chiefly on account of her younger brother and sister, to whom she was afraid she had given a wrong impression of religion, for they had begun to complain how melancholy she had grown, and had attributed it all to religion; "and I am so thankful," she added, "that I have been allowed to live to efface this impression, as I trust I have." After this, too, came all her troubles and sorrows, for which she was now prepared by having thus obtained peace of mind. . . . She said one great reason why she longed to recover from her illness was the thought that she had taken no interest in the spiritual welfare of others; all her religion had been for herself alone, and she had made no effort to assist any one else, which thought was to her insupportable, and she made up for her neglect as soon as she began to recover.

Feb. 14, *Thursday.*—Mr. Ware called this afternoon to talk to papa about the lecture, which is to be delivered to-night.* They had a very interesting conversation. Mr. W. seems a good and intelligent man. He is excessively tall, has a high forehead, and little sparkling eyes; he speaks without opening his mouth, and laughs on one side of it. His favourite phrase of approbation is "Just so," and he has an odd way of mixing up his sentences with "Eh!" when he neither asks a question nor expects an answer. I suspect he is too sanguine about the success of these lectures. Dr. Nichol is to lecture on astronomy, Dr. B. on electricity. Mr. Lowe, a very well-informed man, and conversant with botany and geology, refuses to take any part in the business, partly because his time is fully occupied, partly because he says the researches of science tend to produce scepticism, instancing La Place and others!! . . . .

On coming in, everybody but myself prepared to go to the lecture which papa was to deliver. . . . They set off about half-past seven, and I amused myself meanwhile with
69 Lockhart's "Scott" and my journal. In little more than an hour they returned, together with Mr. W. and Dr. N., who took tea with us—all in high spirits, for the lecture had met with complete success. I never felt prouder of my father.

It seems that the room was crowded, and many were unable to get admittance. The audience listened with pro-

* A course of scientific lectures "for the benefit of the young men resident and visitors" had been proposed, and E.'s father was asked to deliver the introductory lecture.

found attention and great interest, and at the end gave a tremendous clapping. Applauses, too, of the lecture and its delivery were heard on every side, and many persons came up to mamma to express their high gratification. . . . Everybody agrees that it was a beautiful lecture, and admirably delivered. . . .

Mr. Ware sat next me, and we fell into conversation about Cintra, scenery, astronomy, and the two interesting volumes of Professor Nichols. While we were talking, Mrs. Phelps called to us from the window of their house, to say that they could not sleep that night till they knew from what poem papa quoted the lines with which he concluded his lecture :—

> "So should an idiot, where at large he strays,
> Find the sweet lyre on which an artist plays,
> With rash and awkward force the chords he shakes,
> And grins with wonder at the noise he makes.
> But should a wise and well-instructed hand
> First take the shell beneath his just command,
> In gentle strains it seems as it complained
> Of the rude injuries it late sustained ;
> Till tuned at length to some immortal song,
> It sounds Jehovah's name, and pours His praise along."
> (Cowper's "Truth.")

After our visitors were gone, we continued sitting up till very late talking over the circumstances of the lecture, and indeed, I was so happy that I could not sleep till almost two o'clock.

Feb. 16, *Saturday.*—I rode on the St. Gonzalo road for an hour. It was a brilliant, fresh, calm morning, and I never saw the sea so beautifully clear and transparent. From cliffs six or seven hundred feet in height I could see quite distinctly every stone and pebble beneath the water, through which they gleamed like massive emeralds. The rocks here are everywhere clustered richly with prickly pear, geranium, myrtles, and fig-trees almost covered with a tender green mantle. There was a delicious stillness in the air; I heard no sound, except when we occasionally met a peasant, or passed a little hut under the rough stony hills.

The thermometer in the shade is now 68°. No rain, nor indication of rain. The early crops have failed, and the second are likely to be ruined too.

While [our] people were gone out making calls (for these are not yet finished) Mr. Freeman came, and told me that they proposed making use of this afternoon, if we liked it, to take as many of us as liked to go to see the Palmeira. This had been talked of before, Miss Freeman having obtained permission from Lord and Lady Elibank, by whom it is inhabited. Accordingly, at half-past three in the afternoon, both the Freemans came, and papa, mamma, Arabella, and Louisa set off with them, I longing to be able to go too. They partly rode, partly walked, Miss Freeman lending her horse and using it by turns. Papa came home so delighted with Miss Freeman that he said nothing about the Palmeira. "Emily," he said, "I think she is the very personification of innocence. Her eyes are benignity itself, and the way in which she thanks her brother and smiles upon him when he does anything for her is quite beautiful."

. . . By-the-by, the party who went to the Palmeira returned full of the praises of Lady Elibank, who, they say, is a most sweet creature, and very beautiful. They also took a great fancy to Miss Murray, half-sister of Lord Elibank. I have heard the Elibanks called very proud. . . . But no traces of pride appeared to-day. They say Lady Elibank does not appear above eighteen or nineteen years of age.

Feb. 17, *Sunday.*—There are few parts of my life on which I look back with more sorrow and self-reproach than my life in Devonshire. I can see how I gradually changed for the worse during that period. I was led astray by flattery and vanity, by uncontrolled feelings, and, most of all, by a first acquaintance with the everyday follies of the world, and a constant collision with those follies, both in words and actions. . . . Would that I had never been wakened from the happy dream of ignorance in which I lived at sixteen! Would that I had never learnt how different the world is from what I had imagined it! . . . I was admired and flattered (in all sincerity, however) to an inordinate degree, and my vanity fed by every sort of incense. I found myself a sort of *lioness* amongst the whole circle of their acquaintance; I was considered a wonder, a prodigy of talents, goodness, etc. (it was in this light the Warrens first heard of me). And all this awoke in me a new desire of admiration, which I had never had before. The consciousness of obtaining it only increased this desire, which I am sure must have at last betrayed itself. . . .

The consequence of this all was that after my ten months' absence from home I returned a different creature. I had become initiated into a new set of ideas; I was spoilt. The load of remorse I had laid up for myself during those ten months has burdened me ever since, and its weight seems rather to increase than diminish as time goes on.*

I really almost begin to think I *am* making some progress towards health, and may perhaps at last recover. I have felt uncommonly well and strong during the last warm ten days, and my cough is wonderfully diminished. I certainly receive very great benefit from my frequent rides.

Feb. 18, *Monday.*—I finished the first volume of "Os Votos Temerarios," and really became interested in it; the history of Lady Clarendon is actually touching. I can read it now by the eye, as one does English, faster than one can read aloud, only stopping occasionally at some new word.

Feb. 20, *Wednesday.*—I rode up the hill above Hollo-

* The whole of her journal, during these ten months and afterwards, shows how imaginary, at any rate how slight and temporary, was this deterioration believed in by her sensitive conscience. No one else discovered it.—Ed.

way's boarding-house, which is the great north road, the one leading to St. Anne's. It is extremely steep, and the view from it is very noble. From these heights Funchal has almost the appearance of a deserted, uninhabited city. You see no smoke, no moving object; and the bay too, so clear and waveless, without tide or ripple, the vessels sleeping on their shadows. There is nothing to indicate life; all is quiet and solitude. I rode as far up as a sweet little quinta, belonging to some Portuguese, the garden so studded with flowers that I quite coveted it.

Feb. 25, *Monday.*—. . . We had, as usual, a round of visitors. Mr. Hinton led the way, soon after breakfast. He has a handsome face, but an uncommonly reserved, *illegible* expression of countenance, unusually so in such a young man.

March 3, *Sunday.*—. . . After church papa and I took a turn in the church-garden with the Freemans. It was one of the most serene, delicious evenings I have known, and the air was sweet with flowers. The narrow walk up to the church is shaded with two beautiful cedars. There was something quite soothing in the calmness of the air, broken only by the plash of a little stream, and the tinkling note of the goldfinch. The tall datura, covered with its trumpet-like blossoms, now half-faded, the gigantic growth of geraniums and scarlet salvias, and the huge convent that towers high above, all tell that we are not in England. Papa, Louisa, and Mackworth, went to Dr. Nichol's, and saw the procession; and entered also into the Socorro Church, where a sermon was preached in Portuguese. This procession is called "The Procession of Stations." I passed one of these stations, where images were dressed up and tapers lighted. Papa saw only one penitent; they used to be very numerous on these occasions. They are Portuguese gentlemen, and being condemned by their confessors to various penances, perform them in masks and coarse black dresses, that they may not be known. They walk barefoot over the sharp stones, some carrying heavy images, some with their hands tied to immense bars of iron laid across the back of the neck, some wearing tippets stuck full of nails that point inward. These exhibitions are much disapproved by the vicar-general, who seems to be a sensible, liberal man.

March 4, *Monday.*—I found both Mr. and Miss Freeman at home. . . . After her brother had gone out she said that yesterday she felt most melancholy at the thought of leaving him, quite ready to sink under it; but she has made up her mind to it, and feels that she is more wanted at home. I asked her afterwards whether she liked Madeira. She said, "Yes; but still I feel that I am not at home. It makes a great difference, after being a large party at home, to be alone here, and always anxious as I am. But I ought to like Madeira, for I have learnt a great deal by being here. I am very anxious by nature, and formerly, when I was in trouble, I used quite to sink down under it. But here, there is nothing to be done but to trust in God" (*i.e.* when her family at home are ill); "and the affection which *there* would expend itself in sitting by a bedside and other useless little attentions is now spent in prayer; and I have learnt the peace and comfort to be obtained from prayer. . . . I so often wish I could suffer all for others; it is so much easier to suffer sorrow one's self than to see others suffer. One cannot so easily see why another should be afflicted, but when we are afflicted ourselves we can look into our own hearts and see the reason there." She spoke very feelingly about the difficulty of ruling and disciplining our affections, of not loving too fondly; of loving, in short, and yet being able to resign those we love when taken from us. . . .

She read to me several of the Olney Hymns, of which 70
she is very fond, and one in particular, which she had

marked in the year 1830. "It was a very happy day," she said, "when I marked that. There was a pretty little church where we lived then, in lovely scenery; a hill near it was covered with wood, and I sat there one Sunday between services, with my eldest sister, and marked that hymn. I had at that time a sort of shrinking from life—do you know that feeling? I was so happy, without a single care or grief, that I could not understand what was meant by the trials and miseries of life; I thought, 'Is this life, which I have heard is so full of trouble?' I thought it could not last, that sorrows and afflictions must come at length; and I quite dreaded their coming, for I thought I could never support them. And three years after sorrow did come."

March 5, *Tuesday*.—. . . I had the satisfaction to-day of nailing up to the whitewashed walls of my room all my chronological charts, and thus giving it an appearance of comfort, a look of home. Mamma and papa are gone to dine with the Ellicotts. My sisters and Mackie are just departed to their bedrooms. We have had an evening of uncommon merriment; jests and ludicrous anecdotes have been flying round the table, and our laughter has been incessant. M. was looking over the contents of his desk, and found some little tales which I, many years ago, had written for his edification, and I cannot describe the mirth produced by the reperusal of some parts. I am sure neither the party at the Ellicotts' nor that at the Phelpses' opposite are nearly as happy as our own little party have been this evening.

March 6, *Wednesday*.—I was busy most of the day in my room, looking over my portfolios, papers, letters, etc., sorting, arranging, and throwing away. I was highly amused at the curious mixture of every kind of subject which I found in these confused heaps of manuscripts. Fragments of unfinished poems, Latin exercises, and rough reports of conversations, scribbled over one sheet; sketches of epics, translations from Greek plays, notes of sermons, and algebraical calculations, mixed together on a second; on another, grammatical rules for an imaginary language, references to a plan for an invented palace, sums in arithmetic, scenes of unfinished dramas, and lists of *dramatis personæ* are scribbled and scrawled all over with heads and figures of men and horses, likenesses of unconscious sitters, and outlines of trees and flowers. So miscellaneous have been my studies and amusements.

March 12, *Tuesday.*—. . . Charles Parks joined us at dinner; he is now much less reserved and shy, and seems quite at his ease with us, which I am glad of, poor boy! He is much improved in health, and returns to England this spring. He told us that the English merchants here are popular or unpopular according as they acted during the war of Pedro and Miguel, when Miguel's party possessed the island; for the English, being quite unmolested, were not obliged to take either side, and as their houses were never searched, they were able to conceal in their stores and cellars persecuted individuals of the Pedroite party. This many of them did very generously, as Mr. Phelps, Mr. Wallace, and some others. But Mr. —— (such, at least, is the story) voluntarily gave up his best clerk, who had served him faithfully for many years, to the Miguelites. If this is really true, Mr. —— acted basely, and deserves the dislike with which he is regarded by the Portuguese.

March 16, *Saturday.*—A day of expeditions and parties. All of us but myself were to spend the day with the Phelpses at their Quinta on the Mount. . . . At breakfast-time came a note to me from Miss Freeman, saying, "Dear Emily,—The morning is so fine we hope you will be able to go with us in a boat to Cabo Giraô; we will send the horse for you about nine o'clock to spare you the fatigue of walking here; and pray keep quiet, dear Emily, till it comes. In haste, yours affectionately, E. A. Freeman." I forthwith put on my bonnet, and in great delight mounted the horse as soon as it arrived. . . . We pursued our way to Cabo Giraô. Miss Freeman made me lie down on a sofa of cushions they had made for me at the bottom of the boat, and I reposed in luxury, watching the tall cliffs that gradually opened to our view as we glided towards this celebrated headland.

Cabo Giraô is the loftiest precipice in Madeira, and is *said* to be the loftiest in the world. The height (measured to the highest point a little inland) is rather more than two thousand one hundred feet; but the height immediately from the brink is not much less. I think the whole ridge of precipice, nearly of one height and quite unbroken, must be half a mile in length; the highest point is about the centre. . . . We rowed out a little way into the sea, and I gazed with extreme admiration on the stupendous precipice.
71 Had not the "Rambles in Madeira" prepared me for disappointment, I should have been disappointed, for certainly one does not easily realize to one's self its immense height. But looking up is much the least favourable way of viewing a lofty object, because you then only see it contrasted with the sky, which looks the same everywhere; whereas in looking down and seeing the difference in the sea, or whatever object may be below, you obtain an adequate idea of the distance you are above them. The want of objects is a very important circumstance in lessening the effect of an elevation. We were not nearly as much impressed as we should be at the height of Cabo Giraô until we spied some men on the narrow beach below, and the excessive smallness of their figures immediately exalted in our ideas the rock beneath which they stood. The same effect was still more strikingly produced by a ladder, left part-way up the rock after an unfortunate explosion of gunpowder, by which twenty men were killed.

There is a narrow strip of cultivated beach lying beneath

Cabo Giraô, on which are grown the finest vines, figs, and peaches in Madeira. These, contrasted with the huge rock, look strangely tiny; the vine-trellises are like nets, the peach-trees in blossom like small almond bushes, and the fig-trees like plants which you can walk over. Here there is one little hut, the most perfect image of utter and dreary solitude that I ever beheld; shut in on the land-side by the tremendous precipice under which it is built, and with the mighty waste of waters before it, the inhabitants are excluded from all sight of or intercourse with their fellow-creatures except by the accidental and uncertain means of boats. I should think it a most melancholy abode on a howling night of storms and darkness.

The hue of Cabo Giraô is chiefly a dark red; but there is a great variety of dark and purple tints, and streaks of many forms; there are also many tufts of plants and flowers springing out of its inaccessible sides, and the distant summits are crowned with pines and low vegetation. There was another party we knew going by land to the top of the cliff, and they might have been looking down upon us that moment, but it was far too high to distinguish any creature up there.

We now determined to land on the beach. This was a difficult matter, for there is a very steep bank of shingles, on which the waves, even this calm day, broke with sufficient force to dash away the rope from the hands of the two men who had waded ashore, and were trying to drag us up. So we proceeded to another part; the men managed to regain the rope, and pulled the boat up on the black shingles.

We now proceeded to eat the cold dinner which we had brought with us. As Mrs. Hoskyns and I were the two invalids of the party, the rest busied themselves in the most good-natured way to make us comfortable; they spread cushions and cloaks on the shingles for us to sit upon, and propped us up with cushions, supported against piles of great stones. The sun luckily went in just then, so that we were not scorched with heat. We took off our bonnets; the gentlemen opened the provision-baskets; and here, under Cabo Giraô, did we enjoy our picnic-dinner. My first picnic was in the Bradley Woods, in Devonshire; the last was in the New Forest; and now—how little then I should have expected it!—I am at one in Madeira. . . .

Some one—Mr. F., I think—set the example of dipping the hand into the pleasant cool water, upon which we all took to dipping. He next told us that it was very refreshing to wet one's temples with the same; immediately we all began applying our wet fingers to our temples, till a sense of the ridiculous struck Miss F., and she burst out laughing.

On returning to McGinn's we entered the Freemans' drawing-room—all but Mrs. Hoskyns, who was tired, and went up to her own room. Mr. Freeman ordered half a dozen ices, and we enjoyed them mightily. Mr. Shute (who, by-the-by, is very pleasing) soon after departed; then exit Mr. Freeman; and Miss F. took me to her room, where she made me lie down while she changed her dress. She then went up to Mrs. Robinson, saying to me, "Stay there quiet till I come back." On returning she told me that she and her brother were going to eat a little turtle, and asked me to come and taste it with them—which I did; and when this second little dinner was over, as it was growing late, Mr. F. sent for the horse to take me home. So ended a day of much pleasure, spent entirely with the good, kind, delightful Freemans.

March 17, *Sunday*.—I went to church as usual in the afternoon. Mr. ——'s two sermons were both intensely High Church and Puseyite; the most intolerant notions delivered dogmatically and positively, without any attempt at reasoning and argument. In point of fact, he actually anathematized all who did not strictly conform to every rule and ceremony and tradition of Mother Church; and much of both sermons was distinctly aimed at excellent Mr. Langford, who is in the habit of holding meetings for prayer and religious instruction. A great sensation was created by these sermons, which seem to have excited universal disapprobation; every one whom papa met burst out in condemnation of them. . . . How melancholy that religious feuds and factions should be introduced, even into this remote place! Papa has been rather defending Mr. —— to his enemies, on the ground that, as he thinks these opinions matters of vital importance, he is perfectly right to insist on them from the pulpit; but it is the intolerant dictatorial spirit which is so much to be regretted.

March 19, *Tuesday.*— . . . I did not ride, and was all the morning pleasantly engaged in my room. Having finished my devotions and reading, I wrote my journal, and then worked, at the same time learning John xv. Being then obliged to vacate, I went into the drawing-room and read Picciola. On returning I finished St. John, and learnt over again a chart of chronology. Then I worked till dinner. I had every now and then a few housekeeping interruptions.

Dinner over, I worked a little, lay down in my room and read my afternoon portion of Scripture. I then returned to the drawing-room, placed myself on the sofa-chair, and took up Combe's "Phrenology," which amused me not 72
a little. . . . Mackie returned from Caniçal in a state of great delight, and was decidedly of opinion that the reputed fossil-bed cannot be really the remains of a forest. Papa and mamma dined at the Temples', and we had a merry tea at home. After tea I retired to my room, where I am now sitting.

March 21, *Thursday.*— . . . Since I have been in Madeira I have had a strange shrinking from writing letters, even to those I love best. It has now become an effort of mind and body which I dread to attempt, and would willingly avoid altogether. Day after day I have been endeavouring to make up my mind to begin preparing letters which I ought to write by the *Vernon*, but it was not till this day of rain that I have really persuaded myself to do so. I began a letter to Tilla, but it is a painful task, and I find no pleasure in it, as I should once have done. I can hardly account for this feeling, except by the loss of all hope that we shall ever meet again.

March 24, *Palm Sunday.*—. . . Enter Dr. Nichol, bringing us a little packet of fresh dates, no doubt from one of the island palms. We thought them excellent. The doctor brought also a Welsh Prayer-book, for the benefit of Louisa, who is mad about learning Welsh, in which Dr. N. is well versed. He read and explained a little of it, and I was much interested at the resemblance between some of the primitive words and those of the Greek and Latin.

March 25, *Monday.*—. . . Miss Freeman drank tea with us this evening, which is a very unwonted concession on her part, for she generally refuses all evening invitations on account of her brother, and she only came now after as much pressing as we could without selfishness employ. . . . "How happy you are," she remarked to me, "to have had leisure and opportunity to cultivate your mind!" "And how happy I am to have had such a father," I added; "he has taken such pains with me!" "You ought to be happy —you will be happy," she repeated, kissing me. After she had completed the survey of my room and its multifarious contents, she suddenly exclaimed, "Oh, I am so glad that I am not going to stay here, Emily!" "Why?" "Because you would soon find out what an ignoramus I am, and you would not love me." . . .

And this is the only evening that Miss Freeman has spent or will ever spend with us; one of the last few times that I shall see her at all. Like a beautiful vision she has just crossed my path,—oh, for how short a time!

March 26, *Tuesday.*—. . . Mrs. Wynter good-naturedly called to give A. a lesson in German, which she has done two or three times before; and then Dr. N. called to give L. a lesson in Welsh. I am sure languages are popular amongst us. Oh, and I forgot; to make it complete I should have added that Senhor Branco came in the morning to teach papa Portuguese. So the languages we study are no less than eight, including one which only mamma understands: Greek, Latin, French, Italian, German, Portuguese, Welsh, Spanish.

Dr. N. drank tea with us, and was extremely entertaining. . . . Mamma said, "Dr. N., don't you think the Portuguese a very good-humoured race?" "Oh no, ma'am," he replied, with a very decided shake of the head. "Dear! why they always seem so civil and courteous in their manners, I thought they were good-tempered." "Yes, ma'am, if you are civil to them, they are good-tempered to you; but provoke them, and see how their eyes blaze!" He went on to tell us how ready they were to knock down any one with a pole on any provocation, or even to whip out their knives. The Portuguese gentlemen, having each their private enemies, never venture about at night without a large company and a pole to defend themselves. Two men were killed on the spot in a quarrel which took place in a wine-shop just before we came. And these murderers generally escape justice by going to Lisbon, where there is no one to prosecute.

March 27, *Wednesday.*—. . . . I was much rejoiced by the arrival of my book-shelves this afternoon. I immediately set to work to arrange my unfortunate books, which had been lying on the floor for these two months. Having done this to my satisfaction, I proceeded to rout out my portfolios and papers and maps, and put them too in order.

March 28, *Thursday.*—. . . On my way back, I sent away the horse in the Rua João Tavero, and called at the ——s', who, I believe, are somewhat offended at my going there so seldom. Senhor George conducted me upstairs, was very gracious, told me how much better I looked, and gathered me some beautiful flowers of the rose-apple, a large tree which bears these large blossoms, and a pretty fruit like wax, with a poisonous kernel. Mrs. —— meant to be gracious, but was as cold as usual. I cannot bear those cold exteriors which never melt; they give the idea of nothing but ice within. Senhor George insisted on taking me to the cathedral, which is close by, to see the ceremonies there transacting, this being Holy Thursday. I had never been within the cathedral before; it is a handsome building, and seems richly adorned with gilding and carving, but I could not see much of it, because it was darkened, in which state it will remain till twelve o'clock on Saturday night. It was filled with kneeling Portuguese, and I heard the voice of a priest chanting in a very harsh, unmusical voice. We stayed but a minute, and on coming out met with papa in company with Senhor Branco, who was taking him there for the same purpose.

Coming in, I found a stuffed hoopoe which Mr. Page had left for me, having procured it from Colonel D'Arcy.

March 29, *Good Friday.*—I had set my heart on going to church this morning and receiving the Communion, and this, by the use of the Freemans' horse, I was enabled to do. It was proposed to me only to come to the Communion, for fear of fatigue; but I was anxious to join in the whole service, and felt besides unusually strong and well, so I went with the rest. But I had miscalculated my strength, and was so exhausted that I could not enjoy as I had wished and hoped that part of the service to which I had most looked forward. . . .

The moonlight nights are quite heavenly. In England

we do not know what moonlight is. Here there is a brilliancy in the sky, a balm and purity in the air, which cannot be imagined without being experienced. The splendour with which the silver rays of the broad bright moon gleam on the still ocean and the white houses of sleeping Funchal has something almost fairy-like. I can see by it to read the smallest print.

March 30, *Saturday.*—. . . We had seven sets of visitors to-day, whereof I shall mention three. 1. Mr. Lowe, who gave us the curious information that Madeira is just three times as damp a climate as England, but that the damp did not show. (How there can be damp which does not show, I cannot tell.) 2. Mrs. Wynter, . . . who said of Miss Freeman, "If ever any one retained their baptismal purity, it is she." 3. Miss Freeman herself. . . .

March 31.—. . . Being Easter Sunday, this was a day of great festivity among the Portuguese. Amongst other ludicrous ceremonies, the fish which they have been eating all Lent (I forget the species) were buried in triumph, a great procession attending. I understand, too, that at this time they are apt to caricature the English, dressing up people to represent the most remarkable. Last year the eccentric Miss Norton was thus represented, which gave her great offence.

I took up the first volume of Barrow's "Sermons," which 73
I had never opened before, and began the first sermon. . . . The first sentence appalled us by its wonderful length; it is not, however, obscure. It is an eloquent sermon, but I cannot like the way of treating the subject of the redemption; it is the usual way, and papa particularly objects. We talk of its being impossible for God to pardon man on any other terms; but what right have we to say this? How do we know what God could or could not do? it is enough for us to know what He has done. And as to the scheme being analogous to our ideas of justice, it is

no justice to punish an innocent man instead of a guilty, nor was it ever thought so. We cannot, and must not expect to understand how Christ's death saves us; it is sufficient to know that it does. One thing is clear; it shows us as strongly as possible God's horror of sin, which required (why, we know not) so great a sacrifice.

April 1, *Monday.*—After my ride I went to the Freemans'. Mrs. Wynter called soon after, and was shut up with Miss F. for about half an hour in her room, during which time I had a chat with Mr. F. At about twelve mamma called, by agreement with Miss F., who took her up to introduce her to Mrs. Robinson, for we are very anxious to become friends to her, after her ministering angel is gone. I had after this a delightful quiet talk with dear Miss F., perhaps the last morning I shall spend with her. We conversed on the pain of looking back on past happiness; and though I have so often observed it before, I was more and more struck by the entire devotedness of Miss F.'s confidence in our heavenly Father; by her meek and patient submission to His will, even under the heaviest afflictions; the certainty she entertains that all things, whether joy or sorrow, are for our good, so that though she says she dares not look back often to the days before her troubles began, the contrast is so painful, yet she never even wishes anything otherwise. This is a state of mind most beautiful; would that I could attain to something like it! Nothing makes me feel my own defects more painfully than seeing these bright features in the character of another.

May 18.—On the 4th of April I broke a blood-vessel, and am now dying of consumption, in great suffering, and may not live many weeks. God be merciful to me a sinner.

God be praised for giving me such excellent parents. They are more than any wishes could desire, or than any words can sufficiently praise. Their presence is like sunshine to my illness.

May 22.—I have suffered much with lying long, and have just been put on our hydrostatic bed. Relief wonderful. My portrait has just been taken; they say excellent.*

I linger on in the same way, and do not yet sink. Alas! I can never see Richard again.

May 27, *Monday*.—I feel weaker every morning, and I suppose am beginning to sink; still I can at times take up my pen. I have had my long back hair cut off. Dear papa wears a chain made from it. Mamma will have one too.

Here end the extracts; but the writer added a page more to her journal, the last words being written in a tremulous, yet quite legible hand, on June 24th, a fortnight before her release.

* This portrait was taken by a young artist, himself the victim of the same malady, of which he also died in Madeira, not long after his sitter. The painting was very slight, for she could not bear long the fatigue of sitting; but the sweet wasted face was a true likeness. The masses of hair, which she had for weeks during her illness persisted in dressing for herself, having been cut off, made her face look like a child's. The eyes were bright, but gentle; the geranium-colour was fixed on her cheek; and close to her hand, in touching reminder of her lifelong tastes, were a stuffed hoopoe and bee-eater, given her by a friend in Madeira.

Notes

1. Frederick Malkin (1769–1848) was author of a *History of Greece* published in 1830 by the Society for the Diffusion of Useful Knowledge.

2. The Monument became a favorite site for suicides in the 1830s and early 1840s until it was "caged" to prevent further attempts at self-murder.

3. Sir James Thornhill (1675–1734) was a decorative painter who did work at Hampton Court, Greenwich, and Windsor, as well as the famous paintings for the Dome of St. Paul's. Sir Christopher Wren might have liked Shore's comment, since he never wanted his dome to be decorated.

4. In addition to being an engraver, Henry Morland (1730?–1797) was well-known for his portraits and paintings of domestic subjects.

5. Henry Hart Milman's (1791–1868) *History of the Jews,* which first appeared in 1829, was written for Murray's Family Library.

6. John Shore, Lord Teignmouth (1751–1834), was uncle to Emily Shore's father. Governor General of India, he received the title Baron Teignmouth in the peerage of Ireland in 1798.

7. The Juvenile Library, first published in 1800, was one of many sets of books owned in full or in part by the Shores. It contained adventure stories as well as books like Arabella Shore's book on Africa.

8. The second Earl Grey (1764–1845), then prime minister, and Henry Peter (Baron) Brougham were shepherds of the first Reform Bill in 1832. Grey's authoring of the bill and his timing and insistence, and Brougham's speeches in the House of Lords are often credited with its passage there.

9. The Reform Bill of 1832 transferred the voting privilege from small boroughs, controlled by the aristocracy and gentry, to the more populous industrial towns. Smaller property owners were granted the vote, but this first Reform Bill did not enfranchise the working classes.

10. Thomas Cranmer (1489–1556) was the first archbishop of Canterbury, and author of the *Book of Common Prayer.* Archbishop during the difficult years of Henry VIII's reign, he survived the king by nine years only to be executed for his part in the succession plot in favor of Lady Jane Grey.

11. William Frederick, second duke of Gloucester (1776–1834), elected chancellor in 1811.

12. Probably Richard Whately (1787–1863), the archbishop of Dublin, a widely published anti-Erastian divine.

13. Charles Babbage, *The Economy of Manufactures* (London: Charles Knight, 1832). The Shores kept up with new books and current editions.

14. The *Penny Magazine* began in 1832 as an organ of the Society for the Diffusion of Useful Knowledge. From the start, it was a favorite of Emily Shore's and would be the place chosen for the publication of her essays on birds in 1838.

15. Harriet Martineau's stories, mentioned here, are found in her *Illustrations of Political Economy,* 9 vols. (London: Charles Fox, 1832).

16. James Spedding (1808–81) was one of Tennyson's friends in the group called the Cambridge "Apostles." A scholar, in later years he devoted himself to the study of Sir Francis Bacon.

17. *The Architecture of Birds* by James Rennie (1787–1867) was published in London by Charles Knight in 1831 and was part of the Library of Entertaining Knowledge.

18. *Boy's Own Book* by William Clarke (1800–1838), published in London by Vizetelly, Branston and Co. in 1828, was an encyclopedia of diversions, "athletic, scientific, and recreative," for boys and youths.

19. Thomas Bewick's (1753–1828) popular engraved studies of birds are also alluded to in the opening chapter of Charlotte Brontë's *Jane Eyre.*

20. Robert Mudie's *The Feathered Tribes of the British Islands,* 2 vols. (London, 1824).

21. The *Quarterly Journal of Education,* begun in 1831, was another organ of the Society for the Diffusion of Useful Knowledge.

22. The London Zoo was founded in 1826 and placed its collection of

animals on display in 1828. The seven pages about Emily Shore's visit there, which were deleted by her editors, would have been a valuable early reflection by an amateur natural historian.

23. "German Popular Tales" was one of the English titles for Grimm's fairy tales, available in England, with George Cruikshank's illustrations, after 1826.

24. "Netherlands" probably refers to Thomas Colley Grattan's *The Netherlands,* published in London by Longman in 1830 and available in the Cabinet Cyclopaedia (see p. 220), many volumes of which the Shores owned and cherished.

25. Morrison's pills were a well-known and trusted Victorian cure-all.

26. Mrs. Markham was the pseudonym of Elizabeth Penrose. Shore refers to her two-volume *History of France,* published in London in 1828.

27. *The History of Protestantism in France from the Earliest Times to the Revocation of the Edict of Nantes* was a publication of the Religious Tract Society.

28. Bishop Daniel Wilson (1778–1858) was fifth bishop of Calcutta. Many of his sermons and letters were published or reviewed during Emily Shore's lifetime.

29. Madame Campan's (Jeanne Louise Henriette) two-volume *Memoirs of the Private Life of Marie Antoinette* was translated into English and published by Henry Coburn in 1823.

30. Captain Basil Hall (1788–1844) published an account of his travels in North America in 1829.

31. Frances Trollope's book first appeared in 1832. It is characteristic of Shore to be fair-minded and tough in her judgments, as she is here about Mrs. Trollope. She does not, however, point out that Captain Hall was also hard on the Americans and was one of Mrs. Trollope's sources.

32. The New Poor Law of 1834 was the law that helped limit outdoor relief by parishes and confined the able-bodied poor to workhouses. It incensed, among others, Charles Dickens in *Oliver Twist.* From their vantage point in the 1830s, the Shores seem to have thought it would be a workable law.

33. Dr. Thomas Arnold (1800–1853) was a famous educator, headmaster

at Rugby, and the father of the poet Matthew Arnold. Renn Dickson Hampden (1793–1868) was the controversial bishop of Hereford who maintained that the authority of the scriptures held greater weight than that of the church. John Keble (1792–1866) was a poet and a central figure in the Oxford Movement. Keble promoted Anglo-Catholicism but insisted that one should stay within the church of one's baptism.

34. Augustus de Morgan's *The Elements of Arithmetic* was published by John Taylor in 1830 and 1832.

35. "Sir Eustace Grey" by George Crabbe (1754–1832) was available in Crabbe's *Poetical Works,* published by John Murray in 1834.

36. The famous actress Sarah Siddons (1755–1831) was best known for her versatility, her strong characterization of Lady Macbeth, and her association with the Drury Lane of Garrick and Sheridan.

37. *The Bravo* (1831) and *The Waterwitch; or the Skimmer of the Seas: A Tale* (1830) were both stories by James Fenimore Cooper (1789–1851); *Gil Blas* was a novel by Alain René Le Sage (1668–1747).

38. Henry Kirke White (1785–1806), "the boy poet of Nottingham," was a minor poet about whose work most critics have agreed with Shore. "Remains" is an abbreviation for *The Remains of Henry Kirke White with an Account of his Life,* two volumes of previously unpublished poetry and prose compiled by Robert Southey in 1807.

39. Philip Doddridge's *Rise and Progress of Religion in the Soul* was first published in 1745 but saw many editions in the early nineteenth century. Shore refers below to James Fenimore Cooper's *Pioneers* (1823).

40. Joseph Dornford (1794–1868) was rector of Plymtree, Devonshire.

41. John O'Connell (1810–58) was the son of Daniel O'Connell. He too was an Irish patriot, and was also a politician who worked for the repeal of the New Poor Law.

42. James Montgomery was author of *The Wanderer in Switzerland and Other Poems* (1866), a favorite volume of Shore's. She knew the title poem by heart.

43. Edward Smedley (1788–1836) wrote *Sketches from Venetian History* (3 vols., 1831–32). Josiah Conder (1789–1855) wrote *Modern Traveller* (London: Duncan, 1826).

44. Lardner's Cabinet Cyclopaedia was first projected in 1826 or 1828. Edited by Dr. Dionysius Lardner (1793–1856), the series, which ended in 1846, ran to sixty volumes in 133 parts. Each volume dealt with a complete subject and could be purchased separately, but readers were encouraged to buy either the entire set or an entire subdivision such as "The Cabinet of Natural Philosophy," "The Cabinet of Literature," or "The Cabinet of History," many volumes of which were owned by the Shores. Shore here refers to Henry Fergus's *History of the United States of America* (2 vols., 1830–32).

45. *Biographie Universelle* was a popular French dictionary of history, frequently reprinted in the 1830s.

46. Philip Massinger (1583–1640) and John Ford (fl. 1639) were two of Shore's favorite playwrights.

47. Shore here refers to *Thirty Years Correspondence between John Jebb and A. Knox*. 2 vols. (London, 1834).

48. The poet Abraham Cowley (1618–67) was another favorite of Emily Shore's.

49. Shore probably refers to Thomas Bowdler's *A Short Introduction to a Selection of Chapters from the Old Testament*. Swansea: W. C. Murray, 1822.

50. *Rokeby* was a poem in six cantos by Sir Walter Scott (1771–1832).

51. Joseph Blanco White (1775–1841) was a well-known theological writer allied with the Oxford Movement. He entered, on Southey's side, a controversy between Southey and Charles Butler over the relative merits of the Anglican and Roman Catholic churches when he published his "Evidence against Catholicism" in 1825.

52. *The Fair Maid of Perth or St. Valentine's Day* was written by Sir Walter Scott (1771–1832).

53. *Adventures of a Younger Son* was written by Edward Trelawny (1792–1881) and published in London by H. Colburn and R. Bentley in 1831.

54. Racine (1639–99) wrote both *Esther* (1689) and *Britannicus* (1669), mentioned below.

55. *The Penny Cyclopaedia*, 1833–43, was another publication of the Society for the Diffusion of Useful Knowledge.

56. Eyre Evans Crowe's *The History of France* was published in London by Brown and Green in 1830.

57. Shore's new moral and didactic reading included John Foster's (1770–1843) *Essays in a Series of Letters to a Friend,* 2 vols. (London: Longman, Hurst, 1806); Isaac Taylor's (1787–1865) *Natural History of Enthusiasm* (1829); and Joseph Butler's (1692–1752) *The Analogy of Religion, Natural and Revealed* (London: J., J. & P. Knapton, 1736).

58. Mary Somerville's (1780–1872) *On the Connexion of the Physical Sciences* (1834) was dedicated to Queen Adelaide and to the women readers of her day—like Emily Shore.

59. *The Beauties of Beaumont and Fletcher* was published by Beaumont and Francis in 1834 and 1837.

60. The poet George Crabbe (1754–1832) was also author of "The Village" and "Sir Eustace Grey," Shore's favorite poem.

61. *The Course of Time* was a poem by Robert Pollok (1798–1827).

62. Thomas Babington Macaulay (1800–1859) was a famous historian and the author of *The History of England from the Accession of James II* (5 vols., 1849–61).

63. Mr. Nightingale was the father of Florence Nightingale, and Embley was her ancestral home.

64. Jeremy Taylor's (1613–67) *Sermons,* first published in the mid-seventeenth century, were readily available in Emily Shore's day.

65. Isaac Watts's *The World to Come* was first published in 1745 and reissued in a number of editions in the early nineteenth century.

66. Especially popular with women, Mrs. Marcet's *Conversations on Chemistry* was first published in 1806 and achieved sixteen editions in less than forty years. The reference that follows is to Michael Faraday (1791–1861), the famous physicist.

67. Aubert de Vertot D. Aubeuf's *Révolutions de Suède* was a popular history of Sweden written in the 1690s and republished in many subsequent editions. Samuel Astley Dunham's *History of the Germanic Empire* was issued in three volumes by Lardner in 1834 and 1835.

68. Shore has been reading her way through John Pringle Nichol's books on astronomy. She refers here to *The Architecture of the Heavens,* which first appeared in 1837, issued by W. Tait in Edinburgh.

69. John Gibson Lockhart's *Memoirs of the Life of Sr. Walter Scott, Bart.*, was published in Edinburgh in seven volumes in 1837.

70. The *Olney Hymns* by John Newton (1725–1807), an evangelical curate, were a three-volume set of popular devotionals containing scriptural texts and meditations on occasional subjects and on the progress and changes of the spiritual life. William Cowper (1731–1800) was a contributor to the collection.

71. *Rambles in Madeira and in Portugal* was published in London by C. and J. Rivington in 1827.

72. Shore could be referring either to George Combe's (1788–1858) *Essays on Phrenology* (London: Longman, 1819) or to his *System of Phrenology* (Edinburgh: John Anderson, 1825), which was reissued in 1830 and 1836.

73. Isaac Barrow's *Sermons,* popular from the 1680s on, were reissued by Oxford in two volumes in 1810.

The three drawings by Emily Shore that follow are from the 1898 edition of the *Journal of Emily Shore* provided through the courtesy of Michigan State University Library, East Lansing, Michigan.

Frontispiece to the 1898 edition.

THE ARTIST'S FATHER.

Rev. Thomas Shore, M.A., 1793–1863.

THE ARTIST'S YOUNGEST BROTHER.

Mackworth Charles Shore.

Index

www.ingramcontent.com/pod-product-compliance
Lightning Source LLC
Chambersburg PA
CBHW020942310726
48980CB00001B/25

* 9 7 8 0 8 1 3 9 1 3 5 5 1 *